Agile Data Warehousing Project Management
Business Intelligence Systems Using Scrum

Ralph Hughes

AMSTERDAM • BOSTON • HEIDELBERG • LONDON
NEW YORK • OXFORD • PARIS • SAN DIEGO
SAN FRANCISCO • SINGAPORE • SYDNEY • TOKYO

Morgan Kaufmann Publishers is an Imprint of Elsevier

Morgan Kaufmann is an imprint of Elsevier
225 Wyman Street, Waltham, MA 02451, USA

First edition 2013

Library of Congress Cataloging-in-Publication Data
Hughes, Ralph, 1959-
  Agile data warehousing project management : business intelligence systems using
  Scrum / Ralph Hughes. -- 1st ed.
    p. cm.
  Includes bibliographical references and index.
  ISBN 978-0-12-396463-2 (alk. paper)
  1. Data warehousing. 2. Agile software development. 3. Business intelligence--Data processing.
  4. Project management. I. Title.
  QA76.9.D37H84 2013
  005.74'5--dc23   2012030627

British Library Cataloguing in Publication Data
A catalogue record for this book is available from the British Library

For information on all Morgan Kaufmann publications
visit our Web site at www.mkp.com/ or www.elsevierdirect.com

13 14 15 16 17 10 9 8 7 6 5 4 3 2 1

Agile Data Warehousing Project Management

Contents

PART 1: AN INTRODUCTION TO ITERATIVE DEVELOPMENT

PART 2: DEFINING DATA WAREHOUSING PROJECTS FOR ITERATIVE DEVELOPMENT

CHAPTER 9   Starting and Scaling Agile Data Warehousing 303

List of Figures

List of Tables

Preface

I risked a lot professionally when, six years ago, I published a small book suggesting IT departments consider agile methods for building data warehouses. Like many radical ideas, this notion generated a strong storm of negative responses—at first. Within a couple of years the general tone of responses decidedly changed toward the positive. Looking back now, I am glad I persisted in popularizing this particular concept because agile data warehousing is an idea whose time has come. It has been extremely rewarding to have been part of its origins, so much so that with great expectations I am pleased to offer another, more extensive book detailing the practice.

As senior solutions architect and project manager in the field of data warehousing and business intelligence (DWBI), I speak or teach internationally at a half-dozen data warehousing conventions each year. I always ask who in the audience is building a data warehouse with an agile method. When I first started offering classes on agile DWBI at these events, perhaps one person out of a room of one or two hundred attendees would raise his hand. Now, six years later, sometimes half the room will answer yes. Moreover, folks approach me during class breaks to share their experiences with agile data warehousing. By and large, they are achieving wonderful results at some of the largest, best-known Fortune 500 companies in the world, representing industries as diverse as retail, aerospace, health care, insurance, manufacturing, and software.

One of my recent conversations with the director of business intelligence at a major transportation firm for which my company recently started consulting summarized nicely the results these organizations are experiencing: "I can't tell you what a difference agile warehousing has made at our company in just six short months. Delivery speed is up, programmer productivity is up, business engagement is up, quality is up, staff accountability is up." His DWBI department was benefitting deeply from the revolutionary aspects of the agile methods, including time-boxed iterations, embedded business partners, incremental deliveries, regular product demonstrations of truly shippable modules, integrated quality assurance, and frequent attention to process improvement.

The steady stream of positive testimonials I encounter has convinced me that the practice of agile data warehousing is off to a good start. But as strong as these case histories may be, agile methods are still not the pervasive approach for delivering business analytics. A project management style that yields such positive results deserves to be shared well beyond just the core of global companies. This book is powered by the desire to reach the next tier of companies, to introduce agile data warehousing with whoever might benefit among the Fortune 5000 and even the Fortune 50,000.

Answering the skeptics

Embedded within that goal is the desire to provide a counterpoint to those comments claiming that "agile warehousing cannot be done." Over the past several years, I encountered this assessment in print, online, and in person, even at companies that would be wildly successful with the approach only a few months later. These skeptical individuals always had valid concerns that usually fell into one of two camps. One group thoroughly doubted the wisdom of working closely with the customer. "Customers never think carefully enough about what they want. They ask for too much at once. They change their mind at the drop of a hat." With the customer embedded into the development process, programmers might deliver fast but the business partner will only have them chasing their tails, so why bother?

The other group doubted that any team working incrementally could deliver an enterprise-quality data warehouse. "DWBI requires solid data architecture. All data ambiguities must be resolved before you start coding, else you'll have conflicting definitions and transformation rules across the corporation." The business departments might get what they want if the developers rushed incremental enhancements into production, but the corporation will never have a single version of the truth, so why bother?

These objections may sound impossible to answer until one realizes that an agile data warehousing community exists today. We are delivering enterprise data warehouses, and incremental delivery plus close collaboration with business customers is integral to our success. With this book, I hope to illustrate the nature of these solutions so that those listening to the debate will hear both sides expressed well.

Intended audience

I anticipate that there will be three types of individuals listening to that debate, each hoping to hear something different. First, there will be DWBI professionals who are currently leading a development team, following traditional methods. If the statistics cited in the first chapter of this book have any validity, well over half of these team leads already feel that their developers are moving far too slow for their projects to succeed. These readers will be looking for a way to accelerate their programming in the next couple of days. This book provides a quick way to get started with agile methods and then a step-by-step path to enhance the method as each team matures with the practice.

The second group within the audience will probably be DWBI directors. They will be curious as to whether enterprise-level analytics can be implemented using the iterative and incremental approach that many of the agile methods champion. These readers might be willing to make some compromises upon the current methods of their departments, but they will not want to discard all the disciplined practices they have acquired and used successfully over the past decades of their careers. This book plans on providing a balanced approach that offers delivery speed while maintaining just enough process discipline to support corporate solutions.

Last, but not least, the audience for this book may well include project sponsors from the business side of a company. These individuals are undoubtedly afraid that the DWBI projects they have commissioned will be like many of the other projects they have pursued with the help of their IT departments or outside vendors. Development teams demand exhaustive requirements, disappear for months on end, and then return frequently with an application that is missing a large number of the features needed. These business readers are hoping to find a different way to work with IT, one that does not involve so much risk. This book offers a new collaboration model for business and IT in which projects start delivering early and provide frequent checkpoints throughout the development effort.

Parts and chapters of the book

The organization of the material presented in this book tries to answer first the most pressing questions listed earlier, questions regarding how to make developers doubly productive right away. The presentation then steadily pulls back the lens and folds in enterprise-level software engineering disciplines until it addresses the questions of all three of the parties listed previously. Part 1 is to make the reader quickly fluent in a practical, incremental delivery method. Its first chapter describes the problems with traditional methods that an agile approach is designed to address. Chapter 2 sketches a generic agile method called Scrum in order to provide teams with a baseline from which they can begin crafting their own agile solutions. Chapter 3 provides the mechanics of managing the development activity within an agile project room.

Part 2 of the book focuses upon an aspect of agile methods that new warehousing teams invariably find a tremendous challenge: organizing the project for both maximum customer satisfaction and fast incremental delivery. Chapter 4 presents how to author requirements in a uniquely agile way by employing "user stories." Chapter 5 provides an agile approach to defining a DWBI project top down so that it has both the right boundaries and the right connections to enterprise architecture. It then offers an extensive example of writing user stories for a data warehousing project. For DWBI projects with significant data integration requirements, user stories typically prove too large for agile teams to deliver within a short development iteration. Chapter 6 solves this conflict using a slight variation on the user story format called the "developer story." I have always felt that developer stories were the missing ingredient when others claimed agile methods do not work for DWBI. Chapter 7 provides another crucial element for agile data warehousing, namely estimating the level of effort for project work. The estimation techniques presented take place at three distinct levels: the work for the next iteration, the whole project before it is funded, and the remaining project once development is underway. This chapter also outlines techniques that I've drawn upon over the years to achieve early deliveries of the features business customers want most while simultaneously sequencing those deliverables so as to avoid senseless rework.

While Part 2 discusses how to define a DWBI project so that it is ready for agile development, Part 3 turns the perspective around to focus upon how to redefine an agile method for the demands of data warehousing. Chapter 8 outlines several adaptations one has to make to project room activities to successfully navigate the rigors of data integration requirements. Perhaps the most important of these adaptations is to "pipeline" the work to a modest degree so that teammates in each software engineering specialty receive the time needed to achieve high-quality work and enterprise objectives. Finally, Chapter 9 provides a step-by-step means of introducing the modified agile method to a new team and then discusses how to scale up successful implementations for managing a program of multiple projects. It concludes with a survey of further modifications data warehousing departments can make to Scrum, as offered by the lean software community. These modifications may well permit even faster deliveries with a lower method overhead for those projects that can meet the prerequisites.

As this book builds chapter by chapter to a complete solution for the agile DWBI project room, I will call out a few places where innovations outside the walls of the project room could be useful. In particular, there are aspects of requirements management, quality assurance, and data engineering that require resources from and planning by a company's data warehousing department. These topics are addressed by a subsequent volume to this book that focuses upon getting agile data warehousing practices "right" for the enterprise.

Invitation to join the agile warehousing community

It is hoped that project team leads, DWBI directors, and project sponsors will all find substantial elements within this book that address the challenges they face with data warehousing projects in their workplace. I invite all who try the strategies and tactics presented here to contribute back a distillation of their experience by taking the *agile data warehousing adoption survey*, locatable though the companion site for this book. The results of this survey are presented regularly at data warehousing and information management conventions throughout the year. The collective insights the survey offers will be enriched by the input of all practitioners, no matter what the outcome of their projects. If a company performs well with the method offered in this book, as have so many other organizations, then the agile warehousing community will get a glimpse of the factors that reliably make projects succeed. If, however, a company's first few agile warehousing efforts deliver mixed results, then the community still benefits as the survey identifies areas where further refinements to the method can be made. Either way, a more standard, baseline approach to fast delivery of business intelligence applications will emerge, increasing the probability of success for all who follow later.

Ralph Hughes
June 2012
www.agiledatawarehousingbook.com

Author's Bio

Ralph Hughes, former data warehousing/business intelligence (DW/BI) practice manager for a leading global systems integrator, has led numerous BI programs and projects for Fortune 500 companies in aerospace, government, telecom, and pharmaceuticals.

A certified scrum master and a Project Management Institute project management professional, he began developing an agile method for data warehouses in 1996 and was the first to publish books on the iterative solutions for business intelligence projects.

He is a veteran trainer with the world's leading data warehouse institute and has instructed or coached over 1000 BI professionals worldwide in the discipline of incremental delivery of large data management systems.

A frequent keynote speaker at business intelligence and data management events, he serves as a judge on emerging technologies award panels and program advisory committees of advanced technology conferences.

He holds BA and MA degrees from Stanford University where he studied computer modeling and econometric forecasting.

A coinventor of Zuzena, the automated testing engine for data warehouses, he serves as chief systems architect for Ceregenics and consults on agile projects internationally.

An Introduction to Iterative Development

What Is Agile Data Warehousing?

1

How are agile approaches different than traditional methods?
What does it take to make agile succeed for data warehousing projects?
Where do we have to be careful with this new approach?

Faster, better, cheaper. That's the promise that agile methods have been delivering upon during the past decade for general application development. Although they are an increasingly popular style of programming for transaction-processing or data-capture applications, they have not been employed nearly as much for data warehousing/business intelligence (DWBI) applications. It usually takes a combination of project disasters and existential threats to inspire corporate DWBI departments to consider replacing their traditional development methods. Typically, the impetus to change begins after several projects seriously overrun their go-live dates and/or forecasted delivery budgets. Next, the project sponsors in the company's business departments start to grumble. "Our corporate data warehousing department is way too slow and far too expensive." Eventually, one end-user department finds a way to build an analytical application using an outside services vendor and reports to the other business leads that this new system required a fraction of corporate DWBI's typical time and cost brackets. "Should we send all of our business intelligence (BI) work to outside vendors?" the business departments begin asking themselves. It does not matter to them that outside vendors trying to deliver fast frequently neglect to program the many hidden attributes needed to make a system manageable, scalable, and extensible over the long run. All the business sponsors saw was fast delivery of what they asked for. If the business units are frustrated over time and cost, corporate DWBI will survive only if it finds a way to accelerate its deliveries and lower programming expense, restoring its rapport with the customer. This type of predicament is exactly why corporate DWBI should consider agile data warehousing techniques.

On the one hand, it is easy to understand why the popularity of agile for data warehousing lags 10 years behind its usage for general applications. It is hard to envision delivering any DWBI capabilities quickly. For data capture applications, creating a new element requires simply creating a column for it in the database and then dropping an entry field for it on the screen. To deliver a new warehousing attribute, however, a team has to create several distinct programs to extract, scrub,

Agile Data Warehousing Project Management.
DOI: http://dx.doi.org/10.1016/B978-0-12-396463-2.00001-6

integrate, and dimensionalize the data sets containing the element before it can be placed on the end user's console. Compared to the single transaction application challenge that agile methods originally focused on, data warehousing projects are trying to deliver a half-dozen new applications at once. They have too many architectural layers to manage for a team to update the data transform logic quickly in order to satisfy a program sponsor's latest functional whim.

On the other hand, data warehousing professionals need to be discussing agile methods intently, because every year more business intelligence departments large and small are experimenting with rapid delivery techniques for analytic and reporting applications. To succeed, they are adapting the generic agile approaches somewhat, but not beyond recognition. These adaptations make the resulting methods one notch more complex than agile for transaction-capture systems, but they are no less effective. In practice, agile methods applied properly to large data integration and information visualization projects have lowered the development hours needed and driven coding defects to zero. All this is accomplished while placing a steady stream of new features before the development team's business partner. By saving the customer time and money while steadily delivering increments of business value, agile methods for BI projects go a long way toward solving the challenges many DWBI departments have with pleasing their business customers.

For those readers who are new to agile concepts, this chapter begins with a sketch of the method to be followed throughout most of this book. The next sections provide a high-level contrast between traditional development methods and the agile approach, and a listing of the key innovative techniques that give agile methods much of their delivery speed. After surveying evidence that agile methods accelerate general application development, the presentation introduces a key set of adaptations that will make agile a productive approach for data warehousing. Next, the chapter outlines two fundamental challenges unique to data warehousing that any development method must address in order to succeed. It then closes with a guide to the remainder of the book and a second volume that will follow it.

A quick peek at an agile method

The practice of agile data warehousing is the application of several styles of iterative and incremental development to the specific challenges of integrating and presenting data for analytics and decision support. By adopting techniques such as colocating programmers together in a single workspace and embedding a business representative in the team to guide them, companies can build DWBI applications without a large portion of the time-consuming procedures and artifacts typically required by formal software development methods. Working intently on deliverables without investing time in a full suite of formal specifications necessarily requires that developers focus only on a few deliverables at time. Building only small pieces at a time, in turn, repeats the delivery process many times. These repeated deliveries of small scopes place agile methods in the category of "iterative and incremental development" methods for project management.

When following agile methods, DWBI developers essentially roll up their sleeves and work like they have only a few weeks before the system is due. They concentrate on the most important features first and perform only those activities that directly generate fully shippable code, thus realizing a tremendous boost in delivery speed. Achieving breakthrough programming speeds on a BI project will require developers to work differently than most of them are trained, including the way they define requirements, estimate work, design and code their systems, and communicate results to stakeholders, plus the way they test and document the resulting system modules. To make iterative and incremental delivery work, they will also need to change the physical environment in which they work and the role of the project manager. Most traditional DWBI departments will find these changes disorienting for a while, but their disruption will be more than compensated for by the increased programmer productivity they unleash.

Depending on how one counts, there are at least a dozen agile development styles to choose from (see sidebar). They differ by the level of ongoing ceremonies they follow during development and the amount of project planning they invest in before coding begins. By far the most popular flavor of agile is Scrum, first introduced in 1995 by Dr. Jeff Sutherland and Ken Schwaber. [Schwaber 2004] Scrum involves a small amount of both ceremony and planning, making it fast for teams to learn and easy for them to follow dependably. It has many other advantages, among them being that it

- Adroitly organizes a team of 6 to 10 developers
- Intuitively synchronizes coding efforts with repeated time boxes
- Embeds a business partner in the team to maximize customer engagement
- Appeals to business partners with its lightweight requirements artifacts
- Double estimates the work for accuracy using two units of measure
- Forecasts overall project duration and cost when necessary
- Includes regular self-optimizing efforts in every time box
- Readily absorbs techniques from other methods

AGILE DEVELOPMENT METHODS

Adaptive	[Highsmith 1999]
Crystal	[Cockburn 2004]
Disciplined Agile Delivery	[Ambler 2012]
Dynamic Systems Development Method (DSDM)	[Stapleton 2003]
Extreme Programming (XP)	[Beck 2004]
Feature Driven Development (FDD)	[Palmer 2002]
Lean Development	[Poppendieck 2003]
Kanban	[Anderson 2010]
Pragmatic	[Hunt 1999]
Scrum	[Cohn 2009]
Unified Processes (Essential, Open, Rational, etc.)	[Jacobson, Booch, & Rumbaugh 1999]

Scrum has such mindshare that, unless one clarifies he is speaking of another approach, Scrum is generally assumed to be the base method whenever one says "agile." Even if that assumption is right, however, the listener still has to interpret the situation with care. Scrum teams are constantly optimizing their practices and borrowing techniques from other sources so that they all quickly arrive at their own particular development method. Over time Scrum teams can vary their practice considerably, to the point of even dropping a key component or two such as the time box. Given this diversity in implementations, this book refers to Scrum when speaking of the precise method as defined by Sutherland and Schwaber. It employs the more general term "agile" when the context involves an ongoing project that may well have started with Scrum but then customized the method to better meet the situation at hand.

Figure 1.1 depicts the simple, five-step structure of an iteration with which Scrum teams build their applications. A team of 6 to 10 individuals—including an embedded partner from the customer organization that will own the applications—repeats this cycle every 2 to 8 weeks. The next chapter presents the iteration cycle in detail. Here, the objective is to provide the reader with enough understanding of an agile approach to contrast it with a traditional method.

As shown in Figure 1.1, a list of requirements drives the Scrum process. Typically this list is described as a "backlog of user stories." User stories are single sentences authored by the business stating one of their functional needs. The embedded business partner owns this list, keeping it sorted by each story's importance to the business. With this backlog available, Scrum teams repeatedly pull from the top as many stories as they can manage in one time box, turning them into shippable software modules that satisfy the stated needs. In practice, a minority of the stories on a backlog include nonfunctional features, often stipulated for the application by the project architect. These "architectural stories" call for reusable submodules and features supporting quality attributes such as performance and scalability. Scrum does not provide a lot of guidance on where the original backlog of stories comes from. For that reason, project planners need to situate the Scrum development process in a larger project life cycle that will provide important engineering and project management notions such as scope and funding, as well as data and process architecture.

The standard development iteration begins with a **story conference** where the developers use a top-down estimating technique using what are called "story points" to identify the handful of user stories at the top of the project's backlog that they can convert into shippable code during the iteration.

Next, the team performs **task planning** where it decomposes the targeted user stories into development tasks, this time estimating the work bottom-up in terms of labor hours in order to confirm that they have not taken on too much work for one iteration.

After confirming they have targeted just the right amount of work, the teammates now dive into the **development** phase, where they are asked to self-organize and create over the next couple of weeks the promised enhancement to the application, working in the most productive way they can devise. The primary ceremony

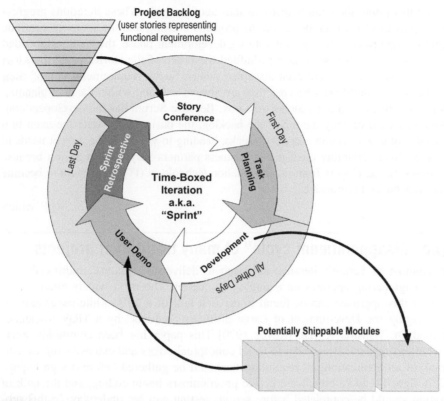

Project Backlog
(user stories representing
functional requirements)

FIGURE 1.1

Structure of Scrum development iteration and duration of its phases.

that Scrum places upon them during this phase is that they check in with each other in the morning via a short stand-up meeting, that is, it asks them to hold a daily "scrum."

At the end of the cycle, the team conducts a **user demo** where the business partner on the team operates the portions of the application that the developers have just completed, often with other business stakeholders looking on. For data integration projects that have not delivered the information yet to a presentation layer, the team will typically provide a simple front end (perhaps a quickly built, provisional BI module) so that the business partner can independently explore the newly loaded data tables. The business partner evaluates the enhanced application by considering each user story targeted during the story conference, deciding whether the team has delivered the functionality requested.

Finally, before beginning the cycle anew, the developers meet for a **sprint retrospective**, where they discuss the good and bad aspects of the development cycle they just completed and brainstorm new ways to work together during the next cycle in order to smooth out any rough spots they may have encountered.

At this point, the team is ready to start another cycle. These iterations progress as long as there are user stories on the project's backlog and the sponsors continue funding the project. During an iteration's development phase, the team's embedded business partner may well have reshuffled the order of the stories in the backlog, added some new one, and even discarded others. Such "requirements churn" does not bother the developers because they are always working within the near-planning horizon defined by the iteration's time box. Because Scrum has the developers constantly focused on only the top of the backlog, the business can steer the team in a completely new direction every few weeks, heading to wherever the project needs to go next. Such flexibility often makes business partners very fond of Scrum because it allows the developers from the information technology (IT) department to become very flexible and responsive.

The "disappointment cycle" of many traditional projects

In contrast to Scrum's iterative approach to delivering systems, traditional software engineering operates on a single-pass model. The most widely cited definition of this approach can be found in the first half of a 1970 white paper entitled "Managing the Development of Large Software Systems" by a TRW researcher named Dr. Winston Royce. [Royce 1970] This paper has been commonly interpreted to suggest that, in order to avoid conceptual errors and extensive reprogramming of an application, all requirements should be gathered before design begins, all design should be completed before programmers begin coding, and the bulk of coding should be completed before serious testing can get underway. In this process, each work phase should "fill up" with specifications before that information spills over into the next phase—a notion that led many to call this approach a cascade or a "waterfall" method.

Many people describe this waterfall process as the "big design up-front" strategy because it requires enormous design specifications to be drafted and approved before programming work can begin. [Ambler 2011] It has also been called a "plan-driven" or "command and control" approach because the big design results in enormous project plans, with possibly thousands of separate tasks, that project managers use to drive the daily activities of the development teams they command. A further name for this style of organizing development is the "big bang" approach because all the value is theoretically dropped upon end users at the conclusion of the project.

Waterfall-style project organization can seem to be a safe approach for large applications, especially those with multiple, intersecting data layers found in data warehouses, because the engineers supposedly think out all aspects of the project thoroughly ahead of time. Scrum, however, simply takes a few requirements off the top of a list and converts them into code before the next set of features is even considered. In contrast to a waterfall method, Scrum can seem very tactical and ad hoc.

For these reasons, when software professionals first learn of agile, they often decide that a waterfall method must be far more robust. Such conclusions are ironic because waterfall methods have had over 40 years to prove themselves, but statistics show that they struggle to deliver applications reliably. The Standish Group's seminal "Chaos" reports detailed the software industry's track record in delivering large systems using traditional methods. [Standish Group 1999] After surveying the results of 8380 projects conducted by 365 major America companies, results revealed that even small projects below $750,000 were unable to deliver applications on time, on budget, and with all the promised features more than 55% of the time. As the size of the applications grew, the success rate fell steadily to 25% for efforts over $3M and down to zero for projects over $10M (1999 dollars).

Data warehousing projects fall easily in the middle to upper reaches of the range documented in the Standish study. Not surprisingly, they, too, have demonstrated trouble reliably delivering value under traditional project management methods. A survey performed in 1994—before agile methods were common—by the data management industry's primary trade magazine revealed that its readers' data warehouse projects averaged above $12M in cost and failed 65% of the time. [Cited in Ericson 2006] Such statistics do not indicate that every waterfall-based data warehousing project is destined to fail. However, if the approach was as robust as people often assume, plan-driven, big-bang project methods should have achieved a much higher success rate in the 40 years since Royce's paper first defined the approach.

Unfortunately, there is a good reason to believe that waterfalls will remain a very risky manner in building large systems: the specifications flowing into any one of its phases will always contain flaws. Being only human, the individuals preparing these enormous artifacts will have less than perfect foresight, especially for companies situated in a world market that is constantly changing. Moreover, in this age of increasing global competition, the engineers producing these specifications are also frequently overworked and given too little time to thoroughly research a project's problem domain. In this reality, developers working from these specifications will steadily encounter the unexpected. Lamentably, waterfall methods contain no back step that allows the developers to substantially revisit requirements if they encounter a major oversight while coding. Testing, compressed to fit into the very last phase of development, cannot call for a major reconsideration of a system's design. With plan-driven project management, the team is locked into a schedule. They must hurriedly span the gaps between their specifications and the actual situation because, according to plan, work must move steadily downstream so that the project meets its promised delivery date.

Rather than mitigating project risk, the waterfall approach actually inflates it. Aiming for a big design up front, waterfall processes are heavy with documentation and encumbered with numerous reviews in an effort to avoid oversights. However, large specification documents acquire their own inertia by virtue of the long procedures needed to update and reapprove them. With this inertia, errors committed during requirements or design phases get "baked into" the application because it is either too expensive or too late to substantively rework specifications when flaws are discovered in them. The phases cannot validate nor contribute to one another's success, making each phase a single point of failure. The entire project will either succeed or fail based on the quality of the requirements package taken in isolation, then the quality of the design taken alone, and then finally the quality of the coding as a whole. Because little flaws cannot be simply corrected when they are discovered, their consequences get amplified to where any one of them can threaten the entire undertaking.

In this light, an iterative approach mitigates risk in an important way. Scrum validates the engineering of each small slice of the project by pushing it through requirements, design, coding, and testing before work on the next set of stories from the backlog begins. Errors detected in any of these engineering steps can provide important guidance on how the team should pursue the remainder of the project. Scrum practitioners note that the method pushes errors to the surface early in the process while there is still time to correct assumptions and the foundations of the project's coding. (See, for example, [Vingrys 2011].) In contrast to the tendency of a waterfall to allow errors to undermine a whole project, the agile approach works to contain failures to just one project slice at a time.

Being large undertakings by nature, data warehousing initiatives pursued with a single-delivery paradigm demonstrate waterfall's whole project failure pattern all too often. A quick sampling of horror stories shared with the author by prospective customers seeking a better approach to building business intelligence systems illustrates the point well:

- A major waste management company complained "We hired one of the world's top systems integrators to build our data warehouse. It cost us $2 million and 3 years of time. All we got was one report. Seems like a very expensive report."
- A Fortune 500 telecommunications company related with alarm "We purchased a 'ready-to-use' enterprise data model from our data warehouse appliance vendor. Once it was in place, their consultants told us they would need 2 years to customize it for our company and 3 years to populate it with data before we could build our first dashboard.
- A Fortune 50 pharmaceuticals company lamented "Our electronic data management project required 150 people for over 3 years and got so expensive it was starting to hurt our share price."

When large, plan-driven projects begin to fail, the managers start taking extraordinary measures to rebalance budgets, deadlines, and intended features. As depicted in Figure 1.2, such a project starts out with a firm forecast of cost, time, and scope. As it becomes stressed by nasty surprises, time and cost estimates start to climb, forcing sponsors to steadily accept less scope in order to keep the project affordable. After several such crises and delays, the company is eventually grateful to push even a small subset of functions into production and declare some level of victory, although the functionality delivered is far less than promised and the cost often double or more than planned for.

Data warehousing/business intelligence departments turn this all-too-common pattern of increasing costs and shrinking deliverables into a *cycle* of disappointment because, still believing that a big design up front is the best strategy, they repeat this basic approach for the next project. They believe the last project failed because they

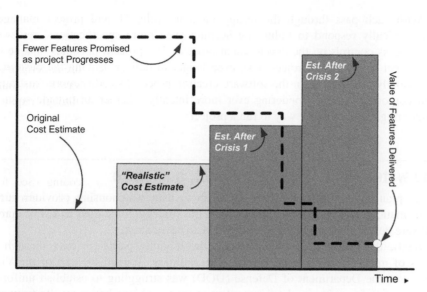

FIGURE 1.2

All too often, waterfall methods yield to the project "disappointment cycle."

did not manage it carefully enough, and start the next project with even more extensive planning and detailed design.

We can rule out unique occurrences of unusual circumstances as the primary cause for failed projects such as the ones sketched earlier. Unlike Tolstoy's unhappy families, failed waterfall projects in data warehousing all seem to be miserable for the same basic reasons. On an average engagement, the project manager specifies work packages in excruciating detail with 5000 lines or more in the project plan. He directs and cajoles the developers relentlessly. Everyone works nights and weekends, and still the project runs months behind and millions over budget, delivering only a fraction of what was promised. When the after-project, lessons-learned session is convened, participants will voice the same rueful observations heard on so many previous efforts:

- We should have done better at gathering requirements.
- The business didn't know what they wanted because they had never seen a warehouse before.
- Design took too long, leaving no time for careful coding.
- Conflicting definitions for data elements made designs worthless.
- Coding went too slow so testing got started far too late to catch some crucial defects.
- Programmers didn't build what was specified.
- Dirty data created nightmares that undermined our schedule.
- By the time we finally delivered, the business had changed and the customer wanted something else besides what we built.

With each pass through the disappointment cycle, IT and project management typically respond to failure by heaping even more specifications, reviews, and process controls on the development process. The process becomes opaque to the project sponsor and projects take even longer to deliver, leaving the customer increasingly alienated from the software creation process, steadily more frustrated with corporate IT, and wondering ever more intently whether an outside service vendor might have a better way to run a project.

The waterfall method was, in fact, a mistake

If the plan-driven, single-delivery approach to data warehousing provides such problematic results, it is natural to ask how the strategy got started and why many software development organizations continue to advocate it.

Sadly, the waterfall approach became the reigning paradigm only through a series of mistakes originating with the U.S. military. Toward the end of the Viet Nam war, the Department of Defense (DOD) was struggling to establish uniform requirements for software development in order to achieve better results from its systems integration contractors. The DOD issued a series of process specifications, including DOD-STD-2167, issued in 1985, which made the single-pass waterfall method as outlined in Dr. Royce's white paper the standard approach for procured systems. [DOD 1985]

As the military's standard for evaluating contractor development processes, DOD-STD-2167 proved to be particularly influential and soon transported the single-pass approach into many further methods descriptions throughout the world. The large-system contractors naturally trained their developers in the approach, and these individuals carried 2167's plan-driven approach to the successive companies they worked for throughout the remainder of their careers. The resulting waterfall methods proliferated, despite the fact that the military's experience with the approach was disappointing to say the least. A 1995 report on failure rates in a sample of DOD projects revealed that given the $37 billion spent on these projects, 75% of the projects failed or were never used, and only 2% were utilized without extensive modification. [Jarzombek 99]

Ironically, DOD-STD-2167 can only be viewed as a grievous misreading of Royce's paper. In its opening pages, Royce identifies the classic waterfall phases, but describes them as only the "essential steps common to all computer program developments, regardless of size or complexity." In the second half of the document, Royce clearly advocates an *iterative* path for progressing through these process steps. Pursuing them sequentially from analysis through coding in a single pass "is risky and invites failure," he warned, suggesting that such a method would work only for "the most uncomplicated projects."

When interviewed in the mid-1990s, the author of DOD-STD-2167 in fact admitted that he had been unaware of the notion of incremental delivery when he drafted his recommendations, even though there were many such methods available at the time. One can only speculate that, in the rush to fix the military's software procurement process for development services, he had read no more than the first half of the Royce's white paper and missed the warning completely. With hindsight, he said, he would have strongly advocated the iterative development method instead. [Larman 2004]

In 1994, DOD replaced STD-2167 with a standard that promoted an incremental and iterative approach. Unfortunately, other governmental departments and several standards bodies had by that time based their methods and operations on 2167 so that the waterfall strategy was the software industry's de facto standard for systems engineering, still in force today. Knowing its origin, however, offers an opportunity to advocate an alternative. One can argue that to persist with a noniterative, document-driven method is to cling to a fundamental error in software engineering, acknowledged by the author of the very approach most the world is following. In fact, switching to incremental and iterative delivery would be simply returning to the methodological direction that Royce established over 40 years ago.

Although the history just described clarifies how waterfall methods got established, explaining why we stick to it after decades of project failures is a bit harder. If the plan-driven, big design up-front strategy remains common, despite its high documented failure rate, it must have a strong psychological appeal, such as

- It parallels the construction industry where buildings are completely blueprinted and costs are estimated in detail ahead of time.
- Those whole project estimates seem to mitigate risk by "thinking of everything" before project sponsors allow coding to begin.
- Fully detailed plans make progress easy to control because project managers can make statements such as "the design work in now done, and we have spent only 45% of the budget—about what we expected."
- The detailed work breakdown structure contained in a plan provides the appearance of a highly controlled process, reassuring stakeholders that the calamities of previous projects cannot occur again.

Perhaps it is important to add one final consideration about why IT departments stick with plan-driven approaches: professional risk. Project managers who take on multimillion dollar projects know they cannot guarantee the engagement will succeed, but they can follow the company's waterfall method in every aspect. If the project later disappoints its stakeholders, the project manager can deflect blame and its consequences by claiming "We followed the method to the letter. If this project failed, then it must be the method's fault, not ours."

Although having a document-heavy, plan-driven method to hide behind might provide some job security, it imposes tremendous risk and cost upon the customer and considerable stress upon the developers who work in the micromanaged environment it engenders. Considering all this risk and the misery of failure, both IT and its business partners can reasonably ask: "Isn't there a better way?" Luckily, with agile methods, the answer is now "yes."

Agile's iterative and incremental delivery alternative

During the 1990s, software programmers were wildly excited about the potential for object-oriented languages to speed up application coding. They became frustrated at first, however, because overall delivery times of their projects remained too lengthy. Eventually, many of them realized that the greatest loss of velocity involved the large specifications they were authoring and the time spent managing work plans based on them. They began to experiment and succeed with blending small amounts of requirements, design, coding, and user review on a small piece of the system at a time. Such an approach kept their projects focused on business value and accelerated their overall development by eliminating the time wasted not only on formally prepared documents, but also on the misconceptions that naturally accumulate during single-pass requirements and design efforts.

In 2001, many of these methodological innovators gathered in Park City, Utah to identify the commonalities among their different new project management styles, which had become known as "agile" methods. The result was the Agile Manifesto, which features four philosophical tenets.

We are uncovering better ways of developing software by doing it and helping others do it. Through this work we have come to value:

- Individuals and interactions over processes and tools
- Working software over comprehensive documentation
- Customer collaboration over contract negotiation
- Responding to change over following a plan

That is, while there is value in the items on the right, we value the items on the left more. (See www.agilemanifesto.org)

With this manifesto, the agile community verbalized their perception that creating shippable code was the true generator of value for their customers. The time-consuming requirement specifications, detailed design documents, and elaborate project plans were only a means to that end and should be kept as light as possible in order to put the maximum resources into solving business problems with coding. The manifesto's authors encapsulated this notion by urging software teams to "maximize the work *not* done."

The signatories of the Agile Manifesto elaborated on the four tenets by providing 12 principles. These principles are listed in the sidebar. Several of these principles clearly indicate an approach where the development team should iteratively build working software, addressing only a narrow swath of breadth and depth from the application's full scope each time.

THE 12 PRINCIPLES OF THE AGILE MANIFESTO

1. Our highest priority is to satisfy the customer through early and continuous delivery of valuable software.
2. Welcome changing requirements, even late in development. Agile processes harness change for the customer's competitive advantage.
3. Deliver working software frequently, from a couple of weeks to a couple of months, with a preference to the shorter timescale.
4. Business people and developers must work together daily throughout the project.
5. Build projects around motivated individuals. Give them the environment and support they need, and trust them to get the job done.
6. The most efficient and effective method of conveying information to and within a development team is face-to-face conversation.
7. Working software is the primary measure of progress.
8. Agile processes promote sustainable development. The sponsors, developers, and users should be able to maintain a constant pace indefinitely.
9. Continuous attention to technical excellence and good design enhances agility.
10. Simplicity—the art of maximizing the amount of work not done—is essential.
11. The best architectures, requirements, and designs emerge from self-organizing teams.
12. At regular intervals, the team reflects on how to become more effective and then tunes and adjusts its behavior accordingly.

Agile as an answer to waterfall's problems

With the outlines of both waterfall and iterative approaches now in focus, we can identify the primary areas where Scrum answers the disadvantages of waterfall while lowering risk and accelerating deliveries. Coming chapters will cite this collection as a means of ensuring that the adaptations this book makes to Scrum have left the practitioner with a method that is still "agile."

Increments of small scope

Scrum's time box allows only a small amount of scope to be tackled at once. Teams validate results of each iteration and apply lessons learned to the next iteration. Waterfall, however, validates work only as the project nears conclusion, and lessons learned can only be applied to the next project. When a waterfall team fails, it fails on an entire project, not just one small piece of the application.

Business centric

Scrum's embedded business partner steers the team and provides much of the validation of work. The business partner sees a steady stream of business-intelligible enhancements to the application, thereby believing he is constantly receiving value from the development team. The business is also validating work as it is completed, guiding the team away from mistakes as they occur and keeping risks minimized. Catching errors early and often keeps the team from losing too much time to a misconception, thus accelerating the overall delivery. With waterfall, the team disappears from business view once it gathers requirements, returning only many months later when the application is placed into user acceptance testing. The business feels locked out of the software creation and perceives a high level of risk.

Colocation

Teams gather in a shared workspace to build each iteration. Colocation allows them to share specifications verbally, eye to eye, thus allowing them to dispense with most of the written to-be specifications that plan-driven methods require. In contrast, because a waterfall project separates the development roles by time and often space, specifications have to be prepared carefully ahead of time and reviewed thoroughly, consuming tremendous amounts of time. Colocation can be relaxed to "close collaboration" for projects involving remote teammates, as discussed in a later chapter.

Self-organized teams

The engineers and programmers on a team are free to organize their work as they see fit. Through sprint retrospectives held at the end of each iteration, they refine and formalize among themselves the working patterns that allow the greatest speed and quality. Waterfall relies on a project manager to direct work, locking out process innovations that do not support the manager's need to control activity. With this constraint, teams do not work as efficiently and delivery speeds suffer.

Just in time

Developers perform detailed requirement clarification, analysis, and design when they start on a module. By locating these predecessors as close as possible to the act of coding, quality and development speed are maximized because the business contexts, constraints, and tradeoffs undergirding each design are still fresh in the developer's mind. Waterfall, however, builds up large inventories of requirements, analyses, and designs that grow stale, costing teammates time to review the documents and allowing them to commit errors when they do not read the specification perfectly.

80-20 Specifications

Scrum teams do research requirements ahead of time, and they draft the overarching design and data architecture of their applications before coding begins. However, they pursue this work only until the solution is clarified just well enough for coding to begin. They understand that as long as the key integration points of the system are clear, the details bounded within the scope of each module can wait to be addressed until that module is actually developed. Therefore, agile teams develop guidelines such as "just barely good enough" [Ambler 2005] or "just enough architecture" [Fairbanks 2010] to indicate how much effort to invest before coding.

It is convenient to call the results of this satisficing approach to investigation and design as "80-20 specifications." Using such specifications, programmers begin coding once they are clear on the most important 80% of engineering details of a module, as colocation and small-scope validation will fill in the remaining details as needed. This 80% clarity needs to be documented only enough to retain clarity until the code is built, at which time the developers will draft as-built documentation that meets the standards of their department. Lightly sketching the most important 80% of a module typically requires only 20% of the time that waterfall would invest in building a polished specification, therefore the 80-20 approach accelerates agile teams.

Fail fast and fix quickly

Contrary to waterfall methods' goal of eliminating project errors through comprehensive requirements and design, agile does not consider failure during software development as bad—as long as such failures are small in scope and occur early enough in the project to be corrected. This attitude has become embodied in a belief among agile practitioners that a strategy of "fail fast and fix quickly" minimizes greatly the risk faced by each project.

Few software professionals have ever witnessed a perfect project. Development teams are frequently surprised by unknown complexities and their own mistakes throughout the entire life cycle of a software application. If developers are going to encounter challenges in every aspect of a project, the agile community argues that teams are better structuring their off work so that these issues appear as early in a project as possible. With each new feature or system aspect they add to an application, agile teams want to detect failure before too much time has passed so that any rework required will not be too much for their streamlined methods to repair quickly.

The incremental nature of methods such as Scrum allows agile teams to uncover flaws in their process and deliverables early on while placing only a small portion of the application at risk. With the incremental approach, a small piece of the solution leads the team through the entire life cycle from requirements to promotion into production. For DWBI, this small slice of the solution will land in each successive layer of the data architecture from staging to dashboard. Misunderstandings and poor assumptions concerning any stage of engineering or architectural stratum will impede completion of the next incremental release in a painfully clear way. The team may well fail to deliver anything of value to the business for an iteration or two. With such pain revealing the major project risks during early iterations, the team can tune up their process. For the most part, because early failures reveal the biggest misunderstandings and oversights, the benefit of fail fast and fix quickly provides large cost savings over the longest possible time. This long payback of early improvements leads some agile methods, such as Unified Processes, to deliberately steer teams into building out the riskiest portions of a project first. [Kroll & MacIsaac 2006] A project employing Scrum can adapt this strategy as well.

By iterating the construction increments, agile teams can steadily reveal the next most serious set of project unknowns or weaknesses remaining in their development process. As developers repeatedly discover and resolve the layers of challenges in their projects, they steadily reduce the remaining risk faced by the customer. By the time they approach the final deliverable, no impediments large enough to threaten the success of the project should remain. Because the fail fast and fix quickly strategy has led the team to uncover big errors in design or construction in the front of the project, the rework to correct the issues will have been kept as small as possible. The potential impact to the business will have been minimized. All told, the team's early failures on small increments of features will guarantee the long-term success for the entire project.

Integrated quality assurance

Agile builds quality into the full span of development activities instead of leaving it to a late phase in the project. Within each iteration, coders write the tests that modules must pass before programming starts. Developers also check each other's work, and the business validates each delivery for fit to purpose. Whereas waterfall identifies defects long after the causal requirements and design efforts have been concluded, agile catches errors early, often while the team still has time to correct both of them. Along with the errors, agile quality practices also provide early identification and resolutions of the erroneous thinking and work patterns that engendered the defects. Each iteration improves the team's quality efforts and progressively eliminates misconceptions, thus Scrum drives defects toward zero over the length of the project.

Agile methods provide better results

Agile methods allow IT to address the discontent among business partners sketched at the opening of this chapter. Each aspect listed previously saved time and effort for the developers, letting them deliver value to the customer sooner. Saved effort also lowers programming cost. Fast iterations coupled with integrated quality assurance allowed errors to be caught and corrected so that these deliveries gain much in quality. With the combined result, IT is servicing its business partners with a method that is faster, better, and cheaper—the three primary components required for good customer rapport.

Business partners also prefer the overall arch of agile projects compared to waterfall efforts. Whereas traditionally managed projects start off being reported as "green" (on schedule) for the first three-quarters or so of a project, their status reports quickly turn "yellow" (challenged) and then "red" (delayed or over budget) as the deadline looms. Agile projects, in contrast, start off red as the teams dive into the tall stack of unknowns of a project and labor to organize themselves within that problem space. The learning that naturally occurs as the teams cycle through their iterations allows them to quickly surmount the challenges, and the project soon turns yellow, then green, and stays green thereon. Customers can quickly forget the chaos at the beginning of an agile project once new features to their applications begin to appear regularly.

Agile for general application development has demonstrated a good track record. A recent survey of over 600 developers whose teams had recently "gone agile" reported that the new method improved productivity and quality for 82 and 77% of the teams. More importantly, 78% of the respondents answered that agile methods improved customer satisfaction with their services. [Ambler 2008]

Agile for data warehousing

Agile methods may well address the fundamental flaws of the waterfall approach and generate some impressive numbers on adoption surveys, but those facts do not automatically make the incremental and iterative approach right for data warehousing and business intelligence projects. DWBI projects are indeed among the largest, most complex applications that many corporations possess. In practice, agile "straight out of the box" cannot manage their breadth and depth. The challenge of *breadth* arises from many warehouses' long data processing chains with components that vary widely in the type of modules being built. The challenge of *depth* occurs when one or more of these modules become a Pandora's box of conflicting data definitions, complex business rules, and high data volumes. Teams will need Scrum's adaptive nature to fashion a method for their project that can surmount these twin challenges.

Data warehousing entails a "breadth of complexity"

The breadth of a warehousing project stretches between the twin poles concerning "dashboarding" and "data integration." These antipodes are so different in terms of the tools employed and the type of work performed that for larger projects they are treated as separate subapplications and are often pursued by distinct teams with completely different staffing. "Dashboarding" is a shorthand label for the front-end components of a warehouse application that end users employ to review and explore the organization's data in an unrestricted, self-service manner. The dashboarding tools available today are quite mature and "nimble," making their application programming typically very straightforward, if not easier than building the transaction-capture systems that agile methods were originally invented for.

Before business intelligence data can be displayed on a dashboard, however, it must be prepared by a data integration system. Data must be extracted from its source, transformed to unlock the secrets it contains, and loaded into a target database that can get increasingly temperamental as the volume of data inserted into it goes up. To date, this extract, transform, and load (ETL) work is still a much larger problem domain than dashboarding. Even with the best of data integration tools, ETL can require far more effort per finished module than dashboarding. For most dashboarding work, programmers can operate within a prepared framework of data structures and semantics and need only build a single application to achieve their desired result. Data integration work, however, requires four or more modules to achieve anything usable. Typically it must traverse several distinct architectural layers, each dedicated to a particular task, including

- extracting necessary data from source systems
- cleansing it of errors and standardizing its formatting
- integrating the cleansed records with data from other source systems
- transforming integrated records into dimensional structures for easy data exploration

Consequently, to place a single new element on an existing dashboard can be as simple as creating a little space for it on a particular window and double clicking from a pick list to drop the desired attribute on the display. In contrast, the data integration work required to make that attribute appear in the pick list can require a team to build, test, and promote four or more separate subapplications.

With such diversity in tools and objects across the breadth of a data warehousing project, dashboarding and data integration naturally require different flavors of agile collaboration. The more straightforward challenge of dashboarding yields nicely to the generic Scrum methods detailed in the next chapter. The more nimble tool set generally allows developers to build dashboards from a loosely defined list of user stories and to place several new enhancements into production every iteration. The embedded business partner can demand wildly different objectives for each iteration, and the team will be able to keep up with him.

The tougher data integration portions of a warehouse project require teams to significantly augment those agile techniques. Even the basics of additional agile techniques data integration teams will require most of this book to present. Not only does data integration require processing modules to move data across the layers of the target database, the data volumes involved may be so large that it takes days to load the warehouse for its next user demo. Because each data element requires considerable time to be presentable to end users, data integration stories do not immediately lend themselves to small, repeated programming efforts and frequent test drives by the customer. To meet the challenges of data integration, Scrum will need the adaptations detailed later in this book, which include

- Creating another layer of functional requests underneath that of user stories
- Adding three additional team roles to facilitate incremental design, including a project architect and a data architect
- Organizing the team into a pipeline of delivery activities
- Conducting two lead-off iterations before development sprints begin
- Splitting user demos into two stages
- Maintaining many small managed test data sets to enable quick data loads before changes arrive at user acceptance testing

Teams will need to incorporate progressively more of these adaptations in their method as the extent of data integration required by their project increases. Projects that are mostly dashboarding will involve only one or two architectural layers and little data reloading. They can employ the generic agile method with few data warehousing adaptations. Projects that must span elaborate data models and complex transformation rules will require most, if not all, of the adaptations listed earlier. Figure 1.3 portrays this relationship between the amount of data integration inherent in a project and the degree to which agile data warehousing techniques must be employed.

Adapted scrum handles the breadth of data warehousing well

The adaptations listed earlier allow agile warehousing teams to dynamically adjust their implementation of Scrum as the changing mix of dashboarding and data

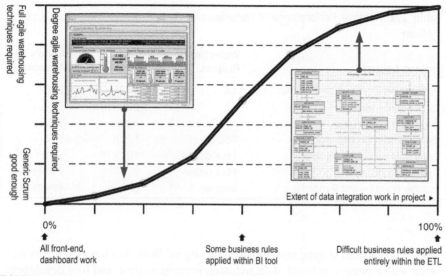

FIGURE 1.3

Complex data integration requires increasing modifications to generic agile methods.

integration will require. Empirical evidence shows that agile data warehousing works. The author has either worked with or interviewed companies with household names in the software, insurance, retail, transport, health care, and manufacturing industries that have implemented their own versions of Scrum for data management projects with great success. As of the time of this printing, the author is collaborating with The Data Warehousing Institute to conduct a survey of the DWBI profession to document the style and success rates of agile warehousing among the practitioners in the field. Results will be accessible soon via a link within the companion Web site for this book.

The author and his company have also had the rare opportunity to benchmark agile data warehousing side by side with another comparable effort that was pursued using a waterfall method. The projects were sponsored by one of the top U.S. telecommunications firms in 2008. They had approximately the same goal of placing sales and revenue of third-party equipment manufacturers into a data mart. The agile team focused on resold cell phone handsets and services, whereas the waterfall project focused on resold satellite video products and programming. Both teams worked with the same business partner and project architect so both started with identical levels of definition.

The agile project had the larger scope, as can be seen in Table 1.1, which compares labor hours as tracked by the official reporting systems of the company's project management office. Because the waterfall project had more difficult extracts to contend with, the numbers in Table 1.1 exclude the data staging effort. Also, because the dashboard applications were funded separately, the work compared in Table 1.1 involves only the design, development, and testing of modules to

Table 1.1 Relative Performance of Waterfall and Agile Projects When Run Side By Side

Project Aspect	Waterfall Project	Agile Project	Agile's Advantage
Project definition (person months)	15	4	3.8×
Target tables loaded	8	20	2.5×
Developer hours/table	1100	400	2.8×
Development expense/table	$66K	$26K	2.5×
Defects found—system test	Four dozen	10	>4×
Defects found—UAT	Four dozen	0	Infinite
Trouble tickets—first 9 months	Scores	0	Infinite

transform data from staging into dimensional targets. Both development teams were staffed with a project architect, data architect, systems analyst, and four developers.

Judging from the numbers shown in Table 1.1, the agile's approach provides a clear advantage to data integration teams. Agile reduced project start-up time by 75%, increased programmer productivity by nearly a factor of three, and drove the project's defect rate to zero. If one is looking for a faster, cheaper, and better way to build data warehouses, the agile data warehousing techniques employed in this benchmark case clearly delivered.

We must note that the agile project cited earlier was led by a very experienced solutions architect who had years of experience as a DWBI scrum master. The acceleration that a new team with a freshly trained scrum master will achieve cannot be predicted from data given previously. Estimating subjectively, however, the author believes that by following the tenets set forth in this book, a new team should be able achieve a 20 to 40% improvement in development speed within its first year of operation, which is in line with forecasts made by others who write on Scrum for nonwarehousing projects. [Benefield 2008; Maurer & Martel 2002] Several considerations for securing the highest productivity gains for beginner projects can be found in the final chapter of this book where it discusses starting a new team.

Managing data warehousing's "depth of complexity"

Dashboarding and data integration define only the breadth of difficulties that DWBI projects will encounter. There is another dimension of depth that an agile approach must sufficiently address if it is to conquer anything more involved than a data mart. This dimension appears when warehousing teams discover that some of their integration modules and even a few of their dashboard components contain abysmally deep problems involving vague requirements, inconsistent data definitions ("semantics"), and intricate business rules. If an agile team were to rush into coding these modules with only a casual understanding of their depths, it could easily produce a warehouse with inaccurate information or data that cannot be utilized for any query outside of the narrow purpose it was derived for. Such deficiencies can cause companies to abandon their DWBI applications, either immediately or after a few years, resulting in a significant waste of funds.

The danger posed by a warehousing module containing a thorny problem can harm a team in two ways. They could stumble into it unprepared and become ineffective as they try to code their way out of the morass or they could be blind to it completely and allow it to sneak into their finished product, only to see end users seriously harmed by the oversight later. This twin danger usually underlies traditional warehousing architects' insistence that warehousing teams should perform a disciplined and thorough analysis of the enterprise before starting design of the warehouse's target data structures. There are many frameworks that teams can use for such a thorough analysis, such as the Zachman and TOGAF. Zachman employs the "Six W's" (who, what, when, where, why, and how) to progressively elaborate an organization's drivers, processes, logical models, physical models, and business rules. TOGAF reveals enterprise-level requirements and concepts by matrixing the business, data, applications, and technology against a company's products, organization, and processes, plus its informational and locational elements. [Reynolds 2010]

The Data Warehousing Institute provides a similar disciplined approach to data architecture for DWBI in particular that drives development teams to completing a robust data model for their projects. This framework requires developers to stretch separate views for business context, concepts, business systems, and IT applications across an organization's transactional, decision, and analytical functions. Executed fully, this framework resolves conflicts in business definitions, yields a fact-qualifier matrix documenting the required analytics, and provides dependable logical models for both integration and dimensional data layers. [TDWI 2011]

Such disciplined analysis before programming has both advantages and disadvantages that an agile practitioner has to weigh carefully. These frameworks generate a lot of information and consequently require significant time and documentation to perform correctly. Optimists would cite that if a team is going to avoid absolutely all mistakes regarding requirements and design, such a large collection of details will be a necessary input. Pessimists would wonder whether a team can dependably sift through such a gob of information to find the details it needs when it needs them. Agilists would question whether the time required to assemble these details will undermine the purpose of the very program they were intended to assist.

Figure 1.4 shows how an agile practitioner could weigh the tradeoff between design risk and time consumed. The solid curve depicts the risk of making an error in the warehouse's requirements or data architecture. With enough effort, a team can drive this risk to zero. The dashed line in Figure 1.4 portrays another, equally important risk—the risk of delivering too late for the company to benefit from the market opportunity that caused the project sponsors to fund the development effort. Whether the application was intended to help capture new revenues, reduce

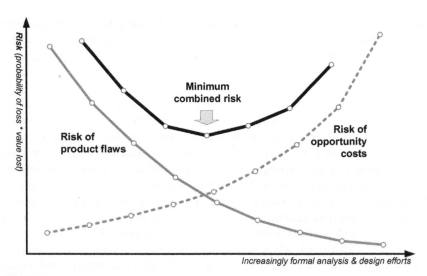

FIGURE 1.4

An agile perspective on the competing risks for DWBI projects.

expenses, or assist in regulatory compliance, the opportunity cost of delaying its deployment can be driven progressively higher by taking too long to put its capabilities online. Just like the risk of error, the value of a warehouse solution can be driven to zero with time. This diagram reveals the rational mix of speed and care a warehouse project should seek. Racing solutions into production places a team on the left side of the diagram where errors will far exceed the urgency of the need. However, investing in a complete enterprise architecture specification places the team on the right side where no need for the warehouse remains once it is finally available. The optimum level of precoding analysis and design the project should take can be found were the total of the two risk curves combine into a minimum overall risk, as indicated by the sweet spot highlighted in Figure 1.4.

Finding the optimum mix between haste and defensive analysis is an art, but there are guidelines for agile practitioners to draw upon. An approach with a good mix for general application development can be found with Scott Ambler's "agile modeling," which presents some practices for economically engineering applications with techniques such as "prioritized requirements," "look-ahead modeling," test-driven design, "document late," and "just barely good enough." Data warehousing teams can derive for themselves a DWBI-specific method for mitigating the risk posed by vague requirements, conflicting definitions, and complex business rules by applying these agile modeling principles and techniques to the TDWI framework discussed earlier for drafting domain and logical models for data warehouses.

Combining agile modeling techniques with a DWBI-specific architectural framework provides a means of deriving a single, static target model for a team to build out, but there will be some projects requiring a more dynamic approach.

Two factors in particular will push a team into work with a progressive set of models, loading and reloading the data schemas that result. The most obvious is that because the business is changing rapidly, no single design will be appropriate for more than a few months. The second is urgency where a business opportunity or threat must be addressed by the warehouse immediately, making the cost of design errors and eventual rework acceptable to the business sponsors. Updating the structure of an existing warehouse table can be painful, however, for a team working with conventional tools. Data already loaded in each table must be converted to match its new purpose. Conversion programs are labor-intensive because they must be analyzed, designed, coded, tested, and promoted like any other ETL module. Unlike ETL modules, however, they are employed only once and thus represent an expensive, nonreusable object for the company. An agile data warehousing program will not be able to maintain its high speed to market if conversion programming is its only strategy for keeping up with quickly changing requirements.

A truly agile method for data warehousing must, then, add a few new facets to its collection of techniques in order to avoid relying on conversion programming.

Agile DWBI practitioners will, then, acquire a set of techniques to add to Scrum that allows them to avoid relying on conversion programming for every transform module that contains a frighteningly deep challenge. The agile team either needs to be able to ferret out those nasty surprises and build them into the 80-20 specification before coding begins or needs the capability to quickly evolve a target data schema and its attendant ETL modules to meet the new requirement that just emerged from the shadows. Answering this call requires both techniques and tools, among them the following:

- a top-down approach that can divide up a project concept into independent data submodels, allowing the team to know that any intertable dependencies they discover later will be tightly localized
- tools that accelerate the collaboration needed to achieve an organizational consensus on the enterprise requirements, definitions, and rules the warehouse will instantiate
- advanced "hypernormalized" data modeling techniques that allow data schemas to be updated as requirements, definitions, and rules change without incurring massive rework and reloading of existing tables
- model-driven warehouse code generators that automate the predictable steps involved with updating, reloading, and reprojecting these hypernormalized data models across a warehouse's integration, presentation, and semantic layers
- data virtualization products that allow DWBI departments to quickly publish new combinations of data assets that meet pressing or transitory business intelligence requirements without having to code, test, and promote data transformation objects

Combined together, these elements will free an enterprise data warehousing program from having to concentrate on programming. The project developers will be able to focus instead on the shape and quality of the information delivered to end

Table 1.2 Spectrum of Strategies for Managing Complex Data Architectures

Project Context	Management Practice	Book and Treatment
Data marts or single-purpose subject areas: Little integration of data assets outside the application being built	Data modeler starts with key data integration points modeled, provides schema details in increments, as needed by the team	Book 1: Data architecture envisioned as another development task for delivering DWBI modules.
Multipurpose subject area or master data elements: Complex requirements, data definitions, or business rules, integration with components owned by other DWBI projects	Data modeler becomes team's interface with enterprise data architecture (EDA), provides team with schemas supporting EDA's data asset road map; applies agile modeling techniques to domain, logical, and physical data model to create target schema increments for team	Book 1: Complexity still managed within the role of the project's data architect who may have to arrange for additional resources or extra lead time to stay one iteration ahead of the programmers. Agile modeling for data warehouses addressed in Book 2
Dynamic industry or compressed delivery time frames: Requirements, definitions, and rules unstable, target data structures must evolve	Embedded data architect pursues data governance and data modeling before providing target schemas to development team(s). Model-driven DWBI application generators make evolutionary target schemas manageable. Teams iterate upon data delivered rather than the ETL code they must build.	Book 2: Fundamentals provided by enterprise data architectural frameworks. Accelerating this process so that it is agile requires hypernormalized modeling paradigms and/or auxiliary tools typically affordable only as part of an enterprise warehousing program

users. Such capability is already taking shape within the DWBI profession, and its practitioners and tool makers describe their organizing principle as "iterate upon the data rather than upon the code."

The overall strategy for resolving the challenge of unpredictably deep complexity within a DWBI project turns out to be a spectrum of choices for teams within an agile data warehousing program. As suggested by Table 1.2, agile DWBI teams do not need to commit to a one-size-fits-all approach, but instead should select the option from this spectrum that best meets their current needs.

Guide to this book and other materials

The strategies and techniques outlined earlier create a long list of topics, so long in fact that it will require two books to fully present all the necessary concepts. This book is the first of two. It focuses on getting agile methods tuned for data

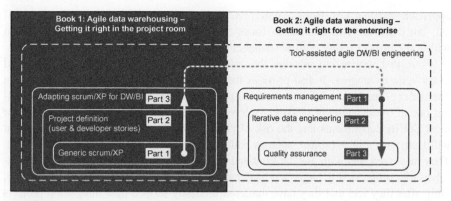

FIGURE 1.5

High-level structure of this book and its companion volume.

warehousing within the scope of the project room. It focuses on answering the challenge of breadth cited earlier, that is, the fact that DWBI projects can vary from complete dashboarding to solely data integration work. The second book concentrates on scaling the method derived in Book 1 up to the level of enterprise data warehousing programs. It explores solutions to the challenges of depth, that is, warehouse components that entail profound problems involving requirements, definitions, and business rules.

Figure 1.5 provides a view to how the material will be split between these two books and the order topics will be presented in. This book is organized into three parts. Part 1 presents a generic Scrum method, one that a DWBI team could employ immediately for a project consisting of primarily front-end, dashboarding work. Part 2 focuses on solving the challenges that new agile warehousing teams all seem to struggle with, namely decomposing projects into user stories ready for development and then packaging them into an acceptable series of incremental releases for end users. Part 3 describes several adaptations to the agile collaboration process that teams working on a DWBI project with extensive data integration projects will find indispensable.

Book 2 begins by discussing frameworks for managing requirements, offering techniques appropriate for a full range of program levels from enterprise data warehousing down to simple data mart projects. It will build upon those requirements management techniques with practices for iterative data engineering, tackling many of the issues introduced in the previous section. It wraps up by describing the components of a robust and agile quality assurance plan for projects both large and small. Throughout all three of these topics, Book 2 discusses the nature of the tools available to streamline and accelerate the work in each discipline.

The astute reader may be wondering why Book 1 starts at the bottom—the recommended process needed within a project team—whereas Book 2 proceeds top-down from requirements, to data design, to testing. A completely top-down approach starting with Book 2 enterprise disciplines would be perhaps more logical, but there are two reasons to focus first upon the reshaping the collaboration within the project room: natural sequencing and progressive perspectives.

First, that sequencing matches the order in which most warehousing teams tend to try agile techniques. It also provides the agile perspective needed to appreciate the remainder of the material. Few companies get started with agile methods by implementing one at the department or program level. The new practices are too unfamiliar for most DWBI departments and the risk of chaos seems too great. Instead a department will start with a pilot project, such as building a single data mart in an agile fashion. They may even start with just the front-end dashboard components and then ease themselves into progressively larger and harder initiatives from the realm of data integration. Only after they feel that they have mastered modestly scoped data integration projects will these companies consider scaling up the agile initiative for the entire department and enterprise warehousing initiatives. Accordingly, this book is structured to start with generic Scrum because those are the practices that DWBI departments will need for their lead-off, single data mart, pilot programs. It then layers on techniques that will equip these departments to tackle the more difficult challenges of data integration efforts. Finally, Book 2 provides techniques for meeting the integrate analytics needed by multiple, loosely related business units requiring enterprise reusable components.

Second, these books start with generic Scrum for dashboarding because it provides the necessary perspective on the fundamentals of agile. The many adaptations suggested after that will draw upon and steadily extend that perspective, downplaying or even discarding many practices cherished by traditional methods and frameworks. These philosophies are easiest to understand when applied to the smallest scope, the work room of a single project. Once the acceleration that these attitudes and behaviors provide for the single project, it becomes much easier to see their advantage at the program and department levels. By the time the DWBI department considers adopting agile as its main method, the cost savings and improved quality of agile projects will have been well demonstrated. With those notable advantages apparent, much of the discussion of the remaining implementation steps usually inverts. Instead of focusing on how to adapt agile development methods to fit into its existing EDW practices, the planners discuss how to adapt those EDW practices to protect and amplify the agile development process that is succeeding every day within the department's project rooms.

Simplified treatment of data architecture for book 1

Given the breadth and depth complexities identified previously, the two books of this set keep their presentations clear by discussing only one of those complexities at a time. Book 1 concentrates on how Scrum must be adapted as a team moves from relatively straightforward dashboarding applications into the challenges of data integration. Although deep questions may arise on those projects regarding cross-project requirements and data architectures, this book glosses over those considerations in deference to Book 2, for which they will be a primary focus. Readers coming from a data architectural background will notice that Book 1, in order to maintain this simplification for clarity, assumes certain solutions at work in the role of the data architect assigned to an agile warehousing project. The solutions packaged into the data architect's station for each level of architectural challenge were included in Table 1.2.

For data marts or single-purpose subject areas, Book 1 assumes that the data architect will start the project with only the most important aspects of the target data model designed—such as the key data integration paths between major topics. He will then progressively spell out the details of the target schema in increments as needed by his team. Later chapters in the book describe how the method creates the time the data architect will need to stay ahead of his team's coders.

For projects that advance to data integration objectives involving shared warehouse subject areas or master data elements, Book 1 envisions the data architect parleying with an enterprise data architecture group as needed. He will then transport into the project room the list of shared components the architecture group plans for the enterprise warehousing program and the roadmap scheduling their deployment. The data architect will then provide his teammates with increments of the target schema as their development iterations progress, and these increments will be compatible with the larger data architectural vision of the DWBI department.

Finally, teams developing enterprise warehousing components in a dynamic industry or under a compressed delivery time frame will have to incrementally design and build out enterprise-compatible warehouse data assets for themselves. There will be no other data modeling process for these projects to rely on. Book 1 defers all discussion of data architectural solutions for this scenario to Book 2, where the solution will involve embedding a data architect on the agile warehouse project and asking him to attend to data governance and disciplined data engineering. Book 2 discusses the advance modeling techniques and tools available that will allow the data architect to incrementally draft the necessary domain and logical models needed to keep his team's deliverables from becoming stove-piped assets that cannot be integrated with or extended to other warehouses in the enterprise.

Companion web site

The topic of agile data warehousing is truly larger than can be presented in even two volumes. Given that these books are published in the age of the Internet, however, the author can maintain a companion site for them at www.agiledatawarehousingbooks.com. This site will contain supplemental assets for the reader, such as

- a continuing discussion of the concepts presented here, often in greater depth and with comments by practitioners who can provide the benefits of their experience
- further best practices, such as ways to combine generic agile practices with data warehousing frameworks and how to address the challenges of formal compliance programs

- links to other books and tools for reengineering data warehouses that will provide essential techniques to the agile teams in the field
- links to agile DWBI professionals, such as solutions architects, data architects, analysts, and testers, who can support the pilot projects of a new agile warehousing program
- surveys on agile warehousing project experiences, their success rates, and the tools and techniques employed throughout our industry
- corrections and elaborations on the contents of this and the author's other agile data warehousing books

These materials should smooth out the inevitable bumps in the road to a stellar agile warehousing implementation and will provide an important touchstone for those hoping to evolve the practice with standards to make iterative DWBI more portable and easier to deploy.

Where to be cautious with agile data warehousing

Although agile warehousing has proven itself very effective and adaptable, it must be introduced into an organization with some care. Keeping in mind a few guidelines will help.

First, everyone needs to be prepared for some chaos during the early days of a project. In many ways, waterfall methods with their long lists of detailed tasks are far easier for teams to follow—until a project begins to implode from unresolved issues a month or two before the go-live date. Agile, in contrast, is simple, but that does not make it easy to execute. The fact that it regularly drives small slices of functionality all the way from requirements to acceptance testing means fatal misconceptions lying hidden within the project concept will bubble to the surface continually where they will stall progress until addressed effectively.

Those planners leading the newly agile program need to warn stakeholders that this steady stream of issues starts with day 1 and that they are not only part of the agile approach, but one of its best aspects. By forcing teams to address crucial issues early and often, agile ensures that project risks are being truly discovered and resolved, not pushed off until acceptance testing when too little time and resources will be available to resolve them.

Second, each agile team will require some preparatory time before they start coding. Everyone may benefit from the defects and misconceptions revealed with every sprint, but coding errors can overwhelm a team if they become too numerous. As explained earlier, Scrum is a collaboration model for fast application programming. It presupposes that someone provides the application's fundamental vision and architecture before programming begins. One of the most common mistakes managers make with agile warehousing is to believe they can simply throw coders at business problems. The agile collaboration model does not suddenly provide magic insight for the developers or the team's business partner regarding requirements and design. Even agile programmers need a moderate amount of guidance on an application's intent and desired component design. A discovery process, which is introduced as "Iteration −1 and 0" later in this book, is still needed.

Finally, agile warehousing teams need the right leadership. Scrum calls for a process facilitator called a "scrum master." Managers new to agile warehousing sometime think that scrum master and DWBI are unrelated and that any good scrum master can lead a team. Unfortunately, scrum masters who have never seen a data warehousing project before can drastically underestimate the complexity inherent in building applications with multilayered architectures and large data volumes. These individuals can make some very basic mistakes when leading a warehousing team, including

- organizing the project around user stories that are far too large in scope
- starting development sprints before enough discovery work has been done
- insisting the developers move data from source to final target in a single iteration
- believing developers can demonstrate each iteration's results using full-volume data loads
- overlooking that the roles a warehouse team can have overlap very little, to the point where many problems can be "swarmed" only by one or two individuals at a time

To prevent this type of faux pas, a company needs to engage scrum masters for DWBI projects who have built warehouses before and understand why the choices can have disappointing results. Better yet, a company should keep the scrum master as a facilitator and provide team leadership from one of the key technical roles, such as the project architect or data architect. Caution needs to be exercised in the opposite direction as well regarding these technical leaders. Modelers and architects that have not worked in an agile environment will be missing many of the practices documented in this book. Without them, these leads will be unable to avoid interdependencies between modules and rework that will slow their teams down. If the first project for an organization is large or highly visible, it may be worth engaging a warehousing architect and data architect who have worked in an agile environment before to join the team. Agile warehousing requires knowing where a team can go fast and where it must go slow. The facilitator and technical leads will only find consensus on which project area falls in each of these categories if they have one foot in both agile and data warehousing worlds.

Summary

For those DWBI professionals who have always felt there must be a better way to pursue application development as a team, agile methods offer an alternative that has proven faster, better, and cheaper for the organizations that have been bold enough to try them. The majority of agile implementations are based on Scrum, which is iterative and embeds the customer within each development cycle so that the business stays fully engaged in the requirements, design, and validation work. This collaborative development process avoids many of the antipatterns noted with the traditional, plan-driven, or "waterfall" approach. Rather than struggling to comprehend and construct a large project in a single pass, agile guides teams toward delivering in small, steadily validated modules. Iterative delivery drives issues of poor development techniques and miscommunications to the surface early so that the software engineers can fix their development processes and customers do not risk waiting too long, spending too much, and receiving too little.

To succeed with incremental delivery, warehousing projects must overcome two primary challenges: the breadth of technical work separating dashboarding from data integration and the depth of thorny requirements, semantics uncertainty, and business rules that can lie hidden in any data transform included in the project. Agile warehousing addresses the challenge of breadth by adapting the Scrum method with several techniques that are covered in this, the first volume of a two-book set. The challenge of depth is discussed in detail in the second volume.

Iterative Development in a Nutshell

What are the basic concepts of a generic agile approach?
How do they assemble into an incremental development process?
Where did the time-boxed method called Scrum come from?

Building data warehousing using agile methods requires a multifaceted approach that implements business intelligence systems incrementally in a way that shortens overall delivery times while simultaneously reducing project risk and driving application defects to zero. As introduced in the previous chapter, agile warehousing is based on Scrum, an iterative collaboration model that accelerates the programming of software applications. By colocating the developers and asking them to repeatedly deliver small installments of the required executable code, Scrum allows a team to build the envisioned system with a minimum of detailed to-be specifications for requirements and design, thus saving time while simultaneously proving out the overall concepts guiding the application's architecture. However, Scrum, as documented by its creators and practiced in general, is appropriate for building online transaction processing systems. As mentioned in the previous chapter, generic Scrum will work fine "right out of the box" for those data warehousing projects delivering mostly front-end, dashboarding applications. Generic Scrum has no specific for building applications with large data integration components. To make Scrum work for those data warehousing/business intelligence (DWBI) projects, we will have to modify some of its patterns and add portions of other agile methods such as Kanban and the Unified Process. These topics get complex and will have to be layered one upon the other throughout the rest of this book. The place to begin such a careful presentation, however, is understanding generic Scrum.

Accordingly, the goal of this and the next two chapters is to familiarize the reader with the basics of managing a project using "plain vanilla" Scrum, as most people teach and practice it today, so that we can begin to adapt it in later chapters for the data-heavy business intelligence systems. This chapter lays out the basic steps of programming a system using the method. The next chapter then outlines the lightweight project management techniques needed to keep a Scrum project on track. The chapter after that focuses on how Scrum expresses its requirements and

Agile Data Warehousing Project Management.
DOI: http://dx.doi.org/10.1016/B978-0-12-396463-2.00002-8

organizes them into a backlog of work to be programmed. The presentation will introduce this agile method not only as it is documented by its creators, but also as commonly taught and practiced by the agile community known to the author. It is hoped that this combination will equip the reader to communicate what is different and advantageous about incremental delivery methods to project sponsors or information technology (IT) managers looking for a means to accelerate a data warehousing project.

Starter concepts

Scrum is one of the simplest of the many iterative and incremental development methods available today. Its creators stripped the traditional software development process down to the core, value-generating activities needed to build an application. Scrum prescribes only enough project management mechanisms to make progress transparent and trackable for both development team members and external stakeholders, and thereafter relies on the team to identify the best means of coordinating construction activities. One of its key features is extremely close collaboration (to the point of colocation where possible) between the business customer and all members of the development team so that they can do away with the vast majority of the "to-be" specifications and time-consuming committee reviews that underlie most waterfall methods. The result is a process so streamlined and unencumbered with low-valued artifacts that an experienced Scrum master can provide a group of uninitiated developers a workable orientation to the method in less than an hour.

When first defined, Scrum focused mostly on how developers will collaborate throughout the construction phase of a development project. It provided surprisingly few practices for actual software engineering. To fill that gap, many Scrum teams incorporated many of the techniques outlined in another agile approach, Extreme Programming (XP), such as user stories and test-led development. [Beck 1999] Early agile teams found that Scrum's collaboration patterns and XP's engineering techniques complemented each other so well that many books and training programs now combine them thoroughly, calling the entire mix "Scrum/XP" or, more commonly, just "Scrum."

Even with the inclusion of XP's coding practices, this "generic" version of Scrum is still a high-level process. Practitioners must bridge for themselves the gap between the approach and their particular situation. In fact, the process of customizing the process to the unique context of each team and project is part of the approach, fundamentally imbedded into one of the steps followed during each development iteration. Accordingly, every implementation of Scrum between any two organizations or even any two projects within the same enterprise will quickly diverge from the generic process to become unique in its methodological details.

In addition to the qualities of lightweight structure, high adaptability, and equal measures of process and engineering, Scrum/XP has several other aspects that make it an optimal starting point for DWBI projects. It stipulates a minimum of processes and artifacts, making it fast to teach. It contains provisions for architecture, scaling, and nonstandard work. It also offers an internationally standardized training and certification program, allowing individuals to move easily with their knowledge of the methods to new workplaces and allowing agile organizations to readily find developers trained in the basics of their method. Because Scrum and XP for nondata warehousing projects are covered well by many writers, this chapter provides a distillation of the generic combination of the two. Readers wanting to delve deeper into the formal descriptions of Scrum and XP will find suggested readings listed in this book's references and on its companion Web site.

Three nested cycles

Because Scrum offers an alternative to traditional, "waterfall" methods, the reader may need a quick outline of a waterfall method for contrast. Figure 2.1 provides a good reference. The main line running diagonally from left to right is taken from the white paper that is widely regarded as having first defined the waterfall approach. [Royce 1970] As this process progresses from system requirements to program design and then to coding, Figure 2.1 depicts the stack of detailed specifications for the engineers and developers each step generates for the actors in the next step to fully read and understand. This accumulating mass of specifications is often the trigger that causes many software professionals to search for an alternative method such as Scrum, because, as the heft of the requirements and design

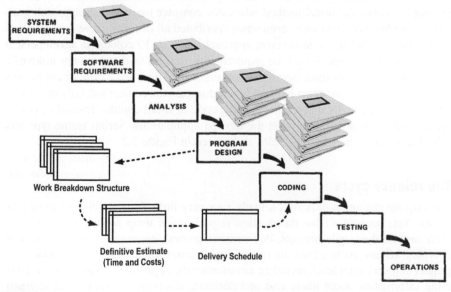

FIGURE 2.1

Typical waterfall method with key project management artifacts indicated.

documents grows, so do their doubts that anyone downstream will actually read and accurately apply all that is specified.

Linking into a waterfall method's chain of steps are a couple of key project management artifacts for which the reader should seek agile equivalents as we explore Scrum in the next few chapters. The first is the *work breakdown structure* (WBS), in which a project manager will gather all the tasks the development team must complete in order to deliver the envisioned application successfully. Software engineers usually provide the technical work items listed in a WBS, although unfortunately the overall process often takes so long that the engineers who forecasted the labor steps are not the developers required to follow them once coding begins. Once the WBS is drafted, the project manager can direct those developers to forecast the labor hours needed to accomplish each work item listed on the WBS, yielding a *definitive estimate* of the time and cost needed to complete the project. The goal of a definitive estimate is an accuracy of plus or minus 10%. [PMI 2008] With such accuracy, the traditional approach stipulates that a project manger should then convert the definitive estimate into a *delivery schedule* predicting the completion dates for key milestones of the project as well as the finished application. Given this chain of engineering events and these project management artifacts, waterfall practitioners consider the process of delivering software on time, on budget, and with all required features as a fundamentally linear and conceptually uncomplicated process: everything is specified, project managers need only to have team members follow the plan. Consequently, waterfall methods rely heavily on a project manager to understand the full list of tasks comprising the project and to assign those tasks to developers as required by the delivery schedule. With the project manager serving as a central dispatcher of work, traditional method advocates consider the waterfall approach scalable to hundreds of developers, even when distributed all over the globe.

In contrast, Scrum is an iterative approach for 6 to 10 colocated developers. It does not attempt to specify all the requirements, design, or development tasks of a project in advance. Instead, Scrum developers start with a list of important project features the application must have and then discover the project's details incrementally as they repeatedly deliver the working code in small chunks. Instead of pursuing a single, linear effort to build the desired applications, Scrum teams typically follow a series of three nested cycles as depicted in Figure 2.2.

The release cycle

The original definition of Scrum actually says very little about the first of these processes. Yet, because all but the smallest organizations wrap some form of *release cycle* around their agile projects, this wrapper process deserves some mention here. A typical release cycle allows the sponsoring organization to manage the phases of a project at a very high level, including envisioning the application's key features, gathering information about likely cost and duration, reserving resources, and planning for the integration of major system components. Release cycles vary in their details, but most have phases equivalent to the components listed in Figure 2.2. Table 2.1

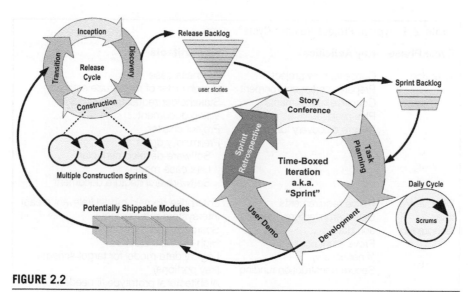

FIGURE 2.2

Three cycles of generic Scrum.

provides a quick guide to the activities and key artifacts included in each of these components. A single-sentence summary of the *inception phase* would explain that it provides actionable direction from the project sponsor, including executive-level requirements. The *discovery and elaboration phase* confirms that the project is feasible given the constraints of the existing business processes, information systems, and corporate data. This phase uses the knowledge gained to create a high- to midlevel architecture for the application's processes and data, and even to prototype the particularly risky portions of the system to ensure that they have workable solutions. The *construction phase* builds out the application, and the *transition phase* moves the resulting components into full operation.

The discovery and elaboration phase is particularly important to real-world Scrum projects. In general, it offers the project architect time to identify the likely scope of the project and to derive a reasonable list of high-level user requirements. This knowledge allows him to collaborate more effectively with the project's embedded business partner to create an initial backlog of user stories, as shown in Figure 2.2. For data-driven projects, such as data warehouses, the discovery and elaboration process also allows the project architect the opportunity to collaborate with the company's enterprise architecture group who may well be pursuing company-wide data governance initiatives or know of other warehousing initiatives that the project's DWBI application should support with its design and information.

Of more immediate concern for the agile warehousing project, the elaboration portion of the discovery and elaboration phase provides the project architect time to confirm the pertinent portions of the corporate domain model and to define key aspects of the application's logical data model. The domain model, often called a

Table 2.1 Typical Project Release Cycle[a]

Cycle Phase	Key Activities	Key Artifacts

Inception	Conceive new project
	Prepare project environment
	Conceive requirements
	Plan project
	Secure discovery funding
		Business case
		Rough order of magnitude estimate
		Stakeholder requests
		Vision document
		Project charter
		Preliminary drafts of:
		    Software development plan
		    Use-case model
		    Software architecture document

Discovery and elaboration	Refine requirements
	Define architecture (process and data)
	Prove architecture (if necessary)
	Secure construction funding
		Enterprise domain model (relevant areas)
		Intersystem requirements
		Source systems list
		High-level architecture
		Logical data model for target schema (key portions)
		Architectural prototype (if needed)
		Largely complete versions of:
		    Software development plan
		    Iteration plans for construction phase
		    Use-case model
		    Software architecture document
		Preliminary drafts of:
		    Design model (process and data)
		    Test plan

Construction	Design components
	Code and unit test
	Components
	Integrate and test Application
		Installable software
		Installation instructions
		Operations guide
		Programmers documentation
		Transition plans
		Largely complete versions of:
		    Design model (process and data)
		    Test plan
		    Installation verification procedures
		Preliminary draft of user support material

Transition	Beta and acceptance testing Package product Support installation Support early operations	User acceptance test plan Installation verification Completed user support material Operating application

[a]Adapted in part from [IBM 2007].

conceptual model, specifies the business entities the project will involve, along with their key attributes, and how they relate functionally to each other. It is useful for resolving uncertainty around and conflicts over the project's central business terms. The logical data model translates the business entities identified by the domain model into data structures and defines the functional relationships between those classes of data. For a data integration project, the key portions of the logical data model for the project would include the primary entities, their natural keys, and the foreign keys that knit the tables together.

Although drafted initially during discovery and elaboration, the domain and logical data models of an agile data integration project will be refined by the development team as the project progresses. Projects invest in the initial versions of these models during the discovery and elaboration phase to serve as a guide for the construction iterations and to reveal whether the DWBI department's standard tools and programming patterns will suffice for the envisioned application. In complex environments, the project may require a couple of preliminary iterations of prototyping to prove out soundness of the planned architecture as well as those programming solution and the project's tool set.

Most companies have a preferred funding and discovery process defined, and Scrum can work easily with the output provided by most of them. For those companies seeking a new approach to the release cycle, many documented processes are available, including several from the agile community. Readers will find considerable detail regarding an agile release cycle for data warehousing in the second volume of this two-book set, especially in the sections dedicated to requirements management and data engineering. This first volume focuses on those topics that tend to be most pressing for most individuals in a typical DWBI project room for the largest portion of a project—how to get the data transformation constructed once the target data structure is largely understood.

Development and daily cycles

Nested within the release cycle is a construction phase, which is composed of multiple instances of the second type of cycle comprising a Scrum process, the *development iteration*. The executable code for a given release accumulates through repeated occurrences of these development iterations. Scrum calls these iterations "sprints," and this book uses the terms sprint and iteration interchangeably. Each iteration represents a turn along the five-step, multiweek development cycle depicted in the middle of Figure 2.1.

In the first step of this cycle, the developers hold a *story conference* where they identify a small set of the project's user requirements that they can deliver within a few weeks. They then determine during *task planning* the detailed delivery work required to build out only the small scope identified during the story conference. These first two steps typically require a full day to complete. All the remaining days save the last one are allocated to the *development* step, where the requirements are converted into shippable modules. For the last day of an iteration, the first half is dedicated to a *user demo*, where the embedded product owner operates the working modules, accepting or rejecting the work. The developers use the remainder of the iteration's last day to hold a *sprint retrospective*, where they explore ways to improve upon their programming activities.

Embedded within the multiweek development iteration is the *daily cycle*, which consists of a brief meeting known as a "scrum," during which team members review and fine-tune their activities and sort out the dependencies between them. This chapter details both the development iteration and daily scrum in a moment after presenting a few more starter concepts essential to the method.

Shippable code and the definition of done

Scrum is designed to deliver a full working application incrementally; therefore, every development iteration should deliver potentially shippable modules of working code. "Potentially shippable" has several implications. First, the modules are not prototypes. They must have all the functional features the business partner has requested within their scope, as well as all the nonfunctional features required to satisfy the IT stakeholders of the project. As an example of the latter set, each module must comply with architectural and coding standards so that the enterprise architects feel that the final application will integrate as necessary into the department's overall collection of DWBI assets. It must also be adequately tested and documented. It must be adequately secure, as well as easily executed and restarted, so that the operations team can manage the application successfully when it is added to the automation schedule. The developers, IT management, project management, and business stakeholders all ensure that the modules delivered are potentially shippable by building considerations such as the aforementioned into a "definition of done" for the developers to employ when deciding whether their work on a given module is complete.

Scrum refers to its deliverables as "*potentially* shippable code," acknowledging that there will always be a portion of the work, such as installation guides, that can be completed only once all the modules for a release have been built. As for the rest of the term, generic Scrum's notion of "shippable *code*" may be a bit too imprecise for data warehousing. The word *code* seems to focus only on the programming of an application. This notion works fine for BI projects that involve mostly front-end dashboarding of existing data, as coded modules will be the bulk of the deliverables. Business intelligence applications involving substantial data integration, however, will require considerable attention to defining and refining the data structures into which information can be loaded for later analysis and reporting. For those projects, a "shippable *module*" may be a more appropriate term that implicitly includes target data structures, as well as coded elements for transformation and dashboards. In fact, some newer flavors of agile methods speak of "potentially consumable solutions" in order to cover the additional elements of usable software, such as documentation, as well as operations and support issues. [Lines 2012] This book refers to *potentially shippable modules* to retain a bit of the original terminology while simultaneously implying that most solutions involve more than just programmed code.

People are often surprised to see documentation in a Scrum team's definition of done. Especially when Scrum first emerged, new teams overemphasized placing working applications into production, neglecting to document the modules as built. This early practice gave agile a bad reputation of never providing documentation, a characterization that the approach no longer deserves today, given the more comprehensive definition of done that most Scrum teams employ. Careful consideration of the Scrum process outlined here should reveal that Scrum contains no inherent opposition to the best practices that IT groups depend on to make their applications dependable and manageable. Whatever best practice an organization wants to implement in its agile method, including "as-built" documentation, can be instilled into the method by fine-tuning the Scrum team's "definition of done" so that it becomes part of every iteration. Of course, a team must assess every suggested add on carefully to ensure that the proposed practice does not undermine its ability to deliver small increments of value quickly and to be responsive to changing requirements. We examine a sample definition of done in a moment.

Time-boxed development

The development sprint is the central, value-generating fly wheel of Scrum. In order to create a steady impetus to deliver deployable enhancements to the organization's business applications within a time frame that has value to the stakeholders, Scrum time boxes these iterations. Scrum teams typically set their sprint durations to somewhere between 2 and 4 weeks and rarely change the duration of that time box. In essence, Scrum keeps this fly wheel turning at a constant pace. Instead of trying to spin it faster and faster with each turn delivering the same amount, Scrum optimizes the development process by steadily increasing the metaphorical gearing attached to the fly wheel so that it produces ever more shippable code with every evenly paced turn until it achieves the team's highest, sustainable pace.

Scrum's short time boxes provide many advantages. First, it keeps the scope of each iteration concise, focusing the team's attention within the near-planning horizon where their vision is accurate. Second, the fact that everything within the time box must resolve to fully usable modules forces the team to resolve complexity and conflicts within the development iteration rather than deferring it until later in the project. Oversights and challenges therefore bubble quickly to the surface during each iteration. Scrum picks up much of its velocity from the fact that colocating the developers allows them to address these challenges in real time through eye-to-eye conversations rather than through the emails, voice mail, scheduled meetings, prepared presentations, and major reviews that waterfall methods rely upon.

This pattern of real-time issue resolution in the project room leads to a third advantage of time boxing. With most issues being resolved by a self-organized team within each iteration, Scrum becomes much easier to manage than a waterfall process. In fact, Scrum was defined as if all the requirements and activity tracking will be performed using index cards pinned to a large cork board. Teams that actually utilize this envisioned paper-based approach find that it works quite well, unless they have remote team members, in which case an electronic equivalent of the cork board becomes necessary.

Finally, time boxing development also enables both the team and management to derive a "velocity" for the team by measuring how much work gets done each iteration. A new team's velocity usually stabilizes within a few sprints, and an established team's velocity translates almost immediately to the next project as long as the work is similar. As presented in later chapters when an agile "current estimate is discussed," once a team establishes its velocity, it can begin to predict when the next release will occur and how much it will cost the sponsors to develop.

Caves and commons

Agile practices prefer colocated, highly collaborative teams, and such teams need a physical space to work in. Scrum practitioners often recommend that companies implementing an iterative method set up a facility of "caves and commons" for their developers. Commons is defined as a large, open plan area, often referred to as a "war room" or "bullpen." It allows the team to collaborate closely, to work spontaneously eye to eye whenever required by the work at hand.

However, we can imagine that providing only one large room to labor in will engender a very noisy work environment. Because loud working conditions make individual concentration difficult and stress developers when they need to attend to their private lives, the agile community also advocates supplying teams with "caves" to run to, either individual cubes or small conference rooms located near the war room.

There are two schemes for caves and commons. The first involves a large war room with a few small conference rooms around the periphery. This plan is most appropriate when the developers will be spending their time working mostly as a team, probably on a single project at a time. Caves provide a place for personal calls and for small break-out teams when they need to hold a conference call that would otherwise monopolize the commons. This "large commons" workspace arrangement lends itself well to programs based largely on contract labor, where the individuals are not accumulating volumes of personal work files to be kept and updated as the years go by.

The second plan consists predominately of individual cubicles with some dedicated conference rooms reserved for collaborative sessions. This "small commons" model implies that teammates will be spending a sizable portion of their work day on individual rather than collective efforts. This arrangement lends itself best to situations where the developers are long-term staff working multiple projects over their tenure with the company or even multiple projects at the same time.

Although agile methods believe that developers are most productive working eye to eye, iterative and incremental delivery does not absolutely require physical colocation. Techniques and technology exist for sustaining an effective *esprit de corps* among geographically dispersed teammates that will be discussed as an alternative to colocation later in the chapter on starting and scaling agile teams.

Product owners and scrum masters

If it were a fully articulated software development methodology, Scrum would prescribe detailed lists of roles and responsibilities. However, Scrum is deliberately only an approach and it emphasizes self-organized teams. Thus it provides us only with a sketch of two roles on the team—product owner and scrum master—placing everyone else in the general category of "developer." Data warehousing requires teams to define a few more roles to meet the demands of data integration, which will be detailed in a later chapter. For now, we need a sketch of just the generic scrum roles to finish presenting the generic method.

Product owner

The person filling this role comes from the business side of the organization rather than from IT. Optimally, she works in the department or division the application will primarily support. Unlike waterfall methods, where users are disjoint from the individuals building an application, this business partner is an integral part of the team in Scrum. Maintaining a high presence in the project room alongside the developers, the product owner will give the team the project's detailed requirements and prioritize the order in which they should be addressed. The product owner is also the person who will accept or reject the team's functional deliverables at the end of each iteration. Close eye-to-eye collaboration with the business through the role of the product owner is key to Scrum's ability to be responsive to the business and to avoid losing any velocity to negotiating a formal or informal contract with the customer.

Being a product owner requires steady involvement with the development team, but the role does not consume 100% of the business partner's time. Participation is naturally high during the first day of iteration planning and the last day in which the sprint demo is held. For the development step, which comprises the bulk of an iteration, the product owner needs only to answer questions regarding requirements as they arise. Because teams typically do not need such consultation every day, the time needed from the product owner adds up to only several hours per week. Many product owners find that their participation averages one quarter time or less with the team. Often they can arrange their work habits to simply start their day in the war room, reading through their email, so that they are present to answer questions that might come up. If quarter time is more than a product owner can afford, agile warehousing teams in particular can provide a *proxy product owner* by moving their project architect into that role on a daily basis and then reverting it to the embedded business partner during sprint demos. This is discussed more in a later chapter where we present the project architect role in detail.

Unlike most waterfall projects, developers on a Scrum project do not answer to a project manager, but instead to the product owner. The product owner directly represents the parties providing the funds to maintain the project and the team, and naturally he becomes very focused on getting the most out of every development iteration. By controlling the project's backlog, the product owner decides what will be built, in what order, and when it will be pushed into production, subject only to technical constraints that the developers will articulate on a daily basis. Fully engaged product owners sometime exert project leadership on a daily basis to the point where they can stand before the task board each morning, driving the team with tough questions that used to come from a project manager:

- Why aren't more task getting completed?
- Why are the remaining labor estimates ballooning?
- What are you folks planning to show during next week's demo?

The product owner must be able to express the reasoning behind the organization's conviction that the business intelligence application is both necessary and needed *now*. He must be able to express all such notions clearly and even provide real-life examples of the business situations at issue. He ensures that the teammates do not fall prey to ambiguity regarding business terms and requirements, which could happen easily given the speed at which the developers are moving and Scrum's minimalization of time-consuming to-be specifications and reviews. Finally, product owners must be prepared to make the tough decisions of which features will be built and which will not and when the functional capabilities he has requested exceed the team's ability to deliver within a given iteration, release, or even project.

Scrum master

This role provides the team with a person who knows the Scrum method very well and keeps the rest of the team on track by reminding them of the details needed to complete each step in the process. As the teammates customize Scrum to better meet their particular project and preferred work style, the scrum master records those policy decisions and ensures that the team abides by them during future iterations.

This role is not a project manager because the scrum master is not responsible for managing cost and funding, team makeup, or hitting preordained milestones. The scrum master does not own the results of the team—that is the role of the product owner. He owns only the description of the process that the team has chosen to follow. As a result, the scrum master role can actually require very little time, especially as the team matures and the developers internalize thoroughly the details of their self-organized work process. Generic Scrum actually suggests that the scrum master be only a half-time role and that he should come from a development background so that he can spend the other half of his days creating potentially shippable objects. For organizations with individuals who specialize in only scrum mastering and provide no technical skills, scrum masters can support two or more projects simultaneously.

Developers as "generalizing specialists"

At first glance, it does not seem possible to establish a fully capable team by defining only two roles and lumping everyone else under the label of "developer." Scrum concedes that the team might stumble a bit during the first couple of iterations as the developers realize the detailed activities and work patterns their precise situation calls for. To adapt, teammates will have to realistically identify their individual strengths and weaknesses, decide how they apply to the project at hand, and fit them together using Scrum's highly collaborative work process.

Few organizations have the resources to staff each team with veteran specialists who cover every technical skill a large project will need. Agile thought leaders often suggest that effective teams will need to be staffed with "generalizing specialists"—folks who start the project with a particular set of technical skills but who can also bend to fill the gaps between the existing specialties on the team. [Ambler 2011] Scrum trusts that self-organization will take over as the iterations progress, leading each person to find the optimal compromise between what he prefers to contribute and what the project needs.

For warehousing projects, integration testing provides a good example of generalizing specialists. Coders can be strong at unit testing but weak when it comes to validating business rules at the component and subsystem level, as well as qualifying that generated data make sense from one edge of the target data model to the other. In this case, the team's systems analyst can step in to define higher level test cases for business rules, as he probably identified the source-to-target transforms for the team. Similarly, the data architect will see that he is the best person to author test cases for overall data integrity, as he knows the function of each table better than anyone else on the team. Scrum's time-boxed iterations and the demo of team deliverables at the end of each one provide the impetus needed to motivate these individuals to expand past the starting definitions of their roles and provide the testing support needed to make each iteration a success.

Improved role for the project manager

As noted earlier, Scrum becomes a very simple process to manage because most of a project's complexity is resolved in real time with each iteration. Consequently, Scrum essentially eliminates the need for a project manager within the project room. Close collaboration and self-organization address many of the day-to-day dependencies that project managers used to resolve on traditional projects. The lightweight, paper-based tracking artifacts examined in the next chapter make team progress readily transparent to developers, product owners, and the larger stakeholder community. The numbers needed can be acquired directly from the team's task board and backlog. Teams that employ electronic task boards can even automate the collation and presentation of status using business intelligence applications. All told, Scrum eliminates the need for a project manager to hold frequent, detailed status meetings.

Scrum projects still need a project manager, however, just not in the project room. The self-organized team no longer needs someone to direct developer actions on a daily basis, but someone still has to marshal resources and information from the department and project's parent program into the project room. For example, if a developer quits, the project manager must work with functional managers to secure a replacement. If the team's velocity slows to the point where they need an extra iteration funded, the project manager takes the change request to the steering committee. Also, if other projects within the program revise the milestone that the agile team must support, the project manager attends all the meetings outside the team room and brings the team the net result after the multiple projects have been realigned. Many project managers appreciate Scrum for removing the burden of daily status meetings and detailed task assignments from their plate, allowing them to work on the more interesting aspects of project coordination. Often, they are pleased to find they can support multiple Scrum projects at once, which they consider job enrichment in the direction of becoming a program manager.

Might a project manager serve as a scrum master?

One person could conceivably fill the role of both project manager and scrum master, but the practice is not generally advisable. The two roles require entirely different personalities. Project managers come from a culture of command and control. That culture depends on detail planning so that control is possible, and planning requires complete, to-be specifications, which is completely at odds with an agile approach. Project managers also commonly believe it is up to them to drive the developers to get work accomplished. In contrast, Scrum provides regular evaluations of the team as a whole so that individuals do not need to be commanded. At the end of each sprint, the product owner either accepts or rejects the deliverables of the iteration, thus informing the developer whether they succeeded or failed as a team. With this whole team motivation, Scrum does not need a project manager to motivate individuals. After a disappointing iteration, the developers can be trusted to understand that their continued funding is at risk. This realization is usually enough to inspire them to analyze and resolve the individual actions that led to the team's failure.

Given that Scrum operates with whole team motivational forces, a scrum master needs to be a facilitator rather than a manger. His role is to remind the developers on his team of the particular adaptation of Scrum they have collectively chosen to follow in order to meet the objectives of each sprint dependably. Scrum masters do not guarantee the process will succeed with every iteration, and this fact is crucial to the long-term success of the agile approach. In order for team members to innovate better ways to build software and to learn self-organization, they must be allowed to risk failure. The notions of whole-team responsibility and generalizing specialists require that the developers take on the hard work of managing the details of the development process in real time. Thus, scrum masters should become at times deliberately passive when developers encounter a problem, letting teammates struggle with issues and plan solutions. Such a hands-off style is antithetical to the command-and-control training of traditional project managers. As a result, most trained project managers carry too much waterfall baggage to make the transition to agile successfully, especially if they are still managing a traditional project outside of the agile team's project room.

Moreover, a project manager's preference for a clear work breakdown structure of tasks and the delivery schedule it supports conflicts directly with the product owner. The product owner is supposed to fluidly create, destroy, and reorder the high-level requirements of the project backlog as business conditions require, leaving the tasks that formerly appeared on the waterfall's WBS to be defined as needed within each iteration. At best, this conflict between a detailed WBS and a high-level backlog will create a perennial source of contention between the project manager and the product owner that will undermine the clarity and *esprit de corps* within the project room. The worse possible outcome of this conflict will be to push the product owner from leading the team, a result that will leave the project without a fully engaged subject matter expert that understands the business situation and can provide accurate requirements.

Finally, project managers have difficulty serving as scrum masters because they must answer for budget overruns. This responsibility causes them to naturally focus on getting the most out of the developers. When this objective emerges, the team can easily sense that their project manager represents the company management and not the developers. The scrum master role has a very different objective when it comes to productivity—to find the sustainable pace for the team, as prescribed by principles of the agile manifesto. Self-organized developers are supposed to identify how much they can deliver every iteration by working normal hours, not nights and weekends. Combining the project manager and scrum master role into a single individual would be to ask one person to achieve maximum return on every programming dollar *and* to protect the quality of life of her teammates. These two objectives are inherently opposed and one will be inevitably compromised.

User stories and backlogs

To understand how Scrum teams can iteratively work through the backlog shown in Figure 2.2, one must first understand the components of the backlog, the user stories. User stories are the central requirements vehicle of Scrum. For the most part, each story states in one or two sentences a small function the business needs the application to fulfill. The product owner authors the user stories, and they take a simple format:

> As {a particular user role in the enterprise}…
> … I want to be able to {perform this function with the application}…
> … so that the organization benefits {in a specific way}.

A typical user story for a business intelligence application might run like this: "As an analyst in the billing department, I want to use the Revenue Assurance dashboard to display trends of monthly billed revenue by product, geographic market, and customer tenure so that we can detect and correct areas where our fulfillment application fails to transfer customer installs to our invoicing systems, leaving earned revenue uncollected."

Because they are so short, user stories can be scrawled by hand on an index card, consistent with Scrum origins as a simple, paper-based collaboration approach. The product owner can draft new stories with a moment's inspiration, as well as remove them from the stack as each story is delivered by the developers or when a particular story is no longer needed. Moreover, the product owner can arrange these short statements to match her order of priority, and she finds it easy to update that ordering as her understanding of the project and its requirements change.

The full stack of product owner undelivered user stories becomes the *project backlog* of features the development team has yet to deliver upon. When the product owner identifies a subset of them that describes the next increment of new application features she wants to deliver to the end users she represents, that subset of stories becomes a *release backlog*. When a team identifies the handful of stories that they will convert into working code during the next sprint, that small set is considered the *iteration backlog*.

Estimating user stories in story points

In order to know how many user stories will fit into the next iteration or how long it will take to deliver all the stories for the next release, teams need to be able to estimate the work implicit in each user story. Developers estimate user stories using an agile invention called "story points." The details of this estimation process are presented in detail across several chapters to come, but because story points are essential to defining each development iteration, we need to consider them briefly here.

Story points express the "size" of a given user story, and the story point unit of measure is defined subjectively by the team. Scrum teams that employ story points leave the precise definition of their unit of measure, never translating it to objectively definable units such as labor hours or lines of code. This vagueness causes no harm because a team needs story points for only two purposes: (a) to express the size of one story relative to another and (b) to appraise quickly how many stories can fit into an iteration.

As an example of relative sizing, we want to be able to know that a user story estimated at "8 story points" is about three times larger than one estimated to be "3 points." For identifying how many stories to plan for an upcoming sprint, we want to be able to state something like "our team has been consistently delivering 24 story points every iteration, so if this particular user story is 8 story points, we can deliver it and 2 more just as big during our next sprint."

Assigning story points is simple. The process is portrayed in Figure 2.3, where a team is building a simple data mart of one fact and four dimensions. Here the team has already finished a preliminary build of the data mart composed of an account and date dimension plus a revenue fact table. The date dimension has been omitted from the diagram for clarity. While facilitating the estimation process, the scrum master in this situation would ask the developers which of the two was the easiest data object to deliver. The developers might answer with the revenue fact table, as it simply loaded the numeric columns of each record in the billing system after finding the right account dimension record to link it to. The scrum master then suggests "Say the revenue fact module was three story points of work. How many story points would you assign to the transform for the account dimension? When you pick a number, ensure that it reflects *how much bigger* this module will be than the fact table, that is, how much more work it you see it needing."

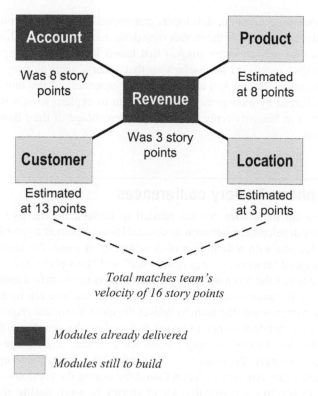

Total matches team's
velocity of 16 story points

■ Modules already delivered

□ Modules still to build

FIGURE 2.3

Estimating story points.

Assume that the team members decide that the account load was eight story points. They now have two references, a three and an eight—one small story and one large one. These references define tangibly for the developers what three and eight story points mean to them. No one else really has to understand it because others only need the conclusions these quantities will lead to. Given the reference points, the scrum master directs the developer's attention to a module they are about to build, say the customer dimension. She asks "How much work will this load module be compared to the revenue fact and the account dimension? That is, how big will it be in story points compared to either of them?"

In this example, the team realizes that the customer dimension will involve some coding of deduplication logic to properly manage records for customers who have opened multiple accounts over time, sometimes with differing names. Accordingly, the developers decide that the customer dimension is not going to be anywhere between the 3 and the 8 points of their reference stories, but larger than both, so they assign it 13 story points. The 13 indicates they think the customer dimension will be almost twice as much work as the account dimension. Given this quick and easy method of estimating the size of the stories that they will work on during the upcoming iteration, developers can appraise their team velocity readily by tracking the total points of the stories they deliver successfully with every sprint.

Veteran scrum masters often suggest that teams keep their story-pointing estimation technique mostly to themselves so that others, such as project managers and IT management, do not feel alarmed by the vagueness of the unit of measures employed. If forced by management at some point to explain what a story point is, the developers can honestly reply it is simply a percentage of their bandwidth for a single iteration.

Iteration phase 1: story conferences

We now have all the starter notions needed to understand the five phases of a generic Scrum development iteration in detail. Having selected a time box between 2 and 4 weeks, and with a definition of done firmly in mind, the team divides the first day of a sprint between a "story conference" and "task planning."

The objective of the morning's story conference is to identify a candidate list of user stories that the team believes it can deliver within the time allowed by the iteration. Because Scrum wants the team to deliver the most important requirements first, it encourages the product owner to revisit and update the priority ordering of her release backlog just before the story conference to reflect any changes in business conditions. Accordingly, the release backlog going into sprint planning during one story conference can look very different than it did during the previous top of cycle.

In order to identify a reasonable set of stories to work during the sprint, the teammates have to derive first a notion of its "capacity," that is, the team's bandwidth in terms of story points. To determine their capacity, they consider the velocity they achieved during the prior sprint and discuss how much more or less they should be able to achieve during the next iteration given vacations, holidays, and special work events that will occur during the sprint's time box. They should calculate capacity in story points to assist them during the next story conference and in labor hours to help them during task planning.

The story conference then begins in earnest with the product owner walking the team down the current incarnation of the release backlog in priority order until the collection of stories reviewed is clearly larger than a single sprint can address. This appraisal is typically done intuitively, without employing story points. If the team delivered at most four user stories in the previous three iterations, then they obviously do not need to consider more than a half dozen or so for the next sprint, unless the current top of the stack contains some unusually small stories.

The team now has a collection slightly larger than what should be placed in its iteration backlog. The developers need to decide carefully how far down this subset they should draw their first notion of a "commit line." The commit line represents the stories they are promising the product owner will be delivered as working modules by the end of the iteration. The developers naturally want to set this line with care. Promise too little and the product owner will start to doubt whether he has employed the right team. Promise too much and the developers will find themselves working nights and weekends in order to honor their commitment.

To set the commit line properly, the team will employ two means of estimating how much work the candidate set of stories represents: story points during the story conference and labor hours during the next phase, task planning. The five-phase cycle depicted in Figure 2.2 shows the story conference completing before task planning begins. In practice, the teammates complete a story conference first, but are free during task planning to move back and forth between discussing stories in story points and tasks in labor hours so that they can get the estimate in story points to agree with the one expressed in labor hours.

During the story conference, developers discuss the requested stories in detail with the product owner, estimating their size in story points, and proceeding until the stories accepted into sprint's candidate backlog have a story point total that equals the identified capacity of the team (as shown in Figure 2.3). New teams will have to guess at their story point velocity, something that is discussed later in the chapter on starting a team. Sometimes the next story in the priority order turns out to be so large that it pushes the story point total far beyond the team's velocity. So that they do not overcommit, the developers will negotiate with the product owner, swapping that story out for a smaller one (close to it in priority) that is small enough to make the story point total better match the team's velocity.

As each story is added to the candidate backlog, the developers and product owner will polish the user story sentence, writing it on a small paper "story card." These cards do not need more verbiage than that. According to Scrum, these cards are not supposed to be fully elaborated requirements. Instead, each card should be only "a reminder to have a conversation" about the requirements implicit in the functionality the card describes. When it comes time to actually develop the feature suggested by the card, the short description will be enough to start a good conversation between the developers and the product owner. Keeping the story cards short avoids investing too much time into to-be specs that could easily conflict with what the team discovers as they build the application.

Although the story cards are kept short, the developers make sure during the story conference that they really understand what each represents so that they can estimate their level of effort. They might jot a few notes down on the back of the card when there are crucial details that everyone will need to recall later. Once everyone feels he understands a story well, the team estimates its level of effort in story points. As shown in the chapter on estimation, the team uses a size-based estimating technique called "estimating poker" to derive a consensus on how many story points the work on a particular card represents.

The story conference progresses until the developers have estimated and accepted enough stories onto the iteration backlog that the story point total closely matches its story point capacity number. A team will base their capacity number on its observed delivery velocity, which is remeasured at the end of each sprint. Velocity is simply a tally of the story points for modules from the prior iteration that the team has delivered as working code and the product owner has accepted as complete.

Naturally, the value of this tally will vary across the project, so during a story conference, the team often draws a second limit on the release backlog somewhere below the commit line to represent the "stretch goals" for the sprint. The stretch goal stories are there in case the team moves faster than expected and a couple of teammates could use something more to do while the rest of their comrades finish up.

Iteration phase 2: task planning

The task planning phase occupies the second half of the sprint's first day. The team's objective is to confirm that the candidate sprint backlog emerging from the story conference is indeed no more than it can deliver in one sprint. The developers work toward this conclusion by enumerating for each user story the development tasks that will be required to fulfill it and then estimating that work in terms of labor hours. They then add up these projected labor hours to ensure they do not exceed the available work hours for the iteration.

If total hours for the candidate stories fall short of available work hours, then the team can go back into story conference mode to push the commit line down another story or two in the release backlog. If instead the total task hours exceed the developers' projected bandwidth, then the developers should move the commit line up, eliminating stories until the project labor hours fall to a doable amount. If the labor hour estimates cause the commit line to move far from where it was set by the story pointing of the story conference, the scrum master should also have the developers revisit their story-pointing process to determine why their first estimate was so far off.

During the story conference, the team placed each candidate user story on a story card. Similarly, for each task identified for the candidate story, the developers will create a "task card" with perhaps a few sentences describing the work involved. The task card gives the teammates a place to jot down considerations that should guide their level-of-effort estimate for the task. Tasks can include analysis, design, development, testing, and documentation efforts. During the development phase of the iteration, these cards will be pinned to a task board, giving the developers easily moved pointers by which they can track progress on their work items.

By the end of the first day of sprint planning, the team will have located the commit line by estimating in both story points and labor hours. Given this double estimation, the team can reasonably expect to complete all the task cards placed on the task board within the time box of the iteration.

Because task planning discussions revolve around technical activities, the product owner is far less central during this stage, but she needs to remain in the room for those moments when the team switches back to story conference mode to adjust the commit line or when developer questions on a story touch upon business requirements.

Basis of estimate cards to escape repeating hard thinking

Thinking of tasks required for a story involves a very different mind-set than estimating how many hours each task will take. In order to avoid switching between these two frames of thinking, teams often take a first pass against the stories in the sprint backlog, defining all the tasks involved, and then undertake a second pass to estimate the labor hours for those tasks.

Thinking up tasks and estimating labor hours are both difficult activities to do consistently and accurately. For data warehousing projects, the list of tasks can get long, but they also exhibit a good deal of repetition from one module to the next. The length, difficulty, and repeatability of these lists lead many warehousing teams to begin gathering "basis-of-estimate" (BOE) cards to accelerate the task planning process. An example of a BOE card for Type 2 slowly changing dimensions, typical of a data integration story, is shown in Table 2.2. This example is taken from a half-year data mart project delivered at a major U.S. telecommunications company using a graphical extract, transformation, and load (ETL) product. Because BOE tasks are highly dependent on a project's tools and computing infrastructure, different teams will derive different task sets for their cards. BOE cards often list the baseline or average person-hours needed to complete a given task. For tasks that require collaboration, total labor hours mean the sum of time spent by all individuals involved, not just elapsed or "wall clock" time.

Warehousing teams typically create one such card for every major type of module that they must build frequently for their DWBI applications. When the product owner submits a user story for consideration during the story conference, the team can usually decompose it quickly into the major feature enhancements required to fulfill it, and many of the indicated modules will match up to a BOE card in their collection. For example, if the product owner asks them to "add a second kind of address—service location—to the billing location already on the revenue fact table," the team will understand that they must acquire a new source, transform its source into a second location dimension, and add links to it in the existing fact table. They should strive to develop BOE cards for each of those major work items: build a new sourcing program, load a dimension, and rekey a fact table. For each type of work, the BOE cards intersect nicely with the definition of done, becoming over time the team's consensus on what is required to consider a given type of module complete.

On dashboarding projects, for example, the collection of BOE cards would include work items such as

- update semantic layer for new data mart tables
- create a dashboard container and menu system
- create query definition dialog box with list of value for parameter fields
- create a trend chart with drill-down capability

For data integration, teams will typically create basis-of-estimate cards for items such as

- add a new reference table for an existing integration attribute
- build Type 2 slowly changing dimension
- build event fact table
- build status-tracking fact table

Table 2.2 Sample Basis-of-Estimate Card

Work Unit: Create New Type 2 Slowly Changing Dimension (Standard Tasks and Typical Labor Totals For all Participants)	
High-level design conference	2 hr
Detailed design conference	6 hr
Define view DDL for initial load sourcing	1 hr
Define view DDL for incremental sourcing	1 hr
Finalize target table DDL	3 hr
Send DDL to DBA and support execution	2 hr
Create **incremental load** mapping	
Row-level meta data columns	6 hr
Replicated columns	3 hr
Derived columns	(depends on business rules)
Create incremental load session	2 hr
Add to incremental load workflow	3 hr
Add **initial load** logic to mapping	
Row-level meta data columns	2 hr
Replicated columns	3 hr
Derived columns	(depends on business rules)
Create initial load session	2 hr
Add to initial load workflow	3 hr
Create parm-setting script	3 hr
Create test data for nightly integration testing	4 hr
Update tarball and version control	1 hr
Move workflows to nightly build	2 hr
Review results for executional completeness	2 hr
Review results for data quality	4 hr
Document as-built design per department standards	6 hr
Perform code and documentation walk through	9 hr

The basis-of-estimate cards for each of these module types would list the tasks typically required and an hour estimate for how long a developer commonly needs to complete each of them. These cards save a team a tremendous amount of time during task planning because they have most of the hard thinking already completed. Instead of trying to dream up tasks and hour estimates from scratch every iteration, the developers can just compare the module they are thinking of building to the appropriate basis of the estimate card and ask only how the next instance they are about to build will be different.

Task planning doublechecks story planning

The task planning session concludes when a consensus has been reached that the team has targeted a realistic set of deliverables that the product owner can expect to

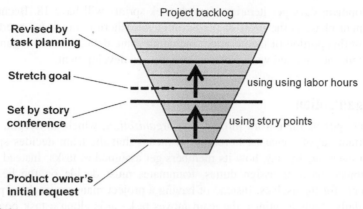

FIGURE 2.4

Identifying an iteration's "commit line" during sprint planning.

test drive at the next user demo. Scrum is truly efficient because, by the end of this first day of the sprint, the product owner and developers alike have arrived at a solid and fairly detailed understanding of exactly what they have promised to deliver and what they must do in the next few weeks to succeed. The story conference represented a top-down notion of what they could accomplish. Moreover, as they prepare to move into the development step of the iteration, they are armed with two estimates in two different units of measure that both demonstrate the work they plan to accomplish is indeed doable. Task planning provides a bottom-up confirmation of the top-down plan's reasonableness.

Figure 2.4 recaps the overall process that typically occurs during an iteration's planning day, showing how the sprint's commit line is progressively defined. The product owner started by asking for more stories than the team could possibly deliver. The developers found a candidate commit line using story point estimation and then refined this estimate to even fewer stories by performing a second estimate of the work using labor hours. They finished by adding a few stories as a *stretch goal* in case they complete tasks faster than anticipated or something blocks progress on one of the stories. In this example, the commit line moved upward with each estimating pass, based on the new information that discussion and estimation provided. The line could have just as easily moved downward during any or all of these passes if the team had realized that they were committing to less than they had capacity to deliver.

Iteration phase 3: development phase

On day 2 of the sprint, the team begins the development phase, which consumes the rest of the time box except for its last day. For 3-week cycles, this amounts to

13 development days per iteration; four 4-week sprints will have 18. Because this development phase is the heart of the Scrum cycle, there is much we need to discuss about this portion of the iteration, including some details on self-organization, daily scrums, accelerated work patterns, and test-led development.

Self-organization

Developers pursue their work through *self-organization*, which, in Scrum, implies an important set of concepts. Foremost, it means that the team decides sprint by sprint, or even day by day, how its members get assigned to tasks. Instead of having a project manager assign duties, teammates must decide on the best work assignments for themselves. Instead of having a project manager tracking progress through daily status meetings, the team moves task cards along a task board. The progress of these task cards allows the developers to monitor status for themselves. They all share the same deadline. If one teammate starts to fall behind, the rest will notice. The fact that they will either succeed or fail in the sprint as a whole team will motivate them to "swarm" upon the issue, altering their individual actions to affect a collective solution to the problem.

Second, close collaboration improves the developers visibility to the quality of each other's work, thus self-organization also involves self-monitoring that everyone's work is meeting the team's self-imposed standards. If one teammate begins to consistently leave work incomplete, per the team's adopted definition of "done," the rest will again notice and must resolve the problem.

Third, self-organization will result in different teams arriving at different patterns for assigning work. Some teams prefer to follow a strict division of labor based on the different technical specialties found among the developers. As long as everyone subscribes to the notion that gaps between the developers must be filled by means of a generalizing specialist, this approach will work fine. Other teams have a greater need to cross train, and thus let people self-assign to a wide variety of tasks depending on their current interests. The skill sets among teammates naturally become more homogeneous over time with this style of self-organization. With fewer gaps between their capabilities, developers on these teams are better able to assign themselves fluidly to whatever tasks have the greatest need at a given moment, accelerating the group to its maximum possible velocity.

Finally, self-organization means that the team is free to invent or adapt tools and techniques as needed, even adopting them from traditional methodologies whenever they make sense. Teams should be encouraged to consider whatever innovations increase their velocity without hurting their work quality. In practice, these criteria will rule out almost every form-based or electronic mechanism for planning, tracking, and reporting because very few tools can meet the blazing efficiency of working eye to eye with paper-based artifacts to deliver a small increment of new code. The primary exception to this observation is geographically dispersed teams, which will need Internet-based "groupware" to sustain close collaboration.

Through self-organizations, most teams do eventually adopt some non-Scrum process elements, such as the formal project definition artifacts and quality assurance techniques that their IT department has defined for all development efforts whether agile or not. Self-organizing can thus imply an eclectic mix of tools and their usage, which is a big reason why each team's implementation of the Scrum turns out to be unique.

Sometimes these elements can help tremendously in integrating Scrum projects smoothly with other departmental projects and IT service groups. They can also cause tremendous heartburn if they impose constraints such as metrics and audits that undermine any of the agile principles incorporated in Scrum. For example, a metric that measures how many times a team's builds fail during integration testing may make sense for a waterfall project where the build is supposed to be near perfect when submitted for testing. But such a metric will seriously hamper agile warehousing teams because they rely on nightly testing rather than a master design review to uncover integration issues. To censure a Scrum DWBI team for amassing a high reject count would pressure them to draft comprehensive design documents before coding just to keep that metric to a minimum. They would abandon the fail-fast and fix-quickly approach that underlies agile's high delivery rates. We will consider a workable set of metrics for agile warehousing teams in the chapter on starting an agile team

Why does agile emphasize self-organized teams so strongly? If we imagine someone trying to perform even the simplest task, such as drawing a cross hair symbol "⊕" on a whiteboard, we can see that having a project manager standing behind him all day long, dictating every tiny motion, is only going to slow him down for several reasons, such as

- the slowness of verbal directions
- the ease of misexpressing instructions or misinterpreting them
- the developer falls idle after completing one instruction while waiting to receiving the next

If instead we transform this manager into another worker, asking them both to just "fill the whiteboard with crosshairs," productivity will go up far more than simply twice as much because they will

- be working in parallel
- lose no time to miscommunications or waiting for instructions
- soon develop muscle memory for the repeated motions
- innovate upon the process, such as using three separate passes, each dedicated to drawing one part of the symbol across the entire whiteboard

Some high-level management is still necessary to ensure that developers are working to a deadline and that work quality remains high, but we can easily see that micromanagement is truly counterproductive and thus a very expensive approach that should be rethought.

Daily scrums

Developing software is a complicated process. In the process outlined so far, Scrum starts with the high-level definition provided by the release cycle's inception and

Table 2.3 Three Questions of the Daily Scrum Meeting

Question	Interpretation
What did you do yesterday?	Can the developers who were waiting for you to finish a particular task now get started?
What are you going to do today?	Do we have two people either planning to perform the same task or about to conflict over the commonly used data object?
What's holding you up?	Who do you need to meet with?

discovery phases and then breaks it down into small pieces that colocated, self-organized teams will program without detailed direction from a project manager. Without some form of coordination during the time between the story conference and the sprint demo, the individual programmers could easily work chaotically and accomplish nothing in their rush to meet the looming deadline defined by the end of sprint. To constrain such chaos, Scrum provides a few elements to keep the team on track during the sprint, the most notable being a brief daily meeting.

This daily meeting is called "the scrum" and is a 15-minute check-in where teammates communicate quickly among themselves. During a scrum, they each take a turn making three easy statements: "What I did yesterday, what I will do today, and what is holding me up." Sharing this information is essential for the self-organized team because it allows everyone to hear crucial information such as which dependencies have been resolved, which two of them are duplicating efforts, and which developers could use some help. These notions have been summarized in Table 2.3.

The scrum master will be essential in ensuring that these meetings occur, start on time, and finish quickly. To keep each developer's check in quick, the scrum master can encourage them to speak only in terms of the task cards they have finished or will start. All other details are relegated for discussion after the scrum. For teams who have colocated as generic Scrum suggests, such follow-on communication takes place easily and spontaneously as needed.

Scrum teams have devised a few tricks to keep these meetings brief, such as

- Don't bring chairs, we're not going to be here long—in fact we'll stand.
- (If the developers are still seated around the project table) close your laptops or turn off your screens—we can't have you reading your email when you should be listening to your teammates.
- Talk too long during your check in and we'll have you hold a heavy binder out in front of you until you're done talking—that will speed you up!
- The scrum master will ask those who are obviously not listening to repeat what the last person just said.

- We've got to start on time if these stand-up meetings are going to be brief—if you're late, you've got to put a dollar in the doughnut jar. If you're late again, then you go buy the doughnuts.

Accelerated programming

The agile principles commend teams to find their sustainable pace, and Scrum employs an interesting combination of opposing mechanisms to accelerate development to the fastest-possible delivery speed that the team can maintain. Two factors in the approach drive a team to program ever faster. First is the embedded business partner who participates regularly in planning sessions and understandably exhorts the team at the beginning of every iteration to take on as many user stories as absolutely possible. Second is the unrelenting deadline pressure represented by the user demo built into every iteration, when all the code must be working so well that the product owner can operate the new portions of the applications himself. The upper limit of the team's delivery speed is revealed by a pair of countering forces. Primary among them is the fact that aiming to deliver too much in one sprint or code too quickly only results in rejected stories during the user demo. A strong second counterforce often manifests itself during the retrospective, where the developers can chide themselves for trying to go too quickly and identify a more reasonable capacity number to base the commit line upon during the next iteration's planning sessions. The net result is that Scrum works to "red line" the team's tachometer—pushing them to gun their application delivery engine up to the point where it might break and then no further.

Scrum's nature to demand the fastest possible delivery out of developers combines well with its reliance upon self-organized teams. Given the steady pressure to accomplish more with every day of programming, agile teams spontaneously find many ingenious ways to work smarter and faster. Figures 2.5 and 2.6 taken together depict a common pattern for faster coding employed frequently by Scrum project teams that can serve as a good starting pattern for new agile teams to consider. Not all of these development steps were part of Scrum when it was first defined. However, the method is so amenable to all beneficial innovation that these techniques from other sources have become part of Scrum as commonly followed so that most practitioners no longer bother to call out their precise origins.

The common accelerated coding pattern begins in the upper left of Figure 2.5. When a developer finishes a task, he needs something new to do. Because he is part of a self-organized team, he does not wait for a project manager to assign him a new task. Instead, he walks to the task board where the stories and their tasks are arranged in priority order, asking himself "What's the next most important item I can work on?" If he selects a coding task, he does not begin programming immediately. To ensure good design, he secures some time from one of his teammates, perhaps the team lead. Together they whiteboard the algorithm or data flow for the module he intends to build. This technique is called a "2-to-1 design" and is an adaptation of Extreme Programming's "pair programming," where two developers

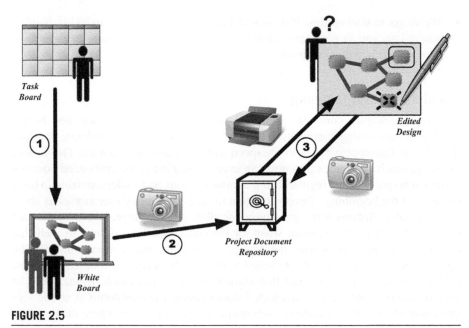

FIGURE 2.5

Common project room pattern for accelerated coding—Part 1.

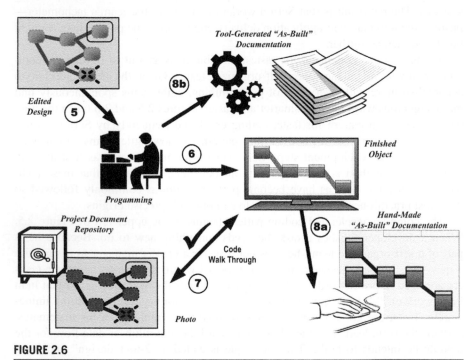

FIGURE 2.6

Common project room pattern for accelerated coding—Part 2.

would code application modules while employing only one keyboard. In XP, one programmer would write the code while the other would watch and critique upon the code's overall design, its fit to purpose, and any programming mistakes it might contain. For business intelligence projects, graphical development tools have replaced the bulk of procedural coding with drag-and-drop module development, making 2-to-1 programming overkill. However, two developers to one whiteboard employ the same technique at a higher abstraction layer where the same advantages can be gained, thus yielding a 2-to-1 design.

Once the 2-to-1 design session is complete, the developer does not proceed to carefully transfer the contents of the whiteboard to a design drawing, nor does he write up a detailed explanation of the design. Such artifacts would represent "to-be" specifications, which can be a huge waste of time should the developer start coding and discover that major revisions to the original thinking are necessary. In Scrum, developers can proceed without polished to-be specifications because the iteration time box ensures that they focus on one small task at a time. With the scope of the programming objective kept small, all the information needed for coding is either on the whiteboard or readily available in the developer's memory. Scrum's reliance on colocation ensures that their teammates are nearby should there be any questions beyond that. A quick photograph of the whiteboard from the 2-to-1 design session will suffice to remind the developer over the next few days of the development pattern he and his teammate desired to employ for the module he is programming. Even an inexpensive 10-megapixel electronic camera can capture the image with enough resolution that every pen stroke from the whiteboard can be revealed by zooming into the photo on a computer screen.

When the developer begins coding, naturally a few oversights will become apparent. To resolve these in the working design, he can print the whiteboard photo on double-sized paper, make corrections and updates by hand with a pen, and then take another photo of the revised objectives to be stored as the next version of the document in the team's artifact repository. Because the amended whiteboard image is a to-be design that only a few people who are intimate with the task at hand will work with, this artifact does not have to be pretty. It just needs to contain all the informational content required to support coding, and the developer's whiteboard drawing and penned-in corrections will suffice.

Or course, for those components of a module that are particularly complex and easily confused from day to day, Scrum has no objection to the developer drafting careful to-be specifications for that area of the application. Naturally, the developer's team will encourage him to scope such detailed artifacts as tightly as possible so as not to needlessly lose delivery speed across a large portion of the project. For data integration modules on warehousing projects, one common place where written to-be specifications are employed regularly is source-to-target mappings. These mappings are usually spreadsheets in which systems analysts detail what source columns flow to which target attributes and the business rules that must transform data involved.

Figure 2.6 depicts the second half of this accelerated coding pattern, which continues with the developer programming the module from his amended diagram of the intended design. Once he believes he has finished programming the module, he can arrange for a code walk through. The teammate with whom he created the original design would be a perfect reviewer. The two of them can print out the amended design photo from the project's document repository and compare it to the module as built, assuring that the code matches design. Once the module passes code review, it may well be worth the developer's time to employ a drawing tool and draft a careful "as-built" documentation of the module just finished. Fortunately in DWBI, many tools have their own repositories from which these as-built design documents can be generated automatically using the tool's reporting features or even a set of SQL commands.

This accelerated development process may appear sloppy to waterfall adherents, but it saves tremendous amounts of time because it invests absolutely as little as possible in polished to-be specifications that often have a very short shelf life. With the work pattern sketched earlier, teams avoid wasting effort on carefully documenting the churn in requirements and design that naturally occur as developers discover oversights and new possibilities while working on a software module.

Test-driven development

The notion of self-organized teams working at an accelerated pace raises natural concerns about software quality. Several agile development approaches, including

Table 2.4 Steps for Test-Led Development

Step	Objective
Add tests	Developer must rethink both a module's requirements and its design to author an effective set of test cases.
Run test suite	Proves that the test harness is working correctly. Also rules out the possibility that the new test is somehow flawed so that it always passes, independent of any changes in the code.
Increment code	Developer programs until the test suite passes. He then stops in order to avoid gold plating the application. He also avoids adding any new functionality not covered by a test.
Rerun test suite	When all the test cases pass, the programmer is done with coding the features the tests correspond to.
Refactor code	Developer cleans up any sloppy programming, ensuring that code complies with project and departmental standards. He also finishes addressing nonfunctional requirements, such as security and performance.
Rerun test suite	Developer ensures that refactoring has not damaged the module's functional capabilities.

Scrum, address much of this risk with a technique called "test-led development." With test-led development, the developer writes the various tests a module must pass before he begins coding it. He then programs until the module can pass the test. [Beck 2002] The formal steps comprising this technique are shown in Table 2.4, which have been generalized slightly to allow for maintaining or enhancing an existing module.

A few practitioners make a distinction between "test-driven" versus "test-led" development in which the former utilizes testing cycles to shape an application's entire concept and design in addition to controlling the quality of its programming. [Astels 2003; Beck 2002] The approach described earlier can be employed on projects where the application's high-level design is provided before development begins, perhaps by a project architect. Thus it might be more accurate to refer to the steps outlined here as "test-first" or "test-led" development. Because so many practitioners frequently refer to all approaches as "test-driven development," however, one has to be careful to divine a speaker's precise definition whenever the exact testing approach is important.

Architectural compliance and "tech debt"

When first introduced to Scrum, veteran data warehousing professionals struggle to see how a development team, building a BI application in small increments through fast bursts of coding, will be able to devise consistent project architecture and faithfully build out components that realize it. Incremental development seems to rule out the creation of an overarching, high-level design that speaks to such notions as reusable modules, standard algorithmic patterns, and nonfunctional requirements such as security and compatible data definitions across the enterprise. A closer look will reveal, however, that Scrum teams attend to project architecture through a combination of context and process, plus several important mechanisms built into the definition of a sprint itself.

Starting with context, projects as large as data warehouses are rarely pursued in a vacuum. As noted earlier, most IT departments have an established release cycle by which they manage their projects, and most large organizations have an enterprise architecture group. In this setting, Scrum teams building a data warehouse release do not have to devise complete project architectures by themselves. The enterprise group, plus the release cycle's discovery and elaboration phase, will have established high- to medium-level target structures and other guidelines for the project to follow. The IT department will provide a substantial list of application standards for the team to comply with as well.

Concerning process, the Scrum collaboration model provides a strong force that helps focus teams on good architecture over the length of a project. The agile principles posit that "the best architectures, requirements, and designs emerge from self-organizing teams." [www.agilemanfesto.org/principles.html] Aligned with this tenet, Scrum relies on the self-organized to pick the proper level of architectural activity. Perhaps a very green team would program the modules of one iteration independently of all others. Reasonably experienced developers, however, will immediately see that the iterative build approach risks a long series of uncoordinated point solutions. Experienced developers will move to mitigate the risk from the very first iteration by asking about overarching design for both process and data during sprint planning sessions. Whenever necessary to maintain the coherence of the project, they will build in architectural and data modeling work items during the task planning of each iteration. Similarly, at the end of each sprint, the product owner is going to operate the current build of the application himself. Because a team would be hard pressed to restrict the product owner's evaluation to only those features just added, the application will have to hold together as a system during the demo. Portions that worked in previous iterations will still need to be functioning in each subsequent product review, providing the team a strong incentive to treat the application as an integrated system, not as a series of isolated features.

More pointedly, the way Scrum is practiced today builds many mechanisms to ensure good architecture throughout the duration of a sprint. Teams with experienced developers or at least strong leadership will reliably employ these mechanisms. Each iteration's task planning session allows the team to discuss building out the next increment as a single effort that is consistent both inwardly and outwardly. Architecture should be part of that discussion; if it is not, scrum masters would be smart to comment upon its absence. The conversations a coder will conduct with his tech lead during the 2-to-1 design should certainly involve many efforts to align each module with the shared and complementary design aspects the team wishes to build into every module. Test-led development should certainly address integration-level quality objectives as well as unit- and component-level concerns. The code reviews mentioned earlier as part of the accelerated development process most Scrum teams follow today should certainly touch upon whether a given module furthers the architectural themes of the overall system. Finally, the sprint retrospective, built into the conclusion of every iteration, provides team members with the opportunity to cite instances of compromised design and to suggest work steps for the team's particular engineering method that will improve architectural thinking and compliance.

To anticipate the material in coming chapters a bit, agile warehousing efforts also staff their teams with a project architect, a data architect, and a systems analyst. Guiding other developers on the team toward good architecture is part of the responsibilities these team leads will have. Furthermore, agile warehousing projects include an "Iteration −1" to provide these leads with a chance to assemble the core of a whole project design.

To doubly ensure strong application architecture, Scrum teams typically add one other mechanism to their method, the *architectural reserve*. Achieving good architecture requires that the team invests labor into compliant, future-proofed, and reusable modules. The fruits of these objectives are usually undetectable to the product owner because they do not manifest as new functional enhancements during a sprint demo. So that the crush of a sprint deadline does not pressure the developers to sacrifice architectural matters for surface features the product owner can directly appreciate, Scrum teams reserve a certain percentage of their bandwidth—typically 20%—for nonfunctional work. During each iteration's planning day, the team retains that percentage of their bandwidth in both story points and labor hours as an architectural reserve. This reserve provides the time needed for developing items the product owner may never understand or value, such as reusable modules and integration test harnesses.

Tucked within that architectural reserve is also the time the team needs to attend to "tech debt." During the development iterations, there will be stories that do not quite get done. Some modules may have small defects that appear when the deliverables are examined by the product owner. For other modules, the team may have finished the coding, but still ran out of time to update the as-built documentation or package the module completely for migration to the system test environment. For still other modules, there may be aspects, including documentation and data quality, that need to be refactored or repaired. When the product owner—or the scrum master acting on his behalf—asks during the sprint demo whether the modules being reviewed are truly "done," the developers will need to mention these omissions and flaws.

For large bugs or substantial gaps in finishing the work of a module, the user story will have to be rejected and placed back on the release backlog for possible inclusion in the next iteration. However, that treatment is too extreme for small gaps that can be remedied in an hour or two during the next sprint. The preferred handling of these small discrepancies is to first secure a statement from the developers that the defects can indeed be corrected in a short amount of time, and then placed upon the project's list of *technical debt*. The story itself is accepted as long as it achieves all the objectives of the user story. The tech debt list enumerates the small cleanup tasks the team still *owes* to the product owner. The scrum master has the solemn responsibility to ensure that the developers pay off their tech debt at the beginning of the next iteration so that the work left undone does not accumulate, grow intertwined, and undermine the team's velocity. The time for tech debt is typically taken from the architectural reserve. Teams will want to keep the size of their debt to a minimum for no other reason than when it grows large, it prevents them from truly using the project's architectural reserve for architecture.

Iteration phase 4: user demo

The last day of a generic Scrum cycle involves a user demo and an iteration retrospective. The user demo comprises the first half of this day. The product owner test drives the new version of the application created during the past few weeks of development and formally acknowledges whether the team has delivered upon each user story as promised.

In order to determine whether each story has been delivered, the product owner should operate the new build for himself. If he were to simply watch the developers operate the new features, a high percentage of them would function perfectly, as the team would simply repeat the unit and component tests they had been working toward all iteration long. If the owner drives the application, however, he has a much higher likelihood of using the software in many unexpected ways, with a higher probability of uncovering the rough edges of the current build. Demonstrations are hard enough for developers to get right, even when they operate the controls. They are doubly or triply hard to survive when one lets the untrained user work the application. By holding its style of user demos throughout the full construction phase of the release cycle, Scrum sets the bar for functional testing far higher than waterfall approaches—one reason that agile tends to drive system defects to zero.

During the demo, the product owner will walk down the user stories of the iteration backlog in priority order, proving to herself that they have been implemented correctly and completely in working code. For data warehousing projects, the product owner will also consider the quality of information loaded into the target data schemas. The scrum master records that stories delivered to the product owner's satisfaction are "accepted." Those the product owner will not accept are labeled "rejected." As shown in Figure 2.7, the scrum master adds the names of accepted modules to the project current release candidate of shippable code. The product owner removes those story cards for his project backlog. The developers are given credit for the story points and original labor hours those stories represent so that the scrum master can calculate the team's velocity in both units of measure at the end of the demo.

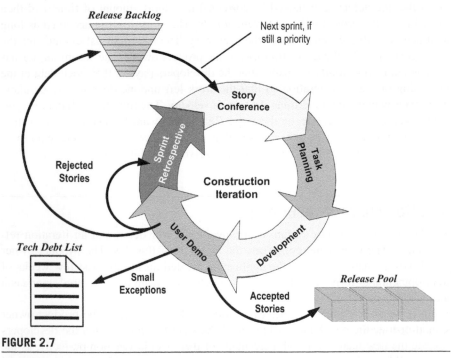

FIGURE 2.7

Handling accepted and rejected user stories.

The product owner's dissatisfaction with a rejected deliverable is often noted on the back of the corresponding story card and the card itself is placed back into the project backlog. If the story represents features that are still important to the product owner, the team will probably see it at the top of the stack when they begin the story conference for the next iteration. If, however, conditions have changed so that the story is no longer needed, the product owner may place its card far down in the stack or remove it altogether.

Many Scrum teams employ a variation on the aforementioned notion of a user demo. As modules are completed during the iterations, the developers request that the product owner examine them and decide whether to accept them at that time. At the end of the sprint, then, most of the modules might already have been accepted, allowing these teams to expand the user demo ceremony. No longer needing the time for a formal accept/reject determination, the product owner invites the larger stakeholder community that he represents to review the new build of the software with him. The user demo becomes a "community demonstration." This variation has the added benefit of bringing to the developers more than just the product owner's perspective on features and design.

Warehousing projects consisting mostly of dashboarding will be able to utilize this community demo approach because the developers can deliver finished modules for product owner review throughout the sprint. For projects involving substantial data integration and long data loads, however, the developers will rarely be able to get their data transformations programmed and a cohesive data load accomplished before the day of the demo. These projects will probably have to dedicate the sprint demo to the accept/reject review of the user stories by the product owner. In that case, the team should encourage the product owner to occasionally hold a community demo independent of the construction sprints so that they too receive feedback from the full cohort of stakeholders.

As mentioned previously, sometimes stories exhibit small bugs or the developers acknowledge that they did not quite meet the team's definition of done because of some minor defect or omission. As long as the developers can assure the product owner that these matters can each be resolved with only a few hours of work, the product owner can safely accept the story, checking that the scrum master adds the missing or malfunctioning items to the list of tech debt, as shown in Figure 2.7.

Iteration phase 5: sprint retrospectives

The sprint retrospective is the element of highest ceremony found in Scrum. Many practitioners consider it the most important of the five phases because it allows the approach to be self-optimizing across many levels. During this final half-day of the sprint, the team does some self-reflection and fine-tunes its use of Scrum so that the next sprint will be both less stressful and more effective. The product owner is included in this retrospective process as well as developers, for the team needs to reflect upon its effectiveness from both the customer's and the producer's point of view.

The retrospective has a precise script to guide each session. Step 1 starts with a teammate reading a short "Retrospective Prime Directive" (see sidebar) to establish an open, nondefensive mind-set among the teammates that will allow an honest self-appraisal. Construction iterations can be pressure cookers, especially at

---

THE SPRINT RETROSPECTIVE'S "PRIME DIRECTIVE"

Regardless of what we discover here today, we understand and truly believe that everyone did the best job he could, given

- what we knew at the time
- our skills and abilities
- the resources available
- the situation at hand

---

the beginning of a project when the team is still struggling with self-organization. Harsh words may be exchanged upon occasion as the weeks go by—sometimes right before the deadline imposed by the user demo. The scrum master needs to bring everyone back to where they understand that each of them is doing the best that they can given the ambitious amount of work they promised to deliver and the constraints imposed upon the project.

In Step 2, the scrum master asks each teammate to think of aspects of the just-completed iteration that went well, placing each one on a separate sticky note. She has them read their observations and gathers them together, perhaps to include them into a written report to project sponsors if need be. Hearing the items that everyone thought went well reinforces the positive thinking established by the prime directive. Without this step, it is all too easy for teams to overlook how much they are getting done and how much they have improved in their development process.

Step 3 is the crux of the retrospective in which the scrum master asks everyone to now think of what did not go so well, writing each notion on a sticky note. She gives them as much time on this step as they can use. When the pace of writing during this exercise tapers off, the scrum master asks each person to read the notes he has written. This reading should be a recital, not a discussion, because working through these observations has its own step, which comes next.

Once everyone, including the product owner, has read his "not so well's" aloud, the scrum master asks the team for help in identifying the major themes found among them. Common themes will be broad categories such as "user stories were vague," "need better source analysis," and "insufficient quality assurance." The scrum master labels sections on a whiteboard for each of these themes and asks the developers to place each sticky note under the theme it most pertains to, much like the process shown in Figure 2.8.

Categorizing these observations is necessary because there is often a lot of repetition of comments between developers, which is only natural as everyone participated in the same process during the time box. Grouping the challenges into shared

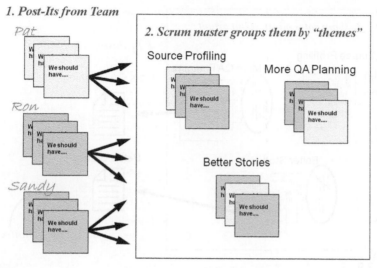

FIGURE 2.8

Identifying areas of improvement during the sprint retrospective (Part 1).

themes allows the team to begin reasoning about the core problems, including those rooted in the team's current adaptation of the Scrum approach. Even with categorization, teams often end up with a half-dozen or more aspects of the development process that could be improved—more than it can fix readily during the next high-paced iteration. The team needs to identify just a couple of areas to improve upon during the next sprint.

In Step 4, the scrum master announces that everyone has 10 or so votes and invites each teammate to spread or clump them alongside the themes so as to reflect how urgently he believes a given issue needs to be fixed during the next sprint. The scrum master tallies the votes after everyone has marked them on the whiteboard and then identifies the couple of areas receiving the most votes, as shown in Figure 2.9. These themes are the areas of improvement the team should discuss in depth during the next step of the sprint retrospective.

For Step 5, the scrum master facilitates a brainstorming session, asking his teammates how they can improve upon most pressing issues just identified. This step can require a considerable amount of time, especially when the team is new to Scrum or a fundamental aspect of the project has changed, such as the technology being used. These urgent themes are discussed until the team has generated a good list of action items.

When he senses the brainstorming session beginning to wind down, the scrum master moves on to Step 6. He recaps the new policies or work patterns the developers have proposed to incorporate into their work habits during the next iteration. He then asks for volunteers who will watch the team work process during the next iteration and remind their comrades of the new approach they just decided

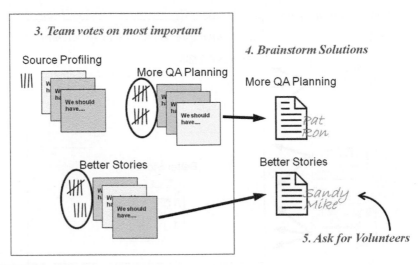

FIGURE 2.9

Identifying areas of improvement during the sprint retrospective (Part 2).

to implement. Calling for volunteers is important. Leaving all new policies to the scrum master to enforce might seem the easy way to implement change, but it rarely works. The participants will not develop a sense of whole team ownership of the new process if they make the scrum master enforce all policy changes. That pattern would also increase project risk by making the scrum master a single point of failure for new policies. Moreover, setting up the scrum master as the enforcer of all decisions pushes his role toward a traditional command-and-control project manager, undermining the agile principle of self-organization.

To wrap up the retrospective, the scrum master can suggest that the team revisits its capacity as an optional Step 7. Purists will say that a team's velocity is simply the story points and original labor-hour estimates fulfilled during the previous sprint, yet this is often too mechanistic. One-off events and big misunderstandings can keep a team from delivering near their true capabilities once in a while. Given all the discussion during the retrospective concerning what could have gone better and what they will do differently next time, the developers have all the information they need in the forefront of their minds to make a realistic appraisal of what story point and labor-hour totals they should aim for realistically during the next iteration.

Retrospectives are vital

New teams often drop the sprint retrospectives. The precise scripting of the ceremony can make retrospectives feel too rigid for a process that is supposed to be adapting constantly. The prime directive can also make them appear too focused on human feelings for a team of technologists. Despite these minor contradictions, retrospectives are absolutely essential for the success of the project for several reasons.

First, retrospectives are where the team's actual method comes from. Out-of-the-box Scrum is only a collaboration model. Details concerning roles and responsibilities, engineering and development practices, plus the linkages of requirements to system validation, all need to be supplied by the team. Scrum's strategy is to land the team knee-deep into the problem space of the project and see how they solve the challenges posed by the particular combination of users, industry, objectives, and technology involved. Where do the ad hoc solutions to these challenges employed during the iteration get transformed into project room policy? It is during the retrospective, not the development phase. During development, the pace is too frantic, teammates may not be in the room all at the same time, and the demo deadline is too close to take time out for long conversations. Innovations are discovered by one or two people at a time, but can only be vetted for universal adoption by the team. If Scrum is going to result in faster, better, cheaper application deliveries, the team must be convened as a group to discuss how they worked as a group.

Second, retrospectives are where developers learn to estimate. Unlike waterfall, where a team gets only one chance to forecast the necessary level of effort and then must wait many months to discover how well they did, Scrum has them estimate every few weeks with feedback at the end of each cycle. This feedback arrives while the teammates can still remember how they derived the estimates so that they are in a perfect position to think through and improve their basis of estimation. For this to happen, however, developers must have a forum such as the retrospective in which to discuss their labor forecasting techniques at length. Although "review the accuracy of your estimates" is not part of generic Scrum's recipe for the retrospective, this discussion is so important to team success that many scrum masters include it as a step just before the team considers what could have gone better during the sprint.

Third, retrospectives are where the team learns to communicate. There are many combinations of producers and consumers within a scrum team: product owner handing off stories to the analyst and data architect, as well as those two providing design input to developer, and developer supplying coded units to integration testers. Working eye to eye requires different skills than writing a specification, and at the fast pace of a Scrum iteration, miscommunications will occur unless teammates are careful. When an iteration fails, it is usually unclear at first where the miscommunication occurred. The retrospective provides the team the opportunity they need to tease apart the chain of events to find the point of failure and devise ways to prevent it from happening again.

Finally, and most importantly from a developer's perspective, retrospectives are where the team's sustainable pace is identified. Measuring the team's velocity only reveals what it was able to deliver. It does not factor in whether the developers were working nights and weekends or whether the workplace was so stressful that most of them are ready to quit the company. When teammates are being pushed too hard, the retrospective is where they can air their grievances and brainstorm ways to ease off the throttle a bit.

Conversely, if the product owner feels that too little is being delivered with each iteration, risking a project that will consume too much money or time, the retrospective is where she can have the team address the situation constructively. By measuring the team's velocity and providing a forum for its review, Scrum provides not only the information the team needs but also the opportunity to have a rational, balanced conversation about what it takes to build a complex software application.

All told, the retrospective is the element of Scrum that guarantees that no party to the process—sponsors, product owners, nor developers—needs to play victim. Waterfall methods, by pushing integration and testing off to the final months of a project, tend to leave developers in a crisis mode before a release, having to make heroic efforts to meet the objectives listed in the project plan. In contrast, Scrum bubbles problems to the surface and demands participants solve them early and often using the retrospective. New teams that skip this valuable process at the end of each sprint risk leaving a fatal issue unaddressed until it is too late.

Close collaboration is essential

Generic Scrum advocates colocating team members in line with the agile principles. When candidate developers for a project start out dispersed geographically, sponsors and project management often frown upon this requirement due to the cost and inconvenience involved with gathering the team in one physical location. Colocation is, in fact, not entirely necessary for Scrum to succeed. The next chapter considers some strategies for working with remote team members, so perhaps Scrum practitioners should speak of "close collaboration" rather than colocation. Either way, we should take a moment here to understand why close collaboration provides such great advantages for speed and quality so that project organizers will realize the effort and expense needed to create a well-integrated team are clearly worth the investment.

Colocation is admittedly an ideal state that many teams cannot afford, but it does accelerate teams greatly by allowing them to get answers to questions as they arise. When an analyst on a colocated team is unsure about the business requirements of a module he is designing, he can call across the table for the product owner to better explain what the business needs. Being able to get an answer eye to eye means developers do not lose time to scheduling meetings and waiting for them to occur. Nor do they lose hours in lengthy chains of email just to get a small point clarified. Likewise, close collaboration eliminates time-consuming roadblocks for coders because they can get the analyst's support as confusion and challenges occur.

Just as importantly, close collaboration allows teams to descope work early and often. If developers begin struggling with, say, an allocation module during one sprint, the systems analyst in the workroom who gave them the algorithm can see and hear the difficulty they are having. He can ponder the situation during the drive home that night and will often return in the morning with a new approach to make the module far easier to code or even unnecessary to program. In waterfall methods, an analyst would have drafted a specification and left the project after transferring it to the developers. With Scrum, he stays close by and will be able to detect opportunities to pull complexity out of scope far more often than if he disappeared to work on another project.

For data integration projects in particular, keeping the product owner colocated with the team allows him to learn about data warehousing and business intelligence far more quickly than if IT had simply interviewed him for requirements and then vanished for many months to build the application. For example, he will learn that Type 2 slowly changing dimensions are expensive to build and consider if the company really needs them for every business entity and whether every attribute of these entities should serve as an update trigger. It is not uncommon for product owners, once they learn about the self-service capabilities of business intelligence tools, to realize that they can get many of their reports from a staging data or integration layer. Such discoveries often allow them to pull entire star schemas out of the project backlog. This occurs frequently during Scrum DWBI projects because product owners have every incentive to descope overly complex requirements whenever possible in order to save money and development time. For these reasons, changes in scope for agile DWBI projects shrink projects as often as they expand them. Downscoping a project or a release is often the easiest way for a product owner to accelerate a business intelligence application the company needs desperately, but he will only understand what can be eliminated or deferred if he has been working closely with the team. Therefore, Scrum's emphasis on colocation and/ or at least close collaboration should be seen as a major strength of the method, despite the fact that it may take extraordinary efforts to arrange for.

Selecting the optimal iteration length

Most Scrum implementations set the time box for their iterations between 2 and 4 weeks. Teams that vary their time box from iteration to iteration find the constant change undermines their perception of velocity, making it difficult to know when they are overcommitting during a sprint's planning day. Varying the time box will also require the team to rederive the unwritten sequence of minideadlines that occurs between teammates within an iteration, an understanding that can take the developers several sprints to work out and internalize. Thus, Scrum practitioners strongly encourage teams to pick an iteration length and stick to it. But how do new teams know what iteration length to try? There are some important tradeoffs to consider.

The longer the time box, the lower the percentage of cycle time top-of-cycle activities such as planning and demos will consume and the greater the portion of time dedicated to pure development. Teams facing complex technical requirements may perform better with longer cycles by avoiding the distraction that frequent user demos and planning days impose upon them.

However, longer cycles are more expensive. Depending on the team size, the difference between a 2-week iteration and a 4-week cycle can be over five figures. If the project starts to run long and the team needs an extra iteration to complete the release, project sponsors are going to experience much less pain funding another

2-week sprint than one twice as long. By keeping iterations short, the team will get extra sprints funded far more easily. Long cycles are also riskier. The iteration demo gives the product owner and team the opportunity to check that the features being delivered truly add value to the company. Similarly, the sprint retrospective allows the team to measure its effectiveness regularly and provides the opportunity to correct any dysfunctional work patterns. By moving from 4- to 3-week sprints, for example, the team will be able to detect miscommunication with the client and learn from their development mistakes 33% faster, driving considerable risk out of the project.

Iteration length has an important impact on the product owner. With long 4-week time boxes, this key business partner will have more opportunities to wander back to his functional department and get swept up in the crises and brushfires he finds there. He can forget about his responsibilities to the development team easily because he only gets to see a demo once a month. A 2-week sprint, however, will keep a steady stream of new features paraded in front of him, convincing him that the business is getting tremendous value out of the team and keeping him motivated to groom his user stories actively because they will be needed in only a few more days for the next story conference.

Although shorter iterations involve more overhead, perhaps this time is well spent because the faster pace gives teams more opportunities to check and correct their estimating techniques and to improve the details of the work patterns. As teams get more experienced, the top-of-cycle phases for shorter sprints will naturally proceed more quickly, to the point where the cumulative time for overhead tends to even out between long and short iterations. However, 2-week sprints often prove far too short for development teams to deliver large enhancements, especially for the data integration side of a DWBI project where multiple architectural layers must be addressed. Trying to get a new source staged, scrubbed, integrated, and dimensionalized all within the 8 work days of a 2-week sprint can be frantic and exhaust a team quickly.

With 2 weeks being too short for the team and 4 weeks being too long for the product owner, 3 weeks often prove to be the right compromise. This time frame also has an appealing, built-in structure to it: 3-week iterations have a clear beginning, middle, and wrap-up segment, each a week long. Moreover, teams working in 3-week iterations can be very clear about the proper intent for each week. The scrum master can summarize the desired cadence of a sprint by stating simply:

> *It's alright to be a bit confused and ineffective for the first week because we'll still be getting organized, but we'd better be making fast headway during that second week, because when the third week starts, it's going to be all about getting ready for the demo.*

Nonstandard sprints

Our discussion so far has focused upon construction sprints, which typically comprise three-quarters or more of a project. Generic Scrum defines several other types of sprints, however, which teams should draw upon as the circumstances dictate.

We refer to all of these variants as "sprints," although some may not be restricted to a standard time box nor a team pursues them with a full five-step Scrum cycle.

Sprint 0

If "Sprint 1" is where the construction work of a project begins, then a Sprint 0 is a time span occurring before Sprint 1 in which the team can get everything ready for development. Acquiring and configuring technical resources, identifying coding standards, and negotiating handoff requirements with the operations team are all perfect activities for a Sprint 0 so that coding can get underway without a hitch when the first iteration begins. This nonconstruction sprint can be pursued easily with a normal time box and the full Scrum cycle, making it a good place to give new teams some practice with the method before the business starts expecting real results from them.

For data integration projects, Sprint 0 allows data architects the opportunity to sketch a whole project data model, at least at the 80/20 level discussed in the prior chapter. Similarly, systems analysts can employ Sprint 0 to research the quality of source data and to define transformation rules for the first modules coded during the first iteration. Because Sprint 0 allows the modeler and analyst to get a head start before coding begins, it also positions to stay one step ahead of the team for all of the remaining iterations. See the sidebar in the chapter on starting new teams for a list of Sprint 0 items appropriate for many DWBI projects.

Architectural sprints

For projects that include some tough technical requirements or involve new technology at their core, an architectural sprint may be necessary. If this is the case, the developers will have to inform the product owner that they will be holding a standard time-boxed iteration using the full Scrum cycle, but that he will see little in terms of tangible modules delivered because the team needs to invest first in the invisible portion of an application, such as reusable business logic, error handling routines, and metadata management calls.

An architectural sprint can also be necessary in those situations where developers were compelled to add a large amount of temporary code in order to get a particular feature into a release well before the necessary technical infrastructure was in place. In this event, the team may need an architectural sprint just to remove all the temporary constructs from the code in order to restore a clean build from which properly designed construction can resume.

No matter what the cause, the team should try to keep sprints that are solely architectural to a minimum because they undermine the agile principle of satisfying the customer with early and frequent deliveries of new features offering a business value. With too many architectural sprints, it will seem to the sponsors that the team has slipped back into a high-risk waterfall pattern of a big deliverable at project's end, even if they are colocated and holding daily stand-up meetings. It will be better to spread the architectural work across the iterations as much as possible where it can be addressed with the architectural reserve discussed earlier, keeping new features as the primary objective of each iteration.

Implementation sprints

Scrum focuses upon delivering shippable modules, yet there are some necessary activities that cannot be pursued until the entire release has been assembled. Examples are final certification runs of system test scripts, user acceptance testing, operational readiness reviews with the production support team, and some final system-wide documentation. For all this prerelease work, a team needs to plan on an implementation sprint before a build is promoted into production. The developers will have to decide on a case-by-case basis whether or not an implementation sprint involves a standard time box and all the steps of a Scrum cycle.

"Spikes"

Sometimes surprises or technical complications can trap a team, making continued progress on user stories impossible until it resolves a fundamental quandary involving data or programming. For example, a DWBI team might be working with a standard ETL tool when it suddenly realizes that they will need to resort to a service-oriented piece of middleware that none of them has worked with before or they may discover that a particular source system does not always provide the parameters needed for an important business rule in the data transformation modules.

In this situation, the developers need to call a time-out from the construction sprints. Maybe the new technology or data puzzle involves only a single layer of the warehouse architecture or perhaps it calls for a "tracer bullet" experiment that carries a sample bit of data throughout all layers of the application. In either situation, the team needs to estimate how many days it will need to figure out and prove a solution to the challenge and then gang tackle the issue until a new norm for the project is proven out. Daily stand-up meetings will still be useful, but the rest of the Scrum cycle is probably unnecessary here. Such a suspension of regular construction iterations is called a "spike," which the Australians, who play a lot of rugby, insist is named after the time-out a referee calls during a game when the field proves too muddy. He sends all the players back to the bench to put on a longer set of cleats (spikes) on their shoes before play resumes. In software development, spikes provide teams with the opportunity to sharpen their tools or understanding to gain valuable traction on a slippery aspect of the project.

"Hardening" sprints

Scrum provides several techniques for keeping delivered modules free of defects, such as test-driven development, the definition of done, and a tech debt list. However, if quality problems do get out of hand, the team can call for a *hardening sprint*—a standard construction iteration dedicated to fixing defects and bringing the current build back to where it is truly shippable code.

Unlike the other sprint variations described earlier, Scrum practitioners speak of hardening iterations not as something to count on, but as an alternative that teams should avoid. Asking sponsors to fund a hardening sprint to fix sloppy code is usually very embarrassing for the team. It informs the business that the project's delivery date will be set back multiple weeks and that the budget will run many tens of thousands of dollars over—all because the developers did not work carefully enough to keep defects to a manageable level.

Where did scrum come from?

The presentation of generic Scrum sketched earlier gives us a starting notion that we can now adapt for business intelligence projects. Before leaving our introduction, however, we should mention some of the rich intellectual history behind Scrum, which will allow agile data warehousing advocates to portray it as a mature and proven method, worthy of pursuing enterprise information systems projects today.

Distant history

Like many good ideas, Scrum arose from the intersection of multiple innovative threads, in this case three from the late 20th century: (1) Japanese advancements in operations research; (2) growing incremental, iterative development investigations in the United States; and (3) the rise of object-oriented (OO) technologies in software. At its deepest level, Scrum draws upon the lean manufacturing movement and quality circles originating in Japanese manufacturing during its economic boom years during the 1980s. The word "scrum" as a project method was, in fact, first employed as a metaphor for better management in product manufacturing companies in a 1986 *Harvard Business Review* article "The New, New Product Development Game" by two Japanese business academicians: Hirotaka Takeuchi (Dean of the Graduate School of International Corporate Strategy, Hirotsubashi University) and Ikujiro Nonaka (professor in the School of Knowledge Science at the Japan Advanced Institute of Science and Technology). [Takeuchi & Nonaka 1986]

During this same time frame, innovative thinkers in the U.S. software industry were exploring project management using iterative and incremental methods. Important milestones in this effort include IBM's NASA Space Shuttle software project that involved 17 iterations over 31 months ending in 1980 and a widely read 1988 paper, "A Spiral Model of Software Development and Enhancement," by a researcher at TRW. [Boehm 1988]

The third thread materialized in the mid-1990s as software managers realized that their object-oriented developers had yet to realize the breakthrough productivity that OO coding technologies seemed to promise. Believing that qualities such as inheritance and polymorphism made OO components far more flexible than modules built with traditional procedural code, they began stripping the procedural aspects out of the current iterative techniques in an effort to make them as nimble as the languages they used for coding. Important moments in this effort include Microsoft's book *Dynamics of Software Development* [McCarthy 2006] and Kent Beck's first XP project at Chrysler in 1997. [C3 Team 1998]

Perhaps the clearest melding of iterative development and OO surfaced with a series of books on the Unified Development Process that aligned a well-described development method with Rational's object-oriented software development tools. (Jacobson and colleagues [1999] provide a good overview of this early flavor of agile.) In 1995, the Standish Group published its seminal "Chaos" study detailing the software industry's abysmal track record in delivering large systems through traditional methods. Their 1999 follow-up revealed that those companies experimenting with shorter time frames and incremental delivery seemed to be turning the situation around, creating some important momentum behind those approaches that utilize quick time boxes and tighter project scoping. [Standish Group 1995, 1999]

Scrum emerges

The three threads described previously merged into the agile approach underpinning this book when two eventual signers of the Agile Manifesto, Dr. Jeff Sutherland and Ken Schwaber, combined the notions in Takeuchi and Nonaka's paper with their own work in iterative methods for OO development, infusing the result with further studies of process theory performed at the DuPont's Advanced Research Facility. [Control Chaos 2007]

The year 1994 saw the first Scrum development project at Easel Corporation, a maker of a fourth-generation language for mainframe data integration. Sutherland and Schwaber formalized their project management approach in a 1995 presentation before the Object Management Group's "Object-Oriented Programming, Systems, Languages, and Applications (OOPSLA)" conference [ADM 1995], after which they began offering Scrum-specific trainings and innovation conferences. In the intervening years since OOPSLA'95, Scrum has gained greater depth and formalization as it cross-pollinated with XP and incorporated research on the theory of constraints [Goldratt 1990], spawning many books, and eventually evolving into a certified scrum master training program for software professionals. [Schwaber 2004]

For the first decade or so, most Scrum implementations were bottom up, but as it steadily achieved more project successes, many top-down implementations sponsored by corporate IT departments appeared. Today Scrum is practiced by many global name-brand companies such as Microsoft, Yahoo, Ariba, Cadence, Adobe, GE Healthcare, Borland, Google, Primavera, Sun, Siemens, State Farm, Philips, IBM, U.S. Federal Reserve Bank, HP, Motorola, SAP, Bose, CapitalOne, and Xerox. [Behrens 2005]

Summary

The internationally defined method called Scrum is a major agile approach that is easy to teach and employ for software development projects. It embeds nicely in an organization's existing release cycle, deriving from that process' discovery and elaboration step an initial project backlog. The five-step structure that Scrum employs for every iteration includes an initial iteration planning day that allows teams to double-estimate the increment of work they are taking on and thereby be sure that they have not overcommitted. The development step in the middle of the iteration benefits from several practical techniques for accelerating coding, such as the 2-to-1 design, and relying on hand-edited photos of designs until the programming of a module is complete. Scrum's iterations end with a day dedicated to user demonstrations of the programming results and a team reflection on how to make the process more effective, making Scrum a continually optimizing process. When it comes to data warehousing, Scrum is a strong method that can be used out of the box for dashboarding and is a good starting point for further adaptation for projects heavy with data integration requirements.

Streamlining Project Management

3

How should we monitor agile teams' overall progress during an iteration?
What patterns should scrum masters be watching for in the project
management tools Scrum provides?
How might we adapt agile for remote team members?

When an agile method unleashes a highly product development team, questions regarding project management will come immediately to mind. Fortunately, because the Scrum method utilized for agile data warehousing requires surprisingly few project management mechanisms, the work of keeping a team on track becomes streamlined greatly. This streamlined approach relies on a pair of simple tracking artifacts, a few best practices regarding sprint lengths and record keeping, and a few adaptations when teams become distributed geographically. The combination preserves Scrum's many strengths, including velocity and responsiveness to the customer.

When agile teams begin delivering at pace, stakeholders will want frequent project status information. At the highest level, the user demo step that occurs at the end of every construction iteration provides a detailed snapshot of the project's progress every few weeks. The cumulative project backlog—where all stories will be marked accepted, rejected, under development, or waiting—can quickly bring stakeholders up to date at the user story level. However, many stakeholders, including the team itself, will be reassured far more frequently that the iteration is on track. They will all want a daily status revealing whether the team will meet its current iteration goals by the end of the given time box.

Scrum provides daily status information using two key coordination tools: task board and burndown chart. These two artifacts will be readily intelligible to the reader, for they build upon notions introduced in the previous chapter, such as user stories, story points, and task cards. The task board allows everyone to see team progress at a task card level. The burndown chart allows a team to view its aggregate progress across all the stories on the iteration backlog. With these coordination tools displayed prominently in the team room, business and information technology (IT) stakeholders can discover for themselves what the team will deliver when

Agile Data Warehousing Project Management.
DOI: http://dx.doi.org/10.1016/B978-0-12-396463-2.00003-X

the iteration concludes, and project managers can learn of sprint progress directly without burdening the team with status meetings. For development team members, the task board and burndown chart minimize the time and effort developers must spend on communicating outwardly. These tracking tools also allow them to assign and coordinate labor tasks among themselves without needing a project manager to control the work room.

Scrum's coordination tools therefore streamline project management for all parties. They work well in their generic form for both dashboarding projects and data integration initiatives. Because they are fundamental to the success of self-organized teams, the reader will need to be familiar with them before we begin customizing other portions of Scrum to better support data integration projects. Presenting these tools also provides the opportunity to resolve three common challenges in managing agile teams with streamlined techniques: what to do when a team is running behind, deciding whether to track actual hours spent on tasks, and how to incorporate geographically remote teammates.

Highly transparent task boards

As detailed in the previous chapter, an agile iteration begins with a day of planning, involving both a story conference and a task planning session. The story conference identifies a few story cards that will serve as the iteration's backlog of work to be done. The task cards are derived from the story cards and enumerate the individual steps developers need to complete in order to turn a given story into a small working piece of the overall application. During an iteration, these cards constitute a rich set of information that could be used to visualize and track team progress toward their goals of each sprint, if only they could be displayed conveniently. The task board answers exactly that need, arranging the cards in a matrix where developers and project stakeholders alike can instantly get an overall impression of progress and look easily into the detailed situation at hand.

The task board is simplistic in its format, but offers a high level of visibility of project progress to stakeholders within and outside the team, making it an essential to display in the project room. At its simplest, the task board is a large wall onto which index cards representing user stories and developer tasks can be pinned. By "large," we mean perhaps an entire wall of a project room. Eight feet tall by 12 feet wide would not be too big, even for a team working with palm-sized index cards. The story and task cards placed on the task board are called "cards" because Scrum was first defined as a paper-based system using a cork board to track team activities. In practice, these cards will be sticky notes for teams tracking progress using whiteboards or some type of screen object for teams employing an agile coordination software package.

Figure 3.1 depicts a generic task board. The column names are appropriate for a team employing plain-vanilla Scrum, but are often adapted by project teams as they customize the method for their particular work styles. For each iteration, story cards

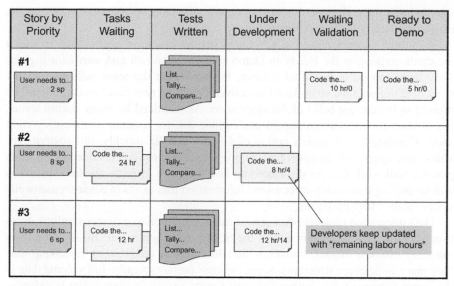

Story by Priority	Tasks Waiting	Tests Written	Under Development	Waiting Validation	Ready to Demo
#1 User needs to... 2 sp		List... Tally... Compare...		Code the... 10 hr/0	Code the... 5 hr/0
#2 User needs to... 8 sp	Code the... 24 hr	List... Tally... Compare...	Code the... 8 hr/4		
#3 User needs to... 6 sp	Code the... 12 hr	List... Tally... Compare...	Code the... 12 hr/14	Developers keep updated with "remaining labor hours"	

FIGURE 3.1

Simplified representation of a Scrum task board in midsprint.

are placed on the task board, using a column running down the left side. The story cards are placed on the board in priority order so that the most important work can always be found at the top of the board. To the right of this vertical line of story cards are several columns dedicated to identifying the status of the associated task cards as the team works upon them: *Tasks Waiting*, *Tests Written*, *Under Development*, *Waiting Validation*, and *Ready to Demo*. Many teams draw a horizontal swim lane across the task board for each story. The story cards will remain fixed to the left-most column as they simply define the swim lanes. As the work of the iteration is completed, the task cards will move steadily toward the right, hopefully all landing in the "Ready to Demo" column by the time the sprint's demo day arrives.

The task board enables self-organized teams greatly. When one of the team's software developers needs work to do, he finds it for himself directly from the task board. Because the story cards define the swim lanes in priority order, he need only identify the task card closest to the top of the Task Waiting column for which he has the skills to complete. By placing his initials on the card, he lets the entire team know who will be working on the task.

Following the principles of test-driven development, the developer then authors the validation scripts for the deliverables he is about to create. He pins that test package into the Tests Written column so that a peer can later find it and then moves the task card into Under Development. When the coding is complete, he can move the card to the Waiting Validation column, at which point a teammate can volunteer to perform with him the validation described in the test package deposited early in the Test Written column. When both the developer and the teammate are satisfied that the task passes validation criteria, the developer can advance the task card to the Ready to Demo column.

As product owner, the team's business partner has been encouraged to watch the cards arriving in the Ready to Demo column. When all task cards for a given story have arrived in this final column, it signals that the team believes that the story card defining the swim lane has delivered and the new functionality should be present in the current build of the application. As practiced by many Scrum teams, the product owner can and should at this time ask for a demo of that story right away. Consistent with agile's notion of fail fast and fix quickly, this pattern provides developers with as much time as possible to fix any defects that appear. This practice will work fine for dashboarding and reporting projects, as the application will be pulling from ready-to-consume information that exists in a warehouse or file system somewhere upstream.

Data integration projects often cannot manage miditeration demonstrations, however, so they must adapt this part of the Scrum cycle somewhat. Business partners can only evaluate extract, transform, and load (ETL) modules by reviewing data they place in database structures. Some business partners require full volume data in the target database tables before they will accept a story involving data transforms. If that information set is large, a full load may well take a day or more before it is complete and the team's deliverables can be demonstrated. Teams working with large data sets rarely have the resources for each developer to load a separate target schema as he programs his module. These teams adopt instead a data load strategy that invests in a full volume target load only at the end of the iteration. Because they must share a single target schema for data that take days to load, the developers will have only enough time during each short iteration to perform a demo load once. They will have to work with a small sliver of data in their sandboxes while performing unit development. Integration testing will have to be executed against a subset of full-volume data that is small enough to allow this level of validation to finish overnight. A few days before the user demo, however, the developers will have to stop programming, assemble a final build, and invoke the ETL for a multiday run. If the developers get the timing right, this full-volume load will end just before the user demo takes place.

Because full-volume data sets are so difficult to work with, teams confronting large data volumes will be able to afford only a single end-of-iteration load. Consequently, they will only be able to provide a single end-of-iteration user demo. On the task board, task cards will accumulate in the last ready-to-demo column until they are all evaluated for acceptance by the product owner on the last day of iteration.

Task boards amplify project quality

As shown previously, quality assurance is built into the very structure of the task board. It demands that each module passes through *three* separate validation points for both functional and technical qualities: (1) the developer must write the tests before coding, (2) another team member must execute these tests for the units delivered, and (3) the product owner ensures each unit meets business needs as part of the user demo. By placing these validation activities on the task board, Scrum incorporates quality assurance into the process of development far more thoroughly than traditional methods.

Traditional IT professionals often paint agile projects as anarchic coding frenzies that pay too little attention to quality assurance. To the contrary, the task board's structure ensures that testing occurs throughout the iteration and consequently throughout the entire project. Waterfall, however, clumps most of its testing toward the end of the construction phase, where it often gets squeezed down to only a few days if upstream phases run long. With this contrast, it is easy to see why agile projects in practice deliver far more trouble-free code than traditional efforts, despite the fact that they allow the developers to build applications much faster.

Task boards naturally integrate team efforts

Not surprisingly, the task board with its prominent place on the project room wall provides a natural focus for the team. In fact, the best place to convene the daily stand-up meetings is with developers gathered before the task board. If all the tasks cards are moving steadily across the board toward the Ready to Demo column, the product owner can simply say "Yay, team! You're making progress." Clumps of cards indicating slow spots will be easy to spot on the board, and in that case the product owner can easily point to the problem area and ask "Why doesn't this story have more cards in Waiting Validation by now? Is there any confusion over requirement that's slowing you down? Are you guys really going to get this feature finished by demo day?" The task board thereby helps keep the business partner engaged in the process and the developers motivated to deliver.

The task board also becomes the primary resource for managing dependencies. Traditional project managers often do not believe that self-organized teams can figure out all the predecessor and successor relationships between tasks for themselves. Typically, these doubts indicated that they are overlooking several factors. First, agile teams rarely start with a blank page, especially on data warehousing projects. The discovery and elaboration phase of most company's release cycles provides a high-level architecture that the agile team can utilize to effectively identify and sequence the major modules it must build. Second, the agile iteration keeps the scope of work small—to the point where it is humanly possible for a team of 6 to 10 software professionals to understand the interconnections between the affected components without needing a project manager to assemble a detailed project plan. Third, the task board spreads all the task cards for an iteration upon a surface, enabling the developers who are wrestling with a complex dependency to point at the cards involved, place colored dots or pins upon them, and write notes on the back of each one. The task board empowers them to see the problem and collectively reason about its solution in real time.

The scrum master can use the task board to accelerate daily check-ins. Daily stand-up meetings often start to run too long when developers go into details about what they are doing and why they are having trouble instead of answering Scrum's three simple questions. In this situation, the scrum master can convene the stand-up in front of the task board and ask each developer to *speak only to the cards*. "What I did yesterday" is answered by pointing to the one or two cards a developer moved the day before. "What I will do today" becomes simply the cards he will be advancing soon and to what columns. Details concerning the hold-ups can be reduced to "I've found a dependency between these two cards, and I need to meet with our systems analyst to clear it up."

Product owners also benefit from the transparency that the task board brings to the formerly obscured coding portion of the software development process. If he pays some attention during the task planning session on the first day of the sprint, he will recognize many of the task cards that appear later on the task board. Once he learns to read the board, he will no longer need to wait for a project manager's summary because he can always derive a notion of sprint progress directly from the task cards. He can compile his own status reports for the executive stakeholders, and at the next stand-up meeting he can ask questions about any pattern on the board that causes him concern. The task board makes the entire software development process transparent to the product owner, who appreciates the knowledge it provides because he must answer frequently to others for funds the project is consuming.

All told, agile's simple task board gives developers the visibility and motivation they need to pull together all the complicated threads of a sprint into a complete delivery. By making slow spots and dependencies more visible, it brings complications that threaten the project to the surface promptly and gives everyone a forum to reason about their resolution before the challenge can affect the team's delivery velocity.

Scrum masters must monitor the task board

Scrum masters must watch for a few developer behaviors that can needlessly impede the progress of task cards across the task board. Let us start with the practice where task boards accumulate dozens of task cards stuck in Under Development with only 1 or 2 hours left on them. Developers cannot bring themselves to close out the cards because they are not quite "done." However, leaving these cards in suspended animation threatens the delivery of the entire sprint because there are other cards waiting for them to complete.

These stalled cards can indicate a few situations, all them needing to be resolved quickly. First, a given card could actually contain more than one task, and it is the last little task within it that is stalled. A common example would be "code the customer dimension ETL." The engineer working on this card might have defined this work to require the module to be not just unit tested but fully integration tested before it can be called done. This card will then end up stuck in the Under Development column until somebody loads and runs a full integration suite, which may not occur until the last day or two of the sprint. To keep the cards moving, the scrum master needs to encourage the team to carefully define tasks to be as atomic as possible, without dependencies. In our example, a simple solution would be to split the task cards into two. The verb on the first would be "code," and the verb on the second would be "integration test."

Coders might also be leaving cards at 1 or 2 hours to go because a feature *might* still be needed. Agile projects work with much of the design kept in teammates' minds, with details provided in real time to their colleagues as needed. In this context, designs are fluid and any developer can rightly believe another feature for his current module is probably coming. He may have even heard a conversation between the product owner and the data architect that makes him sure it will arrive very soon. Unfortunately, the sprint begins to stall while he waits for this requirement to appear. The scrum master should guide the coders to close off tasks once all "actionable feature requests" have been addressed. They can always create a new "add a further feature" task card if an additional requirement is defined later.

Beyond task cards stuck with an hour or two to go, the scrum master might also notice that tasks cards for high-priority stories never advance, whereas those tied to the least important stories of the sprint are making great headway. There are many possible explanations for this. The coders do not consider those tasks as truly necessary but are unwilling to say so or else those tasks represent chores and boring features so the developers are all leaving them to someone else to take on. Also likely is because no one really comprehended the design requirements for those cards during the task conference, they have all chosen to work instead on tasks they understand well.

In these situations, the scrum master truly earns his keep. He must actively inquire about why the cards are stalled, arrange an after-scrum meeting if needed, and facilitate the discussion until the root cause of the delay has been identified and someone has volunteered to resolve it.

Burndown charts reveal the team aggregate progress

The task board, with its swim lanes and its moving task cards, certainly makes it easy for any stakeholder to glean a task-by-task notion of the developers' progress throughout the sprint. The details are all there; however, the big picture is not yet visible. The product owner, the developers, and all interested stakeholders still lack a means of understanding at a glance whether the work of the entire sprint is on track and whether a full iteration's worth of work will be delivered by demo day.

To answer this need, agile provides the burndown chart. It displays a daily total of the remaining labor for all task cards on the task board. Because this number should be steadily trending toward zero, the burndown chart provides a single-glance notion of the status of the iteration. Moreover, any sudden change in the day-to-day trend provides the team with a far more sensitive detections of problems than the task board can offer.

Figure 3.2 depicts a typical burndown chart as it would appear at the end of an iteration. As each developer wraps up his work for the day, he needs to stop by

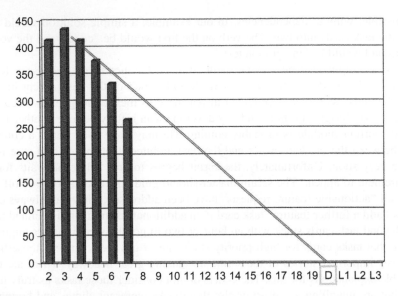

FIGURE 3.2

Typical agile burndown chart with a perfect line.

the task board to update the task cards he is working on with a current estimate of "labor hours to go" before the task is complete. These numbers can be called the remaining labor estimates. Before the next day's stand-up meeting, the scrum master can total up these remaining labor estimates to derive the team's total current forecast of work still in the iteration backlog. This tally becomes the next "burndown bar" added to the chart, representing the team's total labor hours to go before all the stories in the iteration are delivered as promised.

A closer inspection of Figure 3.2 reveals that the first "burndown bar" is drawn for Day 2 of the iteration. This makes sense, as Day 1 of each sprint is dedicated to iteration planning, not development work. One will also note that Figure 3.2 has room for bars up to Day 19 for the 4-week time box it represents and then a day labeled "D" for "demo." If the burndown chart does hit zero on the day of the demo as planned, then all task cards will be in the Ready to Demo column and the user demo will present all stories as done. Some burndowns have a few slots listed after the demo day to represent situations where the team extends the iteration a bit. In Figure 3.2, these slots are labeled L1 through L3 to represent "late" days. There will be more to say about extending iterations a little later.

Scrum masters often fit their burndown charts with a "perfect line" to show where each day's burndown bar should be if the team was to smoothly work off the task cards and hit zero by the end of the sprint. This line is drawn from the top of Day 2's starting tally (the iteration's beginning labor estimate) to zero on demo day. If daily tallies rise above the perfect line, then the team is falling behind. Below the perfect line means that the team is running ahead of schedule. Because the developers

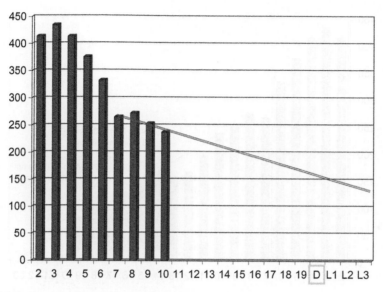

FIGURE 3.3

Midsprint burndown chart showing trouble.

double-estimated the upcoming labor during sprint planning, the sprint should contain reasonable work, making the perfect line a reasonable day-to-day objective.

Detecting trouble with burndown charts

Burndown charts are very good at revealing problems, as shown in Figure 3.3, which has been taken from an actual project that the author led in the late 2000 s. In this snapshot, the scrum master has drawn a trend line that focuses on the 4 days just completed in the middle of the sprint. Drawing such a trend line is more of an art than a science. In this example, the scrum master based the line on the bars for Days 7 and 11 in order to highlight his suspicion that the team was losing traction during this portion of the sprint. With that line drawn, the developers could see easily that they would have no hope of delivering all the stories by demo day if the trend continued. Corrective action was clearly needed.

In this case, the developers conferenced together after the morning stand-up meeting to discuss the forces driving the scrum master's trend line awry. They discovered that one programmer was tackling a Type 2 slowly changing dimension with insufficient training on the ETL tool they were using. He was working without a good coding pattern in mind, and his remaining labor estimates were actually going up day after day as problems with his trial-and-error approach began compounding. With this situation now clearly brought to light, the team was able to reassign the work between them and pull the burndown chart's remaining labor bars back toward the perfect line shown in Figure 3.4.

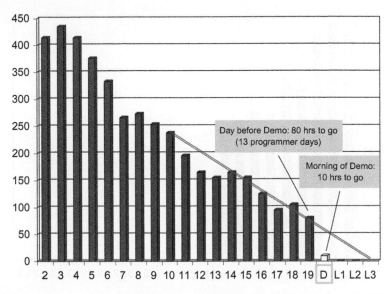

FIGURE 3.4

End-of-sprint burndown chart showing a delivery gap.

This particular case study eventually highlighted the burndown chart's amazing ability to inspire developers to work to their highest potential. The day before the demo was a Friday, and on that morning the burndown chart showed that approximately 13 programmer days of work remained in the iteration—well beyond what the team of five developers could complete in the one remaining day. The scrum master's trend line showed that the team was either going to have to leave some user stories undelivered or extend the sprint by 3 days, as suggested by Figure 3.4. However, when the team convened for the user demo on the following Monday, the scrum master's tally of remaining labor on the task cards totaled only 10 hours, as depicted by the last burndown bar in Figure 3.4.

The product owner was able to test drive the new build and accept all the stories that morning, despite the fact that the team was so far from finished just the work day before. Clearly something extraordinary happened. The developers had taken a good look at the burndown chart on Friday and realized that the choice was between keeping the promises they had made to their business partners during sprint planning or looking like amateurs who cannot be counted on. They may well have also recognized that the product owner reports to sponsors after every iteration and that such reports can easily impact later funding decisions. Due to either of these motivations, the burndown chart had inspired them to put in some extra effort over the weekend and deliver all the promised user stories. No scrum master or project manager had to coax them to do so.

This dynamic is, in fact, a major reason why estimates by agile teams repeatedly prove to be far more accurate than those provided by waterfall teams. Guided by the trend lines drawn on the burndown charts, the developers *make* those estimates come true. Sometimes they must put in extra effort. Just as often, they swarm in the face of a delivery shortfall to figure out how to reduce the hours the remaining tasks will require.

Of course, project leadership must always consider whether a team in this situation has actually cut some important corners in order to meet the deadline. Such shortcuts can create hidden defects in the code or architecture that everyone will come to regret. This possibility underscores the need for teams to put in place strong quality assurance procedures, as discussed in the section on task boards earlier and as explored in detail in the second volume of this two-book set.

Developers are not the burndown chart's victims

While the developers in this case history unfortunately lost their weekend, they are not without recourse to keep that situation from occurring again. The intent of agile methods is to not find ways to make developers work nights and weekends. In fact, one of the principles attached to the Agile Manifesto clearly states that the goal is to help teams find their "sustainable pace" of delivery. No one benefits if agile runs the team into the ground with overwork, leading the developers to seek employment elsewhere.

So if teammates end up working nights and weekends, what can they do to prevent that from happening again? Fundamentally, such an outcome is a function of poor estimating and/or insufficient work methods. The developers need to bring up these topics during the iteration retrospective and have a candid conversation about the forces that have led them to overcommit or underperform. There are at least a dozen aspects of the software development process where they could try correcting the problem with new techniques—from their story point references and programming patterns to their detailed design process and their definition of done. The sprint retrospective affords them the time needed to examine that complex process in detail and find where it needs to be modified.

If the overtime work arose simply from under estimating the difficulty of the work, then the developers should spend a moment during the sprint retrospective to identify a more realistic capacity number to employ during the next iteration planning sessions. As presented in the previous chapter, the team capacity states the amount of work that the developers plan to commit to in the coming iteration. It is tied most closely to the team's velocity, which is the amount of work they managed to deliver during the previous iteration.

Teams that decide to lower their capacity number in the face of too much overtime will need to socialize this adjusted number with key stakeholders. In particular, the product owner and project architect need to understand the new value because it will impact the project's forecasted duration and cost. The necessary revision to the project forecast may well require management to rebalance their expectations concerning the key project parameters of cost, delivery date, and scope. Such adjustments are never made cheerfully. However, if the developers fail to realistically set their capacity when the iterations prove to be too much work, they will have only themselves to blame if they must work long hours regularly. Luckily, as discussed next, the burndown chart offers the team an easily interpreted, graphical means of communicating what their velocity truly is, providing them with the compelling evidence they will need to justify their actions when adopting a new capacity.

Calculating velocity from burndown charts

As introduced in the previous chapter, much of agile project management revolves around the notion of team velocity, which can be measured in two ways: story points and task labor hours. Scrum masters derive a team's story point velocity from a tally of user stories accepted and rejected during the user demo. As shown in a later chapter, teams can use their story point velocity to build a "current estimate" of how many more iterations a release or project will require. Labor-hour velocity has a more limited, but equally important, application. As detailed in this section, developers employ this velocity measure only to set the capacity number for the next sprint, which in turn helps determine which stories they will commit to for the next iteration.

A team's current velocity is defined as the rate of delivery the developers achieved during the previous iteration. A team's capacity, however, is a forward-looking notion of what the team believes it could deliver during the next sprint. Velocity is based on history. Capacity is an educated guess, typically made at the top of the Scrum cycle, and heavily influenced by the developers' recent experiences on the project.

Capacity can be set in terms of story points, as heard when teammates share statements such as the following at a retrospective: "We tried to deliver 30 story points last iteration. We worked night and day and only delivered 25 story points at the user demo. That is still too many story points to commit to. We can't keep working at this pace, so during the next story conference, we should only commit to 20 story points worth of stories."

Capacity can also be set in terms of labor hours, as illustrated by the following statements from the same hypothetical sprint retrospective: "Those stories that we said totaled 30 story points had tasks that added up to 600 labor hours. We completed tasks totaling 500 hours, and again, that was too much work. So, during the next task planning session, we should only commit to 450 hours worth of task cards."

Teams want to have these two separately derived notions of their capacity so that they can check their commitments based on story points against those made based on labor hours. If they do not agree, the developers' two estimates are inconsistent, indicating that at least one of them needs to be reformulated.

With the developers' labor-hour velocity so central to their task planning for every iteration, they will need to show clearly how they derived that measure. Figure 3.5 shows a simple graphical means of identifying the team's delivery velocity in labor hours using the final burndown chart from iteration. In this example, the project is using 3-week iterations. The team committed to 414 hours of work during

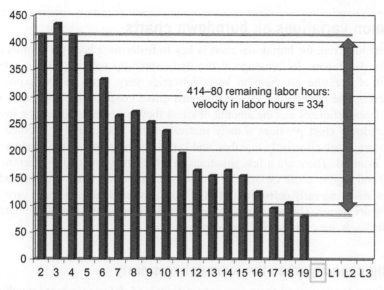

414–80 remaining labor hours:
velocity in labor hours = 334

FIGURE 3.5

Calculating labor-hour velocity using a burndown chart.

the iteration planning session, as indicated by the chart's first burndown bar, but finished the sprint with 80 hours of work still undelivered. The team velocity, then, is simply the 414 hours of originally estimated work less the 80 hours of tasks left undone. The resulting figure of 334 hours is the team's velocity for that sprint.

In deciding what amount of labor this team should commit to for the next iteration, agile practitioners would encourage them to first try the notion of "yesterday's weather." People always want to know what today's weather will be, but if there's no meteorological information available, the best prediction they can possibly make is that today's weather will be about like yesterday's. Agile teams are in the same situation with forecasting how much they will be able to deliver during its next sprint—absent any other information, they should assume they will deliver about what they did during the last iteration, both in story points and in labor hours for tasks.

However, at the top of any sprint, a team may vary its chosen capacity from its historical velocity for many reasons. Most commonly, upcoming vacations or training sessions for some of the team members will cause the developers to lower their target capacity to account for the amount of resource hours they are going to lose during the next sprint. Similarly, it is sometimes clear that the next iteration will be subject to greater distractions from other projects the developers are participating in or, due to a fresh crisis in operations, will sap their time for "production support." Finally, as the aforementioned discussion suggested, a team should adjust its capacity below its velocity if they have been working overtime. In that case, the developers need to set their capacity to reflect what they sense is their sustainable pace.

Common variations on burndown charts

Over the long run, the burndown chart is key to fostering a high-performance team of agile developers. Its presence at the daily stand-up meeting places a healthy amount of pressure on them to keep deliveries very close to the expectations depicted by the perfect line. By creating this direct connection between the developers' labor estimates and the amount of stress they experience during the iteration, the burndown chart provides a daily motivation for teammates to become better forecasters, work effectively together, and keep their promises to the product owner firmly in mind. There are a few situations in which these objectives become challenged and require some variation in the way the burndown chart is employed—situations involving early deliveries, leftover work, and miditeration scope creep from the product owner. This section considers how to adapt one's use of the burndown chart for each one of these challenges in turn.

Setting capacity when the team delivers early

Sometimes teams exceed their own expectations and deliver far more quickly than planned. Although this surprise is a good problem to have, it muddies the notion of velocity, thereby complicating selecting a capacity number to use during the next sprint planning.

It should be stated at the outset that this situation is better avoided if at all possible. Many Scrum projects can maintain an inventory of user stories on the release backlog that are ready to develop. When a team with such a backlog starts to run ahead of schedule, it can simply pull a few more stories into the ongoing sprint and keep working until the conclusion of the current time box. This option is the best choice because it leaves the developers a full iteration's work to base their velocity and next capacity upon. The developers then calculate their velocity as they always do: total story points for stories accepted and total labor hours belonging to tasks that were completed.

In those situations where stories waiting on the backlog are not ready to move into development, the team will be forced to end the iteration early. This can happen on data integration projects because the data architect and systems analyst often work one iteration ahead of their teams (this is the practice of "pipelining," discussed in a later chapter). These teammates may not be finished with the data models and transform rules needed by the next set of stories when their programmers finish the current iteration ahead of schedule, so the developers will have no choice but to end the iteration early. In this situation, the team will have an observed velocity based on a shortened time box. Unfortunately, the team will need a capacity number based on a full-length iteration for the coming sprint planning sessions.

One solution is to simple inflate the velocity numbers measured during that sprint for the number of days that were trimmed from the last iteration. Say a team committed to 24 story points and 240 labor hours for a 15-day sprint that they completed in 12 days. These developers could decide that since 15 is 25% greater than 12, they should aim for 30 story points and 300 labor hours in the next iteration.

This simplistic approach can lead them into trouble, however. Above all, they would be committing to an amount of work based on a calculation, not an observation. They would have to look hard at the root cause behind the past iteration's early delivery. Perhaps the product owner dropped many requirements for a particular user story or perhaps a developer found a reusable module in another data mart that eliminated some of the planned coding on one of his major tasks. Before committing to an inflated capacity, the team needs to be sure that factors leading to a faster delivery during the last sprint will continue to exist.

The safer approach would be to commit again to the same capacity as the previous iteration, but ensure that some extra stories are ready to work on this time. This choice will allow the developers to pull additional stories into the sprint if need be, thereby working a full time box. They can safely adjust their capacity number upward because it is based on a measured velocity of a full iteration.

Managing tech debt

As described in the previous chapter, technical debt comprises the many little aspects of deliverables from previous iterations that were not exactly right or did not quite get "done" by the developers. The product owner accepted the user story despite the unfinished work, but only because the developers promised to attend to those open details immediately at the beginning of the next sprint. Thus it is called "debt" because the developers "owe" that cleanup work to their business partner.

Typically, tech debt is treated like just another set of tasks during the planning of the next iteration. The developers will create task cards for them and estimate the labor hours they will require to resolve. The time to work these tasks will be taken from the team's architectural reserve, as described in the previous chapter. Being the keeper of the work process, the scrum master is responsible for ensuring that her teammates pay off their tech debt right away during the next iteration. This objective may prove tricky to achieve, however, because the next iteration frequently revolves around new, exciting features the business strongly desires, so developers sometime conveniently forget about the lingering tech debt. After all, it usually represents something akin to unpleasant chores for them. Unfortunately, the tech debt can cause serious complications later in the iteration or project if left unaddressed, especially if it involves quality defects, because other developers' modules might start to fail due to this unfinished work.

The burndown chart can be adapted to provide a strong incentive to get the tech debt paid off quickly. As illustrated by Figure 3.6, the scrum master can draw each day's remaining labor hour with the tech debt portrayed on the top of the standard burndown bar in a distinctly different color. With this small change, the burndown chart clearly reveals whether the team is doing its chores before starting in on the fun stuff. If the burndown chart shows tech debt lingering much past the first third of the sprint, the scrum master would be wise to call for a special team meeting after the next stand-up to discuss the problem in detail.

Managing miditeration scope creep

Although the iterative nature of agile keeps the team responsive to changing requirements, the five-step structure to each sprint actually puts some limits on this flexibility. In theory, developers welcome changing requirements as long as the product owner introduces them during the top of cycle, when they can be managed using the standard process, beginning with the story conferences. Should the product owner start pushing new requirements on the developers during miditeration, it would undermine the plan they had drawn up for the sprint, which they are following so diligently, as reflected on their task board. Unfortunately, sometimes the product owner will not be able to wait for the next top of cycle to drop a big new requirement on his team. Typically, this situation happens when an executive suddenly thinks of an essential service the company must get from its business intelligence (BI) system. The executive-level request makes the story more important than any other item on the iteration backlog. If the project is in its final sprint before a release, the new story will have to be addressed during the current sprint so that the executive will see his request fulfilled in production right away. The new story becomes scope creep for the current iteration.

If the developers have one or more stories in their iteration backlog that they have not yet started, and the story points on these items approximately match the estimated points for the scope creep, then the easiest solution will be to have the product owner swap out those stories to make room for the scope creep. Unfortunately, because data integration projects tend to have only a few stories on the backlog for each sprint, often there are too few unstarted stories to swap with. In this situation, the team needs a way to take on the scope creep but avoid looking bad when they cannot deliver all of the other stories they had committed to.

Luckily, agile burndown charts have an answer to this tricky situation. The new demand should be converted into a story, like all other product owner requests. Task cards should be defined and, together with the new story card, should be added at the top of the task board, assuming that this emergency request is considered "priority number one." The developers should then proceed to work the task board as normal, pursuing the highest priority task cards first. To prevent anyone from overlooking the serious impact that the urgent midsprint scope creep will have on the iteration, the burndown chart should be adapted as shown in Figure 3.6. Here, in addition to the tech debt, the scope creep is depicted on top of the remaining labor bars using a third color.

As shown in Figure 3.6, the scope creep appears midsprint and was dutifully burned down along with the tech debt during the remaining workdays. However, progress clearly stalled on the regularly scheduled work that is drawn as the base of each burndown bar. Come demo day, this adapted burndown chart will reveal to

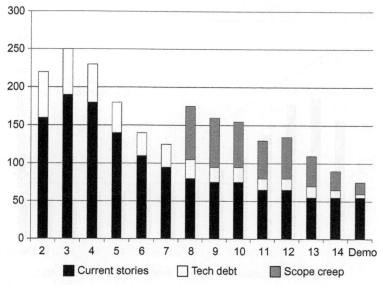

FIGURE 3.6

Burndown chart showing tech debt and scope creep.

everyone that the team worked its highest priorities as expected and that the new requirement pushed on them in midcycle was the reason some of the other stories were not completed. This adapted burndown chart enables the team to be superresponsive to its business stakeholders and still well defended with evidence should its business partners forget why the regularly scheduled stories were not delivered.

In many organizations, urgent events disrupting an agile team's sprints are not so much scope creep but outages in the online applications that demand the developers divert their energies to production support. This same technique can be leveraged to make clear the impact of production support on a team's performance just as well as it can show the affect of midcycle scope creep.

This approach to depicting scope creep or production support work does make it a bit more difficult to determine the team's labor-hour velocity from the burndown chart. To calculate velocity at the end of the iteration graphically, the scrum master must place the segment of scope creep first appearing on the burndown chart on top of the first burndown bar, as shown in Figure 3.7, so that the starting point of the calculation incorporates the labor estimates for all the original stories and tech debt, as well as the additional hours injected onto the backlog during midsprint.

Diagnosing problems with burndown chart patterns

Although Scrum is in structure a simple process, it can be a difficult process for many teams to master. With developers working at their highest sustainable pace,

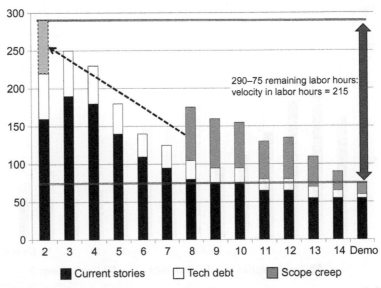

FIGURE 3.7

Calculating labor-hour velocity for sprints with scope creep.

the team's effectiveness is highly vulnerable to misconceptions and counterproductive attitudes among any of its members. Luckily, such issues affect the burndown chart in such a way that a savvy scrum master who is watching for such patterns can detect quickly. Early detection of such troubles is important because it enables the team to take effective corrective action. This section introduces some patterns to look for, both good and bad: early hills, shallow glides, and persistent inflation.

An early hill to climb

In many of the sample burndown charts referenced previously, one should note that the bar for the first day or two went up, not down as the team would have wanted. This is the "early hill to climb" pattern. It is very common; although it should catch the attention of all teammates, it is not a cause for panic. An early hill typically occurs when the team discovers some additional tasks that they did not anticipate during the task planning session on the first day of the sprint. When additional tasks are discovered during an iteration, the developers should create task cards for them, estimate the hours they will require, and add these cards to the task board. If these are sizable tasks, additional hours on the new task cards will make the next day's burndown bar move up.

When an early hill does appear, the scrum master should allow it to worry his teammates. If uncorrected, the growing total for the iteration's remaining work would definitely become a problem. When an iteration's first couple of burndown

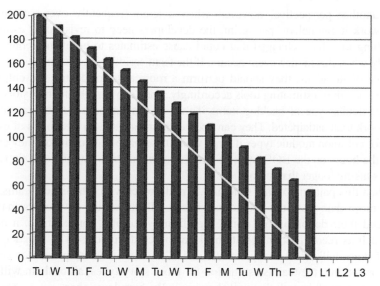

FIGURE 3.8

Common burndown patterns: The shallow glide.

bars immediately begin to hover above the perfect line, the team should become concerned enough to get their work for the iteration fully defined and under control so that they can reverse this trend. Not surprisingly, early hills are much more prominent during the first few sprints on a new project, when unknowns concerning function and design are the most numerous. As the project progresses, the team's vision and their application designs should get steadily sharper, leading these early hills to become progressively shorter, if not disappearing altogether.

Shallow glide paths

The "shallow glide" pattern describes burndown charts in which the remaining labor estimates remain steadily above the perfect line, as shown in Figure 3.8. Here the team is steadily burning off the committed work of the sprint, but not at the rate needed to finish all the tasks by demo day. This is not a particularly pernicious pattern if it happens in isolation. For a new team, it usually reflects that the developers have not realized how hard delivering applications using an iterative and incremental delivery can be. They have overestimated their ability to deliver truly shippable modules.

In one sense, the team need not address this situation because it will rectify itself. When the scrum master employs his regular end-of-sprint calculation of velocity, he will provide the team with the hours for the tasks completed. If the team uses this velocity as the basis for their capacity during the next sprint planning session, they will naturally adjust their commitments lower until they start delivering as planned.

From another perspective, however, when a team frequently overestimates how much work it can deliver per sprint, the developers need to revisit their estimating. Something may have changed that could cause estimates to be off not consistently, but only when this hidden event occurs. If the team seriously overestimates more than a couple of iterations, they should perform a root cause to identify the culprit and then sharpen their estimating tools accordingly. They can recalibrate their story points for a particular type of backlog items if this set has turned out to be categorically more work than anticipated. They can update the steps listed on their basis of estimate cards for common module types if large work items have been omitted. They can also revise the hours on the BOE cards so that they remember to estimate certain types of tasks as taking longer than before.

When this pattern appears suddenly in midproject with established teams, it can signal more than just poor estimating. It can reflect that the developers may have advanced their definition of "done" significantly, adding, for example, a difficult step, such as reconciliation results back to source documents. The tougher definition of done will affect many stories, and if the new work step has not yet been incorporated into the team's estimation for those story types, all of them will be set upon a shallow glide path that will show up in the burndown chart.

Alternatively, the work might now involve an additional tool that the developers are not as proficient in, such as a data quality utility. Another possibility is that they have worked through many easy stories and are now taking on a harder class of modules. Data integration projects that pull data from well-designed sources sometimes find the modules for staging data much easier to build than those that integrate the information later. Consequently, these teams can experience shallow glides on their burndown charts when they begin struggling with the integration layer of their application. Another common cause of this underdelivery pattern to suddenly appear is "organizational friction," where the team members encounter push-back from some of the other IT teams with whom they must coordinate, such as database administrators or quality assurance. The root cause could also be a change in team bandwidth, most commonly due to resource contention. For example, one or more of the team members may have been pulled aside to perform maintenance programming on another system, unbeknownst to their teammates. All these possibilities will suddenly slow the delivery rate of the team. When the burndown bars stop tracking the perfect line closely, the scrum master should explore, with the developers, possible explanations such as the ones just listed.

Persistent inflation

When burndown charts display "persistent inflation," its remaining labor bars drift steadily higher above the perfect line, as shown in Figure 3.9. Here bars keep rising well beyond the point where they should have turned downward if the iteration was experiencing only an early hill to climb. Persistent inflation signals that instead of reducing their remaining labor estimates on the task cards as they work them, the developers are finding steadily more work to do with each hour of work they put in.

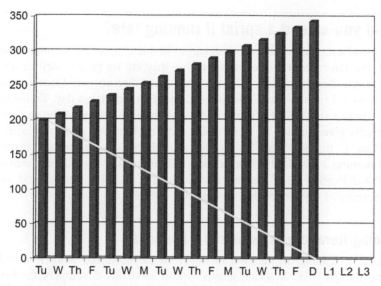

FIGURE 3.9

Worrisome burndown chart pattern: Persistent inflation.

For new teams, this pattern is usually an indication that the work is not arriving to the developers with enough definition. True, agile is based on defining user stories and the implicit technical tasks as needed during each iteration planning day, but one can go too far with this "just-in-time" notion. Most agile teams ask their product owners and scrum masters to groom the project backlog a few days before the start of each sprint. Grooming entails wording the *who*, *what*, and *why* of each user story accurately so that there are no contradictions or confusing overlaps with other story cards. Poorly thought-out stories lead to inaccurate requirements that later change during development. Such requirements can force the remaining labor estimates upward to reflect all the rework it causes. On data warehousing projects, persistent inflation can also indicate that the detailed guidance roles upstream from the developer are not being completed sufficiently. The systems analyst and data architect may be cutting corners on their source-to-target mappings or the attribute definitions of the target schema. The developers find the programming very slow in the face of these insufficient artifacts, and their estimates for finishing the module begin to rise.

Solving this problem may require the scrum master to cancel the current iteration when it is clear that the work has spun completely out of control. The team may well need an extra long sprint retrospective to clearly iron out the roles and responsibilities for the teammates producing the inputs the developers rely upon. Many teams wrestling with this situation decide to draft a definition of done for each of the artifacts from the upstream roles similar to the definitions the programmers employ to ensure that their own work is complete.

Should you extend a sprint if running late?

While introducing the burndown chart earlier in this chapter, we demonstrated how a trend line can reveal to developers whether they are on pace to deliver all of the stories on the iteration backlog by the time demo day arrives. Teams running on schedule would see this trend line intersect the X axis at demo day. Teams running behind would see it intersect to the right of demo day. Many of the sample burndown charts given earlier, in fact, have 3 days on that axis occurring after demo day—"Late 1" through "Late 3"—which naturally begs an important question. If a team is running a few days behind, should a scrum master extend the sprint so they can finish delivering all of the iteration backlog? If so, what limit should we draw on the number of days for such an extension?

Extending iterations is generally a bad idea

In general, extending an iteration to finish up the promised work is a bad idea, tempting though it is. A scrum master would serve his developers far better by guiding them to accept that they failed the current iteration to a small degree. They should simply finish off the sprint and demonstrate to the product owner whatever components they were able to complete. There are two compelling reasons to keeping sprints durations constant: it supports better estimating and avoids undermining team velocity.

Considering estimating first, if the scrum master extends the sprint by, say, 3 days, what would he measure as the team's velocity? The team needs this figure in order to properly set their capacity for planning the next sprint. One idea would be to take the delivered story points and labor hour comprising the stories accepted during the iteration and adjusting them linearly by the number of extra days added. It is not clear how accurate that adjustment would be. During the early days of a sprint, the team struggles with the greatest uncertainty, and their coding rate is the lowest. At the end of a sprint, the developers are coding intensively, given that most of the crucial questions have been answered. With this a natural acceleration in actual coding speed, 3 days at the end of an iteration may be the time band in which over half the demonstrable results of an iteration emerge. In truth, there is no way to accurately "back out" the contribution of the coding accomplished during the few days a scrum master tacks on when extending a sprint. The team's true velocity will remain hidden, and their ability to estimate accurately what they should commit to during the next sprint will be seriously compromised. Without accurate estimating, the team cannot keep from committing to too much work again, requiring another extension. When extensions become the rule, the team has essentially adopted a longer time box. They would be better off just planning on one sprint length and figuring out how much to promise to deliver within that constraint.

Considering team velocity second, if the scrum master frequently changes the length of the team's sprints as needed, she will undermine the team's velocity. Keep in mind that Scrum, as taught in the classroom, is not a method but instead a collaboration framework. The true method that every agile team ends up using develops incrementally from the conversations its developers have during the sprint retrospectives. Although it requires a few iterations to get right, the members of a new team eventually negotiate with each other a complex series of deadlines and handoffs that allow the work to get done completely by the end of the given time box. The complex work pattern they arrive at will be memorized through practice by the developers rather than written down, and it will be based on the precise size of the team's time box. When the scrum master changes the length of the sprint, many of the sequences and timings the developers have internalized will no longer be accurate. They will adapt their cadences to the longer time box only to find themselves out of sync on the next iteration when the time box shrinks back to normal. The resulting confusion and mistakes will consume developer time to resolve, forcing the team's velocity down. Moreover, changing velocities causes uncertainty in the estimation process, which sets off all the disadvantages just mentioned.

In summary, if the scrum master is constantly changing the size of the iteration's time box, developers will never truly know what they can accomplish in a fixed number of days and will not be able to optimize their team work patterns. They will never achieve the long-term advantages of the agile approach, which include product owner trust, stable funding, and minimal interference from program managers. For these reasons, scrum masters need to be implacable and keep the iteration lengths uniform, even when a few days might make the team look good in the short term.

Two instances where a changing time box might help

At least, such consistency is generally preferable. There are two exceptions that may well cause a good scrum master to adjust the time box a little: release boundaries and looming holidays. The former situation occurs when the team is working within the last iteration before the product will be pushed into the release-to-production process. Extending the sprint by a few days in order to get a couple of key features into the next version may well be worth risking all the confusion a changing time box can cause.

In a similar light, the current iteration might be scheduled to conclude only a few days before a major holiday. The scrum master may well realize that starting up a new iteration and working only a couple of days before the team disbands for an extended period will only serve to waste the time spent on sprint planning. In this case, extending the iteration a few days may allow the team to get a little more accomplished before the break. They can make a solid start on the next iteration when everyone returns from holiday instead of trying to remember how to resume a partially completed sprint.

This latter situation is nowhere as demanding as the production release case just considered. If the right open items exist for the project, it might actually be a far better idea to let the iteration run its normal length and use the last few days before the break as a spike dedicated to knocking off some unfinished documentation or clearing out the tech debt list.

In any case, scrum masters will have to choose carefully whenever tempted to extend a sprint; all told, changing the team's time box should be an exceedingly rare event.

Should teams track actual hours during a sprint?

Some scrum masters, especially those with traditional project management training, are strongly attracted to the idea of tracking actual hours spent on tasks. They claim this information will allow the team to estimate labor hours more accurately during task planning sessions. They also desire to compare actual hours against estimates so that they can assist their developers in becoming better at forecasting the labor required for an entire project. Unfortunately, tracking actual hours spent on the individual tasks is ineffective, aims at the wrong objectives, and drowns the developers in detail while undermining agile's pillar of self-organization that is so crucial to a team's velocity. Tracking actuals should be strongly discouraged.

Several considerations undermine the notion that teams will be able to provide better estimates if they had a collections of actual labor hours for past tasks to reflect upon. Scrum masters who begin to fall prey to this hope should be gently reminded of the findings concerning time overruns documented by the Standish Group's *Chaos Reports*, where 84% of the development projects that were either challenged or canceled had an average time overrun of 222%. [Standish Group 1995] If documenting actual labor invested could lead to accurate estimating, the waterfall projects included in the *Chaos Reports* would have demonstrated a far better track record.

Collecting actual labor spent on tasks appears nowhere within the definition of Scrum, and the method performs well for hundreds of teams that do not sink time into this practice. Moreover, statistical inference requires many dozens of data points before one reaches a dependable predictive power. [Cohen 1988] Projects, such as data integration efforts, that deliver only a handful of stories every iteration will not provide enough data points to derive statistically significant averages for task durations, especially when the modest number of collected numbers is divided across dozens of task types.

More importantly, estimating statistics cannot be used without destroying their accuracy. The parameters generated by averaging past events cannot be followed blindly because context is always changing. A developer will have to judge whether a given parameter can be applied to the new task he is estimating, and his mind will be working at the fuzzy aggregate level that we human are inherently limited to. When we mix an incredibly precise number with a rough guess, the result is only another rough guess. All the data gathering and calculation that went into generating that precise estimating parameter are wasted, so we should be very judicious about how much effort we invest in deriving that precise number to begin with.

Beyond the fact that finding a silver bullet for estimating parameters is improbable, we must understand that estimating labor hours with extreme accuracy is the wrong objective. Labor-hour estimates only address estimating tasks. We only define tasks for the iteration immediately ahead of us. We limit our task-level thinking to this near-planning horizon because it is very demanding. On average, software developers only have the mental energy to carefully perform task-level decomposition for a single iteration's worth of work. Beyond that they unconsciously resort back to wild guesses about the actions that will be needed and the time labor will require. This dynamic is exactly why the agile community invented story point estimating—a forecasting technique that operates at a high enough level that our developers can persist with it long enough to forecast effort for an entire release or project. If we were to somehow derive a set of absolutely perfect, labor-hour estimating parameters for tasks, developers would still be able to apply them to only to a handful of stories—a few weeks of work at best. It would hardly be worth the effort required to derive those numbers in the first place.

If the impossibility of deriving and utilizing precise estimating parameters for development tasks were not enough to dissuade us from tracking actuals, we should also consider the destructive impact it will have on the motivations and culture within our agile teams. Agile's entire focus is to deliver production-quality software that provides business benefits within a time frame project sponsors can value. Directing our developers to gather actual hours spent on tasks will swamp them with endless bookkeeping activity. It will divert their efforts away from what truly matters, building working code with such high quality that it can be demonstrated in a few short weeks and then put it into production.

Moreover, as most seasoned scrum masters will attest to, just getting developers to update their remaining labor hours each day on the one or two task cards they have been working is hard enough. Gathering actual hours spent on tasks would require another order of magnitude of cajoling and admonishment to achieve. A more successful approach is to let the developers decide for themselves how long and how carefully they wish to track their actuals. If ignoring actuals causes their estimates to diverge greatly from reality, they will suffer the consequence of their own bad forecasts. They will then have all the motivation they need to get better at estimating by whatever means works for them. The proper recourse may depend on gathering actuals or may hinge on another technique altogether. Developers who devise and pursue their own solution to labor forecasting will become far better at estimating than the scrum master could ever force them to be.

In summary, gathering actuals focuses on numbers that are difficult to gather, impossible to use as intended, and requires busy work that lowers the velocity of an agile team. Scrum masters will do better to stick with agile's simple and effective reliance on story points to perform project planning. This topic is discussed in far more detail in later chapters, where we discuss story point techniques for regularly deriving current estimates for project stakeholders.

Eliminating hour estimation altogether

Indeed, many agile project teams eliminate hour estimating for tasks altogether, seeing the effort as a waste of planning time. They rely instead solely on story point estimates of the user stories to identify a doable amount of work for each iteration. The tasks are still identified during the planning day, but they are defined to be such small amounts of work that there is no point in forecasting them. Ken Collier, the author of *Agile Analytics* [Collier 2011], summed up the attitude embodied by this approach: "All the tasks in a sprint have to be completed, so why spend any effort predicting how much the time they will take? Just get them done instead."

Teams that skip task-level labor estimation also keep their iterations very short so that the total number of tasks do not get out of hand. Consequently, these teams frequently need only a couple of hours to get a sprint planned rather than the full day suggested by the generic agile approach. The hours saved, multiplied by the number of developers on the team, often amount to one or two extra programmer days that go into building more shippable code, completely in line with agile's strategy of maximizing the work not done. That said, other teams are working with stories that will not fit comfortably into short iterations. With bigger stories and tasks to manage, these teams do quite well with the double estimation approach where they use hour forecasts for tasks to confirm their story point estimates, thus ensuring they have not taken on too much work for a given sprint. The right approach for a given team seems to pivot on the type of work a project entails. Projects with mostly dashboarding work typically work well with short iterations and might do well skipping task card estimation. Teams with serious data integration work tend to prefer longer iterations and larger stories, so for them task card estimates are still worth the effort.

Managing geographically distributed teams

Agile methods prefer colocated teammates, as evidenced by 1 of the 12 principles published with the Agile Manifesto: "The most efficient and effective method of conveying information to and within a development team is face-to-face conversation." However, we live in an age of telecommunications and outsourcing. Remote teammates and "virtual" teams that are entirely distributed across the globe are often a reality project planners cannot escape. Luckily, remote teammates do not rule out an agile development method. They require extra effort, as they do in a waterfall programs, but over the years agile practitioners have found ways to make "far location" work successfully. These adaptive strategies and techniques can be combined into a suggested solution path for adapting agile to remote teammates:

1. Consider whether fully capable subteams are possible.
2. Visualize the problem in terms of communication.
3. Choose geographical divisions to minimize communication challenges.
4. Invest in a single colocated sprint to establish the team's *esprit de corps*.
5. Provide repeated booster shots of colocation for individuals.
6. Invest in high-quality telepresence equipment.
7. Provide agile groupware.

These steps are presented in more detail in a moment, but an honest discussion about distributing a team's developers should start by stating the obvious: even with all possible mitigating measures in place, remote teammates will probably reduce a team's velocity and overall chances of success by a noticeable amount. The same is undoubtedly true for nonagile projects, but at least the agile community has some statistics regarding the impact of separating a team's developers. The baseline is for colocated teams, and they achieve an 80% success rate according to a well-respected survey. [Ambler 2008] In comparison, when we allow some "near location" (where teammates can move easily to a shared workspace as needed), the success rate dips six percentage points, as shown in Figure 3.10. In contrast, when one or more teammates cannot join the group in person without travel, the success rate drops to 60%.

To phrase these findings most starkly, when teams dispersed their resources geographically, they effectively doubled their risk of failure, from 20 to 40%. This figure deserves some interpretation, however. First, the 60% success rate still exceeds that measured for waterfall methods operating under their best of circumstances [Standish 1995, 1999], so there is no reason that this increased risk should automatically force teams back into plan-driven methods. Despite the hit to success rates, we would not want to give up the speed to market, higher quality, and improved customer satisfaction that incremental delivery methods provide. Second, experienced scrum masters regularly find ways to make agile work with far location by understanding that it takes extra coordination efforts and requires the adaptations such as described here.

Properly managing remote developers benefits from realizing why colocation helps in the first place. Agile derives much of its advantages over waterfall methods by relying on fluid, informal communication instead of time-consuming formal documentation. Impromptu communication for geographically remote teammates

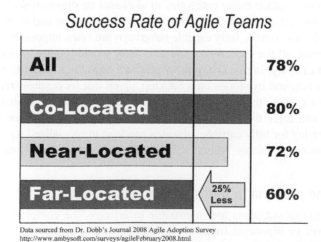

Success Rate of Agile Teams

All	**78%**
Co-Located	**80%**
Near-Located	**72%**
Far-Located (25% Less)	**60%**

Data sourced from Dr. Dobb's Journal 2008 Agile Adoption Survey
http://www.ambysoft.com/surveys/agileFebruary2008.html

FIGURE 3.10

Impact of distributing teammates is measurable.

typically pivots upon speaker phones and Internet-based collaborative software. Even when a company invests in the very best of these tools, they prove to be poor substitutes to actually having a co-worker in the same room. Effective communication is comprised not just of the words employed, but also the tone of voice, eye contact and facial expressions, and body language. Speaker phones filter out all of these components, turning a teammate's voice into a tonally flat dribble, often with enough noise in the background that many of his words are impossible to discern.

Likewise, remote collaborative applications are still very awkward when it comes to sharing a quick sketch—nowhere near the efficacy of two people using a whiteboard. Email exchanges on difficult design points often involve so much back and forth that the parties involved must eventually resort to a phone call to clear up the issues. So, of course, substituting these clunky tools for in-person collaboration is going to hurt communication and productivity, no matter what methodology the team employs. For these reasons, organizations should be realistic and colocate team members whenever possible. When far location is unavoidable, then project planners should follow the steps offered in this section. Readers looking for even further thoughts on working with remote teammates should refer to material found in *A Practical Guide to Distributed Teams*, published by IBM Press. [Woodward, Surdek, & Ganis 2010]

Consider whether fully capable subteams are possible

The best recourse to distributed developers is to colocate subsets of developers into smaller groups that are fully capable for some particular category of work. The project planners can then send each subgroup the user stories they are best equipped to work on. This solution can be hard to achieve and maintain, however, when a project has internationally distributed worksites. For the past decade or so, geographical boundaries often place entire categories of skill sets on opposite shores. It is not uncommon to find all of a project's business analysts in Europe and all its programmers in India. In this context, fully capable subgroups are often impossible to arrange. Moreover, keeping all the specialized subteams busy would require a steady flow of stories in each category. In practice, project planners have little ability to balance the technical skills required by stories on a backlog, given that its business requirements determine what appears there. As a consequence, the demand for subteams can be spotty, which will force most of them to find other projects to work on simultaneously. Thus striving for fully capable subteams can lead to specialized squads that are multitasking between projects. Workable, but hardly the solution one would hope for.

Visualize the problem in terms of communication

When fully capable subteams are impossible to arrange, the complementary roles of the team will be separated from one another. A major approach to minimizing the impact of this separation requires one to understand which roles need to communicate the most so that at least they can be colocated. Figure 3.11 portrays the communication needs of members of a typical BI team. The thickness of the lines

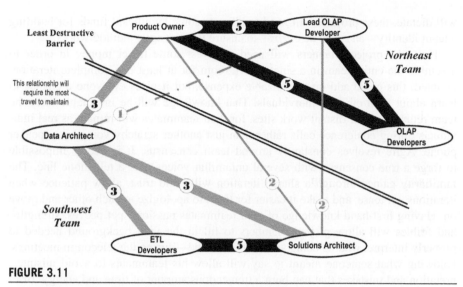

FIGURE 3.11

Geographical distribution's impact on team communications.

connecting each pair of individuals depicts the extent of communication this team expects to occur between those two parties. With such a drawing, one can better plan which teammates most need to discuss matters spontaneously.

Choose geographical divisions to minimize the challenge

Figure 3.11, which visualizes a team's interactions, also shows a dividing line that represents a geographical separation between two subteams. In this case, it is a single line, so the diagram obviously pertains to a project where the developers are split between two office sites. When planning for three and four sites, the diagram naturally becomes that much more complex to draw. Drawing each candidate separation line on one of these communication diagrams reveals which parties will need to travel frequently in order to maintain team cohesion. It may also demonstrate where a formal specification document needs to be reintroduced into the method, despite the impact it will have on some individual's work pace. Modeling separations on the communication diagrams can give team members the advanced warning that they will need to adapt their work habits properly, especially important if their main communication partners are in very different time zones. The divisions on such a diagram can also bolster the business case for implementing the conferencing systems and groupware applications the team is going to need once its members are separated.

Invest in a solid *esprit de corp*

Even with the best of planning, many agile projects will still find themselves having to proceed with a single team spread across many remote sites. As common sense will dictate, these projects will need to allocate some significant funds for building a team identity—an *esprit de corps*—to ensure that the agile method works.

First, the project planners will need to invest some travel money in order to assemble the entire team in a single work room for at least one complete iteration. Granted, this could add up to a sizable expense, but it gives everyone a chance to learn about each other as individuals. That knowledge will be invaluable once the team returns to their distant work sites, for their teammates will remain as real individuals during conference calls rather than just another scratchy voice on a speaker phone. Agile revolves constantly around team consensus. It is nearly impossible to forge a true consensus with several unfamiliar voices over a telephone line. The familiarity gained through a shared iteration will build trust, allow patience when iterations get tense, and make it easier for them to apologize to each other and move on. Having first-hand knowledge of their teammates passions, pet peeves, strengths, and foibles will allow project members to fill in the vital background needed to properly interpret what is being said—and not said—during the telecomm meetings. Knowing what someone meant to say will allow his teammates to avoid misinterpretation and mistakes that can burn a tremendous amount of time and energy. Brief colocation also leads to more effective training sessions and allows far more questions to be asked during the first iteration than would occur over the phone. In all these ways, the familiarity of just one iteration in a single shared space will improve a team's long-term velocity significantly. Given the typical length of many data warehousing projects, in particular, the benefits of increased velocity will often far outweigh the expense of a kick-off colocation sprint.

Provide repeated booster shots of colocation for individuals

The end result of a kick-off colocation sprint iteration will be a more cohesive team sharing the same approach to iterative development, able to communicate quickly and accurately. Unfortunately, this valuable team identity will evaporate once folks return to their remote sites and the iterations wear on. For that reason, team leads should plan on a regular "booster shot" of colocation every few sprints. These repeat visits can be distributed, however, spreading out the cost by bringing back only one or two teammates at a time.

Invest in high-quality telepresence equipment

Perhaps the single greatest challenge to working with geographically remote teammates is not being able to see and hear them adequately. The ubiquitous conference phone in most work places simply does not provide a sufficiently faithful reproduction of a normal conversation to base an entire collaborative project on. Considering the high cost of labor and the disasters that can befall a project budget when a team makes a serious mistake, the expense of high-quality telepresence equipment will seem like a good investment. Of course, because it requires time and money to select and install the right equipment, switching to good communication products takes effort and foresight to make it available in time to help the team.

A particularly important part of planning a remote presence system is knowing what features to look for to support an agile team. At the top of the list is cameras. Images of one's teammates are not a luxury. Voices can be ignored easily, whereas images turn the interaction into a conversation. The images of 6 to 10 teammates have to be managed, however, so an important feature of the telecomm package will be a "Hollywood Squares"-matrixed display of all members' video feeds, as depicted in the upper left of Figure 3.12.

To properly enable effective stand-up meetings, for example, the software must give the scrum master an additional measure of control. As each person takes a turn checking in, the scrum master must be able to mute all other mikes and cause the speaker's image to expand on everyone else's console, as demonstrated in Figure 3.12. Naturally, this causes the remote teammates to focus on the speaker just long enough to truly hear the answers to the three check-in questions employed by the agile stand-up meetings. Because missing a check-in detail can waste an entire programmer day, the scrum master's console needs to remain in the matrixed display so that he can scan the team continuously to spot developers who have stopped listening to their teammates, such as the individual shown reading the newspaper in Figure 3.12.

A further crucial feature for the telepresence solution will be that it is always on. This will require a solid and secure Internet connection, plus software and server units to manage the continuous sessions, but the extra investment will yield

FIGURE 3.12

Good remote-presence tools help distributed teams.

a system that can be fully utilized by the team. Ordinary conferencing equipment, which can take 20 minutes to establish a connection between parties who need to meet for only 15 minutes, is simply not a solution to the team's collaboration needs.

Provide agile team groupware

The final component required to enable geographically distributed agile teams will be the right set of Web-based tools the team will need to work cohesively. Project planners should consider whether the current versions of their software engineering tools will support a distributed team. If a team of warehousing developers is widely distributed, there can be little verbal coordination among them as they make changes to the project's requirements, designs, data structures, and testing documents, as well as ETL code. The software engineering tools they work with will need to be repository rather than file based, so developers can work simultaneously on small pieces of the project without blocking each other with file locks. These tools will also have to support checking objects out and in to avoid inadvertent object overwrites between teammates. They will also have to provide version control and rollback so when the team fails to coordinate effectively, the last working version of an artifact can be restored.

Beyond the engineering tools, a distributed team will need an agile project-tracking package that can make an electronic version of the task board and burndown chart available to everyone on demand. Picking such a package can be a little tricky. Given that there are a dozen different agile approaches available, and that even Scrum has many flavors, the project planners may not find a package that supports the exact flavor of agile they wish to follow. Every package seems to have some crazy limitation, such as constraining story points to 1 through 3 or not having any support for tech debt and scope creep on the burndown chart.

Luckily there is a wide variety of packages on the market today. Several of them support plug-ins, which address the limitations of the base package greatly. A good number of them are also offered in a "software as a service" format, making implementation very fast. With this much to choose from, most Scrum teams seem to be able to find a solution that will support their distributed teammates.

Summary

Scrum provides a streamlined approach to managing a project within the team room. It relies on two simple, yet powerful, tools for keeping an agile team on track during each iteration: the task board and the burndown chart. The task board provides a series of key status columns that the iteration's task cards should progress steadily across as developers work them toward completion. The task board allows developers to find the next set of work on their own and makes project status very easy for all stakeholders to visually surmise for themselves. The burndown chart depicts an iteration's remaining labor hours by day, showing the team whether they are likely to have completed all the tasks in time for the user demo. The burndown chart also allows teams to measure graphically their velocity at the end of each iteration and makes adverse events that threaten that velocity in midsprint very easy to detect. Given the streamlined style of project room management Scrum establishes, there are some best practices identifiable for questions such as whether teams should lengthen an iteration if they are running slow and whether they should track actual labor on tasks in order to improve their ability to estimate. Finally, remote teammates run counter to agile's preference for colocated developers, but there are several techniques for adapting the method to distributed team structures, including an investment in remote presence systems and electronic agile project support applications.

Defining Data Warehousing Projects for Iterative Development

Authoring Better User Stories

4

How do agile's user stories streamline project requirements gathering?
What are the qualities of a good user story?
What techniques can be employed when our team is struggling to write
effective user stories?

The agile collaboration model presented in the last three chapters urges software development teams to forego massive to-be system specifications. It directs them instead to guide their projects' design and development with a collection of simple artifacts called user stories. Like many components of Scrum, the idea of user stories is simple, but not always easy to apply. Understanding their fundamentals and a collection of techniques for honing their accuracy will help teams prepare more effective project backlogs with less effort.

The basic of authoring a user story focuses on the small, that is, crafting single-sentence statements scoped down to a small functional increment that can be delivered within one development iteration. When a story seems too big, agile provides a short hierarchy developers can employ to decompose the notion into appropriately sized statements. A six-component test reveals whether the result is sound enough for the team to start coding.

Unfortunately, the basic approach often teams stymied with too much detail and not enough context to know whether the project's backlog was complete. Over agile's first two decades, practitioners have steadily created and borrowed techniques leading to a more structured, top-down approach that increases team effectiveness greatly when writing user stories. These techniques ensure that a team both realizes the full range of users they must communicate with and understands each category of users in far greater detail. Accordingly, a full presentation of managing requirements in agile project must include a listing of these important extensions.

The result will be a menu of techniques to draw upon for either starting a new project or improving a portion of a backlog that needs polishing. This set of practices, borrowed from the world of agile transaction system development, works well for data warehousing projects that consist predominantly of front-end dashboarding work. Projects involving substantial data integration needs will need to

Agile Data Warehousing Project Management.
DOI: http://dx.doi.org/10.1016/B978-0-12-396463-2.00004-1
© 2013 Elsevier Inc. All rights reserved.

break user stories and decompose user stories down one further step, a process presented in the second part of this book.

Traditional requirements gathering and its discontents

Waterfall projects typically begin with a "requirements bash," where information technology (IT) marshals business users into a conference room for days or weeks at a time, asking them to articulate every function they might possibly want to perform with the requested application. The formal requirements specifications that result from these protract requirement-gathering sessions are complex documents, so involved that organizations frequently employ specialized commercial software applications to manage them. The assumption behind waterfall's requirements bash is that somehow the customer's subject matter experts (SMEs) can accurately specify hundreds of detailed business needs in a single set of interviews. Traditional projects often wisely involve well-trained "user analysts" or "systems engineers" to conduct these interviews, for there are many subtleties inherent in the process, any one of which can undermine the success of the project if overlooked. For example,

- Requirements are fractal and complex, each one capable of having an extensive tree of subrequirements beneath it that must be followed as far as they lead
- Stakeholders often do not know what they want out of an application until they see some working software attempting to fill that need
- Each SME has limited knowledge and tends to describe only the requirements of their part of the enterprise
- No single SME may fully understand both sides of an important interface between two particular departments
- Stakeholders typically speak of their requirements as of the day of the interview and may be entirely unaware of changes that will emerge over the 12 to 24 months it will take to implement the application envisioned
- Users express requirements imprecisely in terminology only the business community understands, which means very little to the technical team who must bring them to life through coded programs
- Even a slight change in wording or interpretation could lead developers into wasting thousands of hours of programming that will have to be thrown away when the misunderstanding is finally detected

This last dynamic is particularly pernicious. Consider the impact that the following change in a stakeholder's wording has on the programming required for a single bar chart on a dashboard of financial data:

1. The graph should show gross margin by product over time.
2. The graph should show gross margin by product *and customer* over time.
3. The graph should show *net margin* by product and customer over time.

These statements are based on well-defined business terms, which often don't exist within the business. They also are based on the business professional thinking through what he needs. The business partner providing these requirements could have easily stated the goal as expressed in the first sentence, then switched to the second 6 weeks later, and the third 8 weeks after that. Each step seems like a basic elaboration to a business person, so simple that IT should have anticipated it. Yet, from the developer's point of view, the appearance of the single word "customer" in the second sentence typically sets off an endless debate between their subject matter experts over the exact definition of a customer. It can also plunge IT into a protracted master data management subproject that frequently takes far longer to implement than the graph it needed to support. Not really. In the third sentence, the change from gross to net margin injects the entire notion of cost allocation of fixed assets and capital projects into the required data transformation, again vastly expanding the amount of coding that IT must complete before it can paint the desired bars on the user's final dashboard.

Agile answers this with fast incremental deliveries. Code base on statement 1, catch it during Q&A or at least the user demo. Solving it will take rewording the request, that is, updating a user story. The better you make your user stories to start with, the fewer rework cycles you'll have to go through. Write good user stories when gathering statements at the user demo and the more effective each of those rework cycles will be.

The disastrous impact set off by small changes in requirements was documented long ago. Many traditional computer systems training courses warn software engineers that there is a 100-to-1 ratio between fixing a mistake after it is coded compared to catching it during requirement gathering. [Haskins 2004] Because business can change its mind so easily and because simple variations in wording can have such horrific budgetary consequences, IT decided long ago that it should gather *all* the requirements from users and "nail down" their wording before starting on a single line of code. This notion was in fact a major motivation behind the design of waterfall methods.

As the waterfall era unfolded, software engineers began constructing careful hierarchies of requirements through which one could drill down through increasingly detailed A-, B-, and C-level requirements. Requirements in these trees were also carefully organized horizontally between a dozen or more categories, such as "user interfaces," "data formats," and "processing business rules." With all this structure and thousand of entries, these traditional requirement specifications became voluminous documents that were difficult to understand and manage for any sizable application. So difficult in fact that analysts frequently had to cross-index its contents into a requirements traceability matrix (RTM) to ensure that nothing was overlooked during the many months it takes to build the system so described. As implementation draws near, a team of users and technical reviewers must wade through the RTM, validating line by line that all requirements have been met. Unfortunately, given the months that have passed since the interviews with the subject matter experts, the people who verbalized and understand the requirements may no longer be with the project or the company.

With all the effort and thoroughness that careful requirement specifications entail, teams should have few complaints regarding the resulting documents. Yet "we should have done better at gathering requirements" is the number one lament made during the lessons-learned sessions at the end of projects. In a study of over 8000 software projects initiated before agile methods became widespread, incomplete or changing requirements and the lack of user input were the greatest causes of project failure, undermining more than one-third of the projects across 365 companies surveyed. [Standish 1995]

Big, careful requirements not a solution

Given this track record, it is clear that the big requirements specification up front never gave software engineers the control over requirements they were striving for. Despite the elaborate hierarchies and traceability matrices, something always seemed to undermine the value of the traditional requirements spec, for all the reasons cited earlier plus a few more:

- User analysts were not actually given enough time to do a thorough gathering because project sponsors demanded to know early on "why isn't somebody coding yet?!" (WISCY)
- User input is spotty at best. Requirements-gathering sessions take a long time and users are under pressure to return to their departments in order to keep up with their own work.
- The single-pass approach causes mistakes in requirements to get "baked into" the resulting designs. Without any feedback on the quality of the requirements, users do not catch the errors in their statements of business need until the code is fully developed.
- Developers were unable to digest the unwieldy document delivered by the user analysts. Under the same WISCY pressure as the requirements team, they proceeded into design with an incomplete understanding of the application needed and did not code what was specified.
- The source systems are changing, shortening the shelf life of requirements even further.
- Moreover, the business itself often changes in fundamental ways after requirements are gathered, often making much of the application based on a single pass at the requirements completely unusable.

It is easy to see that these factors make the "shelf life" of a traditional requirements specifications document too short to be the proper foundation for months or years of expensive software development. Even if IT performs the downstream development work perfectly, the big requirements spec up-front approach will only deliver what the users asked for, not what they and their organizations need.

A step in the right direction

The failings of traditional requirements specification cited earlier spurred a search for a more streamlined manner to capture and manage IT's understanding of end-user needs. An early attempt that is still in widespread use today was "use cases," popularized by advocates of the Rational Unified Process (RUP), one of the first agile methods defined. Use cases demonstrated some advantages, but still did not solve the problems posed by comprehensive requirements documents when they are used as the only requirements artifact for a project.

A use case is a sequence of events that an actor (either a person or an application) performs within a system to achieve a particular goal. [Rosenberg 1999] Over the years, engineers have devised many templates for use cases, and most include sections for identifying the actor, the trigger initiating the interaction, and the flow of events that generates value for the actor. RUP urged developers to gather use cases covering the most important aspects of an envisioned system and then start building the application in iterations, employing the use cases for guidance.

For software professionals desiring the shortest possible time to value for their projects, use cases were a step forward, but incomplete because they often led companies into the same quagmire confounding traditional requirements specifications. Perhaps the developers that first utilized use cases were still too steeped in waterfall's approach to requirements. With time, the use case templates grew heavier, making the cases themselves hard to write and for end users to understand. The flow of events became detailed, requiring additional sections for preconditions, flow of events, and postconditions, as well as variation flows to specify how the system will adapt to varying circumstances. Moreover, system designers wanted to encapsulate reusable components within each other, which turned a set of use cases into a "use case model" with all the complex linkages between cases requiring careful thought. In many organizations, use cases became just another artifact used to construct big designs up front.

Use cases not only became lengthy, but they now had to get reviewed and redrafted until correct, much like a waterfall requirements specification document. The whole process of learning what users want and getting a project started was still taking too long, thus risking all the downsides to the single-pass waterfall approach, namely inconsistent user input, analysts pressed for time, requirements mistakes baked into designs, and complex documents that developers fail to implement accurately. Although a step in the right direction, use cases were still not lightweight enough to help teams avoid overinvesting in careful, deductively derived designs subject to a short shelf life in the face of changing business conditions.

Scrum practitioners today are not opposed to using use cases when a particular flow of events needs to be documented. Their objection is only to employing use cases as the primary requirements vehicle for the project. Use cases, as commonly prepared today, are still artifacts that users have trouble relating to, thus they still keep a team's business partner removed from the development process. Moreover, teams relying only upon use cases are still taking too long to encapsulate an application vision in a usable form. To many agile practitioners, a use case model does not seem aligned with the principle of "working software over comprehensive documentation." Perhaps most importantly, the delay in starting development that compiling a use case model entails means users will still wait a long time before receiving value from the project and developers will wait a long time before their first feedback on requirements and design.

Agile's idea of "user stories"

In order to maximize user involvement and the feedback of vital information, Scrum practitioners want to get their projects started fast and want to be able to make their iterations short. They need a requirements vehicle that captures the intent of a feature without requiring a tremendous amount of time to author. Starting with the use case notion of streamlining the requirements template, they have taken it to an extreme and defined the "user story"—a single sentence identifying a need. User stories accelerate the interaction of the user and the developers so that work can get underway and be redirected fluidly as needed. The contrast with RUP's earlier approach to requirements documentation is so pronounced that even a noted use case advocate has offered that "a user story is to a use case as a gazelle is to a gazebo." [Cockburn 2008]

Traditional software engineers may well scoff at the notion that a team can successfully drive a complex application development project with little more than single sentences scratched on a stack of index cards (as envisioned in the paper-based version of Scrum). Such skepticism emanates from a tremendous misunderstanding. Agile does not employ user stories to replace application requirements. User stories simply identify where a requirement exists in a way that allows that particular need to be managed until it is time to code. User stories do not replace requirements. They only permit the team to defer requirements specification until the time when it can be best accomplished, namely, the moment when developers are ready to code a new or enhanced application module.

User stories move projects toward "just-in-time requirements," allowing avoiding amassing a large inventory of specifications that risk losing value when the business fundamentals of a project start to change. When it comes time to build out a feature identified by a user's story, that is the moment that developers can inquire about actors, triggers, preconditions, and flows of events. All the components of a good use case should still be covered. With Scrum, because this information is communicated orally as much as possible in order to speed its transmission, the sections of a use case are addressed in real time rather than accumulated before coding starts. The fast cycle time the user story allows permits users to see their request in working code quickly and then detect errors in requirements and design before additional layers are coded on top of them.

Users stories were introduce in Chapter 2 as single-sentence statements of business needs. They provide only a good notion of the desired functionality for the application being envisioned, a sketch of a feature that will be valuable to a user or a customer. They communicate this notion via a short little "story" about how someone will actually use the product the team will build. For easy reference, we have gathered in a sidebar the structure and key aspects of user stories presented in the earlier chapter. Because user stories are such a crucial part of the agile approach, we should take some time to understand why they work so well and how to write them well.

USER STORY'S THREE-PART FORMAT

As a <user role>,   (who)
I want to <action>,   (what)
so that <benefit>.   (why)

Business intelligence example: "As a branch manager, I want to start with total asset flows by month for accounts with brokers who've left our firm and then slice and dice those flows by newly assigned broker, call center events, and customer attributes such as tenure and worth so that I can identify important customers who about to follow their old brokers to another company."

Advantages of user stories

Why "stories" rather than "specifications?" First, stories are short—one or two sentences. Teams using a paper-based system can fit them completely on a single index card. Developers using agile project software will have a similarly small space in which to capture a story. This short "story card" format makes them easy to work with. A team can spread an entire project backlog of story cards across a large table and reason about the importance and priority of all the newly requested features at once.

Second, user stories abet the extensive interaction agile wants to achieve on its teams. The short and intelligible format of user stories allows their business partners to fully participate and thus serve as an active member part of the development team. Developers and customers alike can understand what is being asked for. Empirically, we see that people are better able to remember the complex events needed to manage business operations if the steps are organized into stories stating who is doing what and why. [Bower 1979, cited in Cohn 2005]

Third, user stories allow teams to work as the dynamics of the project require. Small cards spread out on a table allow users and developers to move opportunistically between top-down and bottom-up approaches as they sift through the unknowns and dependencies permeating their project. [Cohn 2005] User stories, coupled with iterative delivery, place users in a context where they get quick feedback on not only how they express themselves, but the software that results from their choice of words. This busts apart the old conundrum of users being unable to tell IT what it wants before they see it working in real code. With user stories, the team's embedded business partner needs to tell IT only a small part of what he wants and then gets to test drive the results in a few weeks. This quick cycle allows product owners to learn empirically how precise their vision and self-expression must be, allowing them to get progressively better at both.

A fourth advantage to the user stories short format is that it prevents anyone from overinvesting in the articulation of a requirement. A new business need can be captured by quickly scribbling out another index card, and if the team realizes later the story needs to be revised or dropped, the card can be easily replaced or destroyed. No one will complain that months of hard work had been being wasted when a story card is ripped up. In contrast, one can hear loud protestations in waterfall projects when dropping requirements obviates large sections of binders that took the team several person-years to compile. Employing the extremely lightweight approach of user stories on story cards thus allows the developers to resist "pushing back" when the product owner wants to change directions with the project, permitting the project to stay responsive to evolving business needs.

Identifying rather than documenting the requirements

Developers who are new to agile often think that user stories represent the requirements on a Scrum project. They quickly learn that it is the *conversations* between the product owner and the developers held throughout the development phase of the construction iteration that are the true requirements specification for an agile project. In fact, the agile community frequently encourages practitioners to think of user stories only as a *reminder to have a conversation* about the requirements when it is time to build a particular feature. [Ambler 2003] Users' stories are, then, just the trigger for a just-in-time requirements session. [Leffingwell 2006]

Because requirement conversations can lead anywhere, even to the need to create still more users stories, agile practitioners are very clear that the story-writing process will not occur in a single pass for a project. By making requirements easy to identify, user stories support a process of progressive elaboration that should span all the construction iterations of a project. From this perspective, applications requirements are not somehow already "out there" to be simply gathered as is. The requirements bash that waterfall projects start with is a futile effort to amass a pile of statements that users cannot yet express. Instead, the *roots* of requirements have to be detected and then developed progressively into more detailed functional explanations. Rather than requirements "gathering," agile practitioners prefer to think of the process as "trawling," in which the team must make repeated passes over a vast expanse of ocean with progressively finer nets. [Robertson 1999]

Figure 4.1 depicts a starter notion of a requirements management process for an agile project. Chapter 2 described how most companies will wrap a discovery and elaboration phase around a project during which business needs become enumerated at a high level, yielding an initial "census" requirement in the form of user stories. Everyone involved with the project should understand that this census of the application's requirements is only an incomplete list of "who lives where" that has not yet invested in collecting the inhabitants' detailed life histories. Typically, such a discovery process will identify less than half of the stories the project will eventually consider, and because they were detected at the very earliest stage of the project, many of those stories will have to be polished later by the team as each one approaches coding.

Although high level, this initial census of user stories is still enough information for the scoping and planning needed to get the project funded and resources assigned. It will also allow application architecture and high-level design to get underway. With

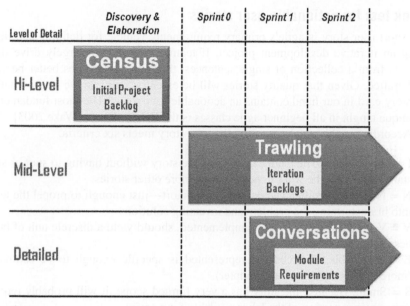

FIGURE 4.1

Agile's three levels of requirements management.

the project underway, requirements management will proceed along two channels, each focused on a distinct level of detail. The first is the midlevel channel, shown in Figure 4.1, which represents the team as it begins trawling for requirements at a medium level of specificity during both preiteration backlog grooming sessions and each iteration's story conference. By revisiting the backlog with each iteration, the team performs the multiple passes suggested by the trawling metaphor. How fine a net the stories must fit through on a given pass depends on how soon each will enter development. Stories considered for programming during the next iteration will receive close attention from the developers, as they discuss whether each is intelligible, complete, and actionable. Stories destined for future iterations may still be discussed, but not in as much detail.

User story definition fundamentals

Although user stories are lightweight in format, no one claims that they are easy to identify or articulate. The process of defining even the initial backlog for a project is hard work. Anticipating that most beginners are going to struggle with writing user stories, most agile trainings provide two mechanisms to facilitate the process: (a) a quick test of story quality and (b) a specific terminology to decompose big stories down into actionable user stories.

Quick test for actionable user stories

The short user story is agile's primary requirements vehicle for defining and managing an iterative development project. If teams are going to largely drive their projects from a collection of single sentences, then those sentences better be very well crafted. Given that quality stories will be essential, how do we know whether the story card in our hand contains an actionable user story? The most fundamental technique taught in all beginner agile classes is the INVEST test. [Wake 2003]

According to this quick test, a quality user story meets six criteria:

I = Independent: The team can develop the story without having to start or substantially revisit the work done on one or more other stories.

N = Not Too Specific: The description is short—just enough to propel the team into brainstorming the problem and inventing solutions.

V = Valuable: The story, once implemented, should yield a discrete unit of business value for the customer.

E = Estimable: The concept represented is specific enough to be estimated (more on this topic in a later chapter).

S = Small: Because the story has a very limited scope, it will probably require only a minor portion of the labor available for a sprint.

T = Testable: The story describes a unit of functionality that is small and distinct enough to be validated once implemented in code.

Like many aspects of the agile approach, the INVEST test is simple and tremendously useful because it can be used repeatedly throughout the life of a project. Data warehousing/business intelligence solution architects working with business partners can employ it during the discovery phase of a project while preparing an initial project backlog. The development team can draw upon it repeatedly once construction has started, during every story conference, to evaluate the stories the product owner wants coded next. The coders can employ the INVEST test during each sprint's development phase to deepen the requirement conversation they have with the product owner before they build out each user story.

High-performance agile engineers repeatedly reapply the INVEST test with their product owner because the users' true requirements may have changed over time or in response to the features delivered by earlier iterations. Take, for example, both independent and valuable. For data warehousing, there are many unresolved dependencies at the beginning of a project, such as "facts cannot be built before dimensions" or "key dimensions cannot be built before their source data have been scrubbed." Early iterations of a warehousing project naturally focus on the precursors involved in these dependencies. As a consequence, far more stories will pass the independent portion of INVEST as the project progresses and more predecessor modules get delivered. Valuable tends to go in the opposite direction. At the beginning of a project, all the users' stories are of course deemed necessary to the product owner; otherwise he would not have authored them. As the project unfolds, however, the product owner will learn more about data warehousing and the team will understand more about the business problem the project has been sponsored to address. A developer might suddenly find a date field that makes customer contact records unique so that call center transactions no longer have to be deduplicated. The product owner might realize that an annual report could be just as easily run from the records in the persistent staging area and that there is no need to build a dedicated star schema for it. The value of many stories will erode as developers build out the planned modules.

"Not too specific" criteria are included because long, detailed stories move the text back toward a full waterfall-style requirements specification, which involves all the disadvantages listed earlier. Moreover, when it comes time to build out the story, long descriptions focus the team on reconstructing old thinking from weeks ago rather than brainstorming the best possible design they can create now. In fact, this test criterion is also known as "negotiable" in order to suggest that everything about a story can be reinterpreted given the team's current understanding of the project.

How small is small?

"Small" is perhaps the trickiest component of the INVEST test. It suggests that stories should imply a bundle of work that will consume only a minor portion of the labor available for an iteration. In some ways, "small" is a secondary concern: one can let the other criteria of independent, estimable, and testable drive the sizing process. But eventually teammates will start asking what the upper limit on story size should be.

There is no one answer for this, only rules of thumb. The easiest such guideline to remember is that developers should be able to deliver more than one story each per iteration. Most teams arrive at a notion such as each story should take the team between half a day and half a sprint to deliver. Perhaps a stronger recommendation is to judge size by its impact upon the team's task board. Stories break down into many tasks each. Stories that are too big generate more task cards than the team can understand when placed in the story's swim lane on the task board. Cluttered swim lanes lower the chance that idle developers will find new tasks on their own, so when a story seems too involved, it should be broken into smaller stories that beget the number of task cards the team seems able to manage.

Reducing the story size to make the task cards manageable is preferable to making the tasks bigger. Although they might clutter a task board, small tasks have great advantages. Tasks that average only a few hours each require less design work and tend to involve fewer dependencies, therefore allowing developers to keep progressing. Small tasks are faster to complete, allowing developers to build a steady rhythm of completing several tasks each and every day. Such a pace lets everyone, including sponsors, know that the team is progressing toward its goals. Problems within an iteration will be easier to detect because they will cause the fast pace of task completion to suddenly disappear. In contrast, if the length of the average task exceeds 1 day, then it may take 2 or 3 days to realize that the team has gotten stuck.

In choosing the right definition of small for stories, the team must decide where the tipping point between manageability and clutter lies. Any initial choice made through this technique will need to be validated by observing how it works for the development team during a real sprint. In the end, each team has to discover empirically—and even revisit frequently—the definition of small that works best for it.

Epics, themes, and stories

Knowing what is small enough for a good user story is very different than knowing *how* to make a story small. Because most functional requests come from business people, candidate stories frequently start as some enormous request, for example, "As a company we want to learn what pleases our customers so that we win in the marketplace." When called on to deliver such miracle capabilities, the development team needs a mechanism for breaking down the request quickly into components that meet the INVEST test's notion of small enough. Luckily, generic agile provides a continuum of terms for focusing business partners and developers alike on the process of story decomposition: epics, themes, and stories.

An "epic" is a user request that is so big that the team has no immediate notion of how many modules it will require take or how many iterations they will take to deliver. This definition is not intended to imply that discussing epics is a bad practice. Agile practitioners regularly recommend that teams start big and progressively refine the functional requests until they arrive at the story level. [Pischler 2010] However, epics are so big they may well need an entire release cycle for the developers to deliver. If the team is going to develop and demonstrate capabilities via short manageable increments, the epic will have to be broken down into smaller units before the team begins work upon it.

Somewhere in between an epic and a story small enough to pass an INVEST test is a "theme." A theme is a user request that will still take more than a fraction of an iteration to deliver, but is still specific enough that the developers can envision a high-level design. With themes, they can ask a few more questions about intent and derive multiple, properly sized stories from the answers. Here is a hypothetical interaction between product owner and developers that makes the epics–themes–stories decomposition path a little clearer:

> Product owner: As director of fulfillment, I want a dashboard that lets me understand operational performance so that we can improve our product delivery times.
>
> Developers: Okay, good to know, but that's a really big *epic*, not yet a short little story. Can you break that thought down to smaller ideas where each one pertains to, say, a particular functional department or type of manager in the company?
>
> Product owner: All right....As a fulfillment manager, I want a summary bar graph that shows me shipments versus orders for each custom-manufactured product by month so that I can see which products our final assembly groups are faltering on.

Developers: That requirement is sure much smaller than the epic you first described, but there's still many numbers involved in every stack displayed on a bar graph. We can call what you just asked for as an important *theme* of the dashboard you're requesting. To get to details, let's think of the graph you described as a stacked bar chart. What measures would each of the colors in the stack for a given month display? Individual products?

Product owner: No, we should display a different bar chart by product type because most types have their own fulfillment manager. The actual "products" are just slight changes in the components used on each unit. I'd use the different colors to indicate the different steps in the final assembly process so that we can spot where in the process a big change has occurred.

Developers: That makes sense. So, let's write a card with the following *user story*: "As a fulfillment manager, I want a bar chart for a given product type that shows orders minus final assembly counts by month with a color for each major assembly step so that I can discover where and when new production problems have appeared."

Product owner: Truly, we've wanted that kind of visibility into production ever since we installed the ERP system 12 years ago.

Developers: Super. Now let's imagine that you spot a big problem on one of these bar charts. You can double click on a colored segment of a given bar to see the numbers inside that segment. What does the dashboard show you next?

Product owner: We need to find out the identities of the individual work groups so that we can figure out what team leader to talk to for a given problem. Can we get a new bar chart showing the same measure by assembly team?

Developers: Yep. Let's write that *user story* down on a card also: "As a fulfillment manager, I want to be able to drill down to a bar chart for a given product type *and assembly step* that shows orders minus final assembly counts by month with a color for each assembly team so that I can decide which team lead I need to talk to about production delays." Let's also put a note on this story card that it's dependent upon the previous one.

In practice, business people warm to this epic–theme–story hierarchy amazingly fast and soon begin thinking in those terms for themselves. For product owners, there is a built-in incentive to express themselves in something close to story-sized concepts because it lets the programmers focus immediately upon how to build their solution instead of wasting time struggling to understand what the business needs. Soon the developers will hear the product owner say something like "You know we need to factor carrier shipment delays into that fulfillment dashboard.... Oh, wait I just gave you another epic, didn't I? Let me start breaking that down for you...."

Once up to speed, product owners should be encouraged to draft user stories on their own, using all three levels of this hierarchy as needed, so that they can walk the team through the project's requirements starting with named epics, drilling down to component themes, and finally small, doable stories. Such a presentation will make the overall organization of the users' needs much easier for developers to remember and internalize. A coherent, well-organized project backlog of user stories also enables application architects to begin a high-level design by listing the major warehouse component the dashboard modules will require.

Of course, a product owner's initial list of user stories will not be perfect. As the aforementioned example suggests, the process of writing user stories requires many decisions and involves important business terms, which often have not been defined consistently across the organization. The product owner will need to write his stories iteratively, using the analysts, architects, and even testers on his team as a sounding board to get the stories small and clear enough to be actionable. Once development begins, this process should happen regularly. The product owner, architect, and analysts on the team should work together on grooming the project backlog several days before each story conference. These grooming sessions will naturally pay closer attention to stories near the top of the backlog because developers will see them the soonest. Stories toward the bottom of the story card stack will be less polished, in contrast to the waterfall approach, where analysts are expected to get all the requirements perfect before coding starts, no matter how far in the future they will be coded. As they prepare for the start of a new sprint, product owners need only review the most important stories from their prioritized list and select enough to keep the team occupied during the coming iteration. While this assignment still requires appreciable effort for this business partner, it is far less onerous than sitting through waterfall's seemingly interminable series of interviews with user analysts, struggling to describe accurately everything a user could possibly want from a new system.

As with user stories, teams will want some guidelines for describing how "big" epics and themes should be. Although no single answer exists, there is some guidance to help a team define the proper boundaries for their particular project and work environment. Table 4.1 lists the rules of thumbs employed by the agile warehousing community that contributed to this book. This collection hinges on notions such as "minimal marketable features," funding processes, solution scopes, and change control triggers associated with level of user request.

Common techniques for writing good user stories

Given that user stories fundamentally structure an agile development project, development teams should drive toward backlogs full of high-quality stories or their projects will be in trouble before the first few iterations end. When agile was young, the only guidance we had for "good user stories" was the notion of the INVEST test plus the epics–theme–story hierarchy. It was not much of surprise then, as agile coaches began doing agile program assessments and project rescues, that the number one complaint from project leaders was "our teams need to know how to write better user stories."

For such an easy idea, user stories are deceptively difficult to get right. As it turns out, writing good user stories is an art, not a science. It takes practice to

Table 4.1 Right-Sizing Epics, Themes, and Stories for Data Warehousing/Business Intelligence Applications

	Epics	**Themes**	**Stories**
Scope of Business Value	Minimal Marketable Feature for Executives and Sponsors	Minimal Marketable Feature for Managers and Users	Minimal Demonstrable Feature to a Product Owner
Project Scope	Used to Define Applications	Used to Define Releases	Used to Define Iterations
Iteration Span	Development will Require Multiple Releases	Development will Require Multiple Iterations	Can be Designed, Built, and Demonstrated in One Iteration
Solution Scope	Requires an Entire Subject Area to fulfill	Requires a Constellation of a Star Schema to Fulfill	Usually Requires just a Slice from One Fact Table and a Few Dimensions
Enumeration	Explicitly Enumerated in a Funding Document	Fully Enumerated after Funding	Often never fully Enumerated before Project Ends
Design Resources	Design Involves an Enterprise Architect	Design Involves a Project Architect	Solution Designed by Team's Analyst and Tech Leads
Change Control Trigger	Program-level Change Control	Project-level Change Control	Change Managed by Product Owner

become proficient at it, and one is never done improving his skill. Organizations new to agile might do well to look outside the company for someone who has written stories before for a full project backlog. Studies of programmer productivity before agile methods emerged reveal that software engineers can be 50 to 100% more productive when they are already familiar with the problem space of a new project. [Bruce 1982] This connection holds for agile settings as well, so business intelligence sponsors should seek veteran story writers with data warehousing experience, preferably in the industry and business function their project focuses upon.

Even with outside support, sooner or later every team—product owner and developers together—must become good at writing their own user stories. While there is no step-by-step recipe for crafting a high-quality story, several strategies have helped many practitioners over the past two decades of agile projects. We list the most commonly shared strategies in the sidebar and describe them in greater detail later, but first a word of caution: teams do not have to employ all of them to succeed. We do not want to return to the days of elaborate waterfall methods with lengthy lists of steps that must be followed before coding can get underway. We want to stay agile, and maximize the work *not* done.

THINGS TO TRY WHEN STRUGGLING TO WRITE GOOD USER STORIES

(Best to try one at a time lest we turn story writing back into a traditional requirements specification process)

- Check team's understanding of each element in the INVEST test
- Review team guidelines for distinguishing among epics, themes, and stories
- Check general agile recommendations for keeping story writing simple
- Adjust the average level of uncertainty left in the stories
- Reverse the order you consider each of the three user story elements
- Deepen team's understanding of "Who"
- Improve team's notion of "What" is being built
- Lightly model the stakeholders' goals to better understand "Why"
- Check that team is not distracted by "How," "When," and "Where"
- Add acceptance criteria to the story-writing conversations

Instead, readers should start simply with the INVEST test and the epic–theme–story decomposition scheme and give their teammates some time to self-organize their own story-writing process. When the developers start to struggle with backlog grooming or story conferences because of vague, contradictory, and not actionable epics, it is time to scan the following list of strategies. By using only one new strategy at a time, the team's leaders, such as project architect, senior developers, or scrum master, can keep the overall process lean and fast. They should then wait for the next bump in the road to introduce another strategy from this list. The right techniques for the team will be those strategies developers come back to repeatedly whenever they have trouble perfecting a particular story.

Keep story writing simple

When iterative development teams start to struggle with user stories, the first suggestions agile coaches make are a fairly common list of basic tactics to keep the story writing simple and effective. [Cohn 2005; Lucas 2011; Pischler 2010]

- Use stories to facilitate a dialog between team and users
- Involve the business as much as possible
- Use stories to precipitate a dialog between the product owner and other project stakeholders for even wider business input
- Write each user story for a single user
- Write stories in the language of business users that's easy to understand
- Use active rather than passive voice so that actors are clearly stated
- Focus on what's important; leave out the rest
- Allow writing stories to be an iterative discovery process
- Make sure they fit on an index card or similarly limited space
- Avoid elaborating upon the user interface or technical details
- Resolve confusion over ambiguous terms
- Hold regular backlog grooming workshops before every story conference

Use stories to manage uncertainty

In order to keep story writing simple, project leaders may have to manage their team's mind-set regarding the goals of the requirements process. When an iteration goes poorly because user stories were vague, developers can often go too far in the opposite direction and focus upon crafting "perfect user stories." This reaction will undermine agility, however, causing them either to imbue the stories with tremendous details or to break the users' requests into subatomic components with no ambiguity at all. In either of these directions, the process of drafting a first project backlog will begin to take months and quarters, seriously delaying the company's projects. Fearing such an outcome, we need to remind our developers of the goal: agile steadily delivers increments of business value in a time frame that lets the business profit from market opportunity. That goal means we have to keep the story-writing process fast. The true strength of an agile team is not the stories, but the behaviors they enable: self-organized development based on eye-to-eye discussions regarding requirements with product owners at the moment coding should begin.

Of course, if the product owner answers most of the developer questions regarding requirements with "I don't know. I'll have to research that," the development phase is not going to accomplish much. Agile is amazingly effective against only a *reasonable* amount of uncertainty, so the proper level of a good story is a balance between uncertainty and detail. To keep the epic–theme–story decomposition process speedy, we need to teach our teams that the objective is only to pare down business partner uncertainty to the point where the rest of the unknowns can be managed by a developer working directly with the product owner. Most teams find a way to express this objective in rough, quantitative terms, such as "Good user stories eliminate 80% of the uncertainty, leaving the remaining 20% to be conquered by the development process." Good user stories still have uncertainty, but only as much as the team can manage within one iteration.

Another way for teams to measure whether their stories are at the right level of certainty is to focus on planning. Ask them whether the entire backlog can be spread out on a large table and provide a solid understanding of the product that has to be built. Moreover, do the story cards provide just enough certainty to sequence the development of the full product? If there are still too many unknowns, then the product owner will not feel he can prioritize and the developers will be unable to advise him about dependencies between the cards. If there is too much detail, there will be too many cards on the table to easily see the modules that must be built and the order to construct them in.

A few quotes can sometimes bring the team back to the mind-set needed to find the right balance between clarity and residual uncertainty:

> "Stories represent requirements, they do not document them." [Davies 2001]
> "The text on the cards is less important than the conversations we have." [Chon 2005]
> "Storytelling reveals meaning without committing the error of defining it."
> **—Hannah Arendt**

We can remind developers who have let "perfect stories" become the enemy of "good stories" that they can rely on agile's ability to fail fast and fix quickly. If the level of uncertainty left in a story somehow results with the product owner rejecting a component during the user demo, it is not a disaster. Agile has kept both the scope of the coding and the time box small in order to ensure that the damage will be manageable. The team can analyze where the confusion occurred in that particular story and tune the level of certainty they ask the product owner to attain with his stories in the future.

Reverse story components

When teams begin struggling to write user stories in midproject, sometimes it is because they are mechanistically following the user story format of who, then what, then why, and it has gone stale for them. [Burton 2011] In this case it can help to reverse the usual format of the user story and ask them to answer these questions in the following order:

- Can we state the discrete value the business will perceive in the work being considered? (Corresponding to the user's stories "why" clause)
- Can we list the actions the user performs with the application to generate this value? (The "what" clause)
- Can we name the individuals or roles that will end up benefiting from this value? ("The "who" clause)

If this simple trick does not help, then perhaps it is time to dig more deeply into each of the three user-story components, as discussed next.

Focus on understanding "who"

The three-part structure to the agile user story can be categorized as who, what, and why. When stories become incomplete, vague, or conflicting, having the developers take a second look at "who" can often resolve the confusion.

Agile developers aim to design applications properly by studying prospective users in typical situations. [Chon 2005] If either the prospective user or the typical situation is not completely understood, necessary information will be missing for the engineers to easily envision an accurate design.

There are two types of confusion agile teams suffer from concerning their customers. First, they overlook some key stakeholders and end up with missing stories. Second, they do not completely understand the users they already have in mind, and thus end up building stories inappropriate for the business. Often this latter case occurs because they are writing from an IT perspective, which focuses on how information will be transformed rather than the business activity the information is supposed to affect. In other words, IT team members ended up writing the user stories for themselves. [Burton 2011]

Agile's primary technique for bringing the business customer of an application project into crisp focus is called "role modeling" in which developers take a moment to list key attributes defining the categories of users they are designing for.

This process is typically performed in a workshop setting and begins with the realization that a product will not have just one user. Role modeling asks teams to first brainstorm all the kinds of users that an application will support and then to organize them into categories such as veteran analysts, computer "newbies," data jockeys, and fraudulent individuals. [Cohn 2004]

Role modeling then invites the team to develop a deep understanding of each user category by analyzing their important attributes, such as:

- The frequency with which the user will use the software
- The user's level of expertise within the focal business domain
- The user's general level of proficiency with computers and software
- The user's level of proficiency with the software being developed
- The user's general goal for using the software

Agile team leaders often extend user role modeling with the use of "personas." Personas were defined by the "father of Visual Basic," Alan Cooper, a thought leader in the software user experience movement. A persona is an imaginary representation of a particular user role. The persona is given a name, a face, and enough relevant details to make him seem real to the project members. A persona should be described sufficiently enough that everyone on the team feels like they know the person. [Cohn 2004] Writing up a bio for this person, adding a photograph, and pinning it up on the project team room go a long way to making this fictional person come alive. The active ingredient for a persona is the bio. It should highlight all aspects that drive the goals and priorities the persona has when he turns to the envisioned application for business intelligence. Common components to the bio would be

- The persona's job title, his boss, and direct reports
- His official and unofficial roles in the organization
- Cross-organizational committees he belongs to
- Criteria that will be used in his annual review
- How his work affects the company's customers
- His upstream and downstream business partners
- What forces him to stay late or work weekends
- His biggest challenges with information timeliness and accuracy

Rich persona descriptions such as just described, even for just the primary users of an application, will empower developers to desk check their product owner's user stories extensively. Not only can they consider the story from the perspective of the individual that the story was written for, say, "Franklin in finance," but they can also discover major oversights and valuable synergies by dropping "Carrie from corporate strategy" into the story's driver's seat and view the situation through her eyes.

Focus on understanding "what"

The second component of the user story that benefits from deeper study is the "what"—the activity the end user wants to perform with the application. Ultimately,

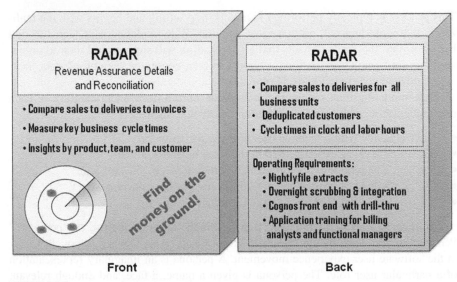

Front   **Back**

FIGURE 4.2

Sample vision box for a revenue assurance project.

the product backlog should enable anyone who reads through the cards to envision both the breadth and the depth of the application's function without drowning them in mind-numbing details. Sometimes the missing ingredient keeping the team from writing good user stories is a coherent notion of function—that is, the developers have yet to picture the nature and extent what the application will look like when finally put online. This can be addressed via a couple of lightweight artifacts.

1. **Vision box.** The first strategy is a generic agile notion called a vision box. A vision box is the package that the compact disk holding the application the team is going to build could be sold in. To draw a good vision box, developers must imagine it will be offered for sales on a store shelf, as if it were a package of cereal or a shrink-wrapped software product for someone's home computer. Teams gain a solid, shared understanding of a project when they collaborate on drawing up the cover of such a box. As visible in the example shown in Figure 4.2, the front of the vision box should have a nice graphic and the major benefits that would compel the project sponsors to buy the product. The back should provide some greater detail on features and benefits, plus some operating requirements that will reflect the project's assumptions and constraints. These boxes are often developed in a half-day workshop between the product owner and the developers. Inviting some of the major stakeholders that the product owner represents to join this team activity can improve greatly the accuracy of the notions placed on the box.

2. **Application wireframes.** Teams can gain a more detailed notion of an application "what" objective if they enrich their story conference or backlog grooming sessions with "low-fidelity prototyping." Also known as "application wireframes,"

these prototypes are simply sketches of the end product's user interface drawn free hand on flip charts with movable post-its representing key display elements.

To keep this process speedy enough for story conferences, the developers must keep in mind that the point of the exercise is not user interface design, but rather to consider the desired application from a customer point of view. Seeing the software through the end-user's eyes may even enable the developers to assist the product owner in improving how his user stories are worded. Every mock-up created needs to be drawn from at least one user's point of view, and the emphasis should be on how to best help him get his job done. Using the goals from the user personas discussed earlier is a particularly effective way to establish business purpose as the point of this exercise.

3. **Lightweight modeling.** As the team collaborates on a vision box and application wireframes, a few of the team leads use that input to draw some quick pictures of the architecture and design elements the application will need. A little bit of this lightweight modeling goes a long way in capturing a rich set of requirements. In particular, as the team drafts these high-level artifacts, they will inevitably say much about source data, quality problems, and integration paths they will have to manage in order to build the product. The project architect can actively place these major processing components on a high-level architecture diagram while listening to the conversation vision box and application wireframe conversations. Similarly, the data architect can get a good start on a *schematic* data model (one that shows entities and relationships, but no attributes) for the target layers as she hears how users intend to use the system once it is online.

4. **Product board.** A product board is a surface (or shareware workspace) where the team can assemble the farrago of "what" information generated by the aforementioned activities. Many of the assumptions, constraints, and validation points that come to light during product discussions are hard to capture using a user story format, but they are valuable information nonetheless. Teammates can ensure the quality of the end product greatly by writing these system aspects on cards of their own quickly as they are mentioned. These cards can be combined with the vision box, wireframes, and lightweight models on a "product board" located alongside the team's task board. [Pischler 2010] The team can also keep cards for the project's epics and themes on the product board, plus cards for system constraints and validations activities. As portrayed in Figure 4.3, this collection of high-level notions will form a readily understandable depiction of the project's destination. Such a picture will be a handy resource to draw upon when the team struggles to articulate a tough user story and to keep it coherent with the other on the backlog. Teammates will be able to add new cards and mock-ups as the project progresses, fine-tuning the picture of their destination as further discoveries are made.

Focus on understanding "why"

The last component of the user story is the "why"—the benefit end users will be seeking when they operate the envisioned application. This topic was touched on

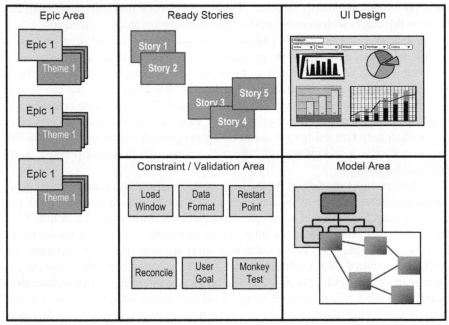

Adapted from Roman Pischler, "The Product Backlog Board," March 2011, http://www.romanpichler.com/blog

FIGURE 4.3

Sample product board.

briefly earlier when we suggested that teams enumerate user goals when drafting personas for them.

A team's understanding of user goals can often benefit from a bit of modeling, which borrows from the earlier agile approaches that relied upon use cases rather than user stories. One can envision a hierarchy of business objectives existing in three levels, portrayed in Figure 4.4: summary goals, user goals, and subfunctions. [Cockburn 2001]

One interpretation of this simple framework could be as follows. "Summary goals" are long-range and high-level desires, often conceived of as the impact the system should have on the operations of the organization once fully implemented and adopted. They are often articulated by the executive sponsoring the application development. For enterprise data warehousing, a typical summary goal that executives might provide would be "higher sales margins."

"User goals" are the first decomposition of summary goals and are more immediate business objectives desired by the folks who will actually touch the workstation the application is operating upon. For example, a manager working for the executive sponsoring the warehouse may wish to explore changes in sales margins by first performing a revenue analysis, then a cost analysis, and finally combining portions of those two studies into a presentation on sales margins. Each of those

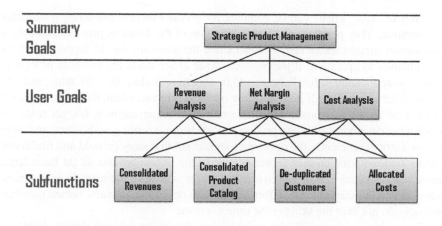

FIGURE 4.4

Three levels of user goals.

steps would be a separate user goal. Any one of them may take all afternoon or several days of interaction with the business intelligence application before the operator arrives at the insight the user goal describes.

"Subfunctions" represent the activities or data sets providing the backup details an operator will need to accomplish a user goal. In our example, the manager executing a revenue analysis would first check that billings were aggregated properly across the overlapping business units of the company and then confirm that payments from customers who have moved between sales territories do not appear twice in the data.

Even a simple model of user goals, such as the one expressed in the examples given earlier, can breathe new energy into a user story-writing process. When this occurs, teams will typically see summary goals yielding epics, user goals generating themes, and subfunctions providing user stories. Once this mapping takes place, teams will often comment that their previous problem in writing stories was that they were trying to express user goals rather than subfunctions as user stories. User goals tend to be too big for a small increment of functionality to address because the user simply needs to do "lots of things" to accomplish a goal. Each of those "things" that eventually achieve the goal is a subfunction. Subfunctions lend themselves to small modules or enhancements, therefore making a better focus for user stories.

Be wary of the remaining w's

A further strategy from the agile community warns teams from venturing too far beyond "who," "what," and "why" while trying to write stories because the "where" and "when" should have preceded the project and the "how" should be deferred until the story enters development.

"Where" and "when" can be complex for product owners managing a distribute organization. They pertain more to the definition of the business process the application should support rather than the interaction the software should support when the user chooses to operate it. If the product owner understands the business process he wants the application to fulfill, he should be able to articulate the who, what, and why required for a user story. If he is not clear on the where and when, the work that needs to be done is business process reengineering. The organization is not yet ready for application development. When product owners begin wrestling with where and when during a story conference, the developers should put that story on hold and find someone to work with the product owner outside of the Scrum process to get these larger questions answered. Diving into *when* and *where* will mire the team in an extensive business process diagramming effort, which, as a development team, Scrum members probably do not have the skills or the time to pursue.

Discussions of *how* will also quickly ruin the agility of user stories. User stories focus on business needs, not their solutions, that is, they should discuss what must happen, not the design of the code that makes it come true. Teams that indulge in design discussions whenever the product owner articulates a desired functional feature will consume so much time that they will never be able to collect a starter list of stories for a full release, let alone a project. True, a couple of team leads can dip their toes into the "how" by performing lightweight modeling during the story conference, but those activities should definitely stay in the background so that the bulk of the team stays focused on the "what" and not the "how."

Add acceptance criteria to the story-writing conversations

As a final technique for improving the quality of a team's user stories, some agile thought leaders advocate adding to them acceptance criteria. [Jeffries 2004] This is a story-level application of the test-led development technique explored for the development phase of a sprint in Chapter 2. For each user story, the team would alternate between probing for clarity on the "who, what, and why" and asking the product owner how she will know the resulting module has been designed correctly. For data warehousing, the simplest of these validation steps usually take the form of checking that all records going into staging actually land somewhere in the warehouse and that key numeric columns in the target table reconcile back to their source systems. As team members identify validation steps for a given story, they might record them on the back of the story card. Some validation plans span multiple stories or themes and should be given a card of their own to be pinned to the product board.

This strategy needs to be managed by the scrum master. It is easy to think of dozens of tests for most user stories. These tests can lead the team to think through the story at a deeper level, complementing the narrative of each story and providing a clear indication of when a story is complete. However, writing tests does take away time from writing stories. Some practitioners suggest that developers strive to identify between just three and five acceptance criteria for every story.

[Pischler 2010] Teams that employ this strategy should ask themselves frequently if they have the balance right or whether they are writing too many tests per story and losing time that could be better spent using one of the other strategies mentioned previously.

Summary

Agile methods such as Scrum rely on user stories for requirements management. User stories are not requirements, but instead are only a reminder to discuss requirements in depth with the project's embedded business partner when it comes time to build out a feature. Although user stories identify rather than document the project requirements, they can still prove hard to write well. Over the decades, agile practitioners have devised many strategies and tools to help teams author better user stories. The most basic tool is the INVEST test, where the most important elements are independent, estimated, small, and testable. There is also a simple hierarchy of epics, themes, and stories to structure the conversation when a story proves far too large. More advanced strategies involve user role modeling, vision boxes, product boards, and detailed examination of the "who," "what," and "why" of every story.

Deriving Initial Project Backlogs

5

How can information technology (IT) help product owners create an initial list of user stories for a data integration project?
What does a predevelopment project backlog look like?
What data integration topics do epics and themes typically link to?

The first part of this book presented a generic style of Scrum as taught and practiced by many organizations for the construction of general computer software applications or—as data warehousing professionals know them—"online transaction processing" (OLTP) systems. For the world of "online analytical processing" (OLAP) applications, "plain-vanilla" Scrum serves as a fine collaboration model for teams building the front-end dashboarding portion of an OLAP system. Teams developing the data integration back ends of those applications, however, will need to adapt Scrum to better fit the unique type of work that they do. As described in the opening chapter, the many hidden architectural layers involved in most data integration applications make delivering value with every iteration of Scrum tantamount to building four or five miniapplications in only a couple of weeks. Most teams find that impossible to achieve consistently. Instead, data integration teams need to adapt Scrum's notion of both the user story and the way it feeds work into the iterative development process in order to make agile collaboration realistic.

The second part of this book focuses on the first of those adaptations: modifying user stories to better support data integration projects. This chapter considers a process for generating the initial project backlog for a data integration project in a data integration context. The next chapter describes how to convert the resulting user stories on the project backlog into "developer stories," small, architecturally specific units of functionality that a data integration team can better manage with its Scrum-based delivery process. Finally, the third chapter discusses techniques for assembling those developer stories together into both a sequence of releases that will deliver increments of value to their business customers and a whole project estimate of an application's likely development cost and duration. In large organizations, this whole project estimate is an important objective for a project because it is typically required to secure the funding needed to begin development.

Agile Data Warehousing Project Management.
DOI: http://dx.doi.org/10.1016/B978-0-12-396463-2.00005-3

The presentation of these three steps is example based so that readers will gain a concrete notion of how a data integration project can be defined and planned for incremental delivery using agile techniques. The example we employ takes a request for a "Revenue Trends Data Mart" from the inception phase of corporate IT release cycle and elaborates upon it until development iterations can begin. This chapter details the work of a project architect who joins the effort before it is even a project. The business sponsor and an enterprise architect have made only a first look at a desired data warehousing/business intelligence (DWBI) solution in order to appraise its feasibility. Enterprise architecture can provide the project architect little more than a sketch of the solution and some high-level constraints. Given that almost superficial starting point, Paula, our project architect, has to interview the project's imbedded business partner and prepare an initial project backlog. As part of the same effort, she will also identify the information members the development team will need to begin an agile elaboration of the project's target data model, source profiles, and transformation rules.

Value of the initial backlog

For Scrum, an initial project backlog is the list of user stories that provides enough definition that teams can start development sprints. It provides an excellent notion of project scope and allows developers to contemplate the technical objectives and labor it will require. The creators of Scrum did not specify where such a backlog comes from, suggesting instead that it is simply originates during the project's first story conference. [Schwaber 2004] In practice, Scrum teams start gathering an initial project backlog as part of the preparatory work performed during "Iteration 0." Many data warehousing projects can start even earlier. Given that warehouse projects are typically large projects, the program management office (PMO) of most companies wraps them in a release cycle. The typical release cycle described in Chapter 2 has two phases before system construction begins: inception plus discovery and elaboration. These phases provide Scrum teams the opportunity to assemble an initial backlog of user stories and perform enough data and process architecture work to support the first development iterations.

Some agile purists might interpret the initial project backlog of user stories as somehow returning to the pattern of big specifications utilized up front by waterfall methods. To the contrary, as shown in the sample project, the project architect will keep the initial set of project artifacts limited to a list of user stories and a few diagrams. The aim is to provide a lightweight rather than a detailed depiction of the project.

The initial product backlog is very much like writing an outline for the author of a book. It takes a short amount of time to build, but saves the author even more time as the next phase of writing progresses and it greatly helps make the resulting book seem focused and linear. The outline itself is not restrictive because the writer is of course free to update it as new ideas occur. Yet it does express a central intent to the work that serves as a soft boundary for keeping wildly irrelevant notions from sneaking into the project. In the agile development context, software developers need the product owner to have such a "guiding outline" for the project. Even with iterative, self-organized teams, coding is still very expensive. Coding without a direction or constraints on scope can be ruinously ineffective. The initial backlog allows the team to perform some necessary architectural work for both data and process so that when the programmers join the effort they do not start programming in circles.

Paula, the project architect in our example, takes the time to derive an initial backlog with the product owner because it provides multiple benefits, including

- The initial backlog allows product owners to arrive at the first story conferences prepared to state which stories should be started, having thought them out well enough to clearly describe what is needed
- It gets the product owner thinking so that she can stay ahead of future sprints as the project moves forward
- It scopes the application so that the coherence of future stories can be considered carefully
- It provides the developers a glimpse of the whole project so that they can do some high and midlevel design based on knowledge gained from generating the list of user stories
- It provides the team's software engineers a first opportunity to include features that address necessary but nonfunctional requirements such as data volumes, processing time, and programming patterns
- It allows the team to make an initial estimate of project cost and duration
- It allows the project to begin coordinating milestones with other projects and programs

It is hoped that the process of deriving the initial backlog defines for everyone the "spirit of the application" so that as the product owner drafts further user stories, all team members can ensure they are consistent and aligned with the project's driving requirements.

Sketch of the sample project

This chapter employs a hypothetical data mart project to illustrate how a team can derive a starter set of user stories for a warehousing project that involves substantial data integration requirements. The sample project used is a distillation of the actual project discussed in the first chapter, which the sponsors ran side by side with a comparable waterfall project and which delivered its application with one-third the programming hours and one-half the cost per data transform module. We use this sample project in the next two chapters also, where we first describe how to translate user stories into programmable "developer stories" and then show how to estimate an initial backlog for project sizing.

Our sample project was commissioned by a large U.S. telecommunications firm, which we can call "PaBell." This company had grown over many decades through mergers and acquisitions from a regional phone company to a conglomerate offering a diverse set of voice and data products throughout much of the continental United States. The author has simplified and "sanitized" our description of the project sufficiently so that the following illustration focuses on the generic challenges faced by any complex firm that must plan and guard its revenues based on a capital-intensive infrastructure.

In our example, the company provides a wide selection of service products to both the consumer marketplace and business customers. Services range from "legacy products," such as phone and data communications based on copper-wire circuits, to more "strategic offerings," such as cell phone service with large data plans. The project considered here came about because PaBell was losing so many subscribers within certain areas of its cell phone business that quarterly revenues were declining noticeably.

The executives asked the corporate strategy team to research the root cause of this "revenue erosion" and to propose ways of mitigating the forces driving subscribers away. Corporate strategy was a small department, staffed with some very clever "data cowboys" who could perform just about any statistical analysis ever invented—as long as they had clean and complete data to work with. Seeing that they needed a steady feed of quality information to run into their data mining applications, corporate strategy approached the business intelligence group of the corporate IT department to build a revenue data mart. The DWBI group had recently adopted an agile methodology based on Scrum and XP, and therefore asked corporate strategy to assign a product owner to work with a data integration team. To help defray the expense of the data mart's development, corporate strategy invited the financial analysis department of the controller's office to participate as a secondary sponsor. In turn, the controller's office provided a subject matter expert with extensive knowledge of finance's requirements and the company's many revenue systems from which data would be sourced. Finance's involvement was considered crucial because the financial analysts regularly groom the revenue and product usage figures that corporate strategy used as the starting point for their analytics.

Fitting initial backlog work into a release cycle

In our sample project, the Scrum team working in sprints will have to fulfill the objectives of the program management office's release cycle. This combination creates an interesting overlap between release cycle phases and Scrum iterations at the beginning of a project. Figure 5.1 presents the overlap employed during the sample project. It maps the Scrum team's iterations onto the release cycle defined by the company's program management office. For waterfall projects, the PMO wants a list of major use cases and a project cost estimate at the conclusion of the inception process. Paula, the sample project's project architect, has negotiated to employ an

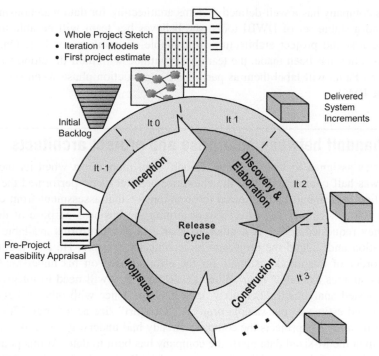

- Whole Project Sketch
- Iteration 1 Models
- First project estimate

Initial Backlog

It -1

It 0

Inception

Discovery & Elaboration

It 1

It 2

Delivered System Increments

Release Cycle

Pre-Project Feasibility Appraisal

Transition

Construction

It 3

• • •

FIGURE 5.1

Fitting early iterations into a typical PMO release cycle.

initial backlog of prioritized user stories as a substitute for the major use cases. She will gather them based on interviews conducted with the product owner before the project officially begins with Iteration 0. She calls that preproject time "Iteration −1." Using the initial backlog from Iteration −1, Paula plans to work with the project's data architect and systems analyst during Iteration 0 to produce several artifacts that will satisfy the PMO's requirements for the inception phase:

- a groomed project backlog of user stories
- a whole project sketch of the logical models for both data and processing
- Iteration 1's physical data model and source-to-target mapping
- a first project estimate

With those artifacts complete, the team can begin Scrum's development iterations. The PMO wants each project to undertake a discovery and elaboration phase where the developers should prove the architectural soundness of their application before beginning the construction phase of the release cycle. Paula plans to use the first couple of Scrum iterations to meet that requirement because she knows that she will have to work with her product owner to either elevate the riskiest user stories to the top of the backlog or start the project with an architectural sprint. Because

Paula's company has a well-defined systems architecture for data warehousing projects and a stable set of DWBI tools, she believes her team will be able to demonstrate a sound project architecture in a couple of iterations or less. Once that demonstration has been made, the team will continue with their development iterations, but Paula will label them as part of the construction phase when she speaks with the PMO.

The handoff between enterprise and project architects

Paula was assigned to the "Revenue Trends" data mart effort when its inception phase was half complete. Eddie, the enterprise architect who performed the initial feasibility assessment, had collected information for that assessment from conversations with executives and directors concerning the business purpose of the data mart they requested. He took a quick look at data and platforms available in the corporation and judged the project to be technically feasible. He also produced a rough order of magnitude estimate for the effort. Based on his understanding of the data sources available, their volumes, and how they will need to integrate into the requested analytics, Eddied drew upon his experience with other warehousing projects and estimated our sample project's "tee-shirt" size as a "large." It seemed smaller than the XL projects the company already had underway, but it is definitely bigger than the M-sized data marts the company has built to date. At this point he is ready to hand off the rest of the discovery work to Paula, who he asked to call him when she was ready to start.

> Paula, the project architect: Hi, Eddie. This is Paula. We scheduled this time for me to get the handoff of the Revenue Trends Data Mart project from you.
> Eddie in enterprise architecture: Oh hi, Paula. Glad you decided to rejoin our happy little telco.
> P: Yeah, had to work elsewhere for 2 years to get some agile data warehousing experience, but I'm happy to be back. The crazy maze of source applications isn't any better than I remembered though.
> E: Nope, afraid not. By the way, I attended the Agile Warehousing 101 class you gave last month. So now I'm familiar with epics, themes, and stories. It'll be interesting to watch this Revenue Trends Data Mart project you're going to do. We've changed the project role names a little since you were here. Let me give you a quick rundown:
> - We now call your position a "project architect." People in that role are still responsible for a solution-level description of the application. They're expected to frame a project's data, processes, and quality assurance plan and then delegate to specialists on their team the work of filling out the details. For warehousing, they also select the upstream systems their project will pull data. You should confirm those choices with me in case I happen to know of a better source, such as a master data application or another warehouse dimension some other project is working on.

- The project's data architect is still called a "data architect." He'll start with your solution-level data model, finish it with detailed logical modeling, and then provide all the physical modeling. He's supposed to coordinate data architecture with my group so we get notions such as master data elements and reusability across data mart projects right from the start. We want you guys to build stuff that further our corporate business intelligence roadmap as much as possible.
- Tech lead is now "systems analyst." He's supposed to validate your choice of sources with some data profiling, research the details to the business trans-formation rules you get from the business experts, and sketch the logical design for the extract, transform, and load application your team will have to build.

So, as project architect you're going to take the lead on defining the solution— both data and process. You were a data architect when you were last here. Did you get a chance to do any ETL while you were away?

P: Yep. 18 months with InformataStage. It was good to see the details on the process side of a project for a change.

E: Well, as you can see from the short packet I sent you on this Revenue Trends Data Mart, I got discovery started with a couple of interviews, just enough to get a few things established, namely:

- I established that they want all company revenues, so you'll have to integrate data from the subsidiaries for some of the dimensions such as product
- I figured out some reusable portions—some we already have and those you'll have to build
- I selected some likely data sources
- I wrote up a "tee-shirt" size estimate of project cost and then put the project on the IT roadmap

Think you're ready to finish off this discovery work for us now?

P: No problem. Of course, coming from an agile perspective, "discovery" means pushing ahead our understanding of data and process through the first 80% of a definition. We need to do just enough to know we haven't made any big mis-takes and to get the first chunk of user stories defined so we can get the project started.

E: You'll still have to do the "elaboration" half of the phase, where you prove out your architecture and mitigate as much of the project risk as possible.

P: True. We'll do that by working with the business to identify the user stories that link up with the high-risk aspects of the application. Then we'll get those placed as high in the backlog as we can while still delivering some stuff that has value to the customer. It's always a balancing act when you take an agile approach.

E: Right. I remember you saying that in class. You want to start delivering value to the customer and getting their feedback on your design as soon as possible. You said that's more important than knowing you've got every last design detail right before you start. That's probably right.

P: "Fail fast and fix quickly."

E: Like I said, it'll be interesting to watch. So, the business departments have picked a couple of subject matter experts to work with you. One's the product owner.

P: I interview them for the first time tomorrow. The objective will be to derive an initial project backlog of user stories and then prepare a budgeting estimate that will let us get the project funded.

E: Those user stories…you made them sound very process or ETL oriented during your class.

P: That's just shorthand. Loading a set of business entities loaded so the business can use data to answer a questions is where the "rubber meets the road," so it's good to define user stories at that level. It makes the whole team focus on delivering value rather than the intermediate, technical steps. But, rest assured, as soon as we're funded I'll start working with the data architect during Iteration 0 to define the logical target data model. We'll also have the systems analysts start in on the source data profiling and business rules. We'll figure the essentials of source and target well before we start designing process modules.

E: You're going to figure out everything about the target model and business rules in just a few weeks?

P: We'll shoot for the most important 80%. For the data model, that's usually all the entity names, their keys and joins, plus a sketch of all the major business rules for the derived columns. We'll leave the details of the rest of the columns until just before each table gets included in a construction sprint. The systems analyst will take his lead from the project architect and data architect regarding when to spell out each set of sources and business rules for the programmers.

E: But you're going to just sketch the business rules for the major columns?

P: Sketching is the right level of definition for most of them if you're going to get the project underway in a business-reasonable time frame. The discovery conversation may reveal some rules that are absolutely crucial. We'll investigate those beyond a sketch. We'll also schedule those as early in construction iterations as possible so that we can get them well validated before basing any other items on them.

E: Hmmm. I'm amazed you wouldn't do all the business rules first.

P: That could delay the project start by 6 months or more. Remember, product owners can usually find value in many of the data mart components even when delivered in increments. For example, seeing "revenue by customer" is worth something to them, even if "revenue by customer and product" would be better. Because we're going to deliver in pieces, we need only have the work immediately in front of us defined in detail. Get the coders working on Iteration 1 and that will buy time for our team's data architect and systems analyst to spell out the details for Iteration 2.

E: So getting back to these discovery interviews you're going to do, the objective for that work is….what?

P: (a) Define a list of user stories that more or less define the application so we understand our project objectives and cost and (b) polish the first iteration's user stories so that they're independent, valuable, estimable, small, and testable.

E: And still negotiable. Right, the INVEST test. Well, I did the interviews for the tee-shirt estimation. I can give you enterprise architecture's version of the business target model and some high-level constraints.

P: "Business target model?"

E: What we used to call the "solutions model." If you're speaking carefully, it's called the "business dimensional model of the warehouse's target data store," but we usually just say "business target model." It's the model of business entities showing facts and dimensions the customer will need for his data mart. (See Figure 5.4 for this chapter's example.)

P: Got it. Tell me what you've got on that model so far.

E: Well, they'll need a revenue fact entity of course, and dimensions for customer, product, and geography. As far as recommended sourcing, the company put shared account and customer dimensions into production a year ago. It's in third normal form using a typical "party" model. [Silverston 2001] Data quality for that topic area is real good so each data mart project only has to transform the records they need from that schema into a customer dimension of their own.

P: Cool. You're making our life easy. Do you have a product and geography dimension for us too?

E: Nothing so far on product, which is too bad because we've got six different product catalogs in this company and no two of them use the same product number for more than 25% of the items they have in common. So your project's going to have a challenge there. For customer information, we've got postal billing addresses for past and present accounts as part of building out the customer party model.

P: Nothing for the location of customer equipment on our network?

E: Nope. The network management department is working on a repository of network service addresses, and I'd love to get your business partners to delay their data mart project until that data is ready, but...

P: Revenues are falling and everyone wants to figure out why.

E: That's right. So, have your data architect coordinate through us in enterprise architecture if and when he models out IP addresses and equipment numbers for end-user services because that will all be part of the network service address topic area we hope to make an enterprise dimension. You'll want to get the grain right so that you don't have to reengineer your data structures when you switch over to shared dimension data.

P: Will do. So here's the business target model that I've been drawing while you spoke. (She emails the simple electronic diagram shown in Figure 5.2.) I'll confirm all those dimensions when I interview my subject matter experts (SMEs).

E: Yep, that's about all I have now. I'm sure it will become a lot more detailed as you folks start working with the product owner. Be sure you and your team send us versions of all your high-level artifacts as you get clarity on them.

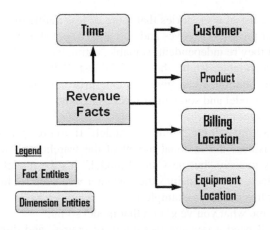

FIGURE 5.2

Starter business target model for sample project.

P: Sure thing. Let me confirm with you the process I'm going to follow to close out the discovery work you started. My goal is to interview the SMEs to get our starter set of user stories, but I'm also going to… (Here she walks him down Table 5.1, pointing out in particular the places where her objective is to confirm the enterprise architecture work and where she will extend or add to it.)

E: That fits with our standard process. I'm a little surprised. I thought agile was "let's just throw coders at every business problem we can find." I would have thought you guys would do without most of the discipline. That's why I was worried that agile data warehousing would lead to a lot of data disparity between applications.

P: We still use sound system and data engineering principles. The real difference is agile warehousing teams acknowledge that a design doesn't have to be perfect before you start coding and getting feedback. We pick out the key integration points within an application and between systems and get those right. The remaining definition work is mostly issues concerning columns and data quality, which can be addressed through increments of code. During our iterations our data architects and analysts stay one iteration ahead of the programmers and provide them the detail guidance they need as they start programming each increment.

Key observations

The conversation between the Scrum team's project architect and the company's enterprise architect touched upon a few key points that deserve highlighting.

Agile warehousing is collaborative even outside the project team. Enterprise architecture typically starts a project, places some definition and constraints upon it, and then hands off to a project team. The project team does not start with a blank slate or proceed without support.

Table 5.1 Major Discovery Steps Showing Collaboration Between Enterprise and Project Architects[a]

#	Representation	Ent. Arch Action	⬅➡	Proj. Arch. Action	Description
1	Business context	**Sketch**	➡	Confirm, add detail	Business drivers, goals, information needs, domain model
2	Business conceptual	**Sketch**	➡	Confirm, add detail	Business information subjects, business questions (epics and themes), facts and qualifiers, business dimensional model
3	Solution schematic	**Sketch**	➡	Confirm, add detail	Source systems model, business target entity model, high-level architecture and data flow diagrams
4	Solution logical	Review	⬅	**Sketch**	Logical data models for integration and presentation layers, business queries (user stories)
5	Solution structural	Review	⬅	**Sketch**	Physical data models for integration and presentation layers
6	Solution procedural	Review	⬅	**Sketch**	Process design and business rules (source to target mappings)

[a]*Adapted from [TDWI 2001]*

As the application is built, the project supports the enterprise architecture's roadmap for the company's warehousing applications. In turn, enterprise architecture supports the project with knowledge of existing data assets, such as reusable dimensions, data modeling patterns, and other architectural standards. The enterprise group also reviews project design decisions to ensure that the data mart will integrate into the data warehousing environment.

With this collaboration in place, the individual warehousing teams rarely have to reinvent the wheel. Enterprise architecture provides them a good starting notion of the project, including how much data integration it will entail, the target data architecture needed, and the major source systems to draw data from.

Architects from both enterprise and project levels understand there will be some rework involved in the project. For example, a perfect, enterprise-reusable dimension is not always available when a project needs to provide those services to its customers. Some of the project's components will be built to answer an immediate need and then swapped out later when the enterprise version goes online.

Some rework is unavoidable, but a major goal for the collaboration between enterprise and project architecture is to minimize it. They must continue to communicate as the agile team learns more about the problem space of the project so that together they can devise the best evolutionary path for the project's data model to take.

User role modeling results

Like many data marts, Paula's project will have multiple stakeholders. Before starting to gather an initial project backlog, she spends a short time performing some initial user role modeling, as outlined in the prior chapter. She makes this effort so that she can better guide the product owner in considering the entire user community during the initial backlog interview. For this initial user modeling, she worked by phone conversations with those who are familiar with the project concept, such as the product owner, the secondary sponsors, and the enterprise architect. She understands that it may have to be repeated in the future as the project progresses. However, by performing this modeling at an early stage, she identifies what the overriding interests of the key users are and where those interest overlap or collide. If she asks those she interviews what systems and user groups they exchange information with, the effort lessens the chance of overlooking a major stakeholder constituency from the start. Even for agile teams, few surprises can muddy the water and derail delivery dates more than discovering a major stakeholder in midproject. For that reason it is worth investing a small amount of effort in user role modeling up front to be reasonably sure that the initial project backlog has not omitted a crucial set of epics and themes.

As shown in the last chapter, we pursue user role modeling by

1. brainstorming the types of users an application will have
2. listing some typical user stories for each
3. grouping similar users and stories together
4. summarizing a list of *who* is after *what* in terms of major functions and benefits

Figure 5.3 depicts the outcome of Paula's user modeling as it appeared at the end of the third step. In addition to users from corporate strategy and finance, her interviews revealed formal and informal data exchanges with the regional BI teams, their executives, and the company's product managers at regional and corporate levels. Figure 5.3 includes a representative user story for each type of user. It also depicts these roles grouped together under user superroles such as product analysts and regional analysts. Figure 5.3 also groups these groups clustered between the interests of the two major user representatives involved in the project: corporate strategy and financial analysis. Having a cluster for finance on the user model soon proved important as the sample project proceeded. As product owner of the application, it was easy for the corporate strategy representative to forget stories pertaining

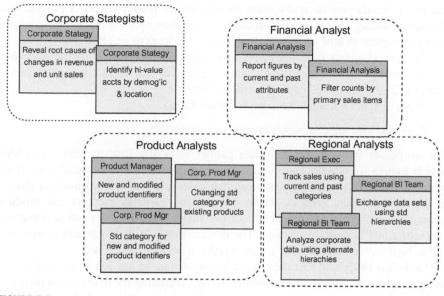

FIGURE 5.3

User role models for the sample data mart project.

to financial analysis. The user model allowed the project architect to continually include the secondary stakeholders in her conversations with the product owner.

Key persona definitions

In our PaBell project, the user role modeling process identified two clusters of user stories that aligned with the two major stakeholders of the project. To safe-guard both side's interests, the project analyst realized that two primary personas were required: one for corporate strategy and another for financial analysis. Once defined, these personas allowed participants in the initial backlog interview and later user story sessions to easily imagine the key the services stakeholders would need from the requested application. This section presents the resulting persona descriptions. Each description follows the template listed in the prior chapter and links their various interests to the notions of "summary goals" and "user goals" also presented there.

Carla in corp strategy

Carla serves as the manager of corporate strategy, reporting to the director of product management and guiding the work of three product analysts with specialties in legacy products, strategic products, and promotional campaign planning. Officially, her group should provide action plans for strengthening the company's product mix through bundling and pricing. Unofficially, she advises network planners and advertising managers on how to make the company's products more attractive.

Her annual review typically pivots upon questions concerning the products her group's guidance made measurably more successful and what competitive situations the four of them helped the company overcome.

Focus of Carla's Annual Review (Summary Goal)

- Have you kept the company's products competitive?

The corporate strategy upstream data partner is mostly finance, which provides usable figures for billings and sales, but her group also receives crucial feeds from network management, fulfillment, customer care, and third-party customer demographic information vendors. Their downstream business partners are product managers, marketing, and senior VPs of two major business units called consumer marketing and business marketing. The downstream parties in particular may turn out to be important stakeholder groups worthy of user modeling later.

Carla has often said that the biggest waste of time in her job is all the hunting and gathering of reference data essential for understanding the many codes involved in finance's information on revenue, costs, call centers activity, and Web site traffic. These codes identify crucial business entities such as products, sales agents, pricing plans, and organizational structures. "It's not so much that there's several hundred codes needed," she often complains, "but that they are changing all the time."

She often cites as well the challenge her teammates have with information timeliness and accuracy. Overlapping customers and product catalogs from the imperfect divisions between company regions and business units force them to sink countless hours in deduplicating the basic reference information before the transactions can be tagged and aggregated.

Typical Business Questions (User Goals)

- Who is buying what products?
- How good is their experience with those products?
- How much do they spend on those products, and how could the company entice them to spend more?

Franklin in finance

Franklin is the company's manager of financial analysis, answering to the director of finance, and responsible for the work of 15 financial analysts with specialties by business unit, product families, and chart of account categories.

His official role is to ensure that all numbers reported to external parties, including the Securities and Exchange Commission (SEC), are complete and correct. This focus reflects the summary goal of the controller's office to provide complete and accurate accounting of the company's financial operations. Much of this work involves managing accrual rules for revenue recognition and expense rules for allocating capital costs. He also manages multiple "realignments" of categorization schemes for product, customer segment, and sales channels throughout the year.

Unofficially, he spends considerable time helping the business units design and implement custom recategorizations of financial figures so their execs can roll up sales and revenue as they prefer to see it.

His annual review typically focuses on the three largest restatements issued by finance during the prior year, and how his team helped detect and mitigate the root cause.

Focus of Franklin's Annual Review (Summary Goal)

- Describe the causes for the major financial restatements our company made this past year and how your team knows they will occur again.

Given his team's role in controlling financial reporting, his upstream business partners are primarily owners of the line-of-business systems, a revenue journaling application, and a set of reconciliation and cost allocation engines. Downstream we find corporate strategy, business unit analysts, and particularly vice presidents, as their compensation is determined directly by the figures Franklin's team adjusts.

Franklin finds himself constantly comparing numbers before and after reference code updates for his downstream business partners. The reference code that gives him the greatest challenge is the "countable" flag. Finance only includes products designated countable when it reports on changes in unit sales. These designations are controlled by business unit product managers who change them steadily as products age and new products take their place. Providing accurate unit counts given the changing categorization consumes much of his work day, so that he often works nights and weekends in order to finish reconciling ledger balances. "Those reconciliations cause me tremendous inconvenience," he laments, "as the raw figures get categorized from the encoding of local business systems to the standard coding for corporate reporting, especially for product catalogs, customer segments, and sales channel."

Data timeliness is always an issue for him because the deadline for monthly reconciliations is the seventh business day of each month, but runs for the revenue journaling and cost allocation engines sometimes do not complete until the fifth day.

Typical Business Questions (User Goals)

- What revenue reconciliation errors did the latest code updates for customer segment and sales channel create?
- What do last period's financial numbers look like when reported through each business unit's alternative product categorization scheme?
- How have the sales unit counts changed given the flagging for issues around countable and uncountable products?

An example of an initial backlog interview

Based on her user role modeling, Paula decided to hold the initial backlog interview with not just the project owner from corporate strategy but also the subject matter expert from finance. This section provides a transcript from that interview, with Paula's counterparts in the business named from their personas, namely Carla from corporate strategy and Franklin from financial analysis. During the interview Paula guides these two

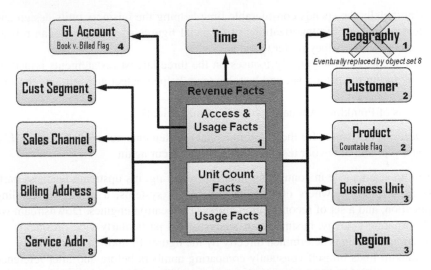

Numbers indicate order in which objects were added to the diagram during the intital backlog interview.
Arrows indicate dimensional data referenced by foreign keys within a fact table.

FIGURE 5.4

Business target model at end of sample project's initial backlog interview.

stakeholders through the process of enumerating the central business problems of the project, stepping them through a series of epics and themes to arrive at solid user stories. Each time Paula believes they have articulated any of these three types of statements successfully, she records it on the initial project backlog. Sometimes this backlog is a set of story cards as originally envisioned by the creators of Scrum, but more often it is an electronic spreadsheet. Table 5.2 portrays the backlog that resulted from this interview session as it appeared at the end of the conversation.

As a business intelligence architect, Paula is also listening for major metrics and qualifiers; when she hears one, she places it on a business target model that will be translated eventually into a star schema by her team's data architect. The business target model was started by the enterprise architect and shows just the business entities that the users will need in their dimensional analysis model and how they join together. Figure 5.4 represents Paula's star schema as it appeared at the end of the interview. Once fully elaborated, this business target data model will express to business and IT alike the interconnected nature of the required facts and dimensions with an economy that even user stories cannot match. For data warehousing projects, both a story backlog and a business target model are absolutely necessary to move on to the next step in project definition.

To keep the process at the right level of detail and moving forward, Paula captures important information that does not fit within the user story format on "constraint" cards, as introduced in the prior chapter. These may well be simply additional lines on the initial backlog. Paula's constraint cards from this interview are displayed at the bottom of Table 5.2.

Table 5.2 Initial Project Backlog for the Sample Project

Item	Primary	Epic	Theme	User Story	Full Text
1	CS	**Drill into revenue by customer, product, locations, and business units.**			As a Corporate Strategy analyst, I need a dashboard of monthly billings with full customer demographics and product details where I can discover...
2	CS		Business Marketing - Eastern Region		...for Business Marketing Group's Eastern Region...
3	CS			Who's subscribing to what services?	...the types of customers subscribing to each service, so we can better design promotions by product type.
4	CS			How long do they stay with us? (How long do customers generate access revenue for us?)	...the length of our business relationships, so we can identify the type of subscriber that is most likely to switch out of our services.
5	CS			How much did they spend?	...the pattern of billings over time, so we can identify the type of customer most likely to reduce spend by downgrading service.
6	CS			Where we should build out better service because we've got demand? (Where do we have high revenue per user, so that we know where we might upgrade the service?)	...the locations where we have the highest revenue, so we can glean some notion of where we need to expand service capabilites.
7	CS		Business Marketing - Central Region		...for Business Marketing Group's Central Region...
8	CS			{Repeat stories from BMG/Eastern}	{Repeat stories from BMG/Eastern}
9	CS		Business Marketing - Western Region		...for Business Marketing Group's Western Region...
10	CS			{Repeat stories from BMG/Eastern}	{Repeat stories from BMG/Eastern}
11	CS		Consumer Marketing - Eastern Region		...for Consumer Marketing Group's Eastern Region...
12	CS			{Repeat stories from BMG/Eastern}	{Repeat stories from BMG/Eastern}
13	CS		Consumer Marketing - Central Region		...for Consumer Marketing Group's Central Region...

(Continued)

Table 5.2 Initial Project Backlog for the Sample Project (Continued)

Item	Primary	Epic	Theme	User Story	Full Text
14	CS			{Repeat stories from BMG/Eastern}	{Repeat stories from BMG/Eastern}
15	CS		Consumer Marketing - Western Region		...for Consumer Marketing Group's Western Region...
16	CS			{Repeat stories from BMG/Eastern}	{Repeat stories from BMG/Eastern}
17	CS	**Identify frustrating customer episodes that lead to service downgrades**			As a Corporate Strategy analyst, I need a dashboard of usage measures from monthly billings with full customer demographics and product details where I can discover...
18	CS			{Same breakouts by Business Units and Regions (Billing Systems)}	...for Business Marketing Group's Eastern Region...
19	CS			Which "large data users" have significantly downsized their service?	...accounts with large usage that are significantly reducing spend, so we know who to build usage histories for.
20	CS			What's the profile of the large data events in the 3 mos before they left?	...usage details for accounts with large usage that are reducing spend, so we can identify the usage that's frustrating these downsizing accounts.
21	CS			What's the typical product that these events occurred with?	...the product mix downsizing, large-data accounts are using, so we can identify products that are frustrating users into leaving our network.
22	CS			What's the location that these events occurred in?	...the service locations for the large data usage for these downsizing accounts, so we can identify portions of the network that need improvement.
23	FA	**Drill into unit counts by customer, product, locations, and business units.**			As a finanical analysts, I need a dashboard of unit counts from monthly billings with full segment, channel, and product details, where I can discover...
24	FA			{Same breakouts for Business Units and Regions (Billing Systems)}	...for the Business Units and Regions (taken individually or altogether)...

		Who's buying what?
25	FA	...the typical purchases of specific customer cohorts...
26	FA	...expressed in current or past business unit assignments for customers	...for Business Units as assigned at transaction time or as later re-aligned
27	FA	...expressed in current or past strategy/legacy indicators for product	...for products as categorized at transaction time or as later re-aligned
28	FA	...filtered for countable unit indicators	...for only those product flagged as countable.

Constraint Cards

29	Need revenue analytics by *standardized*--not local system--product codes
30	Need both access and usage revenues (usage reflects subscriber activity)
31	Must make history on customers optional
32	Must use the standardized product codes in effect at the reporting time point requested by an analysis
33	Need to report using standard or alternative product hierarchies
34	Must allow each business unit-region combination to have distinct sales channel rules.
35	Postal addresses need to be scrubbed and standardized.

The following transcript provides readers that are new to data warehousing a good glimpse of how complicated user stories for data integration projects can be. Note that when the discussion does not identify epics, themes, and stories, it is still a valuable source for design constraints, priorities, or benefits the users are hoping to gain from their stories. This section provides some other aspects on the process, apparent in this conversation, immediately following the transcript.

Framing the project

Corporate strategy (Carrie): We're experiencing serious revenue declines in some major markets. Corporate strategy has done some initial analysis using two consolidated snapshots from the billing systems that span the last 6 months. We think it has something to do with tablet computers and large-volume data users' who get frustrated with our 3 G network's data rates. But that's just what my team of three could deduce from working with the data for a few weeks. We need a dashboard with clean, daily information to find out for sure. That dashboard would let us design some product bundling and network enhancements to improve customer satisfaction. If we can zero in on the right problem, we can arrest or even reverse whatever is driving away our subscribers.

Project architect (Paula): Why do you want to partner with us folks in information technology to work on this problem? Your staff knows SAS pretty well.

CS: We need IT's help because the data cleansing and integration required are beyond what the four of us in corporate strategy can handle. We did a very imperfect job at it during our little prototype. Plus, once we get a way to see what's going wrong by locations, we'll need to follow the trends to see if our corrective actions have had the impact we intended. The four of us don't have time enough to repeat all that data crunching regularly.

PA: You remember from our agile class that product owners have different levels of user stories, right? What you just expressed sounds to me like an "epic": *Drill into revenue over time by geographic regions.* I'll start a list of user stories and build it out as we talk. (Item 1 in Table 5.2.) I can also draw a business target model of the information your users will need for performing this analysis. I've already placed revenue, geographies, and time on it. (Objects labeled with a "1" in Figure 5.4.) Arrows show which type of information points to another as a reference.

CS: I understand the drawing, and I can see already that we'll need to add product and customer demographics for breaking down the revenue numbers.

PA: Let me note that on both the story list and the target model. (She updates user story line 1 and adds business target model object set 2.) Which of our two business units do you need this capability for? Consumer or business marketing group?

CS: We have erosion in both, although I think it's for different reasons. In consumer accounts, I think people are getting frustrated trying to watch movies via the cellular connection on their tablets. They upgrade their home Wi-Fi networks and then cancel the data plan on the tablet. For business, it's probably tablet users with big email attachments that are changing their daily habits. They wait until they find a Wi-Fi hotspot before trying to do email. Of course, when they switch to Wi-Fi, we lose out on data transport revenues.

PA: Of the two, which business unit would be most important for you to understand first?

CS: Probably business marketing because that's fewer customers to contact. We can change pricing and bundling by just sending out a memo to the sales force. We have to link changes in consumer marketing to advertising campaigns and regulatory notices.

PA: Okay, business marketing comes before the consumer market group. I'll maintain that ordering as we fill out the backlog of user stories. How about the three regions? Each has a separate billing system and thus a different pile of uniquely formatted data we need to bring over to you. We won't be able to put them all online at once. What order do you want to understand them in?

CS: I'd go in the order of greatest revenue, so eastern, central, and western.

PA: Often when we're trying to organize user stories for a project, we talk about the "minimally marketable features"—divisions within a backlog of functions the business wants that can be justified separately. These often define a series of major releases that will make up the overall project. Do the notions of business units and the separate billing systems combine in any way to suggest minimally marketable features to you?

CS: Let me think. What if the data mart allowed us to see what kind of customers downsized or disconnected by spend brackets and geographies for just the business marketing group in the eastern region? Yeah, that'd be worth paying for all on its own. We've got major slippage in that market. If we could slow revenue erosion there just by 20 or 30%, it'd probably pay for 50 of these projects.

PA: Super. Let's try using the combination of business unit and billing system to define themes underneath this epic then. I've used the combination of business unit and region to define some themes on the backlog. (Table 5.2, items 2, 7, 9, 11, 13, and 15.) To reflect your priorities, I've placed all the themes for business marketing first and then consumer marketing. With each of those, I've ordered the themes by eastern, then central, and finally western regions. I'll also add both those components to the business target model. (Object set 3.) What do you think? Do these two artifacts cover what you need?

CS: That's going to work as far as this particular crisis goes. But there's a ton of stuff we can learn once we have all the company's revenue from the various billing systems in one place, prepped for analysis. We've got an old data mart now, the Corporate Management Reporting application, but it has only aggregated data. It only goes down to product group, not to the standardized product codes. And it has no customer information at all so we can never answer basic questions about who's subscribing to what services, how long they stay with us, how much they spend, and where we should build out better service because we've got demand. Without answers to those questions, we can't figure out what's happening to revenue in any region.

PA: Those sound like good user stories. Let me add them to the stories on our backlog, underneath each theme (Items 3–6). Also you said *standardized* product codes. I maintain a set of "constraint cards" that help the team remember details. Let me create one here for that notion (Item 29). Now what about the fact that there's two kinds of spend—monthly access fees versus per-unit charges for usage?

CS: We need them both. In general, falling monthly access reflects subscribers who disconnect a service as a whole. Falling per-unit usage charges reflect a decline for a customer using services they maintain an access subscription for.

PA: Let me note both access and usage charges on another constraint card (Item 30). I'll also note that in the *revenue* box on the business target model. We'll have to handle those two sets of metrics differently because one of them needs to link to activities.

Finance is upstream

PA: When we did our user role modeling session by phone last week, you mentioned we'd have some requirements from finance. What's going to be the priority between corporate strategy's needs and those of finance?

CS: Priority's not the issue. Finance is upstream from us. They groom the revenue numbers and control the definition of products. They help the business units clean up their customer hierarchies. You folks in IT need to get those editing rules from finance if you're going to get the fundamental data right. Otherwise corporate strategy will get some muddy results that won't reconcile when we slice and dice the revenue numbers.

PA: Okay. I'm hearing that the project primary goals come from corporate strategy, but we've got to fulfill some objectives for finance first.

CS: Yeah, but you've got to get the corporate strategy analysts some info right away because the company is hemorrhaging subscribers and revenue.

PA: So, I'm hearing corporate strategy wants revenue by all customers, products, and locations with really clean data taken from all six billing systems put online in a hurry.

CS: Yes. We want it all, we want perfect, and we want it now.

PA: You're not smiling.

CS: Because I'm serious. We can't wait very long for these answers. We're losing 10% of our subscribers per quarter in some major urban areas.

PA: Will you accept some compromises in order to get approximate answers sooner rather than later?

CS: It depends on the tradeoffs, I suppose.

PA: That's what project architects like me are supposed to do—explain the choices and work with the business to identify a way to get to your end goal one a step at a time.

Finance categorizes source data

PA: Let's find out from finance how his team contributes to the numbers you're getting now. Franklin, your group is corporate strategy's upstream data provider. They say IT needs to understand the manual adjustments you folks make for them so that we can duplicate that logic in the transformation code we'll build.

Financial analysis (Franklin): I think that's right. We add general ledger accounting to revenue data before it goes to corporate strategy. We spread quarterly charges out across months, which result in the difference between booked versus billed revenue. Also, probably most importantly for corporate strategy, we use reference tables to add several categorization schemes so that revenue from all the business units and regions can be consolidated into a single reporting set.

PA: I'm hearing you'll need general ledger accounts on the business target model. They include the booked versus billed flags, don't they? Let me add that (Object 4). What are the categorizations you just mentioned?

FA: There are three primary ones. We have reference tables for customer segmentation, product code standardization, and sales channel assignment. We manage all of them carefully because they control both of the major types of financial reporting we do. First, we report internally on the performance of business units and divisions. Executive compensation depends on those numbers, so everybody in management is watching every adjustment finance makes to the reference tables for these categories. The second is reporting to external parties, including the SEC, regulatory agencies, and Wall Street analysts. Erroneous changes to those reference tables will force us to later restate revenues and earnings, which leads to all kinds of dreaded audits and investigations.

Customer segmentation

PA: Sounds like our warehouse is going to have to provide an audit trail to every change made then.

FA: Yeah, but be careful—we don't want all that history most of the time when it comes to customer segmentation. Segmentation categorizes "who" a customer is. It has labels such as "Young & Wireless," "Suburban Spenders," and "Mature Mid-Techs." [Nielsen 2011] The segmentation reference table is populated by a special application we run against customer accounts. It uses several purchased data sets as inputs and considers each customer's product mix and monthly spending patterns before assigning a result. The problem here is that the segment assigned to any given customer may change many times throughout the year as they alter their habits. We have over 150 million customer accounts, and when you multiply that by a resegmentation every month or two, the whole mess gets way too big to work with. For 99% of what we do with these data, we need either the current categorization or the one at the end of the prior accounting year. Everything else between those two points is just noise that slows down our analysis.

CS: But because corporate strategy will need those intermediate points for some of our research, please make it available for us as an option.

PA: I better write a constraint card for "Must make full history on customers optional" (Item 31). Also, because the customer segment sounds like it changes often, independent of other customer attributes, we should probably draw it as a separate notion from the customer dimensions on the business target model (Object 5).

Consolidated product hierarchies

FA: Product codes are different. We work with their history all the time. You probably know that we have a different product catalog for each billing system, with a lot of overlaps and contradictions between them. We consolidate these six product catalogs into a single reference table that represents the corporate rollup. We net out all the overlaps and add to the resulting product items an additional, standardized "product code." We then categorize the product codes into a standard hierarchy with finance-created terms such as product class, group, and family. We also add a "countable unit" flag for the big-ticket items that should be included in unit counts for management performance reporting.

PA: Let me note that on the product bubble of the target model…"countable units." (Part of object set 2.)

FA: Unfortunately for everyone, these products get realigned multiple times a year. The CEO and marketing decide some early adopter product families are now *strategic* products worth promoting like crazy or they declare some maturing products should be reclassified to be boring, old *legacy* products. Problem is, executives are tracking sales by product closely, and because every one of them picks a different reference point, finance needs to report numbers aligned to the product scheme that existed when they last took a reference snapshot, including the pattern of which products were strategic and which were legacy.

PA: I'm hearing that this warehouse must support more than just standardized product codes—it must provide data using the standardized coding scheme as of any arbitrary point in time. Let me add another constraint card for that (Item 32).

FA: Don't forget that we need to send performance figures to the business units organized by their particular "alternative hierarchies" each one of them prefers.

PA: That sounds like it still pertains to products, which we have on the target model, but let me add another constraint card for "alternative hierarchies" (Item 33).

Sales channel

FA: Then there's the reference table for sales channel. The channel tells you which part of our organization is responsible for the relationship with the customer. It determines which sales rep, regional director, and vice president gets dinged if revenue falls below a particular amount. We used to track the channel on customer records, but because the right channel assignment was getting changed with every regional reorganization, now we treat it as a notion independent of the customer identity. Plus, channel assignments for the business marketing group are determined by some really complicated rules that involve how big a customer company is, how they ordered their last product, and the mix of technology they're using, plus the level of spend between products. For example, a U.S. company spending mostly on bulk minute plans will move to a particular channel if they start spending more on data, but a completely different channel if they merge with a multinational.

PA: Are the business rules consistent between the regions?

FA: Hardly. Because channel traces back to the organization, each business unit and region maintain their own rollup scheme, and of course those schemes change all the time, just to make life interesting for those of us in finance.

PA: Then I'll write a constraint card for "Allow each business unit–region to have distinct channel rules" (Item 34). Because the channel sounds like it changes on a different schedule than either segment or customer attributes, we'll include it as another separate item on the business target model (Object 6).

Unit reporting

PA: I noticed a minute ago you two mentioned performance reporting based on "countable units." Units would be a new metric. Carla, why have you and I only been discussing revenue?

CS: We need countable-unit categorizations only to validate our data, like when we reconcile back to finance's numbers or link our recommendations back to what the VPs are tracking. Unit counts themselves don't correlate well enough with what customers spend to show us consumer behavior patterns, so we have to run our analysis upon revenue.

PA: Then it's finance and execs that need to look at unit counts in addition to revenue. Units seem to be a distinct set of metrics and suggest a whole set of user stories that will parallel the stories for revenue. So, let's create a new epic to serve as an umbrella for those stories (Item 23). Let me add "unit counts" to the target data model (Object 7). It will link up to the *countable* flag on product. If I look at the existing stories, "Who's buying what?" seems like it could make sense for unit counts as well, so I'll duplicate it under our new epic (Item 25). Franklin, finance is the party interested primarily in unit counts?

FA: That's right. And that's where we'll need to flip back and forth between different time points: current or past business unit assignments for customers, plus current or past strategy/legacy indicators for product. We'll also need to filter counts for countable unit indicators.

PA: Let me add user stories for those notions now (Items 26 through 28). Carla, what about the notion of "How long do subscribers stay with us?" Would you want to answer that using revenue or sale unit counts?

CS: I think that question would be better phrased in terms of billings, as in "How long do customers generate access revenue for us?" We will have to decide each time we do the analysis whether we should use min, max, or average length of service.

PA: And what about "Where we should build out better service because we've got demand?"

CS: That would be better worded as "Where do we have high revenue per user so that we know where we might need to upgrade the service?"

PA: Hmmm. I'll have to reword a couple of the revenue stories (Items 4 and 6).

Geographies

PA: Franklin, what about geographies? Does finance modify or categorize reference tables for locations?

FA: No, but keep in mind the difference between billing address and service location. Consumer marketing analysts tend to speak in term of billing address, that is, people's homes, because 95% or more of consumer cell phone usage is in their home markets. For business marketing, however, everything is tracked by service address, which is recorded in the revenue transactions as the location of the tower a call is originated upon. Billing address wouldn't work for a lot of businesses because the data services for, say, 300 delivery vans west of the Mississippi might be all billed to their holding company in Virginia, telling us nothing about which portions of our network folks are using.

CS: And service location is not a postal address like a billing location. It's a network location, which is defined by the equipment and circuits used to bring a signal to a particular termination point. It's way more specific than the area code or the first three digits of a phone number would indicate.

FA: Postal addresses are handled fairly well by the revenue system, although there's some duplicates due to slight variation in formatting such as "Str" or "St" for "street." The service locations come from a feed from the network management group, and they're kept very clean.

PA: Ooh, data quality. Sounds like I should write a constraint card reminding us that those postal addresses need to be scrubbed and standardized (Item 35). And now, we have two kinds of reference information for locations: service and billing. Because service location is structured differently than billing address, I'll include them as separate dimensions on the business target model (Object set 8). I'll have to replace that simple-mined *geography* object I put on there a while ago. Carla, is service location important for revenue analysis?

CS: Definitely. For the questions we have about falling revenue on big data events, we'll need service location to show us where customers are getting frustrated with their service.

Product usage

PA: I'm hearing another epic at work in what you just said. Up until now we've been talking about identifying *who* has disconnected or downsized. You've envisioned identifying these folks by drilling into the counts of services and the amount customers spend. But when you talk about where big data events occur, I hear you wanting to analyze data volumes and durations, not unit counts and spend.

CS: That's right. The overall objective for my part of the project is to figure out what's frustrating our customers so that we can change our product bundling and pricing, and even adjust areas of our network capacity. For that latter topic, we'll have to focus on the activity of "big data users," where usage is measured in minutes of use and/or megabytes of data transferred. All of it is available from revenue data because we detail the usage they were charged for on every bill we send them.

PA: Then I would suggest a new epic revolving around measures of usage. Could you take a stab at putting it into a user story format for me?

CS: Oh, how about "As corporate strategy, we need to identify frustrating customer episodes that lead to service downgrades so that we can better design our offerings and networks in order to reverse the revenue loss we're experiencing."

PA: That's definitely sounds big, like an epic. Let me add that to our story list (Item 17). Now envision that IT has enabled you to do exactly that. You've sat down in front of the dashboard we've provided. What are the questions you're going to try to answer?

CS: We've already been working on them: Which "large data users" have downsized their service significantly? What's the profile of the large data events they undertook in the 3 months before they downsized? What's the typical product and location that these events occurred in?

PA: Those sound like user stories. Let me add them now—feel free to correct the way I word the "so that" motivations I'm recording (Items 19 through 22). Now is the information available for each business unit and billing system different enough that you think we should work on each combination separately, like in the revenue epics?

CS: Correct.

PA: That gives us some "themes" to place in between the epic and user stories you just articulated. Let me update our story list (Item 18). Also, the epic for usage measures is lower in priority than those for revenue, but higher than the unit counts that finance is waiting for?

CS: Yep.

PA: I should add usage measures to our business target model too (Object 9). With all that, do you think we've covered all the major information that your two departments will need to explore using this dashboard?

CS: I'm sure there's hundreds more user stories possible because revenue and usage information is central to so many of the questions we get asked every month. But you've captured all the basic building blocks that we need to work with. If there's something we've overlooked, it will be minor.

FA: Yes, if finance could access a dashboard matching the business target model you've drawn we'll cut in half the time we hassle with reconciliations every month.

PA: Well, then we've got our initial backlog. We can move on to the next step in project planning.

Observations regarding initial backlog sessions

Knowing when an initial backlog is "complete enough" will be a judgment call requiring consensus between both the architect and stakeholders. As long as it covers the major measures of interest and fully enumerates the qualifiers the business partners want to analyze them by, the early project team can be reasonably assured that no earth-shaking requirements have been overlooked. Moreover, if a major user need has been overlooked, the product owner and stakeholders will be more likely to think of it by working with the team and reviewing application increments than reviewing paper listings of requirements.

Sessions such as the one in the aforementioned transcript generate exactly the sizable list of functional requirements that IT needs to begin high-level design, including logical models for the target data structures. As the project progresses, the team leads, including the project architect, will meet with the product owner on many occasions. Because those sessions will occur after the project has officially started, the team's systems analyst and data architect will also attend. Their presence will allow further discussions of requirements to occur iteratively with elements of architecture and design included.

The project architect conducts an initial backlog interview just to get the project defined well enough to secure funding and engage a fuller team. The next step toward that end will be to convert some or all of the initial backlog into actionable "developers stories." Developer stories result when agile warehousing teams decompose user stories one step further to address the major components of their data architecture. The next chapter examines that decomposition process. To close this chapter, we should take a moment to identify the major lessons for agile warehousing practitioners detectable in this transcript initial backlog interview.

Sometimes a lengthy process

These conversations can be long, sometimes requiring many days, depending on the breadth of the business problem and the number of subject matter experts who must participate.

Note that the project architect is critical to this process and that she is up against a stiff challenge. Much of her facilitation is spent trying to find the right balance between detail and speed. She must elicit enough detail to define, constrain, and scope the project. Some discussion of details will be necessary to achieve that purpose, but these sessions can easily get mired in discussions of business process details, such as information life cycles and data transformation rules. If the project architect allowed the initial backlog interview to indulge in excessive detail, the process would steer back to a waterfall-style requirements-gathering process, the project would have a delayed start, and the business value of the application would be diminished greatly by the time users received its services.

To keep the interview short, it works best to keep the conversation in business language as much as possible, replacing talk of fact and dimension tables with the notions of measures and qualifiers that will be used to analyze them. In our example, the project architect refrained from identifying measures as slowly changing Type 1, 2, or 3 because those are design details rather than requirements. The project architect does have a powerful tool, however, to bring an unfruitful discussion to an end: She can ask "Do the details we're discussing now help define an epic, theme, user story, or another element to place on the business target model?" If not, the team should record the topic on a constraint card and move on. The team can return to that topic when it comes time to build out a story that is affected by the constraint.

Yet the process cannot be overly abbreviated if the project is going to have a cohesive backlog at its center. The project architect will have to use her judgment as to when the backlog is sufficiently complete. She may have to insist that the conversation continue, bucking pressure to "wrap it up" coming from both the business and IT management side.

The initial interview may well require more than the project's product owner. In our example, corporate strategy did not understand all the ways that finance preprocessed the information and was dismissive of the requirements that pertained only to that other department. Sufficient representation of all key stakeholders will be essential. Here too, the project architect must use judgment to simultaneously include all relevant parties participating in the conversation, yet keep the group as small as possible so that the process does not take too long.

One challenge to keeping these interviews moving can be discussions of the source system. Subject matter experts can have a tremendous amount of detail to share about the business systems they've worked with over the years, especially older mainframe applications. Discussions of source details are necessary, but the architect can abbreviate them somewhat by focusing the conversation on whether a particular application's data has value or not. Value here is best defined as contributing to a metric or dimension on the business target model. If a source has value, but is complicated, a constraint card stating that the source must be researched further will suffice. This alternative is especially handy during initial backlog interviews when the systems analyst who can profile data has not yet joined the team.

Sources are often difficult to understand. Thus when the usability of certain data sets cannot be answered immediately, the team may have to adjourn so research can be done. Perhaps the developers will need to declare a Scrum "spike" and take a week to learn about a data source in depth. Staffing projects with a project architect who knows the company's data sources, however, will give the team a resource that will keep the need for such research adjournments to a minimum.

Detecting backlog components

As can be seen from the sample interview, subject matter experts can generate a tremendous amount of detail. The project architect has to listen carefully during these interviews because new stories, objects, and business target model components can get lost in the flood of concepts when SMEs talk intently about solving their business problems. Recordings and transcriptions of these interviews help tremendously because too much goes by too fast to capture it all by hand the first time. The architect must be able to review the discussion again later because subtle choices of wording can suggest whole new facts, dimensions, and stakeholders.

Given the flood of information, the project architect will need some good criteria in order to categorize user requests as epics, themes, or stories. Figure 5.5 presents some notions that might help. It includes a reference to the developer stories presented in the next chapter. Epics tend to be linked to categories of metrics. Placing analytics for these metrics online usually takes one or more releases. In our sample project, the epics were metrics that revolved about very different concepts: revenue versus unit counts versus "frustrated customers."

Themes tend to describe a "minimally marketable feature"—something that may not be a total set of metrics or a business solution on its own, but still a feature that has enough value to warrant a product release. These minimal marketable features can often be found where envision target data will differentiate most readily. With data integration projects, the key question to ask product owners for identifying themes is often: "If we put a given set of information online, what business value could it have all on its own? Can it represent a complete and independently appreciable step toward the larger goal?"

In our example, the consumer and business marketing groups had widely different types of commerce, and within the groups, each regional billing system represented a separate set of accounting books. These source-based divisions made the metrics within each intersection of business group and region separately understandable. In fact, the business had a compelling reason to regularly examine at each such division in isolation from the rest. Such data isolation boundaries frequently make good boundaries between themes.

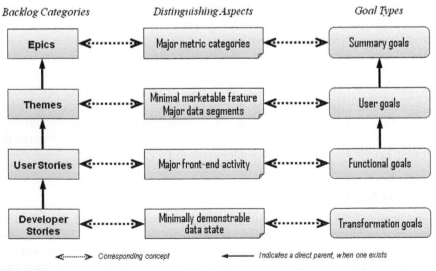

FIGURE 5.5

General functions of backlog items in data integration projects.

Finally, user stories for data integration projects are often detectable when stakeholders begin discussing what they will do with a dashboard once the data set for a given theme is in place online. Note that the user stories produced during these interviews do not have to be perfect because the team will get at least three other chances to consider each story. The first will occur immediately after the initial backlog interview when the data architect joins the early team in order to convert user stories into developer stories and developer stories into a data model. The second chance will be when the team leads and product owner groom the top of the backlog before each story conference. The third will be the story conference with the full team at the start of each construction sprint.

Knowing that the stories will be revisited substantially as the project proceeds, the project architect can be a bit more comfortable limiting excessively detailed discussion during the initial product backlog interviews. Again, the goal of the initial backlog session is only to verbalize epics, themes, and stories with enough detail to generally define, constrain, and scope the project.

Managing user story components on the backlog

The full, three-part format of a user story can be sometimes awkward to manage when working with many stories at once. When authoring user stories, business partners can focus on a given business problem and a given user role for a considerable time while they envision how that person will solve his problem. This mind-set places the focus on the "what" of the stories and leaves the "who" and "why" fairly static for long portions of the conversation. Business users can forget that those two components belong in every story, so the architect will have to occasionally probe for whether the product owner has moved on to a different role or business problem without mentioning it.

Because "who" and "why" can be static for long stretches on the backlog, the project architect will need a shorthand for writing user stories on a spreadsheet or other listing that can highlight the "what" that is changing. The backlog listing from our sample project has such elements. It sets up the "who" at the epic level and uses ellipses to connect it to the "what" portion of the user stories below. Similarly, ellipses on the "whats" can connect them to a "why" clause at the end of a section for an epic or theme. Establishing some system of shorthand for user stories before the initial backlog interview will be important to keeping the resulting listing uncluttered.

Prioritizing stories

A major responsibility of the project architect is to not only decompose this monolithic request into separately appreciable deliverables, but must also get the product owner to express a preference for their ordering. Many customers will insist that they want all data from the source systems, perfectly integrated, in a few short weeks. Such an attitude can be very hard to reverse and, if left uncorrected, will paralyze the development sprints. Accordingly, project architects must get product owners to start thinking about breaking the project into small pieces and prioritizing them, even as early as the initial backlog sessions.

The easiest technique for getting product owners to begin prioritizing is to uncover dependencies between the data components. The project architect can ask, for example, what reference codes and category adjustments occur upstream of usable information. This helps the product owner become more realistic because no one can argue that dependencies do not trump preferences. If the project does involve source-based divisions within the metrics, as discussed earlier, identifying the themes with those divisions will position them as another readily understandable place to segment the project for prioritization.

Prioritizing at epic and theme levels is usually sufficient to get the project framed properly. Many stories often stay contained within themes, and these can be prioritized in small batches as the development work for a given theme approaches. In this way, the product owner needs only to worry about general ordering down to the theme level and detailed ordering for only the theme at the top of the backlog.

Those situations where the product owner insists that two or more epics are equally crucial often signify that the project is bigger than one Scrum team can manage and that there may be a business case for acquiring more development resources.

Unfortunately, all notions of how difficult the individual epics and themes will be to deliver cannot be removed entirely from the initial backlog conversation. Product owners will be confronted with prioritizing between some themes that will be fast to deliver but not as valuable as other items that will take longer to build. The project architect role in these dilemmas will be to provide a notion of fast or slow to complement the product owner's notion of valuable or not. She must also be persistent on getting a priority decision from the product owner in these situations because one team will find it impossible to deliver two big themes at once.

Summary

An *initial project backlog* of user stories is essential to getting an agile warehousing project started. The stories on this list should come from the product owner and sometimes a couple of other key user groups. Because the backlog allows project estimation, and estimation in turn supports project funding, these stories often have to be gathered before Iteration 0 of the sprint and before the full team is assigned. A project architect is a good choice for leading this preproject effort. He should declare an Iteration −1 to create the time to gather the initial project backlog. In addition to that backlog, the architect will also want to derive from the initial interviews a *business target model* of the fact and dimensional entities needed to solve the product owner's analytical problem. This model will later support the work of the data architect and systems analyst during the project's Iteration 0. The business target model and the initial project backlog will evolve as the initial conversation with the product owner progresses. In order to keep the initial backlog interviews to a reasonable length, the project architect will need to employ several techniques for recording information quickly and deferring debate over nonessential details, which can be resolved later during the development iterations.

Developer Stories for Data Integration

6

Why are user stories too coarse for planning data integration projects?
What techniques can we use to discover our project's "developer stories?"
How can we tell if we have a good developer story?

After amassing an initial project backlog of user stories, as presented in the prior chapter, data warehousing teams with a significant amount of data integration work will still not have a list of work items that fit nicely into the small time-boxed development iterations of Scrum. One further level of decomposition between Scrum's user story and development tasks is necessary. Calling this intermediate requirements device a "developer story" indicates its conceptual position halfway between a user story and a developer's work unit. Data integration teams that create developer stories by intersecting each user story with the data warehouse's high-level architecture will transform their user story backlogs into project backlogs that the product owner can still understand and that the developers can also schedule and delivery iteratively.

Data integration teams that employ developers stories will need to evolve their standard story evaluation approach to one that incorporates the data warehouse's data architecture. This evolution will transform the INVEST test for user stories into demonstrable, independent, layered, business valuable, estimable, refinable, testable, and small—a combination known as DILBERT'S test—for data integration developer stories. For any candidate developer story that proves to be too large, there are several secondary techniques for decomposing them one step further. At the conclusion of this decomposition process, the team will have a project backlog of developer stories they can estimate and then assemble into an agile project plan, a process that is described in the next chapter. The techniques employed for defining the initial project backlog of developer stories can also be employed during the development iterations to transform any new or altered user stories from the product owner into actionable work items for the developers.

Agile Data Warehousing Project Management.
DOI: http://dx.doi.org/10.1016/B978-0-12-396463-2.00006-5
© 2013 Elsevier Inc. All rights reserved.

Why developer stories are needed

As defined in earlier chapters, user stories identify small pieces of the business requirements that, among other attributes, can be delivered within one iteration. Data warehousing projects that focus on building end-user dashboards find it easy to define user stories because (a) today's business intelligence (BI) tools allow developers to make big changes to a dashboard's functionality with relatively small effort and (b) even small changes on the dashboard change the way the business can see its operational circumstance, so delivering business value is a straightforward process.

Teams working data integration projects do not find delivering business-appreciable value so easy, however. Figure 6.1 suggests the fundamental challenge they face. The main user story depicted in this example was simple to express, as shown in the sidebar. An abbreviated logical model of the star schema required to fulfill this user story is shown at the bottom of the diagram. Major deliverables needed to populate or to provide end-user access to the data elements in that logical model are shown above as a series of work units leading to the delivery of each logical data component. Shaded deliverables can be thought of "load modules," which include not only a component of transformation code, but also the target data structures and—if the tables are already loaded—the data they contain. In this example,

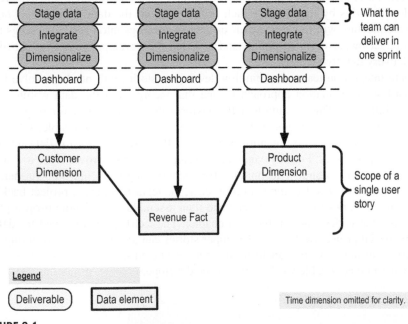

FIGURE 6.1

Most data integration stories cannot be delivered with only one sprint.

the load modules associated with each logical table (a) extract data from various sources into a staging area, (b) integrate data from multiple sources into a normalized set of tables holding a coherent notion of each business entity, and (c) denormalize data into a dimensional model. Each data target, especially the central revenue fact table, will also require some dashboarding to allow users to analyze the information it contains.

SAMPLE USER STORY EMPLOYED FOR THIS CHAPTER

"As an analyst in finance, I want to decompose monthly revenue figures by customer and product so that I can identify the key drivers of our revenue changes."

Dashed lines in the diagram indicate roughly the functionality that the development team can complete with each iteration. Whereas it will take 12 deliverables to provide the target data objects required by the user story, the team can complete only 3 such deliverables per iteration. If the user story listed previously represents the smallest notion of an acceptable end product for business users, this development team will be unable to deliver a business value for end users with every iteration of their project. The product owner will have no user story to review during the user demo until the end of the fourth sprint. Making the customer wait for four sprints for a deliverable does meet the agile principle of delivering working software frequently. The business will not perceive that it is constantly receiving value from the development team. Moreover, waiting so long for a review will deny the team the feedback it needs to stay aligned with the business needs it is supposed to fulfill.

Nor can a team simply switch to organizing its work in terms of the developer tasks that Scrum uses as the next level decomposition for user stories. Developer tasks are the small technical work items needed to deliver a user story. They represent small objectives, such as "update the physical data model," "code an initial load module," and "write supporting shell scripts." If the developers tried to present developer tasks as deliverables during the sprint demos, the business-minded product owner would not be able to comprehend much of what he was reviewing or understand how it contributes to the analytical services requested for the end users.

Some data warehousing professionals believe the situation depicted in Figure 6.1 makes agile methods a poor choice for business intelligence products. Another camp, including the author of this book, believes that the situation requires only a small change in the way teams employ user stories and the product owner's expectations. The small change needed regarding user stories is to decompose them one step further and to use the work units resulting from that breakdown for identifying and scheduling the labor to be bundled into development iterations. These new work units will be intermediate deliverables, not yet demonstrable to the project's full community of stakeholders. The product owner, then, needs to modify slightly the acceptance criteria he follows during the sprint demos so that instead of looking for system enhancements that can each be placed directly into production, he will also accept deliverables that represent major steps toward finished components for end users. With those two small adjustments, data warehousing teams will be able to continue with an agile approach based on iterative delivery and high customer involvement. Both developers and the product owner of a team naturally want to keep the number of intermediate steps required to as small a number as possible—perhaps just a few per user story—so the right level of abstraction for this intermediate container would be something close to the deliverables identified in Figure 6.1.

Introducing the "developer story"

Given that users stories are too large for data integration teams to deliver in single sprints and that developer tasks are an unworkable substitute, agile data warehousing practitioners require an intermediary work container called a "developer story." In data integration projects, a developer story is a unit of work that (a) can be accomplished in a single sprint, (b) represents a major step toward delivering a user story, and (c) is still understandable by the product owner.

Developer stories are called "stories" because each is linked closely to a user story and is also expressed in a single sentence that the product owner can comprehend. Unlike user stories, however, developer stories are authored by the developers, not the product owner. Most often, the developers write these developer stories to describe an important step that data of a warehouse or data mart take in its journey from operational source system to the end-user's analytical dashboard. This orientation was visible in Figure 6.1, which, for each target data object, has information moving from source system to a staging area, then into an integration area, next into a dimensional model, and finally into a dashboard. By writing developer stories as steps in data's journey to the end-user's application, developers remain just barely understandable to the product owner. By providing a simple roadmap for that journey, such as shown in Figure 6.1, the team will enable the product owner to follow along as data move steadily forward. Of course, a small amount of orientation for the product owner covering the macro architecture of a data warehouse may be required at first to make such roadmaps meaningful.

At the conclusion of each iteration, the team can provide a window onto data as it is now stored at a given waypoint along that roadmap. Such a window allows the product owner to review the information and accept or reject the developer story based on the data quality the team has achieved. With both a graphic roadmap of data's journey toward the dashboard and a view of the information at each step along the way, developer stories become largely intelligible to the product owner in a way that completely technical developer tasks are not. By representing progress toward an end-user goal, the completed developer story will then represent a tangible amount of business value to the product owner, allowing him to feel that he is constantly receiving value from the development team. The developer stories are still reviewed by the product owner at the end of each iteration so that the team continues to get the feedback it needs to stay aligned with the business. With the product owner still involved closely with the team and the team still delivering incrementally, developer stories allow data integration projects to be pursued with an agile approach.

Format of the developer story

As described in Chapter 2, the format for a user story is

As {a particular user role in the enterprise}…
…I want to be able to {perform this function with the application}…
…so that the organization benefits {in a specific way}.

Agile data integration teams should follow a similar template for developer stories in order to keep them consistent. A starting template for developer stories would be as shown in the following table. Teams with differing degrees and types of data integration work may well evolve the actual template they use.

Developer Story Component	Approximate Clause in User Story Template
This {this particular data load module},	"who"
will receive {this new set of features},	"what"
so our product owner can validate data loaded into {this target table(s)}, which further completes {this particular user story}.	"why"

The following list provides an example of a developer story from every level of data transform shown in Figure 6.1. These developer stories depict data flowing between the waypoints along the path laid out for product dimension data. Components from the template are set apart using braces. The user story for this sample developer story is abbreviated somewhat to save repetition.

"The {Stage Product Data} module will receive {the ability to detect and load only changed records} so our product owner can validate {that the warehouse is capturing the product records just added or changed in the operational system}, which further completes the {'…decompose monthly revenue figures by customer and product…' user story.}"

"The {Integrate Product Data} module will receive {the ability to include the western region's product catalog for strategic products} so our product owner can validate the {company-consolidated view of all strategic products}, which further completes the {'…decompose monthly revenue figures…' user story.}"

"The {Dimensionalize Revenue Fact} module will receive {the ability link in products records} so our product owner can validate {revenue data by product in addition to customer}, which further completes the {'…monthly revenue…' user story.}"

"Our end-user application's {Product Dimension Dashboard} components will receive {a new strategic/legacy product flag in its query definition screens} so our product owner can validate the {sales orders for the newly added strategic product catalogs}, which should complete our '…monthly revenue…' user story.}"

Two aspects of this template make developer stories easier for the product owner to understand. First, each developer story links to a parent user story that the product owner himself authored for the developers. Second, he directly perceives some value for the business by reviewing the impact on data in a target data object. That value may only be one small step in a chain, but in each review data are meaningful as a component of a larger collection that the end users have requested.

Developer stories in the agile requirements management scheme

Developer stories add just one level more of detail below a user story so that when data integration is required, developers will have the requirements expressed in single sentences granular enough to encompass no more work than will fit within a sprint. When data integration is required and the team authors that work with developer stories, it is developer stories rather than user stories that get added to the project backlog and then enter into the development iterations. With the entire data integration work of a project expressed at that level, the team will have the atomic components needed to estimate the level of effort of a given user story properly and also to organize the project's work into separate iterations and releases.

Figure 6.2 provides a good summary view of where developer stories fit into the full stack of project definition objects that agile data warehousing/business intelligence (DWBI) efforts involve. Working top down, lines 1 through 3, which break portfolios into programs and projects, represent concepts originating outside of Scrum, usually defined by the corporation's program management office. Lines 4 through 6, which break epics into themes and user stories, are defined by Scrum, as is the development task in line 8. The developer story fits in between the user story and the development task and, for data warehousing, is only needed for the data integration work of a project.

Stacking depicted in the diagram is only a baseline, and not as absolute as Figure 6.2 might imply. For example, some teams allow themes to cross epics and releases, where other teams create repeated instances of a given theme so that each instance links only to one epic, as shown in this diagram. Note also that the developer story is now the object directly subordinate to iterations. Because it may take several iterations to deliver all the developer stories that make up a user story, user stories themselves are no longer required to fit within iterations. Most agile warehousing practitioners will still try to bundle complete user stories within a single release, however. For those portions of the project that do not require data integration, the developer story can be removed from this stack and user stories can once again be packaged within the iterations.

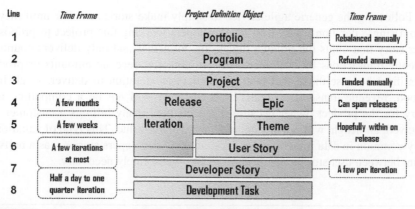

FIGURE 6.2

Hierarchy for agile project definition objects for data integration work.

Agile purists do not like developer stories

Agile practitioners from the world of generic application development often look askance at the notion of developer stories. The major objection they have to the notion is that it provides intermediate results that only the product owner can appreciate. It fails to place new business value online with each iteration, choosing to make two or more small steps forward before any result can be examined in the end-users' applications. The fact that a product owner can understand how several developer stories add up to a delivered user story is not sufficient because product owners cannot employ a developer story to solve real business challenges the way they can with the deliverables defined by user stories. Any feedback the product owner might provide will be theoretical and may well be missing important perspectives that only the wider user community can provide. These agile practitioners would instruct warehousing teams to simply divide up the work into smaller and smaller vertical slices until they identify slices so small that a warehouse team can go all the way from operational source to analytical dashboard in one iteration.

Whenever such a vertical slice of the warehouse can be defined, teams should certainly endeavor to deliver that slice because that path is completely faithful to the agile approach and will accrue all the benefits that incremental delivery to end users provides. This chapter will in fact describe some techniques for defining such small, vertical slices when we discuss secondary techniques for defining developer stories. However, as can be seen from Figure 6.1, there is a limit to how narrowly a team can define a vertical slice and still have it make sense. Say that revenue facts proved too hard to deliver in one iteration because they need a complex business rule for spreading annual payments from corporate customers across the accounting months. Also, assume that the product dimension required complex data integration of the company's six product catalogs that it would take more than an iteration just to load a single series of surrogate keys for that dimension.

Following the generic agile advice to simply make stories smaller until they fit into a single iteration might lead the developers working this project to propose a user story that omits the product dimension altogether and only delivers counts of revenue transactions by customer. They do not offer revenue amounts or product identifiers because those will take longer than an iteration to deliver. In all likelihood, revenue transaction counts by a customer will not be a compelling user story for the product owner because it reflects how many billings a customer has received, an insight without any compelling business value. This type of situation is very common in data integration projects, making developers stories—as a halfway point between user stories and developer tasks—absolutely necessary.

Initial developer story workshops

The need for developer stories on projects involving data integration (assumed hereon in this chapter) creates two important differences for starting warehousing projects from how generic agile development projects begin: the project will need a developer story workshop and it must add a data architect and a systems analyst to the lead-off team.

With developer stories becoming the atomic requirements management vehicle for a Scrum team when data integration is required, they join nonintegration user stories in comprising the project backlog. Consequently, developer stories make up an important portion of the predevelopment work included in many company's project release cycles. Referring back to Figure 5.1, the initial project backlog that the product architect and product owner compiled during Iteration −1 consists entirely of user stories, however. Authoring the full set of developer stories and then estimating the project based on that work will have to take place during an initial developer story workshop, which occurs in the latter portion of the inception phase of the release cycle, during Iteration 0.

Because developer stories link user stories to the major steps data take as it flows toward the end-user dashboards, the team will need to know the warehouse's high-level data and processing architecture in order to translate the project backlog into actionable developer stories. The architectures will not be defined until the data architecture and systems analyst joins the team, so these teammates will be essential for the initial developer story workshop.

The role of the data architect is the easiest to understand. As can be inferred easily from the hypothetical project portrayed in Figure 6.1, teams will need to consider their project's macro data architecture in order to convert user stories involving data integration into developer stories. The lead-off team working to define the project will need a data architect to join the effort because only he can state the exact layers of data schemas the warehouse will comprise.

The systems analyst, too, will be necessary for defining the initial set of developer stories. Interpreting user stories in terms of the project's macro data architecture is often only a first step. The secondary techniques require knowledge of the business rules. Typically, understanding the details and specifying the transforms for a warehouse's business rules are assigned to a role called the systems analysts.

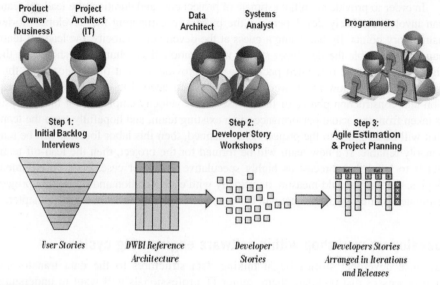

FIGURE 6.3

Defining work units for an agile data warehousing project.

Accordingly, the project's systems analyst will need to join the lead-off team during Iteration 0 as well so that the developer stories do not have to be redesignated later to account for business rules.

Figure 6.3 portrays the overall process of defining work units for an agile data warehousing project. The activity of the developer story workshops is shown in the middle. The product owner and project architect work to refine the collection of user stories coming out of the initial project backlog interviews. The data architect considers each story, using the project's macro data architecture to generate a collection of candidate developer stories comparable to those shown feeding the target objects in Figure 6.1. At that point the systems analyst can inquire with the product owner and project architect regarding the business rules the user story will involve. If significant, he can suggest to the data architect where some of the candidate developer stories will probably have to be split into two or more developer stories. Each of these resulting developer stories will still be demonstrable using newly transformed data. They may just pertain to different sets of columns that each hold the results of a different set of business rules. Because the resulting data can be inspected, the business rule-specific developer stories will still provide some notion of business value for the product owner, as required by the developer story template.

Once the project has been decomposed into a large number of developer stories, the product owner and project architect can prioritize them. The project owner will use the business value for an initial priority order. The project architect will provide guidance on sequencing them according to dependencies, such as the need to build out dimension tables before fact tables can be populated. He will also recommend which developer stories to elevate in the schedule in order to address any major risks facing the project.

In order to provide an initial estimate of project cost and duration, the lead-off team can involve the likely developers for the project in estimating the developer stories using story points. By hazarding a guess at the developer's velocity, the lead-off team can also assemble the developer stories into iteration-sized chunks, as shown on the right side of Figure 6.3. Such packaging will provide a count of iterations and thus a good notion of how many weeks and dollars are needed to complete the elaboration and construction phases of the release. If the velocity employed for this analysis is taken from the actual performance of an existing team, and hopefully from the team that will be assigned to the project being planned, then this labor forecast will be reasonably reliable. If a new team will be formed for the project, then the lead-off team needs to label this forecast as highly speculative. In either case, once development begins, the team should measure its velocity with each iteration and update the project estimate. Estimating the project will be examined in greater detail in the next chapter.

Developers workshop within software engineering cycles

Because developer stories begin linking data structures to the data transformation processes that populate them, senior IT professionals will want to understand where developer stories fit within the enterprise architecture planning processes software engineers like to employ. Table 6.1 presents such a process, one borrowed heavily from the Zachman framework but with elements from the domain of data warehousing clearly added as subrows for each architectural viewpoint. Standard enterprise architectural planning requires that developers analyze and plan in a particular sequence: business modeling, next data architectures, and then functional application architectures. It also stipulates that conceptual thinking precedes logical modeling, which in turn should come before physical modeling. [Spewak 1993] This ordering safeguards that the data designs of applications will support all relevant business entities within the corporation accurately and consistently. This ordering also ensures the many applications that will comprise the organization's processing capabilities across the decades will all support a single concept of company's data, avoiding any conflicts between the representation of information that could make a single, enterprise-wide interpretation of data impossible.

The predevelopment collaboration described among the product owner, project architect, data architect, and systems analyst follows the recommended ordering of development steps. During the initial project backlog interviews, the project architect accumulated a list of user stories and a business dimensional model. These artifacts both belong to the business architectural point of view and represent the functional and data portions of this viewpoint, as highlighted by the shading in Table 6.1. The fact that the business dimensional model and user stories were derived iteratively during the same set of interviews is immaterial to the framework and is, in fact, optimal from a pragmatic point of view in that it saves time and allows each artifact to double-check the findings recorded in the other.

With the initial project backlog interviews accomplished, the project architect involves the data architect to translate the user stories into developer stories. Reflecting upon the user stories and the application's likely source data, the data

Table 6.1 Developer Story Process Derivation Set in a Zachman Framework[a]

Viewpoint (Model Type)	IT Domain	Data Aspects[b]	Functional Aspects	DWBI Role
Business (Conceptual)	Enterprise Architecture	Business Entity Relationship Diagram	Business Process Model	**Project Architect**
	DWBI	**Business Dimensional Model**	**Business Questions (User Stories)**	
System (Logical)	Enterprise Architecture	Logical Data Model	Application Architecture	**Data Architect**
	DWBI	**Application Macro Data Architecture**	**Application Macro Process Architecture**	
		Dimensional LDM (Presentation Layer)		
		Relational LDM (Integration Layer)		
Technology (Physical)	Enterprise Architecture	Physical Data Model	System Design	Systems Analyst
	DWBI	Dimensional PDM (Presentation Layer) Relational PDM (Integration Layer)	ETL Flow Diagrams Source-to-Target Maps	

[a]Adapted for data warehousing from [Zachman 2011], versions 1992 and 1993.
[b]LDM, logical data model; PDM, physical data model.

architect drafts the project's macro data architecture. He may also at the same time begin sketching a logical data model of the application. This work falls clearly in the logical modeling viewpoint of the enterprise planning framework and occurs after conceptual considerations, as preferred. The lead-off team also includes the systems analyst, who is asked to reflect upon whether business rules processing require that a developer stories be decomposed further. That analysis still takes place within the logical viewpoint, but represents a functional portion of the system model so that processing architecture follows data architecture as the framework requires. The fact that, during the developer story workshop, the data architect and the systems analyst may iterate between themselves—or even with the project architect and product owner—as they interpret developer stories is again immaterial to the framework and advantageous as far as the quality of the results matter.

Data warehousing/business intelligence reference data architecture

Developer stories depend extensively on the macro data architecture that the data architect provides to the project. He may be the final word on the direction of this high-level design, but he does not start with a blank slate. Industry norms and even design standards set down by the enterprise architecture group within his company will provide 80% or more of the architecture he will recommend. Although the macro data architectures vary somewhat between companies, all of them are easily recognizable by DWBI professionals, so much so that data warehousing practitioners refer to the typical pattern they follow as a "data warehousing reference architecture." Because reference architecture is required for the first step in defining developer stories, a presentation of a baseline DWBI reference data architecture will facilitate the remaining discussion of this chapter.

The left half of Table 6.2 shows a fairly basic DWBI reference architecture. Data typically progress from top to bottom through the architectural layers represented in this diagram. This reference architecture should not be interpreted as a full-fledged *data architecture*. A complete data architecture specified how enterprise data will be managed within a single, organization-wide approach. It includes design guidances such as a formal naming standard, comprehensive data definitions, reusable data schemas, and physical data structures, plus precise data integrity rules. In contract, a DWBI reference data architecture specifies only the "layers" that exist within the data warehouse.

Each layer within the DWBI reference architecture represents physical data schemas that follow a logical and/or physical modeling paradigm specific to each layer. The staging layer's intent is to make source application data available for transformation. Accordingly, the physical model of the staging layer schemas matches closely that of the source, operational systems, although some provision may exist for meta data as well as before and after images for source records (which would make the element of the reference architecture a *persistent staging* layer). The integration layer provides a persistent workspace for merging comparable data from many source systems. Data architects typically employ a highly normalized modeling paradigm for this layer because it ensures that data supposed to be unique cannot be duplicated. The presentation layer holds data consumable by the business intelligence applications and typically takes a dimensional logical model and a star schema in its physical design, which holds extensively denormalized data. The semantic layer is a collection of join definitions the dashboards require to pull data from the presentation layer. They take whatever form the maker of the BI tool devises, but they typically look like relational models to the designers. Finally, dashboards may contain data structures of their own in order to speed up end-user application performance; often these are memory-resident dimensional data stores that many people refer to as "data cubes."

The right column of Table 6.1 depicts a few common variations on the DWBI reference architecture. The integration layer often includes tables populated with the company's master data elements, such as customer, products, staff members, vendors, and locations. So that the data structures that end-user applications draw upon can be created and adapted quickly, the presentation layer may be comprised all or in part of run-time only "virtual star schemas" that have no persistent physical aspect. For performance, maintenance, and security reasons, presentation layers are

Table 6.2 Typical DWBI Reference Data Architecture: Basic and Extended

Basic	Extended	
Source	Source	Operational Applications Providing Data to DWBI
Staging	**Staging**	Landing Area for Operational Data Extracted from Source Systems
Integration	**Cleansing**	Workspace for Parsing and Standardization of Data Elements such as Names and Addresses
	Integration (Master Data)	Persistent Workspace for Merging Key Data Elements such as Customer and Product. Typically Normalized and Sometimes Expected to Provide a "Single Version of the Truth" within the Enterprise
Presentation	**Presentation (Virtual Stars)**	Data in Star Schemas (Physicalized Dimensional Models), Ready to Consume by BI Dashboard Applications
	Departmental (Virtual Marts)	Subsets of the Presentation-Layer Star Schemas Prepared for Departmental Access in Order to Provide Greater Performance, Security, or Clarity
Semantic	**Semantic**	Dashboarding Tool's Internal Notion of Presentation Layer Objects and how they should Join. Often Masks Complexity, Renames, and Applies Lightweight Business Rules
Dashboards	**Dashboards**	Front-end Applications Displaying Presentation Layer Data

also commonly subsetted into departmentally specific data sets that the BI applications of the end users selectively draw information from.

The layers of the reference architecture make it easy to explain exactly why it takes special adaptations such as developer stories to make agile methods work for data integration projects. To deliver even a single element from source to dashboard requires the data integration team to build not just the dashboard, but also data structures and transform components for the four to six layers of data that must exist behind the dashboard. Delivering a dashboard element is like trying to build four or more integrated applications at once. It is often too much to accomplish in a few short weeks without resorting to a subdeliverable such as developer stories.

Forming backlogs with developer stories

A baseline DWBI reference architecture empowers a data architect and the rest of the lead-off team to easily translate user stories into a starter set of developer stories. The initial developer workshop results in a high-level data flow diagram for the project. An example of such a diagram is provided by Figure 6.4, which shows results for the

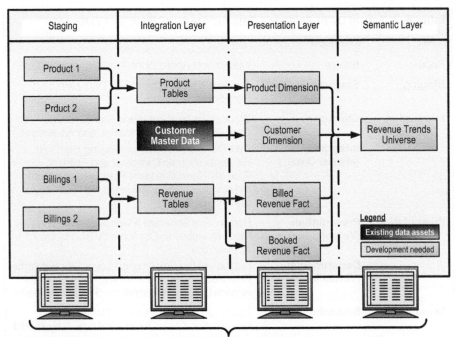

"Product Owner Portals" for Reviewing Results of Developer Stories

FIGURE 6.4

Developer stories derived from the sample user story.

sample user story we opened the chapter with. These data flow diagrams are planning artifacts for the team, meant solely to enable the participants to identify developer stories. Therefore they are drawn schematically to communicate the probable organization of the team's labor rather than in detail as they would be drawn if they were truly design diagrams. When the data architect drafts such a diagram, he is typically working at an aggregate, logical level of abstraction, where each box may represent one or several closely related data objects. He will decide in later design work whether each data object on this diagram translates into one or more physical tables. Fortunately, for an agile approach that prefers to operate with as much just-in-time requirements and design as possible, these schematic data flow diagrams often provide enough guidance that detailed design does not need to take place until the iteration in which each of the objects shown in this diagram will be constructed.

The sample in Figure 6.4 shows three separate threads, one each for customer, product, and revenue transactions. Each thread shows the progression of data across a set of swim lanes that correspond to the layers in the company's DWBI reference architecture. In the sample work presented in the last chapter, the enterprise architect informed the project architect that their company already has a repository of cleansed, integrated customer records, so, in Figure 6.4, the diagram's customer data thread starts in the integration layer with an existing data object. For product and revenue, the team will have to acquire its own data, so those threads start with "new" data objects drawn in the staging area. With these threads, the data architect reveals his plan to first integrate product and revenue records from the two source systems and then dimensionalize it. The semantic layer in the dashboard tool will link the resulting dimensions and facts to make it look like a single data object for the user's front-end applications.

The systems analyst exerted some influence on how the diagram for this example was drawn. Having learned from the enterprise and project architect that many of the company's customers actually pay for their services in quarterly installments, he realized that revenue data actually take two forms—what was billed to the customer every 3 months and the monthly break out of those quarterly payments. The data architect had suggested only a data object called revenue fact for the presentation layer. Realizing that the team would need to apply some complex business rules for allocating quarterly billings to monthly revenue bookings, the systems analysts asked that billed and booked revenue be represented as two separate data objects so that the team would treat them as separate developer stories. When the revenue data structures are later fully realized, each of these developer stories may pertain only to a distinct set of columns within a single physical table or may become a separate physical table each. Given that the developer workshop's data flow diagram serves as a work-planning rather than a design artifact, the data architect was happy to draw two data objects, understanding that he would be later free to realize the objects differently in the application's design if need be.

Once this schematic data flow diagram was complete, the team could see that viewing the single user story of our example through the lens of the DWBI reference architecture resulted in 11 developer stories. In practice, a multiplier of 10 to 1 or even higher is not uncommon for data integration projects. There is a further multiplier for translating developer stories into development tasks, as demonstrated earlier by Table 2.2, which listed the typical steps to building a common dimension object for a data warehouse. The combined effect of these two multipliers reveals why many teams that try to utilize generic Scrum can find data integration projects overwhelming. Working with only user stories, they may plan to deliver three or four stories per iteration, only to see the work explode by a factor of 200 or more tasks per story—far more than can be handled easily on a task board by a self-organized team of a half-dozen developers. Introducing the developer story and conducting development planning there bring the objectives of each iteration down to a reasonable number with no hidden multiplier involved, making the work far more manageable.

The aforementioned discussion focused on identifying developer stories during the initial stages of a project in order to scope the whole project and to provide an initial project estimate, as required by the inception phase of the release cycle. The team will repeat developer story workshops as necessary through remaining phases of the release cycle, often as part of the backlog grooming process that precedes each story conference. Typically the product owner will meet with the project architect a week or two before a story conference to groom the backlog of user stories.

These two will then support the data architect and systems analyst as they convert the new and modified user stories at the top of the list into developer stories so that the team can conduct the next story conference with well-defined developer stories and form a reasonable commitment for the iteration. For those stories that the team will most likely work during the next sprint, the data architect and systems analyst also need to provide data and process designs at an 80/20 level of completion so that the programmers can move to coding without delay. These specifications do arise instantaneously; we will discuss in Chapter 8 how to create the time the data architect and systems analyst will need for this work.

Evaluating good developer stories: DILBERT'S test

Whether at the start of a release cycle or at any point during construction, the team will need a repeatable means to judge whether each developer story is defined sufficiently. For user stories, Scrum provides the INVEST test to give a team a quick notion of whether the user story is workable. Because developer stories are decompositions of user stories, much of the INVEST test will still apply, but we will need to add a component to acknowledge the crucial role the layers of the DWBI reference architecture play in their definition. After adding a couple of new components and renaming a couple of others, the test for a good developer story becomes a checklist that includes demonstrable, independent, layered, business valued, estimable, refinable, testable, and small. With those modifications, INVEST criteria for user stories become "DILBERT'S" test for developer stories, as detailed in Figure 6.5.

With this second guideline in place, a team will continue to use INVEST for testing its user stories, dropping down to DILBERT'S test whenever it comes time to draft developer stories by stretching the user story across the DWBI reference data architecture. A quick description of each component of DILBERT'S test is found next.

Demonstrable

"Demonstrable" indicates that the deliverables for each developer story should result in something that can be demonstrated to the product owner during a sprint's user demo. Therefore, each developer story can be accepted or rejected at the conclusion of the iteration.

The greatest challenge to delivering data integration services incrementally is that it can take two or more iterations to move all the necessary data elements from the operational source systems to the dashboard where they can be reviewed by the product owner. Using the DWBI reference data architecture to segment a user story is a great technique for making data transformation steps manageable for the developers. The danger with that approach, however, is that teams become largely occupied developing pieces for the invisible layers behind each end-user dashboard and neglect to review them with the product owner.

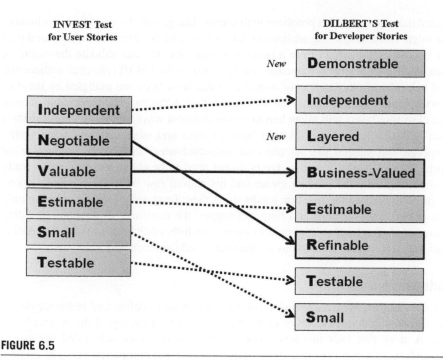

FIGURE 6.5

Deriving DILBERT'S test from the user story INVEST test.

Waterfall methods incur tremendous risk when their teams stop communicating with the end-user community for months at a time while programmers construct the application. Agile warehousing teams want to avoid this practice and instead keep the users involved tightly with the project as the application takes shape. As they standardize, deduplicate, and merge operational data, adding history and derived columns, they need stakeholder feedback every few weeks to tell them where they have misunderstood the requirements or failed to apply a transformation rule properly. Without this regular feedback, they cannot hope to "fail fast and fix quickly."

Luckily, the remedy requires only a small amount of effort. Every developer story must be defined so that it is demonstrable. Simply pushing data from one layer to the next is not enough. The team must also conclude every developer story with a display of results that the product owner can review. As shown in Figure 6.4, developers need to provide a simple dashboard for each layer of the reference architecture so that the product owner can examine the results of the developer story for himself. At the conclusion of each iteration, the developers should update these "product-owner portals" so that their business partner can review whatever new transforms have been added, no matter how small, and provide feedback.

Whereas on first thought it would seem that business users would have little interest in these intermediate steps data take, in practice the normally hidden data layers can prove very useful to the product owner. For example, by looking simply only at staged data, he can detect problems with source data quality the team had overlooked. He might run a simple reconciliation back to source to determine if the acquired data are complete and correct from a business perspective. He can validate the output of data cleansing transforms in the data quality layer of the DWBI reference architecture and help identify those areas of source data that have been too mangled by the data entry operators for a programmed routine to repair. A dashboard connected to staging and cleansing layers will allow him to try out different ways of joining the company's data on business keys and discover business rules and other insights buried within corporate information that no one ever suspected was there. These product-owner portals to the intermediate data layers do not need to be elaborate, production-ready dashboards. Only the product owner and his chosen few from the business departments will evaluate the iteration results using these front ends. Often displaying only one or two table's of data at a time will support the necessary evaluations. Building these simple front ends so the product owner can fully participate in validation during each sprint is a small price to pay for the user-based feedback they generate.

Independent

For developer stories, *independent* means teams need to define and sequence developer stories so that each can be coded when it arrives at the top of the project backlog. A story that fails this test cannot be worked on when scheduled because it depends on one or more other stories that have not been completed yet.

The independence of developer stories can be enhanced greatly by the way the data architect and systems analysts define them. In the sample data flow diagram presented in Figure 6.4, the team may find itself delayed in starting on the revenue trends universe because it depends on the booked revenue fact table, which involves some complex business rules. To make sure that the developer story is independent, the team leads could split it into two developer stories—a universe each for billed and booked revenue—allowing a good portion of the project to be developed before the allocation business rules were finished.

Layered

The "layered" criterion indicates that a single developer story shows development in only one layer of the DWBI reference data architecture. Focusing on one layer will also help considerably to make each story *independent*, especially if all its inputs and outputs connect to data objects located outside the layer in question. If developer stories scoped to either the integration or the presentation layer still do not feel "right sized," the team can extend the layered concept and try restricting the story to a single rank of a tiered data model, as discussed in the next chapter.

Business valued

"Business valued" reminds the developers that they must define and communicate every developer story so that the product owner appreciates it as a significant step toward delivering the overall application. This criterion will probably be the one that requires the most effort and creativity from the technical members of the team. Many DWBI professionals believe this objective cannot be achieved. In their vision, business partners want to perform their analysis using fully dimensionalized data and could care less about what each dimension looks like individually. This interpretation is true only in a minority of projects and can be reduced even further if the team manages its rapport with the product owner properly.

Far more common are product owners who have struggled with one or more IT projects in the past, maybe even a data warehousing effort. They hated the fact that developers disappeared for months on end, only to return with an application that tragically failed to meet key business requirements. These project veterans comprehend all too well the tremendous risk a large data integration project represents, both in terms of expense and opportunity costs. Instead of being dismissive of the incremental steps involved in delivering data, the product owners will be thrilled at the chance to see and manipulate warehouse data at each step in the reference architecture, for such demonstrations assure them progress is being made and the risk they run by associating their name with the project is being reduced steadily.

True, the team may have to educate its product owner some regarding the reference architecture that defines the waypoint along which data added must reach as it moves through the warehouse. Most business partners these days have worked with data applications so they will understand readily the fact that data must be staged before it can be scrubbed and integrated before it can be arranged nicely for analysis. If the data warehousing terminology interferes with understanding, dimensions and facts can be reexpressed in business terms such as metrics and qualifiers to make them business meaningful.

Once the product owner is oriented properly, the team should keep the schematic data flow diagram for each user story on the project board. With such a graphic, the team can check off each element as demonstrated to the product owner so that progress toward the final objective—the dashboard—can be visualized and tracked easily.

Furthermore, the project architect can take on the role of finding business-relevant queries that will communicate to the product owner the progress represented by each intermediate delivery. As the product owner test drives a dashboard connected to one of the data layers of the warehouse, the project architect could provide the following commentary in order to underscore the business value of the developer stories being reviewed:

- I remember you had your doubts whether any team could actually get usable data out of our new enterprise resource planning system. However, in this simple dashboard here, we can see staged data showing purchase orders and the line items linked to each. Why not take a moment during this demo and see if you can filter for the orders given to your most troublesome vendors during the month of December?
- I recall your concern about whether the service addresses in the western region's call center system were usable. Let's look at the dashboard we built for you

showing customer account records that we just finished cleansing. You'll see we can now aggregate 99% of the service locations by census block, based on standardized postal addresses. That puts us in a position to consider the special business rules needed for the remaining 1%, which would make a good developer story for the next sprint.

- I wrote in my notes that you were worried we would not be able to trace customer orders to shipping dock activity in order to get fulfillment cycle times. In this dashboard for the integration layer we just built for you, we can show that less than half a percent of sales cannot be traced to an outgoing tracking number. Does that seem like a big step to providing the traceability you're looking for?

With a little creativity, the technical teammates will be able to fine-tune each developer story so that an interesting demonstration can be presented to the product owner. The small minority of stories that cannot be given a business-intelligible interpretation can be declared part of the 20% architectural reserve described in earlier chapters on generic agile project management.

Demonstration ideas are especially easy to come by if developers keep in mind that the product owner is being held accountable by company executives for the project's enormous burn rate against budgeted funds. Like anyone in that situation, he will have a strong interest in seeing business-intelligible evidence that the team is making progress. It will not matter if that proof of progress comes through a hastily created BI portal connected to data on a system test server. As long as he can trace it to a waypoint on the high-level architecture diagram and perform some business-meaningful operation with it, he can make a compelling report to his management that the project is moving forward. We will explore how teams can even give their product owners an approximate percentage completion to report when we discuss project estimation techniques in the next chapter.

Estimable

This component of the test is borrowed directly from INVEST, where we stated that the story must describe work specifically enough for the team to be able to estimate the level of effort required to complete it. The next chapter discusses estimation at length.

Refinable

"Refinable" means that the wording of a developer story should be meaningful and well scoped, but the details are left to be filled in later. This component of the acronym is primarily a simple rewording of INVEST's *Not-Too-Specific* criterion, but may actually be the more useful of the two notions. True, a team may waste valuable time by gathering too many specifics up front for a story, but, more importantly, the accuracy of one's vision improves as the project progresses. Stating a story loosely at first and refining it close to the moment that its build-out begins positions teammates to discuss requirements and design at a time when their knowledge of both will be at their peak. Overall, product owner and developers will make the fewest mistakes if they organize the project with short statements of intent, planning to refine those statements into a fuller expression of requirements when they start transforming work upon a module.

One way to keep developer stories from descending into too much detail is to instruct teams to focus on only the "what" of a story, that is, *what* has to be accomplished, deferring the *how* for discussion within the development portion of the iteration in which the module will be built. For example, it will be enough to write a particular developer story stating that addresses will be cleansed, leaving out the details of how street and city names should be actually parsed into tokens and what lookup tables should provide the replacement strings need to standardize the components identified. The fact that the team includes a data architect and systems analyst who will be providing 80/20 specifications for the programmers when they begin to code a developer story ensures that the project will have a coherent data and processing architecture. Within that context, if a developer story provides just enough information that the team can determine if it fits comfortably within the time box of a sprint, all other details can be deferred until later.

Testable

This element is borrowed directly from the INVEST test, which stated a story should describe a unit of functionality that is small and distinct enough to be validated in a straightforward manner.

Luckily, developer stories are fairly close to the "units" that developers have in mind when they consider "unit testing" their code. This proximity makes validation of developer stories fairly easy for them to envision. We discuss testing for data integration projects in much greater detail in the enterprise volume of this two-book set.

Small

This criterion is also borrowed directly from the INVEST test, which suggests that every story should have such a limited scope that the work implied will consume only a fraction of the team resources available during a sprint. Fortunately, if the team applies the earlier criteria of *layered*, *independent*, and *testable* properly, "small" usually results. When this combination does not achieve that effect, there are secondary techniques for further decomposition, as discussed next.

Secondary techniques when developer stories are still too large

What happens if a developer story meets all the criteria of DILBERT'S test except for *small*? The story is perfectly layered, business valued, and demonstrable, yet the team does not believe developers can complete it within a single iteration. Letting developer stories exceed a single iteration will seriously undermine a team's ability to manage its work. If all stories spread across three or four iterations regularly, problematic stories will no longer be detected quickly. The team also risks ending an iteration with unfinished stories and absolutely nothing to demonstrate to the product owner. Velocity will be impossible to measure and, without a metric for work accomplished, retrospective will become effete for process improvement. Clearly, if the developer stories created by pressing a user story through the sieve of our DWBI reference architecture yield stories that are still too big, the team will need another battery of tactics to achieve the granularity required for smooth, iterative development. Luckily, the data architect can take the lead on further decomposing the work into smaller developer stories by splitting their target data objects between separate sets or rows, columns, column types, or tables.

Decomposition by rows

Breaking out candidate developer stories by identifying separately loadable sets of rows is possible when each source added to the warehouse results in an additional, independent set of records in the target tables. As long as each new source does not require updates to the rows already loaded, the team will find further substories packed within the candidate developer story that can be pursued in different iterations.

This technique is particularly useful when rows resulting from each new source derive from very different sources or transformation rules. By decomposing the candidate story into these distinctly transformed set of rows, the team allows itself to focus on just one complex transformation at a time, with probable gains in module testability and data quality as well.

Figure 6.6 depicts this decomposition technique using the example from our initial backlog discussion of the sales channel in the last chapter. During that conversation, stakeholders warned the team that each region of the company used very different business rules to determine which part of their organization was responsible for maintaining the relationship with a customer. The "load sales channel dimension" developer story suddenly appeared to the team as a module that would take many iterations to load.

Here the team drew upon the skills of the data architect. As part of the design process, data architects determine how dimensional data will be stored and how data will be joined to the records of the fact table. In this example, the data architect was able to assure the team that each region's business rules will result in a new independent set of records in the sales channel dimension table. Furthermore, because there will be no snowflaking of the dimension involved, these records will link only to fact records sourced from the transaction systems of that region.

With those assurances, the system analysts could determine that each transaction source would simply layer another set of records into the sales channel dimension table without requiring modifications to previous load rows. That said, the "load sales channel" candidate story could then be subdivided into separate

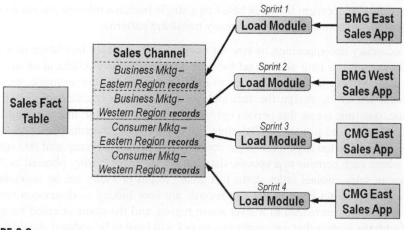

FIGURE 6.6

Developer stories by sets of rows.

developer stories for loading the sales channel records from the unique source for each of the company's sales regions. With the channels assigned according to the particular business rules of the region a sale belongs to, each of these developer stories dealt with only a single transformation pattern. Each developer story now appeared small enough that each of them would fit within a single iteration.

While performing this secondary decomposition, the team quickly revisited the other key points of DILBERT'S test besides *small* for each new developer story:

- Each story remained *demonstrable* because with a changeable filter on region code, the product owner could zero in on the new records loaded by each successive story.
- Each wave of source records resulted only in inserts upon the target table and no updates so the stories were *independent*.
- The secondary stories all pertained to the integration section of the reference architecture, even a stratum of records within the sales channel table, making them tightly *layered*.
- Each such demonstration would allow the product owner to report to his management that yet another region's sales channel was now stored correctly in the warehouse and the scope of transactions his portal can analyze is expanding steadily, making the story *business valued*.
- By decoupling the complex transformation rules, the logic involved with each substory could be considered separately, making them all the more *estimable*.
- The conversation with the data architect touched only lightly on the transformation rules for each region's segment records, leaving the details to be managed during the development work specific to each regional source, thus keeping the new stories *refinable*.

- Smaller independent modules based on a single business rule are always more *testable* than modules involving many transform patterns.

Secondary decomposition by row set works equally well for fact tables as it does for dimensions, as long as the load for each additional source results in an insert of new data without necessary updates to existing records. In our example, the data architect intends to design the fact table to hold revenue transactions. These are atomic, one-time events that pertain only to a particular region so that the record sets can be loaded independently. Therefore, should the "load revenue fact" developer story prove to be too large for a single iteration, it too can be decomposed into substories where each pertains to a specific data source. However, a story phrased as "load corporate sales channel order status fact table" would probably not be segmentable by regional row set because the fact records are now linking to dimension records that have been generalized to a level above region, and the status-oriented nature of the fact table implies that a previous fact record will have to be updated should a later transaction push it into another sales channel category.

Decomposition by column sets

The second of these techniques by which the data architect can further downsize developer stories is by splitting target data objects by the sets of column set to be loaded. This approach can be a bit trickier to think through, however. Load modules can be devastated by a change in the data structures. Because a large amount of code has to be updated, retested, and then promoted to production even if a single column name or its width changes, teams in general are very wary about changing the columns making up their target tables.

In some circumstances, however, the team can safely alter a table structure, allowing it to defer design decisions and constructively evolve a target schema as they work through a series of developer stories. In particular, as long as each new story requires that columns only be added, not changed, dropped, or renamed, then a series of developer stories based on distinct column sets can be pursued independently. Such stories will not entail reworking existing code, for any new column was not present when existing modules were developed, and therefore could not have been referenced by them.

A series of column-based developer stories can be envisioned using the example depicted in Figure 6.7. This example pertains to the product dimension table of the sample outlined in the previous chapter. Each new source system would provide product identifiers employing a unique set of native keys—keys that end users would want to reference in the dashboards. For this requirement, the data architect decided that each set of native keys would load into their own set of columns in the target table, exactly the design revealed in Figure 6.7. Over time the column sets will fill out moving left to right rather than top to bottom as occurred with the row sets of our previous technique.

There will be, of course, some shared columns pertaining to surrogate keys, a standardized identifier, and both warehouse and source meta data that will be

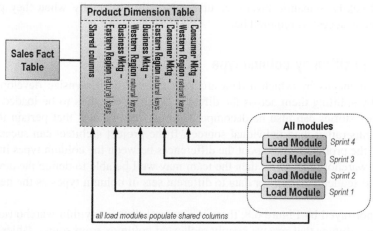

FIGURE 6.7

Decomposing developer stories by sets of columns.

populated no matter which data source is being processed. As long as the loading of shared columns remains consistent, no rework of existing code will be required. In fact, such consistency can be achieved easily by asking the developers to employ a reusable subprocess responsible for loading these shared columns.

As shown in Figure 6.7, the transforms populating the regional native keys can be decomposed into separate modules. Each of the modules will provide values for both its own specific target columns and the shared columns along the left edge of the table. The specific columns will hold the source system's native keys for products, which will be convenient for the developers, as the source systems have wildly different formats for their product identifiers. The shared columns will receive the corporate product code that will allow rational consolidation of the separate product catalogs.

The decomposition by column set scheme allows developers to build separate load modules one at a time for each new source system rather than having to digest all the product identifier transformation rules in one iteration. The data architect can even defer specifying the attributes for each successive column set until the team is ready to build the transforms needed for a given source system, making even data design work incremental.

While decomposing the "load product dimension" story into developer stories for specific column sets, the team repeatedly applied DILBERT'S test to the new developer stories. Their analysis paralleled that of the row set approach given earlier, with exception of *demonstrable*. When working with a progressive set of rows, the team needed to provide only a changeable filter to allow the product owner to view the accomplishments of each story in turn. With column sets, however, the team will have to add new columns to the semantic layer of the product owner's portal after every story so that the product owner can see data loaded into those new fields. Luckily, semantic layers are updated easily, especially when they provide single-table access as required here.

Decomposition by column type

The third means by which a data architect can further downsize developer stories is by splitting them across the different types of columns to be loaded. Large developer stories can also be decomposed along column sets that pertain to *types* of columns rather than individual sources. If the project architect can successfully educate the product owner about the differences between the column types included in most warehousing tables, then the team may well be able to define the developer stories to sequentially deliver data to different sets of column types as the iterations progress.

As portrayed by Figure 6.8, there is a natural division within warehouse tables between columns that receive simply replicated columns from source tables versus columns receiving derived values created by complex transformation rules. There are also columns for primary keys, foreign keys, and aggregates, as well as meta data from source or meta data generated by the warehouse itself.

Although a product owner instinctively wants all data made available immediately, project architects can share with them that there is a different business value provided by each type of column. Keys alone will enable counts to be calculated for the entities in the dimensional model. Counts are often the first business value stakeholders need to have when they begin working with newly loaded data.

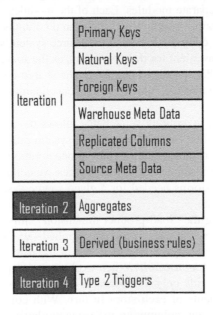

FIGURE 6.8

Different column types found in data warehousing tables.

Textual replicated columns allow those counts to be filtered and combined selectively by values found in the source system. Numerical replicated columns can be summed and averaged. With such counts, sums, and simple filtering, the product owner can generate a first set of business insights to review. True, the capability is limited, but most product owners will agree that working with some information now is preferable to remaining blind to business operations until everything needed is in place.

By providing the column types needed for such simple analytics, developers will have bought themselves some time to work on delivering the derived columns that will need complex business rules coded. They can even consider dividing groups of business rules into distinct subwaves in order to make the remaining developer stories small enough to fit into sprints.

In the initial user story interview session described in the last chapter, finance had mentioned that postal addresses needed to be scrubbed before they would be reliable. In order to decompose the "deliver addresses" developer story, the team can consider segmenting the work between directly loadable columns versus columns needing scrubbing. In particular, postal address lines one and two (which typically hold street number, street name, and living unit identifier) will need standardization, but the city, state, and postal code attributes are well controlled by the source systems and can be loaded as is. Thus the work can be distributed across two iterations, the first delivering immediately replicable columns such as CISTAZIP, which will allow transactions to be analyzed down to the postal code level. In the second sprint, the team would finish up the scrubbed columns, allowing metric disaggregation down to the street and census block level.

In reaching *small* via this technique, the elements of DILBERT'S test largely track the pattern established in the previous two examples. For *business valued* in particular, however, the team needed to work a bit harder to explain for the product owner the new set of analyses made possible as each column type is populated in the target tables. *Demonstrable* required repeated updates to the product owner portal as new column sets became available. Separating transformation rules from other column types led to substories that make the developer stories independent. The tighter scopes of these new stories made the delivery increments more estimable and testable.

Decomposition by tables

The fourth technique by which the data architect can further downsize developer stories is by splitting the target tables they focus upon into special purpose objects. When faced with time-oriented entities such as a customer with so much history that queries began to run long, DWBI data architects realized long ago that they could separate these large tables into two versions: one table holding all history and a smaller one with only the last image for each native key. For many BI applications, because the vast majority of analyses focus on recent events or current status, these queries can be answered from current data only. Furthermore, queries reporting on trends are often based on only a few time points, such as the end of each month over the prior 3 years. Only rarely do the users truly mine the full life cycle of a topic and require information as of any arbitrary point in time. Given this natural division in usage, data architects can provide fast performance for the bulk of user queries by designating a "current history" table that holds data for only the most recent, frequently used time points. Such tables contain considerably less data to be processed by each query, allowing the system to return results far more quickly.

When a project involves a set of user stories requiring current data and others based on full history, the developer story for some of the larger dimensions can be split between "deliver current data" and "deliver full history." This design pattern actually reflects what is commonly called a "type 4" dimension. [Kimball Group 2011] Developer stories for deliver current data typically require less complex logic than full history routines because old records for a native key can be simply replaced rather than marked inactive. Often the data volumes for current data sets are low enough that the developer story can require only a full refresh ("kill and fill"), making the load logic very straightforward.

Figure 6.9 depicts the decision to break a developer story for a large dimension into two. The data architect first adds a "current-only" version of the dimension entity to his data models. The team then defines a developer story for "deliver current customer data" and another for "deliver full history customer data." Whereas the original

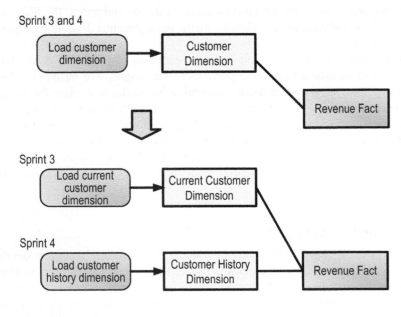

Other dimensions omitted for clarity.

FIGURE 6.9

Decomposing developer stories by target tables.

developer story was considered so large it would take two sprints to complete, the new developer stories can each be delivered and demonstrated in a single iteration.

As far as DILBERT'S test is concerned, delivering the current table is clearly *demonstrable* as long as the project architect actively scopes the product owner's review to questions involving latest customer segments. The *business value* will be certainly apparent, as the first developer story will provide data that address nearly all of the questions users have in mind. Because the fact records have separate foreign key columns linking them to the two versions of the segment dimension, those foreign keys can be loaded in separate processing runs, making the stories *independent*. As with the other segmentation techniques, the tighter scope of the new developer stories makes them both more *estimable* and *testable*.

Theoretical advantages of "small"

With the techniques considered earlier, we now have a deep toolkit for decomposing user stories as much as necessary to prepare them for iterative delivery. Our overall process is progressive by nature:

- The methods of the last chapter let us move from big statements of user needs down to clearly scoped *user stories*, all sized properly for the product owner to track.
- The decomposition process documented in this chapter breaks those user stories into *developer stories* where the work is right-sized for software developers to pursue using a time-boxed, iterative development process.
- Once a development sprint begins, developers will further decompose the developer stories into tasks small enough for an individual to complete within a matter of a few days.

This process steadily reduces the scope or "size" of the request confronting the developers, yielding two important benefits. First, by reducing scope we steadily drive uncertainty out of each product owner request until the unknowns that remain can be managed successfully via the eye-to-eye collaboration that agile methods rely upon. By addressing detailed requirements and design through direct conversation, development teams can do without the large, up-front specifications that consume so much time and effort under waterfall methods.

The second benefit of steadily reducing the scope of a given developer story is that the size of the work units becomes increasingly homogeneous; this convergence allows the development process to proceed far more smoothly. Figure 6.10 depicts two projects, both being pursued iteratively, but taking very different approaches to the definition of their work packages. In both, the work bundles are trying to thread through a small aperture in a wall. This constraint represents each team's finite capacity to turn requirements into working code during a single iteration.

In the first project, the developers have spent no time at all trying to break the work bundles down to a consistent size, especially one appropriate for the size of

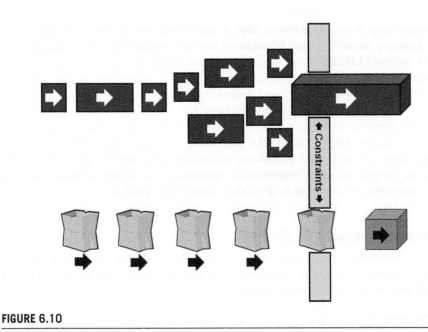

FIGURE 6.10

Consistent story size improves an agile team's velocity.

their aperture. As can be seen, such an approach is a prescription for delays and frustration when a particularly large work package plugs the opening for more than one iteration. These developers can expect to frequently appear at their user demo with nothing appreciable to show for the prior sprint. With sprints for a team of six coders costing somewhere between $75 K and $150 K per iteration (2010 dollars), such disappointments will increase the anxiety of the product owner and his sponsors quickly.

The second project, however, has taken a different approach. Its developers have taken the time and acquired the skills to decompose their work steadily until it sits in their backlog as a collection of more or less homogeneously sized work bundles. We will see in the next chapter how they can quantify module and work package size, but for now we can say that the developers acquire an intuitive sense of the complexities of their modules so that they can continue decomposing them until they all feel consistent and appropriate compared to their team capacity. As shown in the previous chapter, the team moves toward consistently sized user stories using the INVEST test and then to right-sized developer stories using DILBERT'S test.

The payoff is apparent in the bottom portion of Figure 6.10. By measuring their velocity each iteration, these developers have discovered their capacity to convert requirements into working code. They can think of their capacity as the aperture in the wall that is just right for a, say, 10-pound sack to fit through. Using the decomposition methods discussed in this chapter they have broken the work down into units of 10 pounds or less so that they can fill each sack with close to that exact amount of work. Once packaged in this way, they can move the sacks steadily through the aperture. By taking each request through the chain of epics, themes, and two kinds of stories, they know that there is no oversized request in any of the sacks that is going to clog up the gap in the wall. They will be able to steadily convert user needs into working code free of any complications due to work package size. Moreover, the team can optimize their work habits for the 10-pound sacks and acquire far more velocity than if they had to keep their work habits able to manage a wide range of work package sizes.

Readers should be careful not to interpret the story preparation described in the chapters of this part of the book as somehow returning to waterfall's notion of "define everything down to the last detail" before a team begins system construction. Instead, the stack of project definition objects displayed in Figure 6.2 remains a single-sentence requirement identifier. The initial project backlog interviews and developer story workshops attempt to identify a whole project's worth of work, but only for scoping, estimating, and scheduling purposes. The product owner and team expect the stories in the bottom half of the list to have considerably more precision than those at the top. Moreover, the data architect and systems analysts provide specifications only for developer stories that will be programmed in the next iterations, and those artifacts will be 80/20 specifications at that.

Of course, occasionally teams will underestimate a package. Agile accepts some surprises as the price to pay for faster project starts and higher delivery speeds. Agile's iterative structure and sprint retrospectives give a team the chance to discuss the pain caused by such misestimation so that they can steadily improve their work-definition techniques. Yet, such misestimation will be the exceptional occurrence for agile warehousing teams that employ developer stories. By driving the work definition past the level of user stories, down to the developer's notions of work units, these teams will uncover a good deal of the technical work hidden in a project's user requirements. They will see this implicit technical work in enough detail that the risk of such nasty surprises becomes sufficiently small.

With developer stories and their decomposition techniques now illustrated, all that is left of our three-step project definition process is to estimate the size of the work packages so that a team can recombine them into the "10-pound sacks" described earlier. Techniques for such estimation and packaging are precisely the object of the next chapter.

Summary

A backlog of good user stories defines a project well, but data warehousing efforts involving significant portions of data integration need to develop those user stories one step further into developer stories in order to arrive at a list of work units that will fit easily into Scrum's iteration time box. Developer stories are user stories decomposed using the macro data architecture that the project's data architect specifies. Each developer story represents a work unit that developers can plan and deliver easily within an iteration, and it is a deliverable that will be valued by the project's embedded business partner.

The primary means of identifying developer stories is to conceptually stretch a user story across the layers of a data warehouse's high-level data architecture, often called the "DWBI reference data architecture" by data warehousing professionals. A typical DWBI reference architecture has layers for each major data modeling paradigm within the warehouse: staging, integration, presentation, semantics, and dashboards. Teams can generate a starter list of developer stories by inspecting the intersection between the layers of a company's DWBI reference architecture with each user story in the project backlog. Agile warehousing practitioners can employ the "DILBERT'S test" to appraise whether each resulting developer story is sufficiently defined and actionable.

For any candidate story that is still too large, there are several secondary techniques for decomposing them one step further. These secondary techniques subdivide developer stories by considering the sets of rows, columns, column types, and tables required by the candidate story. At the conclusion of this decomposition process, the team will have a project backlog of developer stories they can estimate and then assemble into an agile project plan.

Estimating and Segmenting Projects

Why do development teams frequently overcommit and how does agile's "sized-based estimation" avoid this trap?
How can story points and project backlog enable us to predict how long a project will take and how much it will cost?
How can we group the estimated components into major deliverables, given that we cannot build everything at once?

All software development teams must estimate labor requirements in order to plan their work and communicate project trajectories effectively with their stakeholders. Although no software developer can predict the level of effort work units will demand with perfect certainty, accuracy in estimation is worth some study and effort because the more dependable a team can make its estimates, the easier it will be for them to deliver according to the resulting plan. Accurate estimating also lessens the chance a team will have to disappoint project stakeholders with schedule and cost overruns.

Previous chapters detailed an agile approach to defining projects with just enough detail to understand the work required, both at the outset of an effort and then repeatedly before each development iteration. The result of that definition process provides a backlog defined at two levels: First from a business perspective, the backlog begins with "user stories" authored by the team's product owner. Second, this backlog also contains a decomposition of those user stories into "developer stories" that are small and technically explicit enough that developers on the team can begin delivering the required system components. As presented in this chapter, agile provides a novel technique called "size-based estimation" for predicting the level of effort the stories on a backlog will require. Teams can employ this new technique upon only the leading edge of the backlog in order to define just the next iteration. They can also use the technique to estimate the entire backlog in order to forecast the labor a complete release or full project will require.

Once the backlogs are estimated, data warehousing teams will naturally want to group the components of work into iterations and releases. Teams can draw upon three techniques for assembling the developer stories on a project backlog

Agile Data Warehousing Project Management.
DOI: http://dx.doi.org/10.1016/B978-0-12-396463-2.00007-7

into both reasonably scoped iterations and a series of releases that will provide end users with a steady stream of valuable business analytics. Compared to the estimating approach taken by waterfall projects, agile estimation is mentally easier and repeated far more frequently as part of the method, allowing teams to forecast a project's labor requirements far more dependably. This ability to estimate accurately requires both a solid understanding of the work implicit within a project and a well-tune delivery process. Because failings in any part of this chain will prevent the team from delivering as promised, the agile team can employ the accuracy of their estimates as a highly sensitive metric for tracking the quality of a team's overall delivery process.

Failure of traditional estimation techniques

The Standish Group's *Chaos* reports, published before agile techniques were common, documented that less than one-third of information technology (IT) projects over $750K are implemented on time, within budget, and with all the features promised. The reports cited "underestimating project complexity and ignoring changing requirements" as basic reasons why these projects failed. [Standish 1999] Such findings clearly suggest that if developers receive only one chance to estimate a project, they will rarely forecast accurately, allowing sponsors to expect far too much functionality while budgeting far too little funding for the project. Despite the growing sophistication of our industry, inaccurate estimates continue to vex information systems groups, leading one long-time observer to sadly ask "How can experts know so much and predict so badly?" [Camerer 1991]

Empirical evidence shows that developers forecast only half the effort their tasks will take, with a large amount of skew in the distribution above this mean. [Demarco 1982; Little 2004] Figure 7.1 shows this distribution and provides an

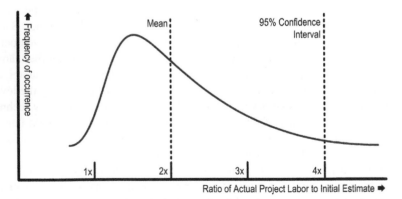

FIGURE 7.1

Empirically, waterfall estimates are difficult to rely upon.

instant insight as to why traditional estimation techniques regularly undermine project success. To understand this dynamic, one must keep in mind that project sponsors and managers absolutely despise exceeding their budgets and can make life very unpleasant for developers when a project threatens to do so. However, the long tail to the right in Figure 7.1 reveals that these managers should be requesting not twice, but *four time*s as much funding as the team estimates in order to be 95% confident they will not have to make "another trip to the well."

Few managers are willing to quadruple their project estimates, yet when they only double their team's labor projections, they instill unavoidable disappointment into the future of at least every other project. Somewhere long before the expected delivery date, these projects are going to appear undoable as defined. Developers will be pressured into making heroic efforts involving working nights and weekends. Quality, moderately neglected as soon as overtime started, continues to fall as developer morale sinks. The cost of the overtime work will exceed the project budget long before the first release sees production, resulting in unhappy project sponsors. Scope will be cut in order to restore some measure of feasibility, adding horrified customers to the disgruntled sponsors. Downstream teams that had been depending on the project to deliver will find important prerequisites for their applications delivered late with less than expected scope. All this pain occurs because, as revealed in Figure 7.1, traditional estimating is congenitally blind to the time and resources a software project truly needs.

As the logistical, financial, and political strains of an underfunded project reverberate throughout the company, the organization enters, crisis by crisis, the "disappointment cycle" sketched in Chapter 1. The project's final costs ends up greatly exceeding the value delivered. At the project postmortem, frustration and conflict will swell as the team zeroes in on the root cause of the problem, one that many of them had seen before: "Why did we promise *again* to metaphorically force 10 pounds of fruit into a 5-pound sack?"

Traditional estimating strategies

What are the estimating approaches used by traditional projects that perform so poorly? The profession has taken two main strategies for forecasting level of effort: *formal estimation models* and *expert judgment*. Formal estimation models are parameter-driven formulas that supposedly will predict, when provided sufficient measures describing the software envisioned, both a mean and a variance for the level of effort required to build it. Expert judgment, however, involves providing a system description to experienced systems professionals, then relying upon their intuition to provide a probable labor estimate and a range of uncertainty.

Formal estimation models are appealing because they seem to encapsulate years of lessons learned into formulas that one can inspect and fine-tune. In practice, however, such models have been expensive to build and disappointing in results for the simple reason that, for all their cost, they are no more accurate than expert judgment. One survey of a hundred IEEE papers regarding software effort estimation methods indicated that "…estimation models are very inaccurate when evaluated on historical software projects different from the project on which [they] were derived." [Jorgensen 2000] Unfortunately for data warehouse projects, business intelligence applications within a given company differ constantly from previous efforts due to evolving sources systems, innovation in tools, and the diversity of business areas within an enterprise.

A second reason that formal models often disappoint their sponsors is that software engineers will subvert them once they become too complex to understand readily. The author has observed many instances where engineers became frustrated while working with complex estimating spreadsheets with thousands of cells. Instead of requesting an update to the logic of the estimating utility, these users would simply open a hidden worksheet of the tool and overwrite an intermediate result with a value they found more believable. In choosing an estimating approach, planners must accept that the entirety of an estimating technique must remain easily intelligible to the staff members employing it, or they will simply draw upon their intuition, often without much discipline to their approach.

If the effectiveness of formal estimating models is limited, then one must rely upon expert judgment. To its credit, expert judgment can be deployed in very short order and "… seems to be more accurate when there [is] important domain knowledge not included in the estimation models, [or] when the estimation uncertainty is high as a result of environmental changes…." [Jorgensen 2004] Traditional project management offers several methods for gathering input from many individuals and collating it into an expert judgment forecast. Some of these methods can yield reliable estimates if followed carefully.

Business pressures frequently undermine these more disciplined methods, however. Instead of being asked to follow a careful, deliberate approach, developers are ordered more frequently to produce an estimate by an arbitrarily close calendar date. Faced with a tight deadline, developers will gather into a single conference room and "hammer out" an estimate for management as fast as possible. This approach can be called the *estimating bash*, where developers simultaneously draft a project's work breakdown structure and forecast the work effort required, task by task, using any means they see fit.

Some projects make an effort to gather expert judgment in a more deliberative style. They parcel out aspects of the project to individual developers and then invite them to present their findings at a consolidation meeting. Although the prep work was performed carefully, the collation process involves reviewing the reasonableness of the component estimates. This consolidation meeting often becomes just another estimating bash as folks challenge each other's forecasts over a conference table and revise them based on hasty, not-so-expert judgments. Given that the failure rates documented by the *Chaos* reports actually increased with the size of projects, this consolidation process appears to be just as vulnerable to the unreliable, ad hoc techniques that dominate the estimation process of small projects.

Why waterfall teams underestimate

What are the dynamics occurring in projects large and small that push traditional projects into the grave underestimates considered earlier? Four counterproductive patterns are regularly at work: single-pass efforts, insufficient feedback, rewards for overoptimism, and few reality checks.

A single-pass effort

According to the Project Management Institute's (PMI) outline of the standard waterfall practice, planners should work through a series of cost estimates as they envision, fund, and finally plan their projects in detail. PMI expects project managers to work with software engineers to produce and estimate a "work breakdown structure" (WBS). Forecasts based on these WBS should start as *order of magnitude* predictions (–25 to +75% accuracy) and eventually become *definitive estimates* (–5 to +10%). [PMI 2008] Only once the team has produced a detailed WBS and a definitive estimate can development work begin. The project manager will employ this last work breakdown and estimate as a comprehensive project plan to which he will doggedly keep the project team aligned. When cost and schedule overruns grow too large, he will be forced to "rebaseline" the plan, but, because hard and fast promises to stakeholders were based on this "definitive estimate," such adjustments are made only rarely.

In this common approach to development projects, labor estimation is something developers are asked to do only once in a long while. Producing a definitive WBS is tedious work, and many months pass before the project concludes and estimators discover how well their forecasts matched actual results. Given these factors, developers naturally view accurate estimation as a secondary priority requirement for their careers, nowhere near as important as technical skills and even political acumen.

Project managers essentially discount estimation also because of this single-pass approach. Obtaining an estimate from the development team is simply a milestone that must be achieved before they can finish their proposals and hold a project kickoff. They approach the developers with a detectable emphasis on getting the estimate done quickly so it can be presented at the next steering committee meeting, often giving the team insufficient time to make a proper assessment. Furthermore, estimation is a cost, and once a (supposedly accurate) estimate is in hand, there seems to be little reward in continuing to invest in an effort that has already delivered its payload. Like developers, management sees estimation as something done rarely—an occasional, necessary evil.

Insufficient feedback

In the single-pass approach, the reward for estimating well is remote and indirect. Accuracy in these forecasts is measurable only many months later as the system approaches implementation. Because the actual work eventually involves a mix of tasks very different from those foreseen, the quality of the many small predictions that went into the overall forecast is difficult to ascertain. Tallies of actual labor hours eventually arrive, but they are usually aggregated across major components so that the root cause for forecasting errors ends up hidden in averages and standard deviations. Furthermore, troubled projects often get cut in scope, making it impossible for developers to match much of their earlier level-of-effort forecasts to the project actuals. In this context, little natural learning occurs and the developers cannot improve at estimating.

Moreover, the slow and obscured feedback on the quality of their labor projections means that the developers are not subject to forces encouraging accuracy in estimation. Developers, working line by line through a tedious work breakdown during an estimating bash, must envision in detail the steps required to complete each task before they can consider how long that work will take. Processing such details is possible for a small number of components, but envisioning the hundreds of items comprising a typical project consistently is beyond the capabilities of most developers. As mental fatigue sets in, what immediate consequence keeps them from estimating each subsequent task a little less carefully? As teams tire half-way through their first pass on estimating a large project, the urge to finish up eventually outweighs their wish to be thorough. They rush through the rest of the list and, thrilled to be done with such tedium, making little effort to conscientiously cross-check the results.

Overoptimism rewarded

Compounding the inaccuracies introduced by a single-pass context with little effective feedback, developers feel pressure to whittle down their best guess at labor requirements for several reasons. Whether projects are proposed to internal boards or external customers, everyone involved with the estimate realizes that too high a tally will cause the proposal to be rejected. Consequently, a "price-to-win" mentality takes over where each developer begins quoting each task at the *largest acceptable estimate* that the organization will accept. This approach avoids many microconflicts with the project manager organizing the estimation effort. These managers often arrive at the estimating bash with strong opinions on how long most efforts should take and can wield autocratic powers to override the estimates provided by developers. Even worse, research has documented that managers view high estimates not as an indication that the project may be too ambitious, but rather as a signal that the developers are less qualified than they should be. Surprisingly, these executives do not correct this misconception when the lower estimates turn out be wrong. [Jorgensen & Sjoberg 2006] Over the years, developers learn of this bias and become reluctant to forecast accurately because of the negative consequences such estimates send.

Few reality checks

The factors just discussed combine to give preeminence to the overly confident participants within a team. There may be several bright developers in the group who can see the enormous harm that bad estimates can cause, but there are some powerful forces that keep them from correcting the situation when one or two dominant teammates take over the estimating process.

As research has shown, the problem with incompetent people is that they lack the ability to recognize their own incompetence, a blindness that allows a highly assertive developer to thrust upon a team his hasty estimates for each task. [Goode 2000] Lamentably, groups engaged in a shared effort such as estimating under a time pressure often fail to push back upon improper impulses due to *group think.* Group think is defined as a "mode of thinking that people engage in when they are deeply involved in a cohesive in-group, when the members' strivings for unanimity override their motivation to realistically appraise alternative courses of action." [Janis 1971] Whereas many would expect a project manager to guard the team against this unfortunate pack mentality, her priority is typically to get the estimate done, and the same research defining group think revealed that "directive leadership" from the top of the group's hierarchy usually exacerbates the problem.

Conscientious members of the estimation team may wish to correct the error-prone process unfolding within an estimating bash, but they typically have no alternative to propose because many organizations do not teach a standard estimation process or at least one robust enough to undercut dynamics as pernicious as overconfidence and group think.

Criteria for a better estimating approach

Agile practitioners have innovated upon labor estimation considerably in order to address the weakness in the approach waterfall projects typically employ. Given the pivotal role that forecasting effort plays in setting stakeholder expectations, it is not surprising that several thought leaders have studied labor estimation in great depth. Over the years, research has amassed more than a hundred possible improvements for the practice. Recently, one researcher was kind enough to consolidate them into 12 key recommendations. These recommendations are listed in Table 7.1, along with aspects of agile data warehousing that align with each recommendation. A moment's reflection will reveal that agile's methodological elements, and the estimating techniques explored shortly later, incorporate well all of these lessons learned.

In general, there are four primary objectives that agile estimation must support. First, Scrum teams must estimate the top of a backlog in order to decide how many user or developer stories to take on during the next iteration. Second, most teams need to estimate an entire project during the inception phase of a project in order to secure go-ahead approval and necessary funding. Third, throughout the construction phase of a project, teams must revisit their whole project estimates in order to confirm for stakeholders that the project is still doable. Fourth, when the backlog must be changed, teams must be able to tell stakeholders the impact of including or excluding any number of stories from the backlog.

These objectives certainly drive the agile estimating approach presented here. Agile's new approach to labor forecasting includes several innovations. First, it adds size-based estimation to complement the labor-hour forecasts, whereas waterfall methods restrict themselves only to labor-hour estimates. The size-based technique, which is presented in a moment, offers the team greater speed, accuracy, and validation for its labor forecasts.

Table 7.1 Twelve Objectives for Good Estimation[a]

Goals (Numbers Indicate Supporting Objectives)	How Achieved in Agile Data Warehousing
Reducing Situational and Human Biases	
1. Evaluate estimation accuracy, but avoid high evaluation pressure.	With sprint demos, developers succeed or fail as a team, not as individuals.
2. Avoid conflicting estimation goals.	Teams can focus upon achieving 95% accuracy as their only goal.
3. Ask estimators to justify and criticize their estimates.	Built into estimating poker, and reviewable during sprint retrospectives
4. Avoid irrelevant and unreliable estimation information.	Estimating poker brings in information only as needed. scrum master also keeps discussion on topic.
5. Use documented data from previous development tasks.	Reference stories and basis-of-estimate cards
6. Find estimation experts with proper background and experience.	Members of established agile teams will have worked similar stories and tasks in previous iterations.
Supporting the Estimation Process	
7. Estimate top-down and bottom-up independently of each other.	Employ both story points and task labor hours
8. Use estimation checklists.	Employ both reference stories and basis-of-estimate cards
9. Combine estimates from different experts and estimation strategies.	Story points and task labor hours
10. Assess the uncertainty of the estimate.	Can be made part of every sprint retrospective
Provide Feedback and Training Opportunities	
11. Provide feedback on estimation accuracy and task relations.	Daily burndown charts show whether team is moving fast enough to meet iteration goals. any overtime required is a strong reflection on the quality of the team's estimates.
12. Provide estimation training (learning) opportunities.	Sprint retrospectives provide a frequent opportunity to discuss and improve estimating skills. the start of every iteration provides a frequent opportunity to try out new estimating guidelines.

[a]Adapted from [Jorgensen 2004].

Second, the agile approach involves frequent estimating sessions instead of following waterfall's style of a single estimate at project start and perhaps a couple further estimates when the project has veered so far from plan that the entire forecast must be "rebaselined." In contrast, agile includes estimation as part of every iteration, and this frequent repetition causes developers to get good at estimating quickly, and then keeps them good at that skill.

Third, agile estimation requires that teams steadily accumulate their project experience into selecting key reference stories and standardizing developer task lists for important, frequently repeated types of work. These references help developers improve estimation accuracy by encouraging them to apply project knowledge they already possess consistently.

Fourth, agile estimation cross-checks the leading edge of its story point estimates with the labor-hour forecasts for each iteration. This practice asks the team to perform two passes at forecasting the same work, each done in a different unit of measure. Developers naturally reflect upon and resolve any conflicts between the estimates, revealing for them any errors in their approach to forecasting labor.

Finally, agile estimation provides prompt and thorough feedback on the accuracy of developers' estimates. By comparing the actual labor an iteration consumed versus the forecast the team had made a few weeks earlier, developers can steadily improve their estimating accuracy.

An agile estimation approach

All told, agile estimation addresses the weaknesses observed in the waterfall approach; as a result, agile labor forecasts throughout a project prove to be far more accurate than observed for traditional projects. In effect, agile estimation narrows the curve of actual labor versus initial estimates shown in Figure 7.1, reducing the problem of the fat tail to the right. The increased accuracy of agile forecasts allows teams to avoid overcommitment on both an iteration and a project level, while simultaneously giving management the information they need to fund and coordinate properly across multiple projects. Because estimating within an iteration is more different than estimating a full iteration, both deserve to be presented separately.

Estimating within the iteration

The agile approach is rooted, naturally enough, within the development iterations. Table 7.2 shows how each phase of the normal sprint incorporates estimation. The team performs a top-down forecast for only the handful of stories requested by the product owner during the story conference. As discussed in the prior chapter, these items will be user stories for front-end modules and developer stories for data integration work. Estimates made during the story conference will be in story points, first introduced in Chapter 2. When the team moves into the task planning phase of the sprint, they break the candidate stories into development tasks and estimate those

Table 7.2 Estimation Incorporated into Every Step of Scrum Iterations

Iteration Step	Estimating Focus	Details
Story Conference	Forecast	Use epic–theme–story decomposition to derive standardized user and developer stories.
		Estimate level of effort in story points using "estimating poker."
		Use team's story point velocity to identify maximum stories deliverable.
Task Planning	Verify	Derive standard task list for each story type from BOE cards (see Chapter 2).
		Forecast tasks' labor requirements in "ideal hours."
		Use team labor-hour velocity to identify max stories deliverable.
		Results may indicate current sprint backlog is too large.
		Teams alternate between story point and labor-hours estimation until they yield the same result.
Development	Watch	Mark remaining labor estimates (hours) on task cards worked.
		Retally all remaining labor daily and plot on a burndown chart.
		Compare trend in remaining labor plots to a "perfect line" to reveal iteration status.
User Demo	Validate	Credit team for the story points and labor hours associated with stories accepted.
		Tally them into a velocity in both units of measures.
		Calculate percentage of labor hours delivered successfully.
Retrospective	Learn	Tally them into a velocity in both units of measures.

work items in labor hours, that is, the total developer time required to complete the work identified by the task. For the major development modules that they must deliver frequently, agile warehousing teams will often gather a typical list of tasks and approximate labor hours onto basis-of-estimate (BOE) cards, also described in Chapter 2. These BOE cards provide the team's consensus on the pro forma tasks needed for each type of developer story. Teams often record on them starter notions of how many labor hours each task should take. With BOE cards, the developers greatly standardize and assist their own efforts in estimating labor hours accurately with a minimum of mental effort.

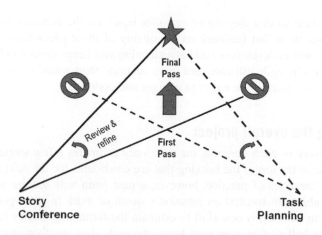

FIGURE 7.2

Two units of measure increase accuracy of agile estimates.

By measuring the estimated story points and task hours contained in the stories accepted during the user demo of the previous sprint, developers know their team's current velocity in both points and hours. When they estimate stories during the story conference, they add stories to the sprint backlog until the total story point matches their velocity. When they break the stories into tasks, they add up the work time forecasted for the tasks and compare that to their velocity, this time measured in labor hours. If the labor hours of the tasks come close to the team's labor-hour velocity, then the two estimates made during the story conference and task planning agree, and the developers will be as sure as they can possibly be that they have not overcommitted for the coming iteration. When the forecasted labor hours do not come close to the team's velocity, however, the developers must suspect that either their story point or their labor-hour estimates are wrong. They revisit their iteration plans, estimating changes in story points and then labor hours until they resolve the discrepancy, as shown in Figure 7.2.

Unlike the single-pass approach of waterfall projects, the agile sprint provides developers with important feedback on the quality of their estimates, as listed in the bottom half of Table 7.2. During the development phase, a burndown chart that lags above the perfect line tells them that they committed to too much work. If the product owner rejects any stories during the user demo, they learn that they probably took on too many stories to deliver them all with sufficient quality. During the retrospective, complaints of working nights and weekends tell them they set their sights too high for the sprint. Most importantly, during the retrospective, the developers can discuss in detail why the estimates made 3 or so weeks before were inaccurate. They can then explore how to increase the accuracy of their labor forecasts for the next story conference, which will occur the following work day.

In short, agile incorporates estimating as an integral part of being a developer. Forecasting accurately becomes a priority in their job. Agile leverages its short iterations to give developers a tremendous amount of practice at estimating.

It positions them so that they thrive or suffer based on the accuracy of those estimates. It gives them fast feedback on the quality of those predictions. In essence, agile quickly makes developers good at estimating and keeps them good at it. There is no wonder why agile estimates are more accurate than waterfall, and why agile projects are consequently far easier to manage and coordinate.

Estimating the overall project

Within the work of each iteration, the team only estimates a few stories at a time, namely those at the top of the backlog that are candidates for the next sprint. With a couple of iterations of practice, however, a new team will acquire a reasonably dependable ability to forecast an iteration's worth of work in story points. At this point they can utilize this new skill to estimate the remaining stories for the entire project. Even better, if management keeps the agile data warehousing team intact across projects, an established team arrives at a new engagement with their forecasting skill already honed, allowing them to provide a first estimate for a project at the end of the project's inception phase, before the first development iteration.

However, many agile practitioners who specialize in the development of "online transaction processing" (OLTP) applications bristle at the notion of providing a whole project estimate. Taking a "purist" position, they commit to nothing more than delivering the next set of stories requested by the product owner into working modules, one iteration at a time. When asked for a project estimate, an agile purist will push back, saying "If you like what we're doing and the speed we are going, then fund us for another iteration. We work at the highest, sustainable pace. The application you desire will appear as fast as it possibly can. As long as that's true what possible value could knowing the eventual completion date have?"

The logic contained in such a stance might work well for OLTP and even warehousing dashboard projects. For those types of applications, users do receive new features every few weeks. They can at least steadily benefit from the enhancement, even if they cannot get the team to predict when the whole project will be complete.

More moderate agile practitioners will partake in "release planning," which is a workshop that provides likely duration and cost predictions for the entire project. However, even moderate agile developers for OLTP applications will hesitate to perform whole project estimates. They will caution sponsors that stories beyond the next release and at the bottom of the project backlog are those items that the product owner has groomed the least, making them too vague to even estimate.

For data integration projects, however, both the purist and the moderate position will be incredibly frustrating for sponsors. In the absence of the data warehousing/business intelligence (DWBI) component and application generators explored in the next volume of this book set, even the world's fastest developers will need months to deliver the first slivers of a new data mart into a production release. Thus, users will not receive an instant flow of new features and sponsors will not have the opportunity to judge project progress based on usable results at the end of every iteration. With a burn rate of $100 K to $200 K per iteration, the project simply consumes far too many resources for the organization to take it on faith that something of value will be delivered eventually. For the sake of their own careers, sponsors need to be able to provide executive management with a good notion of how much the project is going to cost and how long it will take.

Realizing that the data warehousing context demands whole project estimates, agile warehousing teams follow the process outlined in the past two chapters in order to derive a good backlog of user stories. The project's architect, data architect, and systems analyst then translate that backlog into a fairly complete list of developer stories where data integration work is involved. This refined backlog is still composed of stories, so it is not the big-design up-front specification that makes waterfall projects take so long to get started. However, this backlog does give a clear enough picture to serve as a solid basis for whole project labor forecasting.

Once the application development has started, the team will naturally learn more about the project. The team's velocity will also be revealed during sprint retrospectives. As this new information becomes available, the team's leadership incorporates it into an updated "current estimate," typically prepared at the end of each iteration. By providing current estimates regularly, the team can keep the product owner and other stakeholders steadily apprised of the latest information on the project's remaining scope and probable completion date.

Quick story points via "estimation poker"

Before looking at the details of deriving whole project forecasts and refreshing current estimates, readers will need to be familiar with the special method agile teams employ to quickly estimate the labor requirements of backlog stories. Additionally, they will need to understand the two styles in which these estimates can be made: story points versus "ideal time."

As important as forecasting labor requirements is for running a project, agile teams still want estimation to consume as little time as possible. They want a quick and easy way to derive good story point estimates so that their story conferences proceed smoothly and their whole project forecasting sessions do not turn into protracted, mind-numbing estimating bashes. Fortunately, the agile community has perfected a particularly streamlined means of uncovering the story points implicit in a story, a technique called "estimating poker." This practice is summarized here, with further details available in many agile project management books (such as [Cohn 2005]). Luckily for data warehousing teams, the estimating poker technique works equally well for estimating dashboarding development work as it does for developer stories for data integration work.

Before estimating begins, the scrum master gives each team member a small deck of cards. Each card has a different number printed on it, so that for any story being considered, a member can express how many story points he thinks it represents by simply selecting the appropriate card from his deck. Often, these cards have pictures from a particular class of objects, such as fruits, African animals, or transportation vehicles, to remind the developers that they will be estimating the size of the work unit, not its labor hours. Figure 7.3 displays one such card deck

FIGURE 7.3

Typical card deck for agile "estimating poker."

with numbers ranging from 0 to 40 associated with the pictures of purebred dogs ranging from 4 to 200 pounds in weight.

Note that the deck does not include every number between the two extremes. Agile developers do not like to lose time debating whether a particular story is a 6 or a 7. By spreading the numbers out a bit, card decks make group decisions easier and keep the process speedy without losing too much accuracy. The typical agile estimating deck employs an expanding series of numbers. The most popular pattern is the Fibonacci series, which starts with 0 and 1, and then assigns to each succeeding card the sum of the numbers on the prior two cards. By convention, agile teams employ this series up to 13 and then switch to rounder numbers such as 20, 40, and 80 beyond that. Typical decks also include a card with a question mark (the "mutt" in Figure 7.3) so that a developer can signal he does not believe the team has enough information to provide an accurate estimate.

The process for using these cards to make an estimate proceeds as follows:

1. Have the product owner and other team leads present the story.
2. Each developer selects an estimating card expressing the size of the work required by the story.
3. All developers show their cards at once.

4. The scrum master identifies the highest and lowest individual estimates and asks those developers to discuss their outlying values.
5. Teams reselect and display estimating cards, discussing outliers and reestimating until a consensus is reached.

Before the estimating session begins, the team must identify or review its reference stories. As described earlier in Chapter 2, these stories pertain to a few work units already completed that the developers know quite well. The team only needs a couple of these reference stories, ranging from small to fairly large. The team gives the smallest of these stories an arbitrary number on the low end of the number line, such as a two or a three. The team then awards points to the other reference stories that reflect how much more work they represent compared to the smallest unit. Say a team has picked three such stories to serve as their references and assigned them three, five, and eight story points. The developers do not obsess about how many hours went into each module built, but they are very clear in their minds that the module built for the five-point story was nearly twice as much work as the three and that the eight was nearly three times as large.

To estimate a story from the top of the project backlog, the team discusses the requirements with the product owner and then considers briefly the technical work it will entail. As they talk, they should be striving to pick a card that best represents the size of the new story compared to the reference stories. The scrum master watches the developers during the discussion, and when it seems they all have a card selected, he asks them to "vote" by showing their cards.

Even in established teams, these votes will not match at first, but they often cluster closely around a particular value. At that point the team needs to discuss and revote until the estimates converge upon a single value. What if a team of nine developers voted a particular story with one 2, seven 8s, and a 20? Instead of going with the majority, the scrum master immediately polls those with the outlier estimates, asking "What do you see about this story that the rest of us have overlooked?" In a typical data integration estimating session, the developer voting 20 might say something like "To build this customer dimension, we'll have to deduplicate the account records from three different sources. We've just upgraded the data quality engine, and the new version is a nightmare. The labor it will take to deduplicate our account records now is going to kill us." This comment will undoubtedly spook the other developers, who will frantically start searching their decks for the 20-point cards. But the scrum master should turn to the developer voting 1 story point and ask "What do you know that the rest of us don't?" This developer might reply with "The data quality engine may now be a nightmare, but the accounts receivable team just put a new service online that returns a golden customer record. All we have to do is send an account list to the right Web address and it will send back a set of standard customer IDs." Convinced by this suggestion, the other developers will search instead for their 1-point cards so they can revote the story.

In the estimating poker technique, as long as teammates disagree over labor-hour requirements, the scrum master asks them to place additional evidence and analysis before the team so that the disparity can be resolved objectively. The emphasis on outlying votes and objective resolution works to avoid group think, ensuring that important information is not overlooked and that no one person dominates the process. Although several iterations of voting may be needed before the team reaches consensus on a story, the time involved is mostly dedicated to analyzing the situation. The actual process of polling the team for an estimating process does not take very long, typically between 3 and 5 minutes per story. The poker technique can move at this quick pace because it is using pair-wise comparisons between the unestimated work and the reference stories. This is an intuitive process that draws upon the best parts of the human mind. The waterfall alternative is to break work down into microscopic tasks and estimate the labor hours for each—an excruciatingly detailed endeavor that quickly exhausts even the best software developers.

Because agile estimating is fast and easy, teams can achieve remarkable consistency and accuracy with their agile story point estimates. With estimating poker, agile estimating sessions stay fun and retain the attention of all developers, for they know that the estimates they provide will directly determine whether they work nights and weekends during the coming sprint. Although it is fast and easy, the estimating poker "game" is not an undisciplined approach. It is actually a lightweight version of the "wide-band Delphi" estimating technique, which has considerable research vouching for its effectiveness. [McConnell 2006]

Occasionally, teammates will split into two irreconcilable groups on a particular story, one voting 8, say, and the other voting 13. If the discussion is no longer revealing any new information addressing the disparity, then the scrum master can propose they just split the difference, call it an 11, and move on. Two story points one way or another should not make or break a sprint. If the team frequently divides into such implacable groups over estimates, then the scrum master should inquire as to the root cause during the next retrospective. A frequent divide within the group can represent a deeper division, such as two incompatible architectural preferences (such as Inmon versus Kimball) or the fact that the project involves two completely different types of work (such as dashboarding versus data integration) that might be better pursued by two separate teams.

A high point estimate for a story—say a 40—can indicate to the developers that they are discussing not a story, but a theme or an epic. This outcome should spur the scrum master into having them discuss how to break the story into smaller deliverables. Once teams get established, they often develop a "resonant frequency" with the estimates for their backlog stories. The bulk of their stories fall within a range of three consecutive cards, say 3, 5, and 8. This tendency reflects a dynamic scrum masters should encourage because it means the product owner and project architect are looking past epics and themes and bringing consistently defined user and developer stories to the story conferences. Such consistency is welcomed because it will allow the developers to optimize their development process for these standard-sized stories. They will achieve maximum velocity by sticking to common story sizes, keeping out of the backlog the oversized stories that will only "gum up" their DWBI application delivery machine.

Story points and ideal time

As discussed in Chapter 2, because Scrum/XP is really a collaboration model and not a complete method, there is tremendous diversity between agile teams. When it comes to estimating, the most fundamental variation observed is whether a team employs story points in addition to labor hours, as outlined in this book, or skips story points entirely to estimate work only in labor hours. The latter style is called the "ideal time" approach. Because ideal time estimation certainly works for many teams, one would be hard pressed to say its advocates are committing an error. However, there are several reasons to think that employing story point and labor hours performs better. A list of the pros and cons for each approach will allow readers to decide for themselves which choice is right for their teams.

Table 7.3 sets forth the major poles defining the diversity in estimating styles. Other variations exist, but they become readily intelligible once one understands the differences portrayed here. The primary contrast is depicted in columns 1 and 2, that is, between the two approaches taken by generic agile teams: story points or ideal time. For clarity, the table also lists in columns 3 and 4 the approaches recommended in this book for agile data warehousing, where the variation is driven by whether a team is pursuing mostly front-end, dashboarding work or back-end, data integration work using data.

Column 1 in Table 7.3 depicts the generic story point agile team as estimating user stories in story points and then tasks in labor hours. Column 2 shows that an ideal-time team estimates user stories in work days for an anonymous developer operating under ideal conditions. The ideal-time team estimates in "anonymous" labor time, whereas the other three approaches use personalized labor hours at the task level, a point discussed in more detail in a moment. Often ideal-time teams will only enumerate the tasks within each iteration, keeping them so granular (2 to 4 hours) that the team need not waste any time estimating them. They believe it is more efficient to simply work those tasks and get them done. Because both columns 1 and 2 portray generic agile teams building OLTP applications, neither of them need to concern themselves with developer stories.

Columns 3 and 4 of Table 7.3 depict our recommended approach for agile data warehousing. If the developers are pursuing front-end, BI stories only, their work is very much like that of OLTP projects. Although the work will entail mostly user-interface elements that must be moved about the screen and enriched as the product owner requires, the team can deliver user-appreciable results with every iteration. These teams can safely pursue the project with just user stories estimated in story points and tasks estimated in hours. For data integration projects, however, teams will not be able to regularly deliver results that end users can work with or value. These teams will find their work much easier to understand and estimate if they utilize the developer story decomposition scheme suggested in the previous chapter. For data integration stories, then, teams award story points to developer stories rather than user stories. For development tasks, they will still estimate in labor hours as done for dashboarding work.

Table 7.3 Summary of Contrasting Agile Estimating Approaches

Approach Employed⇒ *Object Estimated* ⇩	Generic Agile		Agile Data Warehousing	
	Story Point Teams (1)	*Ideal-Time Teams* (2)	*Dashboard Work* (3)	*Data Integration Work* (4)
User Story	**Story Points**	**Anonymous Ideal Days**	**Story Points**	*Stated, Not Estimated*
Developer Story	*Not Used*	*Not Used*	*Not Used*	**Story Points**
Task	**Personalized Labor Hours**	*Stated, but so Small there's no need to Estimate*	**Personalized Labor Hours**	**Personalized Labor Hours**

Story points defined

With the contrasting styles of story point and ideal-time estimation now outlined, readers will benefit from a more careful definition of the two fundamentally different units of measure they employ. As described earlier, story points are a measure of magnitude or size of the work a story implies. Divining the labor implied by a particular story is analogous to guessing the weight of a piece of fruit, be it a cherry or an orange. One cannot specify exactly the object's mass through simple visual inspection, but by knowing that an orange is half a pound and a watermelon is five, he can come reasonably close to predicting the weight of a cantaloupe. On a data warehousing project, developers may decide that a slowly changing dimension is an eight given that they have agreed that a simple transaction fact table load module is a two. Such a statement is analogous to saying that a cantaloupe weighs about the same as four oranges. Moreover, when a team decides that two eight-point stories will "fit" within a 2-week iteration, it is on par with saying that two cantaloupes and four oranges will fit within a 10-pound sack.

When teammates really press for a more scientific definition of story points, scrum masters can always suggest that a story point is simply a percentage of a team's bandwidth, that is, its ability to deliver new application functions within one sprint time box. If the developers are currently delivering 20 story points every iteration, then 1 story point is 5% of that capability.

Ideal time defined

When teams estimate stories in labor hours, they will state that something as unalarming as "Story 126 will take 45 hours," but it is important to remember that they are speaking in terms of "ideal time." Ideal-time estimates are labor forecasts based on the assumption that whoever ends up developing the deliverables for a story will work only on that story until it is finished, and work under ideal conditions. There will be no interruptions or time drained away by departmental meetings, emergency emails, or idle chatter with one's teammates. Ideal-time estimates also assume that working conditions will be perfect—every tool and datum needed to build the code will be readily available, and every piece of information needed to guide the coding will be supplied without delay. That these conditions will actually occur is highly suspect. Perhaps even more dubious is the fact that ideal-time teams estimate these work durations not for any one teammate in particular, but instead for an anonymous developer. By defining the labor forecasts for an ideal programmer in an ideal situation, developers can continue using a single team velocity for setting sprint goals rather than having to track velocity for each role on the team. [Cohn 2005]

The advantage of story points

As long as a team can reliably forecast a backlog's labor requirements without investing too much time, the choice between the story point and the ideal-time approach will not matter. However, research and experience suggest that most teams will perform better using the story point approach.

The primary advantage of ideal-time estimates is that they are in hours. Hours are easier to explain to stakeholders outside the team, including project sponsors, the project management office, and team members' function managers. No one outside an agile project understands "story points." In fact, teams using story points cannot tell you the precise unit of measure they represent, and one team's story points certainly do not match that of the next agile team.

The problems with ideal-time estimates appear immediately, however, and many of them are implicit in the definition of "ideal." Ideal-time estimators forecast labor for an anonymous developer. During the estimating process, however, one developer might state that an ideal programmer can complete a story in 2 days whereas another insists it will take 4 days. To resolve the issue, they will have to identify a particular person to use as an example of programming style so that the notion of an anonymous programmer suddenly disappears. Now that they are discussing particular individuals on the team, they should start tracking the velocities for each teammate in order to avoid overcommitting during each sprint. More importantly, by pegging estimates to the precise programmer they think will do the work, they have instilled a tremendous constraint on the iteration. Programmers cannot share or exchange stories during development, else they will undermine the estimates and risk working nights and weekends in order to deliver new features as promised. Ideal-time estimation thus discards the advantages and speed achieved through a spontaneously self-organized team.

Research has shown that the human mind excels at comparing the relative size of two complex objects, but does poorly at identifying absolute magnitudes if there are more than a few abstract factors involved. [Miranda 2000; Hihn, Jairus, & Lum 2002] Ideal-time estimates consist of the absolute magnitudes that humans struggle with. It is possible for developers to estimate labor hours reasonably well for a small number of tasks, such as those making up a single iteration. Estimating more items than that, however, causes their minds to tire and the accuracy of their estimates to fall. Story point estimation requires the pair-wise comparisons research shows humans are good at performing. Being easy to generate, story points then make a far better choice for estimating an entire release or project.

Ideal-time estimation also suffers in the area of resolving disputes. When two developers provide wildly divergent forecast for the same work item, they are tempted to discuss the actions they believe each task will take. Discussions regarding step-by-step actions are far too granular. Such detail will slow estimating to a crawl, preventing the team from getting through a story conference quickly, not to mention a whole project estimating session. When the estimating effort required for individual work elements goes up, it saps the energy of a team working a long list of items, driving overall forecasting accuracy down.

Contrast these lamentable aspects of ideal-time estimates to the advantages of story points and the choice should become clear. Story points equal not hours but a more intuitive notion of a story's size, such as its "weight" or "mass." The hours the work requires are implicit in the size, so teams can work at this higher unit of measure and skip all the disagreements over detailed technical tasks and their proper durations. The developer who will pursue a work unit is not implicit in that module's size, so the developers are free to swap roles during the sprint and share the load as necessary in order to get the job done in the shortest possible time.

The size of a story is also independent of the nature of the team. Ideal-time hours can shrink as a team gains experience with the problem space of the project or can grow when external factors make work more difficult in general, such as when developers begin using a new tool or a personal matter impacts the effectiveness of a key member of the team. With story points, such vicissitudes simply make the velocity rise or fall. The estimating units themselves do not vary, making story point forecasting much simpler for developers to keep consistent over the life of the project. Perhaps more importantly, the invariability of a size-based estimate allows a team to forecast an entire project and avoid revisiting that forecast constantly because the unit of measure has changed.

Story points can also tap an important second estimate that validates the programmers' forecasting skills and quickly makes their estimating more accurate. Story pointing teams set the points for their work during the story conference and then corroborate them with the labor-hour totals assigned to component tasks during the task planning portion of the sprint planning day. Teams typically bounce back and forth during the planning day between story points and tasks hours until they get them both right. Ideal-time teams estimate immediately in hours, leaving them no other unit of measure with which to verify their projections. Without a double check, spurious factors can warp their estimates unimpeded and undermine their forecasting accuracy.

Crucially, story points do not mislead project stakeholders into misinterpreting the team's estimates. When a team states a project will require 1000 ideal hours, the rest of the world hears only "1000 hours" and decides quickly that four developers should be able to deliver the whole application in less than 2 months. When a project is estimated in story points, stakeholders must ask what the team's velocity is before they can infer a delivery date. This links everyone to the reality of the team's performance and insulates the developers greatly from other parties' tendencies to build unrealistic expectations. Story points also do not invite management overrides. When developers decide that a particular story will take 60 hours, project managers and functional supervisors can easily double guess the estimate, claiming that a "reasonably competent" programmer should be able to get it done in half that time. Story point estimates must be interpreted using the team's velocity, thus again forcing everyone to utilize the historical facts that actual project experience provides, avoiding distortions caused by wishful thinking.

Finally, story points are just plain easier to work with. By avoiding issues such as who will actually do the work and how fast they should really code, teams can estimate each story in a few minutes once they understand the functionality desired. This enables them to keep story conferences brief and efficient, making it much easier to keep everyone involved. The ease of story pointing also makes it reasonable to estimate an entire project, allowing teams to provide regular forecasts of remaining work that sponsors demand from projects as lengthy as data warehousing efforts. Moreover, with ideal-time estimating, the team loses the accuracy and speed needed to regularly provide current estimates for the project. Without story points, it is difficult to provide the team's prediction of how long a project will take, allowing stakeholders to develop contrary notions, which often result in developers having to finish the project under an extreme time pressure to meet an arbitrary deadline.

Estimation accuracy as an indicator of team performance

Team estimates provide a handy summary level measure for assessing the effectiveness of an agile team. When teams are executing their agile method effectively, they should be able to reliably deliver 95% of the work they take on with each iteration. To achieve this high level of performance, they must do everything right. They first understand the features requested, decompose them into properly sized stories, plan their delivery, collaborate well with each other, validate their work as they go, and provide working software so robust the product owner can evaluate the results using his own business questions to guide him. If the team fails to execute well on any portion of this chain, the ratio of accepted results to amount of work promised at the start of the sprint will take a rapid dive. Fast delivery of quality applications may be a primary goal for agile teams, but the accuracy of their estimates is the "canary in the coal mine" indicating whether something has deteriorated with the process in the project room.

The ratio of accepted-to-promised work can be calculated for every iteration in story points and labor hours. The possibility of two different units of measure adds some subtlety to working with this metric. The ratio for story points is simply the story points of accepted stories divided by the story points of stories promised at the start of the iteration. The ratio for labor hours is the total of labor hours on tasks that were completed—according to the team's definition of done—divided by the total hours for all tasks associated with the promised stories. If the team delivers upon 95% or more of both story points and labor hours, they can be assured they are performing well. The ratio for story points can fall dramatically if even one story gets rejected. When this happens, the team must consider the ratio for labor hours. If the labor-hour ratio is also below the 95% mark, then it indicates that the team had trouble somewhere in its process and did not get all its work done. The drop in the story point ratio may be simply due to the amount of task work not completed. If the ratio for labor hours is above the 95% level, then the story must have been rejected for quality reasons, and the team should focus on that aspect of their process rather than on whether all the work was completed. The sprint retrospective is the natural forum for determining the root cause when either of these ratios falls, and exploring their movements often reveals the rough edges in the team's development process.

Value pointing user stories

As described earlier, story points provide a sense of how much labor a given developer story for a data integration project will likely require. In that light, story points reflect a notion of cost, to wit the programming resources the organization will have to invest to acquire the capabilities described. Any estimate of cost naturally gives rise to a complementary question: how much will a particular unit of work be worth once completed? That is, how much will its promised functionality be valued?

Many agile teams use the estimating poker technique to derive not only story points but also "value points" for the components on the project backlog. Instead of obtaining those value points from the programmers, the team leads will hold a value-estimating session for the product owner and the project's major stakeholders. Whereas it may seem natural for the stakeholders to award value points to the user stories, sometimes they are too granular. In that case the business partners will only be able to value point themes. They might ask "What's the value of slicing revenue by customer? I can't tell you. But understanding where we're losing revenue, that's worth twice as much as being able to review our costs." If the stakeholders can only value point the themes, then the team can ask the product owner to finish the job and distribute them across the component user stories. As a default, he can award value points proportionate to the story points the developers set if no other way to proportion the value suggests itself.

The payoff of value pointing a project's themes or user stories is severalfold. The result gives the team, including the product owner, a set of numbers they can utilize to place the user stories in priority order. Value points provide a notion of business benefit to consider when it comes time to rescope the project or contingencies require the developers to delay the delivery of a particular feature. The team can also prepare what the agile community calls a "burn-up chart," a chart of benefits delivered by the project over time using the value points of the stories delivered against time.

If the project has been assessed a return-on-investment (ROI) measure, the value points contained in each major component can lead to a dollar measure of benefit by simply distributing the ROI across stories in proportion to the value points assigned to each. This practice will make the project burn-up chart of value delivered to date all that more compelling by putting it in dollars, a unit of measure that everyone can understand. A dollar-based graph of value delivered to date will allow the product owner to quantify the benefits of the project to sponsors whenever the project's future funding is discussed. Value points translated to ROI dollars even allow the contribution of several projects within a program to be aggregated.

Finally, when the slope of the burn up from one project begins to level off, the program can consider whether the company would be better off transferring those resources to another project. Thus value pointing enables companies to allocate their programming resources far more effectively, making them well worth the small amount of time they take to gather. The burn-up chart will be considered again in the last chapter of this book.

Packaging stories into iterations and project plans

An earlier discussion in this chapter mentioned that some agile teams will refuse to provide their stakeholders whole project estimates. Unfortunately, the length and high expense of data warehousing projects invariably require a labor forecast if the project is to be funded. Sponsors may provide a little "discovery" money to get started, but soon the executives will require a cost target and a calendar goal for the project. Data warehousing stakeholders commonly insist upon such estimates so that they can judge as the project progresses whether a team is performing and whether the scope of the project is under control. The product owner, under heat from the sponsors, will also demand a schedule of iterations listing the features that will be achieved with each sprint. These demands require that agile warehousing teams learn to bundle user and developer stories from the backlog into attractive releases, where each provides valuable new services to the business departments of their company.

Fortunately, a project backlog with story point estimates provides the raw material for preparing these major artifacts. They require only that the story points have been estimated and a measure of the team's velocity. Both the story estimates and the velocity must be in story points. To derive an estimate for a whole project or for just the release ahead, the team must group the stories in the backlog into iteration-sized chunks. Figure 7.4 shows the end result of this process for a data integration project, where the backlog's detailed lines represent developer stories.

In Figure 7.4, user stories are shown as headers over the related developer stories. They have been "appraised" by the stakeholder community using the "value points" in order to facilitate their prioritization. Story points are visible on each developer story, and they are what the team has used to group stories into iterations, using in this case a velocity of 16 story points, which they must have achieved during the prior iteration. At this point, developers can communicate to stakeholders that the entire deliverable represented in Figure 7.4 will require four sprints. If they

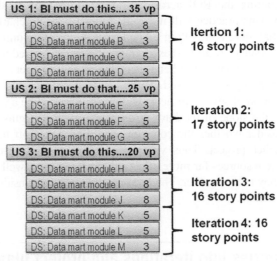

US: User Story   DS: Developer Story   VP: Value points

FIGURE 7.4

Deriving a current estimate from a project backlog.

are using a 3-week time box, simple math allows them to state that four sprints will take them 12 weeks. To derive a cost projection for the sponsors, the team can simply multiply its per-iteration burn rate by the number of necessary sprints that the bracketing process has indicated. If, in our example, the project is consuming $100 K per iteration, simple math again reveals that the team will need $400 K to deliver all the modules listed on the current project backlog. By this means, agile teams can provide stakeholders an answer to "how long is it going to take and how much is it going to cost?"

As each iteration concludes, the team will acquire a new measure for its velocity. To prepare a current estimate of the cost and duration for the remaining development work, the team needs only to bracket the remaining stories on the backlog using their existing story points and the new velocity. This step will provide an updated count of the necessary iterations, which in turn will indicate a new forecast for the remaining development cost. Occasionally, teams will realize that they misestimated an entire class of stories and need to adjust their story points. For example, a data integration team might decide that all slowly changing dimensions need to contain the previous value for certain fields on the current record rather than just tracking history with inactive records, that is, they should be Type 6 rather than Type 2 dimensions. This decision will increase the typical story point for many of the project's developer stories involving slowly changing dimensions, say from a five to an eight. Such an adjustment is again easy to include in a new current estimate by simply revising the story points for that class of stories and rebracketing the backlog using current team velocity. Agile's current estimates, based on

> **Table 7.4** Six Steps for Prioritizing Project Backlogs
>
> Agile has only one priority: Business Value
> Teams can Lower Risks by Considering Additional Criteria:
> **1.** Predecessor/Successor Dependencies
> **2.** Smooth out Iterations
> **3.** "Funding Waypoints" in Case Resources Disappear
> **4.** Architectural Uncertainties
> **5.** Resource Scheduling

story points and team velocity, are quick to create and update, plus they are readily understandable by all stakeholders.

Criteria for better story prioritization

Bracketing a backlog's stories using team velocity to derive a current estimate presupposes the team has placed the stories into the right sequence. In practice, teams usually alternate a bit between sequencing and bracketing in order to derive a delivery plan of iterations that all roughly match the team's velocity. Additional factors also come into play as the team discusses ordering of the stories. All told, there are six considerations for sequencing the stories of a backlog, as listed in Table 7.4.

Generic agile recommends that the product owner sequence the stories according to business value, and certainly this is the place to start. By sequencing in business priority, the team will ensure that it delivers the maximum value possible should the project get canceled before it is completed. However, if members of an agile warehousing team did not look beyond simple business priority, they would be risking several other factors that could easily make the project fail. Table 7.4 lists five prioritization criteria beyond the simple business value necessary to mitigate these risks. The next consideration should be ordering the stories to account for data and technical dependencies. For example, the product owner may insist upon slating the "load revenue fact table" developer story at the top of the backlog, so the team will need to gently assert that at least some of the dimensions need to be delivered before loading a fact table makes any sense.

The third consideration on the full list of prioritization criteria would be to swap developer stories in and out of iterations in order to "smooth" each bracket down to match the team's velocity. If the team has a velocity of 15 story points, it makes no sense to have a sequence that requires 12 points in one iteration and 18 in the next. A better solution would be to swap a 5-point with an 8-point story so that both iterations match the team's velocity of 15. Naturally, the product owner needs to be included in these discussions, but unless the team is starting the last iteration before a release, such "horse trading" between iterations will have no impact on the stakeholders the product owner represents.

The next sequencing criterion focuses on "funding waypoints," which are the places within a project plan where the organization might reconsider whether to continue funding the development of the application. This criterion asks the product owner to consider the value of the project, assuming it is not funding past each release boundary. This consideration can lead him to spot a user story far down on the list that the business cannot live without, even though it made sense somehow to develop it later in the project. The story could be a tool supporting annual reconciliations between warehouse data and operational systems. The product owner did not feel he must receive it right away, but he knows the company will need that feature eventually if the product is going to be complete. When faced with funding waypoints that might cause the bottom of the list to be dropped, such stories should be moved up before the release boundary in question in order to minimize the impact of a possible project cancellation.

At this point, the stories are in a logical order and reflect the highest possible value to the business. The project architect should now search for the technically riskiest stories on the backlog and consider elevating them to earlier iterations. Take, for example, a profit margin data mart project in which the product owner has placed the revenue fact table at the top of the backlog. The project architect might realize that the transformation for the cost fact table will require a standard costing subprocedure and have serious doubts whether data available are complete enough to power the algorithm everyone has in mind. Accordingly, he should advise the product owner to elevate the story for the cost fact table above that for revenue facts so that the team can build enough of the allocation engine to prove the technical feasibility of the entire project.

Finally, resource availability can often impact the optimal ordering of a project backlog. Say the product owner has organized the backlog to steadily deliver a series of dashboards with each iteration, but the BI developers will not be released from another project for another 4 months. Here it would make far more sense for the team to build all of the dimensions before the fact table behind even the first dashboard, because without a BI front end there is no compelling reason to rush the fact tables into production before all their dimensions are ready.

Segmenting projects into business-valued releases

The criteria presented previously work well for ordering a project backlog, but ordering alone does not provide a full project release plan. To get the necessary feedback on requirements and to maintain project funding, agile teams must regularly push new capabilities for end users into a production environment. For this purpose, good sequencing is not enough. To plan out a steady flow of valuable features for end users, the team will need to devise ways to package the project's stories into a series of functional enhancements for the application that end users value. "Project segmentation" is the practice of selecting points along a project backlog where an intermediate version of the software can be placed into production for end users to benefit from. Effective project segmentation balances sequencing stories in order to avoid rework for developers against bringing forward certain features that will please the end users and project sponsors. Project segmentation first occurs at the end of the project's inception phase as part of deriving the whole project vision and cost estimate required by the project funding process of many companies. Once the project's construction phase begins, teams frequently revisit project segmentation whenever business or technical needs change in order to redefine the sequence in which features will be delivered.

Segmenting a project defines a series of production releases where each provides a compelling stakeholder benefit. However, incremental delivery means all but the last release will be missing some features, so any proposed release schedule will mix benefits with frustrations for users. Negotiating an acceptable series of releases can be very difficult when working with a stakeholder community that wants all data, wants it perfect, and wants it now. There also may be certain milestones a project must achieve to coordinate with other IT projects in the company. The team must find a set of natural dividing lines within the stakeholder's notion of "the data warehouse" along which reasonable, partial deliverables can be defined.

While planning their project segmentation, agile data integration teams usually cycle through three steps utilizing three artifacts: dividing up the project's *star schema*, finding corresponding divisions on the project's *tiered integration data model*, and summarizing project releases using a *categorized services model*. To keep the presentation of this process clear, the following text first recaps the data engineering solution engineering approach by which teams derive the data models employed, then describes three artifacts employed, and finally illustrates how they are used to segment the project into an incremental series of application releases.

The data architectural process supporting project segmentation

Because project segmentation determines customer satisfaction directly, it is a primary practice needed to make agile data warehousing projects succeed. Conceptually, it occurs at the end of a long chain of activities pursued by the data architect with wide support from the other teammates. In waterfall methods, these activities follow a precise sequence, as prescribed by enterprise architectural planning and standard system engineering. On an agile team, the data architect iterates between them while reviewing the results with the rest of his team, providing greater detail with each pass. Typically, agile teams work an architectural plan until the artifacts cover the most important 80% of the project. In the interest of getting the project started and to begin learning from actual results, the team considers these 80/20 specifications "good enough" and leaves the remaining details to be specified when the developers begin building modules during an iteration. Although agile teams move between engineering steps as needed to achieve a workable design, it helps to know the logical sequence these steps should occur in helps understand project segmentation. That ordering can be summarized as follows:

- **Business modeling** in order to identify required informational entities and to resolve any conflicts in terminology and semantics through data governance. In agile projects, authoring user stories that describe the desired application is included in this step.

- **Logical data modeling** in order to represent the data entities and attributes indicated by business requirements, but to depict them independently of how they will be implemented in the physical tables of the database. In agile projects, decomposing user stories into developer stories occurs during this step.
- **Physical data modeling** in order to specify the precise tables, views, indexes, constraints, and other database elements the team will need to create and populate in order to deliver the services depicted in the logical and business models.

Artifacts employed for project segmentation

In an agile data warehousing project, the data engineering steps listed earlier result in a set of artifacts that assist greatly in project segmentation. For data integration projects, project segmentation must be preceded by a good start on developer story decomposition, story point estimating, and whole project planning, as presented in the past few chapters. In addition to a prioritized and story pointed project backlog, segmentation requires a few additional artifacts to enable the team—including the product owner—to fully envision various alternatives and reasons about the advantages of each. These artifacts are as follows.

Business target model

The business target model is a business-oriented presentation of the application's dimensional model. It depicts major business entities as a set of facts and dimensions the customer will need for his data mart. The team uses this model to understand the purpose of the data warehouse it is building for the end users. This artifact was first introduced in Chapter 5, and Figure 5.4 provided a good example of such a model. As in that diagram, the business target model is often drawn schematically, with only the entities identified, or at most a few key attributes. Because the objective of dimensional modeling is to provide business-intelligible data stores, often a data mart's subsequent logical data model closely resembles the relevant portions of the business target model.

Dimensional model

The dimensional model is a logical data model of a DWBI application's presentation layer (introduced in Chapter 6) from which the end-users' dashboards will draw data. It lists the entities and attributes the envisioned dashboards will require. Those entities providing measures are called *facts*. Those providing qualifiers by which facts can be disaggregated, filtered, and ordered are called *dimensions*. The top half of Figure 7.5 provides an example of a dimensional model. Typically, facts appear central in these models with dimensions surrounding them. Again, because dimensional modeling strives to make presentation layers intelligible for business users, dimension models appear very much like business target models, only with more details regarding the attributes of the entities. In the figures discussed later, dimensional models are depicted schematically (entity names without many attributes specified), which is often the way agile warehousing teams will draw them while planning projects on team room whiteboards.

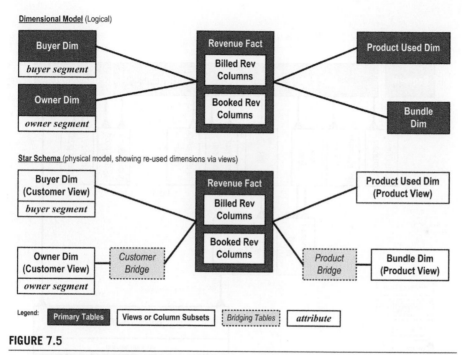

FIGURE 7.5

Sample dimensional model and corresponding star schema.

Star schema

A star schema is a physical model of the database tables needed to instantiate the logical dimensional model discussed earlier. The bottom half of Figure 7.5 provides a schematic depiction of the star schema employed by the examples in this chapter. Star schemas can often appear very much like their corresponding dimensional models occurring upstream in the definition process and also very much like the business target models that occur upstream from that. However, as can be discerned in Figure 7.5, the physical star schema can provide additional information covering the substitution of views for physical tables and the role of "bridging tables," both of which are discussed during the example given here.

Tiered integration model

The tiered integration model is a physical model of the integration layer. It differs from a standard physical model in that (a) its tables are often depicted schematically with all table names, but attributes only where necessary, and (b) tables are arranged in levels that reflect the number of parents each has so that the team can identify dependencies between them easily. Figure 7.6 depicts tiered data used in this chapter's examples.

Categorized service model

A categorized services model is a diagram that identifies a few important categories of service for end users that the development team can add to the application

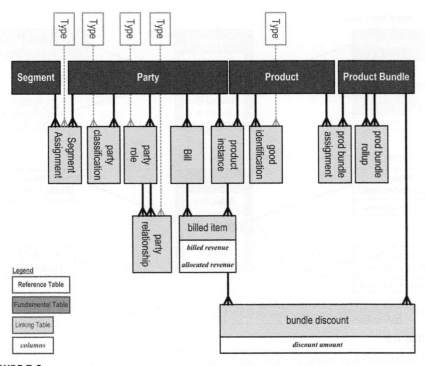

FIGURE 7.6

Sample tiered data model for an integration layer (drawn schematically).

in increments. This model also displays major steps along each of those categories that define intermediate levels in the richness of service provided, allowing teams to select which level to include with a given release. Figure 7.7 depicts a categorized services model for the front-end "domain" of dashboard components for a data warehousing project. Figure 7.8 presents a similar model for the back-end domain of data integration work that many business intelligence projects also require.

Each of the sample diagrams has divided the services of its particular domain into four categories. It is important to realize immediately that every team will probably select a different number and set of categories for its service models. In the examples provided in these figures, the front-end model uses for its categories the "user-friend-liness" of the dashboard, the access user will have, transformations embedded in the front end, and the frequency with which the BI tool will refresh its data subsets from the presentation layer. The back-end model defines its first two categories using the layer from the project's macro data architecture (discussed in the previous chapter) and the style in which it refreshes the tables in those layers with new data from the operational layer. The other two categories match that of the front-end model.

Each category provides its own collection of progressive service increments. These increments will be used to define the intermediate waypoints within the categories that the team can use to define a series of incrementally better product

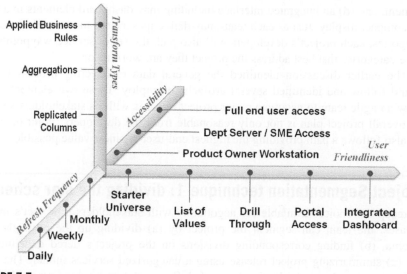

FIGURE 7.7

Front-end project categorized service model.

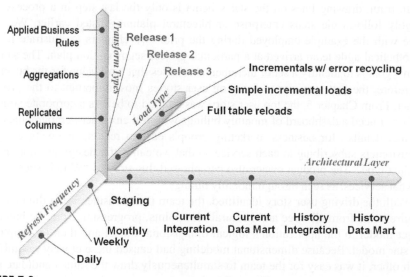

FIGURE 7.8

Back-end project categorized service model.

releases. The front-end category for user-friendliness, for example, defines a series of waypoints that progress along four levels of service, including (a) simple models for the semantic layer, (b) a list of values for query definition screens, (c) the capability to "drill through" a display to listings of data values behind a dashboard element, and (d) an integrated interface including may dashboard elements in a single compact display. Just as each team may define its services model with different categories, each project's developers will also pick the set of service waypoints on those categories that best address the project they are working on.

The earlier discussion identified the general data engineering process teams should follow and identified several artifacts to employ. These two elements will allow an agile team to negotiate major project releases with its stakeholders so that the overall project plan is not only reasonable from the developers' point of view, but also follows a path providing the highest end-user business value possible.

Project Segmentation technique 1: dividing the star schema

To recap the choices available for negotiating with stakeholders a project's major releases, the team can segment the project by (a) dividing up the project's star schema, (b) finding corresponding divisions on the project's tiered data model, and (c) summarizing project release using a categorized services model. The first of these approaches is fairly simple minded. Segmentation by dividing up the star schema occurs when the team draws the project's star schema on a whiteboard and begins drafting lines around the tables to define a series of project releases.

In truth, drawing lines on the star schema is only the last step in a process that roughly follows the steps enterprise architectural planning listed earlier. We continue with the example employed during the prior two chapters to illustrate how a hypothetical agile team arrived at a particular project segmentation plan. The sample team's goal is to identify a set of incremental releases that have value for the business. Therefore, the first step was to focus on user stories most important to the product owner. From Chapter 5, the top user story was worded to be "As a corporate strategy analyst, I need a dashboard of monthly billings with full customer demographics and product details…for business marketing group's eastern region…allowing analysis of customers subscribing to each service so that we can better design promotions by product type." The product owner also paraphrased this story as "Who is subscribing to what services, as seen through monthly billings?"

With the driving user story identified, the team then considered the dimensional requirements from all three architectural viewpoints, progressing from the business target model to the application's logical dimensional model and then to the physical star model. Because dimensional modeling had caused these closely resembling each other, it was easy for the team to simultaneously draw the same candidate segmentation lines on all three. Figure 7.9 shows how the final set of candidate lines appeared on the physical star schema. Note that most table column and several dimensions, including date, have been omitted for clarity.

The dialog that led to the lines displayed in Figure 7.9 unfolded as indicated in the following transcript, stylized to keep the presentation short.

Paula, project architect: Okay Carla. You're our product owner so I've got to tell you that the full data mart the business has requested cannot be delivered in one iteration or even in one release if we want to put something into production

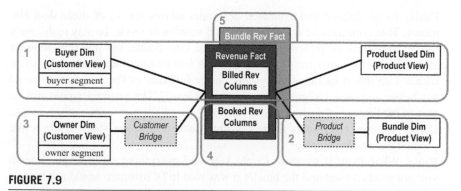

FIGURE 7.9

Project segmentation lines drawn on a star schema.

every couple of months or so. Your highest priority user story focused on "Who's buying what?" Consider the group of objects I've identified with Circle 1 on our set of dimensional models. You can look at the business target model, and the rest of the team will be looking at the physical star schema, as the circle is approximately the same on each. Circle 1 says we will push a build onto the production server that will allow your users to analyze billed revenue columns by the party that bought a service and the product that they are using.

Carla, product owner from corporate strategy: Will the first release allow me to see the market segment the customer belongs to?

Dale, team's data architect: Yes, but only the segment of the buying company. We know you have a business rule requiring that the segment of a buying company should be overridden by the segment of their owners if the owners are considered a "global account." You won't have any information on owners if we segment this project according to Circle 1.

Carla: How about product bundling? Our customers buy packages of services and equipment called "bundles," but the billing system charges them for the atomic components within those bundles, applying a discount later at the bill header level for the bundle.

Dale: We'll be limited by Circle 1 on that aspect, too. With this first release, you'll only be able to identify the charged products, not the product bundle the customer ordered.

Carla: And what about the allocation of billed revenue to monthly components for customers paying quarterly?

Dale: Circle 1 will only give you billed revenue, so the metrics your user will see will be a bit "lumpy." According to our systems analyst who profiled data for the Easter business marketing group, omitting allocated revenue will affect about a quarter of the customers.

Carla: We can wait for the allocated revenue, and even revenue adjusted for bundle discounts, but I would really like to get owner segments, product bundles, and allocated revenue in the first release.

Paula: We've defined and estimated developer stories for all of those data elements. That collection of features is about 8 months of work. To stay agile, we'd like to have three incremental releases in that time frame, not just one, in order to provide some value for your end users as fast as possible. What if we drew Circle 1 so that it included everything on the left side of the diagram so you'd get buyer and owner segments in the first release? The product would not be part of the first set of dashboards.

Carla: No, owner segments are not as important to that user story as the actual product a customer's using.

Paula: What about if we drew Circle 1 around everything on the right side so you got product used and the bundle it was sold in? Customer would not be part of that first release.

Carla: Bundles are more important than owner segment, but not more important than knowing who the buying customer is.

Dale: Then we hear that the first version of Circle 1 is the best collection of analytical capabilities we can give you as a first release at the 2-month time mark. We should then aim for providing product bundles next and then customer owners. After those are both delivered, we can work on the data transforms for allocated revenue. Let me draw Circles 2 through 3 on the model here.... You'll notice on our physical star schema that I've included the bridging tables in those other circles. The one on the left allows us to do the rollups from buying company to a holding company, even if there's several layers in between. [Kimball 1998] Likewise, the one on the right allows us to do the rollups for products into bundles. We'll be using views so that in the long run we can provide buyers and owners from a single set of customer tables and products used and bundles from a single set of product tables. [Kimball 1997]

Paula: The story point estimates we made using this project's developer tell us that with the team's current velocity from its last project, we'll be able to deliver each project segment circles in 2 months.

Dale: I'm drawing two more circles for releases we'll deliver after that. Circle 4 involves business rules for allocating revenue, and Circle 5 will provide a second version for all revenue tables that includes the discounts for bundles.

Carla: So, I'm taking your word on how long each group on this diagram is going to take, but you've drawn those boundaries in the right order.

Paula: We'll maintain a current estimate for you. If the team's velocity improves, we'll be able to recalculate and tell you how much earlier we can deliver.

Project Segmentation technique 2: dividing the tiered integration model

With the negotiation just given, the team established an acceptable series of end-user features with the product owner. Unfortunately, this series is defined only in terms of the presentation layer of the project. When the project architect cited team estimates suggesting that each delivery group would require 2 months, she had to be taking into account the integration layer that the data architect has stipulated for this project. In our example, the team concluded its user-level negotiation with the product owner using the set of dimensional models and then convened an integration-layer segmentation workshop involving the project architect, data architect, and systems analyst. At this workshop, the team will concentrate upon the integration-layer segmentation needed to support the desired segmentation identified for the presentation layer. By drawing a corresponding series of candidate deliveries on the integration's tiered data model, the team can decide quickly whether the implicit integration work of the negotiated schedule will be indeed reasonable for the programmers.

Figure 7.10 shows the project segmentation the team from our example drew upon the tiered, physical data model for its integration layer. The conversation was led by the data architect, as he authored the tiered integration model and could best link its components to the elements and groupings drawn on the star schema. A transcript of Dale's comments while applying this second technique follows.

> *Circle 1 on the star schema requires us to have billed revenue, buying customers, and charge products. On the tiered integration model, billed revenue is found in the billed item table. The buying customer is found in the party table, and the charge product in product. To link these tables together so we get data needed for Circle 1 on the star schema tables, we'll need everything in Circle A1 on the tiered data model. That won't be enough for the first release, however. We must provide the segment for the buying customer, so we'll have to have records from Circle A2 as well.*
>
> *The second project segment we negotiated with the product owner was for product bundles, and that would be this Circle B that I've drawn on the tiered integration model. Likewise, owner market segments will require the tables included in Circle C on the diagram. I can see that the allocated revenue will be a second set of columns in the product instance billing table, whereas bundle discounts come from a bundle discount table. In both cases, we're fortunate. Adding the features for Circle B, C, and beyond will not require us to include any new parent tables for bottom-level tables we already populated, so there will be minimal rework with this segmentation plan.*
>
> *So now we can easily figure out the data transform modules we'll have to build in order to get the required data loaded. Let's see if the work defined for the three releases making up the first full version will doable given the time we have:*
>
> - *We'll have nine target tables comprising two reference tables, three fundamental tables, and four linking tables.*
> - *I'll have to model them in detail and get the DBA's to create them in the target schemas.*
> - *The systems analyst will have to specify any data transforms needed by any of the target columns.*

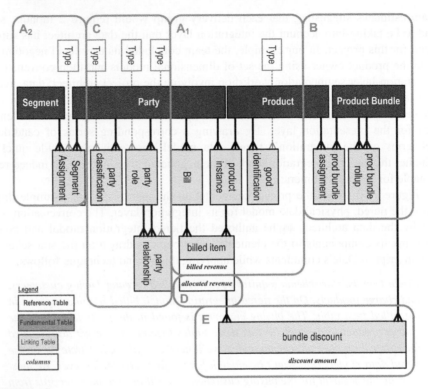

FIGURE 7.10

Project segmentation using a tiered integration data model.

- *The programmers will have to build both initial and incremental load modules for all nine tables, which is approximately 18 modules.*
- *We need to reserve a good week for our tester to load full volume data and conduct the system tests before we can promote onto the near-product server for user acceptance testing.*

   Paula said two and a half months for all the developers' stories in Circle 1. That's 9 weeks after subtracting a week for system test, or three iterations with our 3-week time box. Nine weeks for coding 18 modules after all the 80/20 specifications are prepared. Judging from how things went on the project we just finished, it seems tight, but doable.

The data analysts reasoning just described reveals several important aspects of performing this second segmentation step with the tiered integration model. First, the analysis occurs at a predominantly physical modeling level, but because the business and logical modeling preceded it, the team did not risk overlooking business semantics or logical requirements that would have invalidated the planning performed using the physical, tiered data model.

Second, much of the required information for this second step in project segmentation was prepared ahead of time and made possible by the developer story workshop described in the previous chapter. Because the data architect had been able to prepare a tiered data model based on the developer stories, it was ready when the team reapproached the product owner to negotiate project segmentation. Similarly, the story points that allowed the project architect and data architect to rapidly appraise the labor requirements for each circle had been derived earlier by working from the list of developer stories. Of course, as further discussions and analysis such as outlined in the aforementioned transcripts occur, the team may have to improve upon its collection of developer stories and/or their story point estimates. For the most part, however, project segmentation utilizes existing knowledge; therefore, developers can resegment quite responsively during conversations with the product owner.

Third, as the circles on Figure 7.10 reveal, tiered data models allow the team to define small vertical slices of the overall project that are deliverable independently. This pattern is the core to agile data warehousing, making it possible to identify and plan for incremental deliveries that entail a minimum of rework. If, contrary to our example, the data architect had found that elements in later releases required parents to be added to already loaded tables, then rework would be required. The degree of rework implied may have precluded a particular candidate segmentation plan, but in either case the tiered data model would have allowed the team to reason about whether the rework was worth the accelerated deliveries it would have supported.

Project Segmentation technique 3: grouping waypoints on the categorized services model

Some qualities that teams can use to define project segments cannot be depicted on any data model. To segment a project using these qualities, a team must employ the categorized service models. The application qualities that these artifacts model frequently determine the level of service that end users will receive from a DWBI application, such as the frequency of loads, the volumes it contains, and the types of columns that have been populated with values. Figures 7.7 and 7.8 portrayed the notion of categorized services for both the front-end, dashboard service domain and the back-end, data integration service domain of a data warehousing application. The categories that defined each of these domains provide the team with a set of service waypoints with which a series of increasingly service-rich releases can be identified. The concentric rings in Figure 7.8 depict a series of releases for back-end services that the team in our hypothetical project negotiated with its product owner. Because such negotiation sessions sometimes touch upon the different types of columns that each release will have populated, the team's data architect is usually included. But the full set of service decisions involved in these negotiations address how the various releases will represent solutions to the end-user's business needs. Discussions at the solution level require the project architect, who usually leads these meetings. The dialog that established the releases identified on diagram in Figure 7.8 followed the following transcript.

Paula: Carla, there's other categories of data mart features that we can compromise at first so that the developers can deliver some partially working systems very quickly. See if you can follow along on this services model diagram. Each of these categories provides several choices, and I need to find out from you which combinations of those choices would represent usable versions of the application for your users.

Carla: You mentioned this before concerning the back-end capabilities. Didn't you suggest the team place only current data in the warehouse first and then later beef up the data transforms to place history records online as well?

Paula: Yes, that choice has to do with the "architectural layer" category in the diagram. We're planning on using some views and our company's "virtualization software" to split the current data into two deliveries. In the first release, we can populate only the integration layer and then create a virtual data mart of current data on top of that. That will provide your users some analytical capabilities. It will also give the developers time to build a full data mart of current data for the second release and then add in history records for the release after that. The compromise the virtualization tool will force on us for the first release is that your users can only submit queries that return a limited volume of data and don't involve any advanced business rules.

Carla: Well, if we load just the eastern and central regions for the business marketing group, we should have only about a tenth of the full data, so big queries won't be an issue. The limitation of basic business rules shouldn't pinch too much, either, because at first we'll be just performing counts and building lists as we get to know the data.

Paula: Okay, great. So that defines three steps concerning the project's architectural layers. We'll also want to take three steps along the "load type" category. We'll start Release 1 with full table reloads—"kill and fill" loads—as long as we have small volumes because full reloads are easier to program. When we get to larger volumes, we'll have to switch to scanning the sources for changed and new records, so Release 2 will have simple incremental loads of whatever has changed since the last ETL run. After that, we'll add in some error recycling features for Release 3 so that you can see the source records that won't load because of data quality issues occurring in the operational systems.

Carla: Didn't you want to defer the complex business rules also?

Paula: Yes, that has to do with the "transform type" category. If okay with you we'd like to build Release 1 for just columns that get replicated as is from the source system. That would cover just billed revenue. For Release 2, we'll populate the columns holding aggregations, such as Top 100 Customers. We'll finish with Release 3, which will handle the complex business rules, such as allocated revenue and applied bundle discounts.

Carla: Well, the first set of user story is essentially "who's buying what" in the business marketing regions. We can get close enough to an answer for that question on billed revenue alone. Allocated revenue address user stories were written for finance and regional executives, and they are pretty far down the project backlog, so it's okay to defer those until the third release.

Paula: Super. The last type of service we'd like to deliver in steps is the frequency we refresh data in the data mart. Because we'll be running the loads by hand at first, I like to give the first release just a load on the first of each month. We can get the load process mostly automated for Release 2, but it will still take some manual support for the reference tables. Given that, we'd like to move to only weekly for that release. By the time we get to the third release, we should have the kinks in the load routine worked out, making daily loads possible.

Carla: Daily loads are also of interest to finance only. The rest of us can live with weekly and even monthly at first while we're getting to know the data.

The concentric lines on Figure 7.11 connect up the waypoints that Paula selected on each category for each of the three releases she proposed. She followed the back-end conversation given earlier with another discussion of the waypoints for the front-end service model. By connecting those waypoints with lines, the project architect can provide a clear grouping of the feature set that will make up the incrementally expanding capabilities end users will enjoy. Should new information or requirements arise during the project, the architects and product owner can easily revisit the categorized service model and draw a new set of feature sets for the releases they plan, making resegmentation of application services an easy, fluid process.

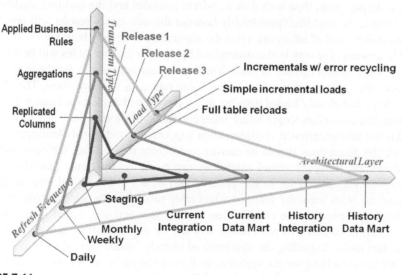

FIGURE 7.11

Project segmentation lines on a back-end categorized service model.

Embracing rework when it pays

One aspect of the incremental delivery approach that will cause traditional data integration developers to bristle is the notion that a team might deliberately choose to load fact tables when only a few of its dimensions are available. As portrayed in Figure 7.9, the team in our example defined an incremental release that would have only the customer and product dimension ready for use, planning to back fill the revenue fact table later with the keys for the many other dimensions defined for that set of measures. Traditional developers will claim that such an approach only causes unnecessary rework. "It's just as much effort to link in all the dimensions for a fact table as it is to do one," they will insist. "So let's wait until the complete set of dimensions is ready and link them all in at once."

This might be a compelling argument when true, but it rarely describes the full situation confronting the team. To release fact tables with their full complement of dimensions requires that all the dimensions be developed before fact tables are delivered. Depending on the business circumstance, this can delay the delivery of crucial business insights to the end users for too long a time. It is a return to the big, single delivery paradigm that waterfall methods advocate.

Traditional developers are correct, however. Implementing dimensions incrementally can require significant rework. The degree of rework depends on context. If the new dimensions change the "grain" of the fact table, then the rework can be considerable. The grain of a fact table is the level of atomicity implicit in the table's data. Measures of sales by sales agent and product are actually aggregates compared to sales by sales agent, product, and customer. If adding new dimensions gives the fact table a deeper grain, then both data transform modules and the end-user dashboards may have to be modified considerably because the new query results will provide a more detailed level of information that the application is already built for.

The amount of rework is also determined by whether the fact tables will be reloaded or have existing data updated in place. The former case is far easier for the team, but if the fact tables contain large data volumes, it can take days to reload them. The alternative is to update already loaded data, but this approach will require the team to program and run data conversion scripts, which takes considerable effort as well.

All the aforementioned considerations support the traditional developer's view that all the dimensions should be constructed before loading fact tables in order to avoid rework. However, actual conditions can be far less extreme than those considerations suggest. As far as the grain of fact tables is concerned, the additional dimensions often leave the grain of a fact table unaltered. In our example, revenue records are defined by the combination of customer account, billed item, and bill date. Their definition will not change whether or not the billing address is linked to the fact table. Regarding the challenge of already loaded fact table data, projects that are slowly adding source systems, such as occurred in our sample project, start off with small amounts of data, making full reloads less onerous.

In practice, teams will have to provide their product owners with an outline of the cost and benefits of adding dimensions incrementally. The costs are easy to focus upon, but teams must be careful not to overlook the benefits. Data warehouses provide insights into the operational performance of the company. The harm of delaying the availability of a fact table can be that it forces the organization to "fly blind" in the face of such urgent conditions as fast-developing competitive pressures or ruinously large cost overruns. For the telecom company of this chapter's example, losing 10% of a $15B customer base every quarter represented a revenue fall of over a billion dollars *per year.* Yes, the rework that adding dimensions incrementally to the revenue fact table may add up to $20,000 or $30,000, but that cost pales in comparison to the opportunity cost of not understanding the forces driving customers away.

Compelling business situations usually lead agile data warehousing teams into project segmentation plans that involve an appreciable amount of deliberate rework. The true objective of the agile team should be not to eliminate rework, but to avoid design *churn*, which can be defined as needless modification in construction plans due to mistakes in requirements and analysis. In the approach outlined in the past few chapters, the agile team has followed disciplined enterprise architectural planning guidelines by pursuing business modeling before logical modeling, and logical modeling before physical design. The recommended decomposition of the agile epics and themes established user stories before developer stories, which aligns with business modeling before logical design. As long as agile teams persist in this ordering of their analysis, they will reduce project rework to its practical minimum. The rework that remains will make business sense, as long as the opportunity gained by an early release outweighs the extra cost of delivering the solution in increments. By planning on incremental deliveries and the rework it entails, the data warehousing team will be able to meet one of the primary goals of agile methods: a delivery process through which the business stakeholders constantly receive new value from the development team.

Summary

The infrequent attention that waterfall methods pay to estimating project labor leads regularly to grossly inaccurate project estimates that hurt both developers and stakeholders alike. In contrast, because agile methods build estimating into the fabric of every development iteration, it quickly makes developers capable of estimating accurately and maintains their skills. To bolster the accuracy of their predictions, an agile team estimates using two units of measures—story points and labor hours, cross-checking and revising both viewpoints until their predictions agree.

Agile also provides the notion of sized-base estimation using a technique called estimating poker that allows teams to assign story points to backlog stories quickly. Being fast and accurate, this forecasting technique enables a team to estimate the stories of both an iteration and an entire project, allowing agile teams to predict how many iterations a project will require. Because all aspects of the developer's collaboration must go right for teams to regularly deliver upon all that they estimate they can build each iteration, tracking the accuracy of a team's estimates can quickly reveal adverse changes in the collaboration patterns within a project room.

The ability to estimate a full project accurately enables agile teams to group the stories on a backlog into a series of intermediate releases. There are three techniques for planning this project segmentation: divisions drawn upon the application's star schema, its tiered integration data model, and its categorized service model. Proper project segmentation may well include some deliberate rework, which—far from being the anathema that traditional software engineers may regard it—makes perfect business sense when it allows teams to deliver crucial analytical capabilities to end users early and often.

Adapting Iterative Development for Data Warehousing Projects

Adapting Agile for Data Warehousing

8

How can we adapt the generic agile process to better support projects with significant data integration work?
What new work roles and handoffs should we teach our agile warehousing teammates to employ?
How can our fast delivery teams ensure high-quality results, even when they must evolve their target data schemas frequently?

The material in the first two parts of this book only carries a data warehousing team part way to their goal of delivering high-quality business intelligence (BI) applications quickly. Part 1 presented Scrum as a generic agile collaboration method for developers. Part 2 then described a means for decomposing a complex project into a list of bite-sized work units ready to submit to that agile development method. If the envisioned project entails predominantly front-end, dashboarding modules, then the material presented so far will probably suffice because the work matches the general, transaction-capture application development work that Scrum was invented to accelerate.

Data warehousing projects, however, frequently require significant data integration, so they differ from front-end applications in that they must transform and move data between multiple, radically different data schemas before it's ready to be consumed by end users. Teams that try to employ generic Scrum "out of the box" for data integration projects will find that the method has not prepared them completely for the challenges of data integration projects. They will discover that without staffing a self-organized team with specific skills, they will not have the necessary leadership onboard. They will find that without a bit more structure, the development step of each iteration tends to force one or more technical specialties on the teams to fall idle while others are overloaded. They will also witness that wrestling with large data volumes will cause their developers to undermine each other's work. They will realize that generic test-led development does not address well enough the full-application integration issues of their project. Finally, they will feel totally unprepared for the work required to adapt a previously loaded set of data warehouse tables to cover the next set of business needs waiting in the project backlog.

Agile Data Warehousing Project Management.
DOI: http://dx.doi.org/10.1016/B978-0-12-396463-2.00008-9

In order to prevent this remaining gap from causing new Scrums to flounder through their first few iterations or even suffer a failed project, the last part of the book discusses adapting generic Scrum to better support data integration work. This chapter focuses on several basic techniques that will make incremental development for the data integration aspects of a data warehousing/business intelligence (DWBI) project appreciably easier to complete. The next chapter describes how to introduce the adapted method to a new team and how to scale it up for a multiproject program. The end result will be a starter method with one foot planted firmly in agile principles and the other fixed squarely in the world of data warehousing. It is this combination that will allow DWBI teams to achieve the goal described in the opening of this book: fast delivery of BI applications with few defects in a way that keeps the business both engaged with the process and delighted with a series of valuable, incremental releases.

The context as development begins

Recapping the project context established by earlier chapters will help the reader relate the adaptations to generic Scrum suggested here to the larger data warehouse engineering process that most large companies employ. The techniques described in this chapter are appropriate for a team that has just finished the inception phase of their company's release cycle and is ready to embark on the development activity that comprises the phases of system elaboration and construction. These phases were described earlier in Chapter 5. Table 8.1 provides a summary of the inception activities described in the previous section of this book, participants, and key resulting artifacts. The inception effort generated for the team a reasonably good knowledge of the application they must build. Although all participants in this early work realized there would still be holes in their knowledge, at least the major items defining the solution's data and process will have been illuminated. The remaining gaps are small enough that the team can fill them in as individual work units are fed to the Scrum iterations for development.

As the first technical person assigned to a project, the project architect pursued several activities and artifacts during the inception phase that culminated in order a high-level description of the solution and a labor estimate for building the application, as required by most companies before they will fund a project. Pursuing even this early work with an agile mind-set, he aimed at completing "80/20 versions" of these artifacts, that is, he planned on investing 20% of so of the effort waterfall methods typically dedicated to them in order to uncover and specify the most important 80% of the specifics needed to guide the project. The 80/20 goal made perfect sense because he was preparing the project for an agile team. When he and his future teammates would later start the project, they would reapply the definition and estimation techniques repeatedly on increasingly smaller scopes for each user story as it approached the development step of a Scrum iteration. The project architect's 80/20 groundwork during the inception phase included many aspects of generally accepted enterprise architecture planning methods. By working top down and focusing on the most important aspects of each topic, he assured that the project definition did not

Table 8.1 Groundwork Already Completed When Agile DWBI Development Begins

Activity	Participants (Leads in Bold)	Results
Feasibility assessment	**Enterprise architect**	Highest level business requirements; major data source systems, including existing data warehouses; "T-shirt size" project estimate
Initial project backlog interviews	**Project architect** Product owner	Initial backlog of uses stories; business target model
Initial developer story workshop	**Data architect** Project architect Systems analyst Product owner	Developer stories for data integration work; project's macro data architecture; high-level version of dimensional model and star schema for presentation layer; high-level logical and physical models for integration layer; notes on key business rules
Project story point estimation	**Developers** Data architect Project architect Systems analyst Product owner	Initial "current estimate" of project's labor requirements; backlog bracketed by team's velocity (velocity being speculative if team is new)
Project segmentation workshop	**Data architect** Project architect Systems analyst Product owner	Incremental release plan

overlook any large aspects of the application. As described in the middle part of this book, the project architect collaborated with the company's enterprise architecture group to discover intersystem requirements, existing data assets the new application could leverage, and corporate data architectures. With the project's product owner and other business stakeholders, the project architect held initial backlog interviews where he iterated between user stories and business modeling in order to define the scope of the project and gather the context needed for further discovery work. The result was an initial backlog of user stories, prioritized by value to the business, plus a business target model reflecting the analytical information the end users would need.

Once the business modeling was complete, the data architect and systems analysts joined the conversation. They held a developer story workshop intent upon deriving a similar 80/20 understanding of the project at the logical level. With the product owner attending as a business requirements resource, these three technical leads iterated among users stories, target business model, and the project's likely macro data architecture, which the data architect provided. They transformed user stories into DWBI-appropriate developer stories so that the project backlog now contained work modules that would fit within short Scrum time boxes. Developer stories also provided the data architect with enough guidance to provide first-cut, 80/20 versions of the application's logical and physical data models.

With the project backlog now transformed into developer-appropriate work units and some data modeling completed, the developers joined the conversation the inception effort long enough to estimate the backlog in story points. With those story points, the project architect leveraged the developer's velocity from another project to produce the project's first current estimate so that the sponsors could make a funding decision. If the team was just being formed, then the project architect had to infer a velocity (see sidebar). In either case, this current estimate will be revisited at the end of every iteration using the actual velocity that the team achieves.

SURMISING A NEW TEAM'S VELOCITY

For the most part, agile teams want to measure their velocity and use that empirical information for setting goals and updating "current estimates" for their project. Utilizing an existing team's velocity on a project they are finishing to estimate a project they are about to begin works well enough for the rough estimate needed during the new project's inception phase. Everyone should understand, however, that this estimate will be inaccurate to the degree that the work of the new project differs from the work of the old. Later, the team should insist on providing an updated current estimate for the new project based on their actual measured velocity after every iteration.

Estimating a new project that will be developed by a new team is so risky that it is inadvisable. It would be better to call the first two iterations an elaboration or prototyping phase so that the team can establish an actual velocity before providing a current estimate for the project. However, many large companies absolutely require a labor estimate for a project before they will allocate any development funds. In that case, the following approach is the best a new team can manage.

---

1. Calculate the developers' availability to work on the project for the first iteration by subtracting from their total work hours the time they will put into other projects and office activities such as email and meetings.
2. Divide that number by two to reflect the inefficiency they will experience while they are learning Scrum. This calculation yields their "capacity" for the first iteration.
3. Estimate the top of the project backlog in ideal hours (discussed in the previous chapter) until enough stories have been identified to consume the team's capacity.
4. Pick the smallest and largest stories accepted for the iteration's backlog. Assign the smallest item two story points. Have the team estimate the largest one using estimating poker (covered in Chapter 7).
5. Have the team estimate the remaining stories using as references the two they just assigned story points for.

With a green light on funding, the project architect, data architect, and systems analyst convened a project segmentation workshop with the product owner where they iterated between the 80/20 versions of the business, logical, and physical models, grouping the modeled objects for various combinations of end-user services, until they arrived at a plan identifying a series of incremental application releases that were simultaneously business-acceptable and technically feasible.

All these activities resulted in an action plan with medium-level detail, bringing the team to the point where developers can begin to build the application. The goal from this point on is to deliver small slices of the application. Perhaps the first couple of iterations will focus upon reducing the remaining major project risks (the elaboration phase), but quickly the goal will be providing fast, incremental delivery of valuable information services for the end user (the construction phase). If the first few iterations produce immediately usable services, the team will have succeeded. If those results are less than perfect, the team will still succeed in that errors in requirements and design have been uncovered while there is still time to fix the oversights. The secret to this "fail-fast and fix-quickly strategy" is the ability to quickly deliver usable application modules that can be evaluated by the team's business partners. To adapt Scrum to achieve fast, incremental delivery for a project involving data integration, the team will need several elements beyond generic Scrum. They will need to retain the additional leadership roles that powered the inception work described earlier, a strategy for keeping big data from slowing down its developers, a collaboration model adapted to multilayered architectures, a means of continually assessing whether they are delivering quality product, and a means for evolving target schemas once loaded with data so that intentional rework does not undermine the schedule and economics of the project.

Data warehousing/business intelligence-specific team roles

Regarding explicit roles, generic Scrum specifies only that teams will have a product owner and a part-time scrum master. All other teammates are simply "developers." Staffing is left to the project organizer to find the appropriate skills. As considered throughout this book, if a project involves data integration work, the delivery team will need additional skills in order to get project components defined well enough for developers to begin work. Accordingly, agile data warehousing has adapted the definition of a Scrum team to explicitly include four additional team members: the project architect, the data architect, the systems analyst, and a system tester.

Perhaps generic Scrum is wise not to spell out too many team roles, preferring instead to rely on the principle of "self-organized teams." Once they accumulate a decade or so experience in the field, many BI professionals have worked on several diverse aspects of building a data warehouse, such as data extraction, extract, transform, and load (ETL) development, data quality utilities, Web services, and visualization packages. Teams that are so lucky to have well-rounded teammates can gain tremendous productivity by letting them work together in the best way they can devise for themselves without forcing them to stick to specific skills. Even if each teammate develops a particular technical strength or preference, agile practitioners believe teams will still succeed through self-organization by utilizing a strategy of "generalizing specialists." [Ambler 2011] The common metaphor is a baseball team playing defense—each player must cover different portions of the field as the situation changes or as their teammates get pulled out of position.

Self-organization unleashes a tremendous amount of latent productivity, and teams should cleave to it as much as possible. Data warehousing tends to stretch the boundary of self-organization, though. Because each type of work on a data warehousing team tends to have its own tool set, members of a data warehousing project tend to specialize considerably. Data definition requires data modeling tools. Teams employ large packages for data profiling and cleansing. There are even larger software suites for ETL. Front-end work has comparable packages. Most of these products have their own scripting language or programming framework, making it very difficult for most individuals to be simultaneously adept at more than a couple of them. As a consequence, data warehouse projects of any size end up with more specific roles than general agile teams.

In the world of waterfall methods, "roles and responsibilities" are defined so that project planners will know how to staff a team correctly from the start. Given the detailed specialization needed for data warehousing projects, agile warehousing planners could benefit from even a small amount of the same preparation. Typically, agile data warehousing projects need the following roles and handoffs to occur.

1. A project architect who will understand the driving requirements, propose a business model for the application, and sketch a balanced technical solution.
2. A data architect to translate the solution vision into a series of logical and physical models for target data repositories.
3. A systems analyst to define high- and medium-level processing patterns plus the details of the transformation rules the coded modules will affect.
4. A systems tester who can assemble a daily validation process that will inform the programmers when defects have been introduced.

These four roles, plus the product owner, can be considered the leadership subteam of the project, for they make choices that determine the direction in which the team's developers will labor in for many hundreds of hours. These roles have been discussed in earlier chapters without careful definition, but to understand how to adapt Scrum to better blend their activities, a more careful description of the responsibilities of each will help. Table 8.2 provides one possible configuration of major responsibilities of each of these leadership roles; the following sections touch upon the highlights for each role.

Project architect

The project architect's goal is to deliver a solution in a timely and economical fashion. Given that solutions are technical applications solving business needs, the person in this role must envision and communicate the application to both the business

---

Table 8.2 Suggested Responsibilities for Agile DWBI Technical Leads[a]

Section 1: Responsibilities Common to All Roles
- Self-organize to ensure team success during each iteration
- Attend ceremonies of Scrum iteration, especially the sprint retrospective
- Attend daily stand-ups
- Update task cards with remaining hours
- Support product validation from component to user acceptance testing

Section 2: Project Architect
Project inception phase
- Conduct Iteration −1, including
  - Definitive business requirements from project sponsors
  - 80/20 business requirements* from others
  - 80/20 data governance*
  - 80/20 business modeling*
  - Initial user story backlog
  - Selection of data source systems, including reusable company data assets
  - Analysis of impacted systems beyond product boundary
  - Nonfunctional requirements
- Drive Iteration 0, including
  - Initial developer story workshop (other resident resources participating)
  - Story point estimation
  - (First) "current estimate"
  - Project segmentation workshop
  - Maintain list of intentional rework

Construction phase
- Refresh aforementioned artifacts with each iteration
- Support user and developer story grooming before start of each iteration
- Ensure coherence between major project elements, including
  - current estimate and intended funding
  - project segmentation and project milestones, including external ones
  - requirements, data architecture, process design, and system testing plan
- Identify project risk and mitigations, including resequencing project backlog
- Serve as "proxy product owner" when product owner participation is insufficient
- Represent product and team to architectural review and change control boards
- Orchestrate sprint demos

Product validation
- Draft solution-level test cases for each sprint demo with product owner
- Lead definition of user acceptance testing if product owner does not
- Certify product delivered as a solution to the business need

Transition phase
- Draft disaster recovery plan
- Monitor releases once in production

(Continued)

Table 8.2 Suggested Responsibilities for Agile DWBI Technical Leads[a] (Continued)

Section 2: Data Architect

Project inception phase

- Support Iteration −1, including
  - 80/20 data governance
  - 80/20 business modeling
  - Initial user story backlog
- Support Iteration 0, including
  - Define project's macro data architecture
  - Draft 80/20 logical and physical models for presentation layer*
  - Draft 80/20 logical and physical models for integration layer*
  - Participate in initial developer story workshop
  - Support business rules definition
  - Design data views for external, impacted systems
  - Participate in story point estimation
  - Drive project segmentation workshop

Construction phase

- Revise artifacts authored above as needed
- Maintain project's data dictionary
- Pursue data governance to completion where needed
- Coordinate data models with enterprise architecture
- Communicate DBMS requirements and DDL to DBAs
- Provide completed data models for stories entering development

Product validation

- Direct source data subsetting for unit and system test data sets
- Provide data quality test cases

Transition phase

- Direct data conversion scripting to support intentional rework

Section 3: Systems Analyst

Project inception phase

- Support Iteration −1, including
  - 80/20 business rules*
  - Initial user story backlog
- Support Iteration 0, including
  - Conduct 80/20 source data profiling*
  - Participate in initial developer story workshop
  - Participate in story point estimation
  - Support project segmentation workshop

(Continued)

Table 8.2 Suggested Responsibilities for Agile DWBI Technical Leads[a] (Continued)

Construction phase
- Revise artifacts authored above as needed
- Draft application's midlevel ETL data flow*
- Draft team's standard coding patterns
- Finish data profiling for modules entering development*
- Specify data integrity rules to control which data will be loaded into warehouse
- Draft source-to-target mappings for modules entering development*
- Maintain projects reference model
- Document team's reference modules
- Set as-built documentation standards

Product validation
- Design source data subsetting for test data sets
- Codesign and direct construction of test harnesses
- Provide source-to-target test cases, especially for business rules
- Provide nonfunctional test cases

Transition phase
- Maintain build plan for each release
- Draft implementation plan

Section 4: System Tester
Inception (when possible; often joins project after inception phase)
- Infer system testing requirements given project architect findings:
  - Impacted systems beyond product boundary
  - Nonfunctional requirements

Construction phase
- Set unit and component test result documentation standards
- Lead consideration of INVEST test's "testable option" during sprint planning
- Sets many expectations for programmers regarding type and depth of unit testing
- Ensure testing incorporates into team's story point estimates
- Gather test scripts from teammates
- Maintain test defect tracking
- Vocalize new defects and standard test metrics at daily stand-up meetings
- For project opting for automated testing:
  - Define, prepare, execute, and assess automated daily testing
  - Configure test scripts for automated test engine where appropriate
- Sets requirements for test suites to incorporate in a nightly integration testing suite
- Certify to product owner that data reviewed during sprint demo were loaded:
  - via a single, unassisted process run
  - from a single set of coherent production-comparable data
  - and was not hand altered after landing in target data structures

(Continued)

Table 8.2 Suggested Responsibilities for Agile DWBI Technical Leads[a] (Continued)

Product validation
- Collect integration and system test cases from all teammates
- Derive test cases from source-to-target mappings as needed
- Promote developer's test cases to integration and system test where appropriate
- Maintain repository of test assets, versioned by build and release, including
  - test source data (both subsets and high-volume data sets)
  - expected results
  - actual result (summaries)
- Codesign and validate test harnesses
- Conduct high-volume testing of every iteration's build
- Contribute nonfunctional test cases
- Plan production-readiness testing (system testing)
- Support definition of user acceptance testing
- Observe developer's preparation for story demonstrations
- Validate source data subsets and other test data sets
- Provide test coverage and status metrics to stakeholders

Transition phase
- Plan and conduct system and regression testing for release candidates
- Represent team to operations during production-readiness reviews
- Automate system and regression testing as necessary

Section 5: Scrum Master *(often joins project after inception phase)*
Construction phase
- Guides teammates through:
  - standard agile process
  - adaptations made for DWBI projects
  - further adaptations adopted by team during project's sprint retrospectives
- Reminds teammates as needed to:
  - apply INVEST test to user stories
  - apply DILBERT'S test to developer stories
  - resolve tech debt before starting new programming
- Ensure best-possible estimation process, including consistent reference stories
- Lead Scrum steps when other teammates do not volunteer
- Gather and visualize performance metrics adopted by team, including
  - daily burndown, including tech debt and intrasprint scope creep
  - delivery velocity
  - accuracy of estimates
  - distribution of story points

[a]*Responsibilities are presented in order discussed in the text, not importance. "Stories" refer to developer stories for data integration modules and user stories for other work. Items marked with an asterisk indicate major components of the "iterative analysis and design" referred to throughout the chapter.*

stakeholders and the technical members of his team. For data warehousing, solutions also involve matching source data from operational systems to target data in a presentation layer, plus devising the major functions of the front-end dashboards. Matching source to target will involve conceptualizing major data processing objectives for both front and back ends of the application. In essence, the project architect is the one person who states to both business and technical stakeholders "I understand the need, I've devised a solution, and I guarantee that if we construct what I have in mind correctly, it will solve the business problem."

With this broad responsibility, the project architect naturally focuses upon getting three key aspects of the project right:

1. requirements (corresponds to understanding the need)
2. design (corresponding to the nature of the solution)
3. quality assurance (corresponding to constructing the application correctly)

It is common to summarize this role as the person who must "drive" these three key aspects of the project. There are too many details in each of them for the project architect to deliver directly, but he can set the objectives for each aspect, get the work started, delegate to and support others who specialize in each, and approve their deliverables.

Some organizations just starting with Scrum make the mistake of elevating the scrum master to be the primary lead upon a team. For agile data warehousing at least, a quick comparison of the responsibilities of the project architect with those of the scrum master (also included in Table 8.2) reveals that project success rests far more heavily on the experience of and the direction provided by the project architect. Agile teams want to emphasize self-organization and collaboration so they do not need formal hierarchies within the project room. When a team falls short of these goals, however, the scrum master on a warehousing project needs to be ready to yield the lead to the project architect. He, in turn, must yield ultimate authority to the product owner, who represents the sponsors of the project.

There are several other key aspects of the project architect's role on an agile warehousing project. He balances opportunity versus cost. In addition to being responsible to the product owner for solving the business problem, the project architect is responsible to the team for segmenting the project so that it involves as little rework as possible. He also translates his understanding of business requirements into a selection of the correct operational systems from which warehouse will source data. He identifies the major risks of the project, such as questionable data quality and really tough business rules. With that knowledge he must plan for mitigating any major points of project risk. Above all, the project architect must find a way to push the project forward and get new features delivered to end users sooner so that the business receives value early and often and so that the team gets the feedback it needs to know the application is moving in the right direction.

Given the diverse aspects of the project for which he is ultimately responsible, the project architect will need to have substantial experience with the full life cycle of several business intelligence projects in his past. The other technical members of the leadership subteam will have deep knowledge of their specialties, but they will need someone with a breadth of experience to select a single solution from the many technical approaches available. He will also need to have studied the discipline of data warehousing so that he can identify and explain the proper options for many tough and pivotal design decisions, such as the perennial "Inmon/ Kimball" debate. [Inmon 2001; Kimball 1998] Moreover, he must possess a reliable method for working through these issues, either the company's standard architecture approach or the one offered by the Data Warehousing Institute, or even one adapted from a non-DWBI framework such as the Zachman, RM-ODP, or TOGAF. [Zachman 1987; Mowbray 2004; OMG 2003, 2004]

Finally, the project architect must guide his teammates in sufficiently addressing a long list of "nonfunctional requirements"—the quality attributes of a system beyond the surface features that users interact with directly. These notions represent solution constraints that often appear on the project board in an agile team's project room, as discussed in Chapter 4. Sometimes they are referred to as the system's "abilities" such as scalability, extensibility, and recoverability. Table 8.3 offers a representative listing of these desirable system aspects.

Data architect

The first consumer of the project architect's vision will be the data architect. For data integration work, this individual must design a data repository for the application's presentation layer that will support the desired analysis and, if necessary, for an integration layer to precede that. (Both layers were introduced in the previous chapter.) As was the case for the project architect, the team needs an individual in this role who possesses a strong architectural method for data analysis and design. Before designing the warehouse's target database, he must ensure that business meanings ("semantics") of all data elements are clear, accommodating any conflicts in entity and attribute definitions between business parties. The target data design must support and even enforce the correct relationships (cardinalities) between the entities it supports. Should the project architect stipulate that the database enforces business rules within data, the data architect will design the mechanisms to affect those constraints.

Regarding the design process, the data architect needs to meet four major objectives. He must advise on the proper paradigm for the warehouse as a whole, manage distinct and complementary data models for all data layers, advise on the proper grain for the presentation layer, and implement the proper level of normalization for the integration layer.

First, the choice of paradigms refers back to supporting the Inmon, Kimball, or a combination of the two, depending on what the project architect selected as a solution for the business requirements. The data architect should understand the reasons for the project architect's choice and even challenge the decision when called for.

Second, managing complementary data models refers to maintaining both logical and physical viewpoints of the target database. Without strong leadership from the data architect, teams can confuse these two viewpoints. The logical view defines

---

Table 8.3 Important Nonfunctional Application Requirements

Extensibility
    System is prepared for future growth in functionality, that is, it includes mechanisms for expanding and enhancing its capabilities easily without having to make major changes to its low-level code.
Adaptability
    System can be reconfigured for reasonable changes in operating contexts with a minimum of reconfiguration or recoding.
Scalability
    System is prepared for future growth in data volumes.
Reliability
    System performs as planned with a minimum of unscheduled downtime.
Maintainability
    Flaws found after implementation can be located quickly and corrected without excessive expense.
Interoperability
    System can exchange information and services with other applications as the need arises with a minimum of reconfiguration or recoding.
Isolatability
    The boundaries of the system once implemented are well known and its actions intelligible without reference to the operations of other applications.
Affordability
    System provides intended services with reasonable development, implementation, and support costs.
Understandability
    Users and IT personnel can comprehend the intended use and actions of the system without excessive training or outside support.
Recoverability
    System reestablishes services after major system outage with little or no intervention by IT personnel.
Auditability
    Systems actions are evident and understandable by reviewing a transaction log, even months after the actions occurred.
Manageability
    System can be kept in service without excessive monitoring or IT support, even when conditions change within reason.
Supportability
    System services end users without prompting many calls to the IT help desk.

---

data in terms of its business use, whereas the physical view focuses on the specific structures in which it will be stored. Should a team neglect one of these models, the complexity of the transform logic can become needlessly complicated or the usefulness of the warehouse data can be seriously compromised. [Burns 2011] The data architect ensures that both viewpoints exist and that the team employs them properly.

Third, although advised by the project architect, the data architect will have the final say on the grain of the entities in the presentation layer. The grain is the level of detail stored by a (logical) entity or a (physical) table in the data warehouse dimensional models. Data architects want to match the grain to the most atomic use of the data planned for the long term so that the application will allow all analyses the users plan to conduct both for the present and in the future. They do not want to specify a level of detail deeper than what is needed, however, because the cost of building the warehouse increases dramatically with finer grains. Choosing the grain is usually hard work requiring understanding the short- and long-term business intent plus the nature of source data.

Finally, the topic of proper normalization relates mostly to the logical design of the integration layer and determines the degree to which entities in the logical data model are broken into single-themed tables. The collective purpose of these single-theme tables is to specify a data repository that can hold any information consistent with the business' operations and that will not distort the information stored during update operations. Data architects achieve normalization by following a now standardized set of rules that steadily moves a logical design to higher levels that offer greater flexibility at the cost of steadily more entities to manage. [Kent 1983] Until recently the primary question regarding normalization was whether the third "normal form" was sufficient and whether the situation required a fourth or fifth.

In the last decade the normalization question that a DWBI data architect must answer has evolved to whether warehouses should employ the newer and still developing "hypernormalized" approaches, such as sixth normal form, data vaulting, or anchor modeling. (For information on these advance normalization patterns, see [Date, Darwen, & Lorentzos 2003], [Linstedt, Graziano, & Hultgren 2011], and [Rönnböck et al., 2010], respectively.) Although still a nonstandard approach with nascent support among the data warehousing profession, these hypernormalized paradigms are important for data architects to offer their agile teammates because they can avoid a large portion of expensive rework when the structure of loaded tables must be modified, thus allowing existing warehouses to adapt to new customer requirements. By picking the correct level of normalization for the project, the data architect determines whether the data warehouse as a database can be truly agile in the long run.

Systems analyst

The systems analyst is responsible for specifying the transforms implied by both the source and target databases. This responsibility requires him to understand not only the intent of the system as provided by the project architect, but also the selected data sources in detail and the data models provided by the project's data architect.

The need to understanding the sources requires the systems analyst to perform data profiling on relevant portions of the source systems. These data profiles provide extensive information on such notions as the cardinality of records between source tables (i.e., whether the relationship is one to many or many to many), the domains and consistency of values within the columns, and the ability to join source data dependably to other source tables. The need to understand the target makes the systems analyst one of the first and most important reviewer of the data models provided by the data architect. That position allows him to request columns as needed to support the data transformation the project architect's solution objectives will demand.

The responsibility to specify the data transforms for the developers requires the system analyst to comprehend the user stories provided by the product owner thoroughly. Moreover, he must understand just as well the developer stories so that he can detail not just the end-to-end data transforms, but also how to transform data as it moves from one layer of the warehouse's data architecture to the next. The systems analysts must collaborate with the data architect to specify the data integrity rules that determine which records from one layer, including the source systems, will be accepted by the warehouse into each of these architectural layers of its database.

In addition to profiles of source data, the primary work product of the systems analyst is source to target maps (STM). Often there is one STM per target table in each physical model of the data warehouse. The simple items on these mappings are the columns that are simply replicated between source and target. More complicated are the meta data columns and aggregates. The most involved STM elements are usually the derived columns, for which the systems analyst must specify the inputs, the transformation algorithm, and the target columns. Systems analysts must pay particular attention to a few special situations occurring on the source systems, such as instances (a) when records get deleted in the source systems, (b) when certain columns trigger the need to update slowly changing dimension records, and (c) when foreign key values for a target record do not identify a record in the related table. Source-to-target mappings become even more complex when the systems analyst adds in rules for the disposition of records that cannot be loaded, as well as variations for initial load versus incremental loads of a table.

Systems tester

The final member of the leadership subteam on an agile DWBI project is the systems tester. This individual takes the project architect's high-level quality assurance plan for the project and provides details on how to put it into effect when the construction iterations begin. He also defines how any given release candidate will be validated as an integrated system, both in terms of business-requested functionality and its compatibility with other applications in the shared production environment. Especially for agile projects, which are delivered incrementally, such validations must be repeated often. Accordingly, the system test provides a strategy for organizing the numerous test cases for the project into reexecutable scripts, whether they be applied against the application by hand or through an automated test engine.

In general, the system tester has three moments of truth: daily, at the end of each construction iteration, and when the team delivers a release candidate. On a daily basis, he needs to tell the team whether the current build is complete and correct, and if not, approximately where the problem occurs. At the end of each iteration, the system tester needs to certify to the product owner that the collection of data he is about to review was actually loaded by the application being built and not patched together by developers desperate to have something to demo. For each release, the system tester must certify to the operations group that the application the programmers have delivered will operate dependably and can be restarted by following the team's written instructions when it suspends abnormally.

The relationship of an agile system tester to the project's individual test cases is very different than one observes on waterfall projects. Because agile teams work with a minimum of to-be specifications, the agile system tester will have no documents from which he can derive test cases independently. Accordingly, the role of system tester on an agile team is no longer writing test cases but instead gathering the right test cases from all the other parties in the team. In addition to collecting unit test cases from programmers, the system tester actively solicits story tests from the product owner, plus functional and nonfunctional test cases from all other resident resources. Often these parties do not know how to write tests, so the system tester becomes a leader in that he sets quality standards for the test scripts his teammates will write and coaches them on how to meet those standards. Finally, the system tester should transform whenever possible the test suites he assembles into machine-executable packages so that they can be invoked overnight by a computer center scheduler in order to thoroughly validate the team's current build without manual labor.

The leadership subteam

The project architect, data architect, and systems analysts are obviously upstream from the programmers in terms of the work they must accomplish. In many ways, the system tester is upstream from programmers as well. He sets many expectations for the programmers regarding the type and depth of unit testing plus requirements for test suites that can be incorporated in a nightly integration testing suite. These four technical roles are typically individuals with the most data warehouse experience on the team, and they provide crucial direction to the programmers on a daily basis. Combined with the product owner, these four are in fact the team's leaders.

Now that each role has been described in some detail, there are some overarching considerations regarding the list of responsibilities provided in Table 8.2. First, roles are not people. Big teams have the luxury of assigning a separate person for each position, but small teams will have leaders wearing multiple hats. Second, the responsibilities suggested here have been assigned to one role each, but as discussed in earlier chapters, teams deliver faster when its members innovate, so it is best to treat this chapter's lists of responsibilities as only starting points to get a team staffed and moving forward. Given the high experience of the leadership subteam, they will self-organize in ways to get the definition work completed as needed. Third, as suggested starting points, these were kept abbreviated. They will grow considerably as teams learn more about agile warehousing.

Probably the most important aspect of starter responsibility lists is that they define the forward-looking aspects of an agile warehousing team. With the sprints' stiff deadline pressure always upon them, agile teams tend to become overly myopic, focusing no further than the next set of deliverables. Sprints are stressful, especially when an overnight integration test fails or tech debt starts to grow, so getting everything finished by the next demo is typically all the programmers have the mental bandwidth to contend with. For applications such as data warehouses, which have many interacting layers and components, such a limited vision could result in some very expensive oversights when locally optimized design choices prove unusable across the entire arc of a project. The leadership roles suggested here have the responsibility to look beyond the programmer's near-planning horizon and anticipate broader design objectives such as extensibility, scalability, performance, and ease of promotion. They are the teammates that ensure the sum of all the iterations adds up to a coherent whole that the business will value. This forward-looking, anticipatory aspect of their roles is another reason why these leaders need to be experienced warehouse professionals.

Resident and visiting "resources"

There is some risk in referring to the new roles suggested in this chapter as team *leaders*, as the word can denote an element of hierarchy. Hierarchy can undermine the sense of equality that self-organization requires and thus might lower team velocity. In the last analysis, it is the programmers with their fingers on the keyboards, creating shippable code, who generate the value for the business. It is hoped that the leadership subteam does not try to direct the programmers on the team through any command and control mechanisms, but rely instead on the natural authority that their greater knowledge and experience with the data integration project should impart to them.

For that reason, the word *resource* may be a better choice because it is devoid of management overtones and emphasizes instead that these experienced teammates must be ready to provide answers as needed to keep the programmers stay productive. Moreover, individuals filling these pivotal roles need to remain accessible to the programmers throughout the project. Instead of swooping in and dropping off specifications, these leaders need to live in the project room, to be *resident resources* wrapped around the programmers as a support structure, as shown in Figure 8.1.

There are other skills the team will need from time to time, such as database administrators (DBA), platform administrators, storage manages, and Web service architects. Folks with these skills are also informational resources, but do not need to live in the project room full time. An occasional appearance to stay abreast of the project will suffice, plus longer conversations when there is an issue they can help with. These folks can be referred to, then, as "visiting resources," which is also depicted in Figure 8.1. These individuals should participate in the project room when needed and should be free to work elsewhere when their contribution is over.

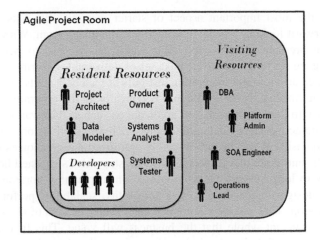

FIGURE 8.1

Expanded team roles for agile data warehousing.

Table 8.4 Key Traits For Agile Team Leaders

- Willing to work incrementally to a reoccurring set of deadlines
- Willing to proceed to next process step when only 80% sure
- Able to sense the most important unknowns
- Experienced enough to see the whole picture
- Able to hold a workable architecture in mind
- Can compartmentalize and decouple major units of the application
- Accepts "good enough" at first
- Works steadily toward perfect for each incremental release

Because some of them may need to participate extensively during various portions of the project, their availability and level of time commitment need to be planned for when starting a new agile warehousing project.

New agile characteristics required

The aforementioned resident resources may feel challenged by the iterative context when newly assigned to an agile DWBI initiative if all they have is waterfall project experience. The incremental and collaborative style of the agile project's nature requires a very different mind-set from traditional software engineering. Project planners should understand these differences up front while staffing a project because they will need to assemble a set of resident resources with the right temperaments, or give them the right agile orientation, for the project to succeed.

Table 8.4 lists key aspects of the required mind-set for team leaders to contribute effectively to an agile data warehousing project. Some of these traits call for a higher tolerance for uncertainty and risk, as is implicit in agile projects where the development effort is packaged into many small, loosely coupled work units rather than one completely specified, monolithic deliverable. In general, team leaders need to embrace the Deming/Shewhart cycle of "plan, do, check, and act." This cycle allows that a project plan is probably not perfect to start with, but can be perfected with feedback provided by the results of putting the plan into action. By leveraging such feedback, the team can proceed after pulling together only 80% of the most important details before the team moves ahead. Consequently, a key skill will be to know more or less the most important aspects of a particular work bundle that must be covered ahead of time and which aspects can be safely left to elaboration when programmers start to build out a module. These leaders will need to provide these details to developers just in time to support coding and actively validate the results throughout every iteration of the project

These members on the leadership subteam will need to guide the team in defining and sequencing work in a way that keeps intermodule dependencies from blocking progress. Such acumen comes from building many warehouses before, so experience is doubly important for agile DWBI team leads. If the company does not have an internal resource with sufficient experiences, then this is an area where engaging some solid consultants for a short while will increase the project's chance for success greatly.

Avoiding data churn within sprints

As the more experienced members of an agile warehousing team, the "resident resources" described earlier need to be alert and guide the programmers around common mistakes that will undermine their effectiveness. One of the most taxing of such "antipatterns" is *data churn*, an occurrence that stems from a team's haste to build the modules of iterations without preparing ahead of time for demonstrating results.

One of agile's central objectives is to increase the proportion of time that programmers spend creating new value over administrative work. Faced with agile's tough and repeating deadlines, many data warehouse teams assume it will be fastest to simply load production data as each module is completed, leaving the product owner to evaluate whatever data are found in the target tables by the time the iteration ends. However, if source data used for demonstration purposes are not managed carefully, the inefficiencies of grabbing production data as needed can explode quickly and consume half or more of a team's available time, especially as the deadline for the next sprint demo draws near.

Figure 8.2 reveals how easily data churn can occur if the individual developers focus exclusively on getting only their piece of the warehouse programmed and loaded for demonstration. The target model in this case is a simple star schema with a sales fact table, a dimension for customer, and another dimension for product. Table 8.5 lists the actions the team takes to load data for a demo and the amount of time each step can waste if the team does not preplan and manage its load data.

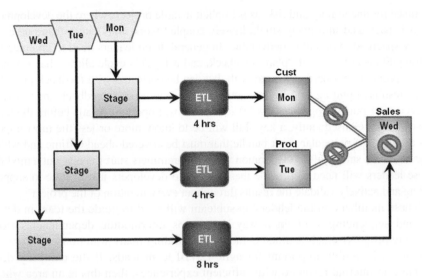

FIGURE 8.2

Data churn wastes agile team productivity.

Table 8.5 Time Lost to Unmanaged Data Churn

Day	Developer	Action	Action Hours	Cumulative Hours	Cumulative Hours Lost
Mon	Alex	Load CUST DIM with Mon data	4	4	0
Tue	Barb	Load PROD DIM with Tue data	4	8	0
Wed	Chet	Load SALES FACT with Wed data	8	16	16
Thu	Deb	Reload all with Thu data	16	32	16
Fri	Alex	Update CUST code, full reload	16	48	32

Percentage loading time to do-overs: 67%.

The cost of data churn arises from two factors. First, loading production data can consume too much time simply due to its volume. Second, loading uncoordinated snapshots from source will lead to relational integrity problems. If, as our example shows, Alex loads up his *customer* dimension using Monday's production data, Barb uses Tuesday's for *product*, and Chet grabs Wednesday's for the *sales* fact table, the product owner will be bound to reject at least the *sales* module because it will contain sales events from Wednesday that have no corresponding records in the supporting dimensions that were loaded with data of earlier days. To achieve relational integrity within data in this case, the team will have to reload all three tables in order to have a coherent set of records placed within them, essentially wasting the 16 cumulative hours it took to load them previously.

Unfortunately, the story rarely ends there. Programmers always seem to overlook something crucial for the upcoming demo and need to make a tiny modification to the ETL code that obviates existing data and necessitates a full reload. As shown for the Friday action in Table 8.5, if Alex has to modify and reload the *customer dimension*, the net result will be to waste two-thirds of the team's cumulative load time. Teams racing to get the ETL ready for a sprint demo can easily make a half dozen or more little changes to the code, compounding the problem illustrated and leading to an inordinate waste of programmer time. Although data churn wastes time for projects following any methodology, its impact upon agile teams is amplified because they integrate the applications and load data for user demos every few weeks, whereas waterfall projects tend to undertake integration activities only as they approach their single delivery date. Although "just grab production data" is an easy policy to articulate, warehousing teams realize eventually they cannot be agile with this development data sourcing strategy.

Solutions to data churn are typically twofold: (a) take a snapshot of all the required source tables and load from that static data repository and (b) subset data down to where it takes only a half-hour or so to load the tables needed for a demo so that coding changes do not consume too much time for reloads. Although these recommendations may sound reasonable, it can be very difficult to secure the external support needed for this strategy. First, creating a static snapshot of production that the team can manage often requires allocating a considerable amount of storage, especially since more than one snapshot is inevitably required if the team desires to keep their snapshots relatively current. DBAs will resist granting this storage because it is a scarce resource, and the program manager controlling the agile project's funds will resist because more storage will manifest higher costs. Second, this approach can require giving the team developers some high-level privileges over that development space and table structures because they will need to evolve their source data repository frequently as they incrementally expand the sources they pull from and the additional columns they add for managing data. Although the team's data architect is probably more than capable of adjusting table structures in a disciplined manner, this privilege is often one that database administration groups frequently want to retain for themselves, even for development environments.

When it comes to reducing the size of actual data loaded, developers themselves frequently push back because subsetting the production snapshot down to a manageable size requires work. Subsetting a big data set involves identifying a core set of records in a few tables and then bringing along the records from all other tables related to them. This culling of records can involve a considerable amount though, especially if the source comes from a complex application with many intersecting combinations of primary and foreign keys.

The fact that demo data sets need to be refreshed occasionally requires the team to repeat some of this work regularly. Product owners feel better if demo data are reasonably current and teams steadily discover new business rules for which they need data from new source tables to implement. Because demo data sets need to be refreshed occasionally, a team's subsetting routine will need to be a repeatable process, thus requiring a bit of programming in and of itself. All this prep work must occur before the first iteration it hopes to assist. If the team does not attend to this matter during Sprint 0, it will have to declare a *spike* later to get everything in place, necessarily causing the next demo to be delayed.

Solving data churn is an example of a tough problem where the resident resources of a team need to lead. They will have to insist that preparing a small managed data set will save time and thus merits the planning and scripting that subsetting data will probably require. They will need to pursue greater storage from the database administrators, plus some privileges over development schemas so that the team can improve its test data repository as the project progresses. Moreover, their skills as architects, modelers, and analysts will also be necessary to get the proper subsetting scripts written, validated, and executed.

Table 8.6 repeats the events of the previous example, showing how the situation improves when the team works with a small managed data set. Most notably, there is no need to reload the target schema on Thursday because the developers have each populated their modules from a coherent set of data and avoided relational integrity problems. Moreover, when Alex has to make his small update on Friday, he has to obviate only the time spent loading small data into the customer and sales objects—1.5 hours instead of the 16 hours in the previous case. The percentage of load time wasted is still higher than one might like (around 40%), but the magnitude of time lost has been reduced greatly, making the situation manageable, and agile warehousing now possible.

Table 8.6 Far Less Time Wasted with Small Managed Data Sets

Day	Developer	Action	Action Hours	Cumulative Hours	Cumulative Hours Lost
Mon	Alex	Load CUST DIM with managed data	1/2	1/2	0
Tue	Barb	Load PROD DIM with managed data	1/2	1	0
Wed	Chet	Load SALES FACT with managed data	1	2	0
Thu	Deb	Reload all with Thu data	0	2	1.5
Fri	Alex	Update CUST code, full reload	1.5	3.5	1.5

Percentage loading time to do-overs: 43%.

Pipeline delivery for a sustainable pace

The full set of roles suggested for the aforementioned agile warehousing team follows the software engineering value chain that traditional BI teams have used for decades: architecture, analysis, data modeling, process design, coding, and then testing. Whereas waterfall methods typically spell out many further engineering steps beyond simply listing these roles, agile prescribes little more than "self-organization" and "test-led development" from this point on. For teammates who have not worked on an agile project before, Scrum's lack of detailed step-by-step directions often leads to the sense of chaos in the project room during the first sprint or two. In fact, Scrum's nickname is "controlled chaos." Most new teams instantly begin to experiment with ways to structure the handoff between roles in order to make the work within a sprint more efficient and predictable. For data warehousing, the most common experiments turn out to perform poorly, but there is a third innovation that seems to solve the problem.

Figure 8.3 depicts the two work-sequencing approaches that do not work too well. They are actually "mash-ups" of waterfall and Scrum. The first is called "scrummerfall" in which a team tries to pursue each stage of a waterfall engineering process using a Scrum-style collaboration in the work room. A scrummerfall proposal is often expressed as something like "we'll do two iterations of requirements, three of design, then four for ETL coding, two for BI development, and finally one sprint for testing."

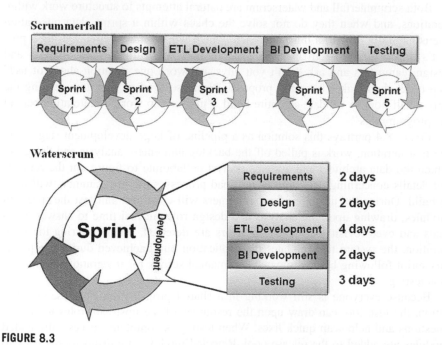

FIGURE 8.3

Agile mash-ups that do not work.

A moment's reflection reveals that this process has clearly lost all the advantages of an agile approach. These developers may be holding stand-up meetings in the morning, but they are still attempting to perform a big design up front and to drive a fully scoped objective through their process according to a plan. Moreover, how should the programmers keep from falling idle during the long requirements and design process? Where is the mechanism for the programmers to request further requirements and design when they discover a large oversight when modules enter the programming stages? How does this approach avoid compressing the time dedicated to system testing out of existence when development stages start to run long?

The second half of Figure 8.3 depicts waterscrum, another common experiment that arises when teams try to rigidly sequence the distinct work phases within a single iteration. Waterscrum proposals typically sound like "if we've got 13 days before the next demo, then let's do 2 days of requirements, 2 days of design, 6 days of development, and 3 days of testing."

This approach at least works on a small slice of project scope, but is still challenged to keep all resources busy throughout a sprint and tends to compress coding and testing if the upstream activities do not finish in time. In fact, waterscrum typically destroys a team's *esprit de corps* because programmers start nagging the analysis and design roles to "hurry up with the data model" and testing is perennially demanding that programming "speed it up and finish" before the time box ends.

Both scrummerfall and waterscrum are natural attempts to structure work within iterations, and when they do not solve the chaos within a sprint, data integration teams naturally drift to a third approach, which works much better. During a project's third or fourth retrospective, programmers will turn to their analysis and design teammates and ask "can't you guys just work one iteration ahead of us?" The tester then makes a similar proposal: "I am so tired of you guys leaving me only a half hour to validate an entire build. I'm going to work one iteration behind the programmers."

Figure 8.4 portrays this solution as a pipeline of large development stages. On the first iteration, work is pulled off the backlog and enters analysis and design in which the data architect and systems analyst collaborate to figure out the remaining details concerning data objects and load processes the programmers will have to build. During the next sprint, programmers will code and unit test the specified modules, drawing upon the analysis and design roles in real time to answer questions and even revisit the "specs" if errors are detected. Finally, during the third iteration, the system test validates the application build achieved during the previous sprint following both automated and manual scripts for integration and regression testing.

Because everyone is still working in a shared project room in close collaboration, the test, too, can draw upon the resources of the upstream roles to answer questions and help with quick fixes. When testing is complete, successfully coded modules are added to the release pool. Rejected modules are dispositional back to earlier work stages or even the release backlog for reprioritization.

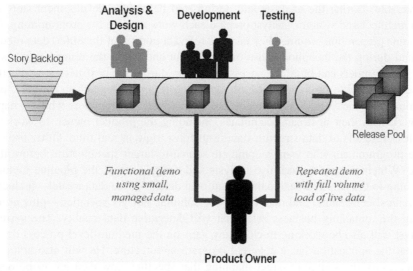

FIGURE 8.4

Pipelined delivery technique.

This pipelined delivery technique solves the time squeeze that the various team roles experienced during scrummerfall and waterscrum. Each role gets a full iteration to apply their craft to the application being built and no one falls idle. By decoupling the roles within the structure of the sprint, the team has eliminated waterscrum's endemic conflicts over handoffs, removing a tremendous amount of stress that formerly undermined team collaboration. Moreover, once the pipeline is filled, the team loses nothing in terms of velocity because the work bundle will flow out of the end of the pipeline with one sprint's worth of developer stories delivered every iteration.

The pipelining diagram is sometimes misinterpreted to mean that the agile team is returning to waterfall methods or that it is focused on programming only, neither of which is true. This approach is still agile for many reasons. The product owner is still embedded in the process rather than excluded until a final delivery is ready. The team is laboring to deliver upon a small slice of the application, not trying to fulfill a big design up front. It is hoped that the teammates are still colocated so that they can support and answer each other's questions in real time instead of communicating through large specification documents. Finally, their intent is to deliver value with every iteration. Although there will be a delay as the pipeline loads up, afterward the product owner will see tangible progress with every development iteration.

As for whether the pipeline focuses only on programming, the middle station of this arrangement is indeed a "development" step. However, "development" means bringing both data and process design together into a single data warehousing deliverable. During the analysis and design step before the development step, the data architect and systems analyst prepare each work module for programming. For both this preparation requires they take the relevant portion of the 80/20 data models created during the inception phase of the project and fill in the remaining gaps so that programmers can build the necessary system during the next iteration. Whether these gaps need to be filled 100% or something less will depend on the ETL programmers on the team. Some projects are staffed with programmers who are happy to work with their upstream teammates, including the product owner, to work out the lesser details of data structures and transform logic in real time. Other projects have programmers who want a complete source-to-target specification before they code. Whichever is the case, the analysis and design step of the pipeline includes finishing to the required degree the definitional details of the data model—including semantics, constraints, and data typing for columns not yet specified—plus articulating the remaining business rules that will determine data quality. The systems analyst will also be working to close any gaps on the medium-level process design so that the application has a coherent program architecture. He will also complete as necessary the source-to-target mapping that specifies how data are to be transformed. Given this list of activities, data architecture and data integrity are as much components of each "module" on an agile team's backlog as is programming.

New meaning for Iteration 0 and Iteration −1

One disadvantage to the pipelined delivery approach depicted in Figure 8.4 is that it takes two iterations to fill the pipeline before the team begins delivering shippable code. Whereas there is no impact on the *eventual* velocity of the team, the process does introduce a delayed start for the team. This initial delay is worth bearing because the strategy allows the teammates to work throughout the rest of the construction phase at a more sustainable pace with greater attention to the quality of their work. However, the delayed start does need to be negotiated with the customer and IT managers who were promised that "agile means fast delivery." Accordingly, it must be presented to the project stakeholders in a way that justifies the time needed to get a project started right.

The previous part of this book discussed Iterations −1 and 0 as times during which the team completes the inception phase of the company's IT project release cycle (see Figure 5.1). The term "inception" is hard for many business stakeholders to understand instantly. The pipelined delivery approach provides an alternative way to envision and justify these two lead-off iterations that agile warehousing teams require. Figure 8.5 lays out a grid of pipelined work stages and project iterations. Each block arrow symbol represents an iteration's worth of developer stories. The first package the team will program is labeled as "A," the second as "B," and so on. Naturally enough, programmers will begin coding package A during sprint 1. During sprint 2 they will work on package B, and a systems test will evaluate package A. The packages follow a predictable diagonal path as they move from role to role while the iterations progress.

Iteration	Project Architect Solution Reqts	Data Modeler / Sys Analyst Technical Reqts	Developers Potentially Shippable	System Test Shippable Code
-1	A+			
0	B	A+		
1	C	B	A	
2	D	C	B	A
3		D	C	B
4			D	C

"+" indicates lead-off package that the indicated role should scoped to entire project, not just iteration 1

FIGURE 8.5

Pipelined work stages across project iterations.

The implications for project start-up appear when the first work packages are projected backward in time. From where do the programmers get the definition for package A in order to build it during sprint 1? This package comes from the data architect and systems analysts, who must have worked on it during the prior iteration. The iteration before sprint 1 happens to be Iteration 0, discussed earlier. Continuing with our story, the analysis and design roles needed package A envisioned before they could detail it. They will receive the package's vision from the project architect, so that role must have worked package A the sprint before Iteration 0. Pipelining, plus the role of the project architect, implies that projects require an "Iteration −1" to get started, as shown in Figure 8.5.

During Iterations −1 and 0, the scope of the work packages for the leadership subteam is larger than for other sprints. If the project architect, data architect, and systems analyst focused only on the developer stories that make up package A during these lead-off sprints, the team could suffer from any aspects of later packages that were not architecturally anticipated during the definition of the first work bundle. These lead-off roles can lower project risk by expanding their notion of package A to include a healthy amount of "whole project thinking" as they prepare the first set of stories for programming. Whereas it would be nice if these two precoding sprints would fit into the same time box the team will use for development, the whole project scope of package A implies that the leadership subteam will need a bit more time than a regular sprint to conclude their work during Iterations −1 and 0.

Projects should not be lavish with the extra time allowed for precoding sprints, however. In order to get the project started as soon as possible, these lead-off teammates should not aim to provide an absolutely complete and bullet-proof specification for the whole project. As mentioned earlier, 80/20 specifications will serve quite well because agile's iterative delivery approach will allow the little errors in requirements and design to be discovered and corrected as part of a sprint. The leadership subteam can reduce the start-up time greatly by defining just the project's overall framework plus the details of package A. Future iterations will allow the up-front roles the time they need to think through the details of packages B and beyond. To time box Iterations −1 and 0 properly, project planners should therefore ask the architect, modeler, and analyst to estimate how long they'll need to pull just the most important 80% of the project into focus. Typically, this amount of definition takes about a fifth as long as a full waterfall discovery and specification process requires.

It is crucial that agile data warehousing leaders insist on time for Iterations −1 and 0. The most common mistake that IT managers make with iterative approaches is to think that agile somehow allows them to deploy programmers to address a business need instantly. One can almost hear the impossible promises they make to business partners: "Your department needs to understand the cost numbers coming out of our three ERP systems? I'll have six developers over there building a solution for you starting Monday." Skipping Iterations −1 and 0 dooms the project from the start. There is nothing about agile that eliminates the need to think through requirements and design a bit in advance of programming, so time for this preparation needs to be allocated.

Pipeline requires two-step user demos

The pipelined delivery approach changes not only the timing of analysis and design, but the nature of agile's user demos as well. So that miscommunication and errors can be caught and even corrected as soon as possible, programmers still need to demo their deliverables at the end of each development iteration, before the build enters the system testing station on the pipeline. However, as seen earlier, programmers need to work with small managed data sets if they are to avoid the time-wasting effects of *data churn*. Consequently, when the product owner evaluates whether to accept each developer story during the sprint's user demo, data he will review will be small data the developers normally work with.

However, one or two records out of a million can reveal an arcane error or oversight in ETL coding, especially when complex transformation rules or boundaries between time periods are involved. The product owner can detect such errors only by reviewing a module loaded with a snapshot of full production data. With the pipeline approach, system test has chosen to validate each build one iteration after it is completed by the programmers. Because he is working with a static build and has a full iteration to perform this validation, it is reasonable to ask him to load it with full production data. The resulting full volume load should be shown to the product owner to assure him that the ETL delivered the previous iteration does not fail when exposed to production-level data. As a consequence, pipelined agile data warehousing teams typically perform two demos of each build for the product owner, as shown in Figure 8.4. The first will occur during the user demo of the iteration where the code is completed, and it will be based on a small, development data set. The second will occur when the system test is ready sometime during the next iteration and will employ a full volume, production-comparable data set.

Keeping pipelines from delaying defect correction

When either of the two demos occurring during pipelined delivery reveals a defect in the code, the team has several choices on how to disposition the "bug," depending on the severity of the defect. Some of these choices allow the product owner to see corrections quickly, whereas others involve longer cycle times.

As shown in Figure 8.6, small defects can be sent to the programmers immediately. If discovered during the demo at the end of the coding stage, they can be added to tech debt and corrected during the next iteration. If discovered by a system test working with large data, they can be sent to the programmers during the ongoing iteration. In both cases, the defects are small and the labor needed to correct them can be drawn from the team's 20% reserve for architectural work and tech debt.

Another category of defects is midsized coding mistakes that do not need any additional analysis or design, but are too large to fit within the tech debt reserve. Teams should place these defects back upon the release backlog as a developer

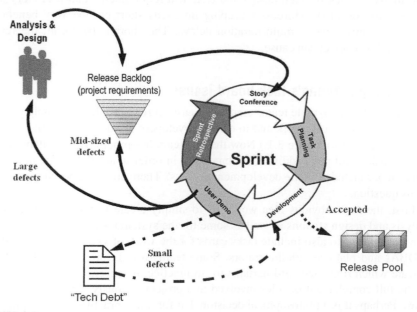

FIGURE 8.6

Disposition of defects depends on severity.

story. The product owner and developers can decide together whether the resulting story needs to be included in the coding work of the next sprint or deferred. When the defect is accepted back onto a sprint backlog, the product owner will see the corrections in the small volume demo at the end of that iteration after it was discovered.

Truly large defects will require the analysis and design roles to rethink the definition they originally embedded within one or more developer stories. In this case, the defect must travel all the way to the beginning of the pipeline so that the data architect, systems analyst, and even the solution architect can reprocess the requirements and design. It may be one or two additional iterations before the product owner sees the corrections made to this level of defect.

Table 8.7 summarizes all of these levels of defects and their implicit resolution delays and offers a few insights worth noting. First, because little errors can be handled in the next iteration by developers, they have little impact, but big errors can involve a long delay. Consequently, teams should structure their particular adaptation of Scrum in ways that keep errors small. The groundwork performed by the leadership subteam during the inception phase is designed to eliminate large errors, and therefore Iterations −1 and 0 are essential in keeping the size of errors manageable. Moreover, the work invested in decomposing user stories down to developer stories is very much worth the effort, as small scopes typically limit oversights to small defects, especially when preceded by the whole project thinking included in the inception phase. The developer story process also gives the team an extra opportunity to think through design and technical requirements that user story discussions do not allow. Moreover, keeping iterations short can be very beneficial because big errors cause multi-iteration delays. The shorter the sprint, the fewer days of delay a defect can cause.

Resolving pipelining's task board issues

As seen in Chapter 3, agile teams employ an easy-to-read task board to help participants track each others' work and to enable developers to find work for themselves as needed. (Refer to Figure 3.1.) Now that the team has pipelined its collaboration, will the task board need additional components in order to align with the new division of labor included in the development process? There are three possible answers to this question.

First, the most obvious idea would be to simply create task cards for the new analysis and design stations as well as some for the system testing role. Some teams even go as far as to also include tasks cards for the work of visiting resources such as DBAs and platform administrators. Some teams use different-colored cards to indicate which role each card pertains to. In practice, however, creating task cards for the full complement of roles involved in a project seriously clutters up the task board. Perhaps it is a philosophical decision, but for many practitioners, the primary goal of agile is to keep programmers with their fingers on the keyboards creating value for their business partners. If the task board becomes too complex, developers

Table 8.7 Defect Levels and Associated Pipeline Resolution Times[a]

Case # (1)	Size of Defect (2)	Project Architect (3)	Data Engineer and Systems Analyst (4)	Developers and Small-Volume Demo (5)	Systems Test and Large-Volume Demo (6)	PO-Observable Feature Delay (7)
1a	Needs small coding change	n/a	n/a	Iteration +1 (via tech debt)	Iteration +2	One iteration
1b	Needs technical redesign	n/a	n/a	Iteration +1 (via dev story backlog)	Iteration +2	One iteration
2	Needs new data structures and/or STM mappings	n/a	Iteration +1	Iteration +2	Iteration +3	Two iterations
3	Needs new conceptual design or sources	Iteration +1	Iteration +2	Iteration +3	Iteration +4	Three iterations

[a]*Notes by column: (3) through (6): Lists when the named role will address the defect, where "iteration" signified the sprint in which the defect was discovered, for example, "iteration +2" means that if the defect was discovered during Sprint 3, the role will be correcting it during Sprint 5. (7): Quantifies the number of sprints between the moment the embedded business partner rejects a story due to a defect and the sprint demo in which he sees the correction. "One iteration" means he will see the correction at the user demo of the next sprint.*

who approach can begin to despair, claiming "I can't find my work. Can the scrum master please tell me what to do next?" When this occurs, cluttering the task board has destroyed the all-important agile resource of self-organized teams.

A second option is to create a column somewhere on the left of the task board for analysis and design and a second column on the other side of development for system testing. This solution is workable but does suffer from the fact that cards moving through analysis and design are developer stories. They must become task cards when they enter the middle realm designated for coding work and then become developer stories again when they move on to system testing. This proves to be a complicated transition that many teams have trouble tracking easily. Task boards should also be lucid to nontechnical project stakeholders, and the transition from stories to tasks back to stories undermines that objective as well.

The third approach is by far the simplest means of evolving the task board for pipelined delivery. This choice is to remove the analysis and design plus system testing work from the board altogether. If keeping programmers coding is the primary objective, it makes sense to dedicate the task board to tasks for programmers alone to assure that nothing gets in the way of self-organization or the clarity of the board. Scrum masters should ask the upstream and downstream roles to take command of their own work. If they want to create a task board of their own, they are free to do so. Because noncoding work involves only a few individuals, they can maintain their own project organization artifacts without scrum master support.

The key to making this developer-centric approach work is to ask the upstream and downstream parties to coordinate their work with coding work by watching the programmers backlog and task board. "Organize your activities any way you want," the scrum master can suggest. "Analysis and design just has to have its work ready to use when the programmers need it to start programming. The system test just needs to be ready to validate each build after it is demonstrated to the product owner at the end of a coding sprint."

These suggestions will be eminently doable with the agile artifacts already employed. The data architect and analyst can watch the current estimate presented in the previous chapter to know what stories the programmers will need when. These two upstream roles need simply to find the next iteration's bracket on the project backlog as shown in Figure 7.4 in the previous chapter to discover what stories they should be currently preparing. They may want to keep an extra 20% or so ready to go as well in case the team gets a sudden burst of energy and increases their velocity.

The system tester has an even better vantage point because, in addition to the bracketed project backlog, he can observe in the project room exactly which stories are being coded and the issues they are encountering. This exposure should allow him to prepare for his next sprint accurately. If the work upstream in this highly transparent pipeline looks like it will be particularly demanding, the testers in many companies can request some extra resources from the IT department's pool of testers.

Pipelining as a buffer-based process

In essence, pipelining the data integration work asks the programmers' upstream and downstream teammates to work not to a time box but to a buffer. A buffer is an area where work items can wait until some party is ready to begin laboring upon one of them. Teams will often place a limit of how many items can collect in a buffer so that the overall system is forced to start work on the modules in the buffer rather than letting more accumulate. In our example, if the developers are regularly converting 30 story points of developer stories into shippable code every iteration, the analysis and design team must then keep at least 30 story points or so of work ready for them to start programming. Analysis and design may, in fact, choose to keep a slightly larger amount in the buffer, say 36 story points, so that the developers do not fall idle if they suddenly progress faster than planned. The system test has the opposite challenge—keeping its buffer sufficiently drained rather than sufficiently loaded. The tester can see that the developers complete about 30 story points of work per iteration, so he must staff the system test up to a point where it can regularly perform integration and regression test on builds with that many story points of new features every iteration.

Projects that break the analysis, design, and testing function into separate teams are faced with the difficulty of not only matching work rates between the different skill groups, but also of keeping all the teams hitting their iterative top-of-cycle phases on the same day. Unfortunately, something always seems to happen to throw one or more of these teams off the shared cadence. Programming might run long just before a holiday, system testing might lose a validation host for a few days, or analysis and design may simply finish its next-iteration artifacts 5 days early. Coupling these work stations through time boxes only leads to headaches. Having the upstream and downstream roles work from buffers is far simpler. If any of these resident resources has satisfied their buffer requirements before the programmers are ready for the next handoff, they can either assist the programmers with the coding work or perhaps work on spinning up another agile project.

The end result is shown Figure 8.7 where only the programming squad operates in a time box. The upstream partners need only have one short list of stories they have prepared for the programmers and a prebuffer with one iteration's worth of stories they could spec out depending on how much the programmers pull from the buffer at the beginning of the next sprint. The system tester has a short list of new stories coded during the previous iteration that need to be validated and a growing postbuffer filled with stories already cleared for implementation as part of the next release.

A team working with this type of pattern has entered into a blend of time-boxed and buffer-based self management. Details regarding time-boxed techniques come, of course, from Scrum. Pointers on how to manage pull-based, buffer-oriented project management come from another agile method called Kanban. By combining both time boxes and buffers, the team employs a particular agile mash-up called "Scrumban." This combination is a mash-up that works, and, as presented in the

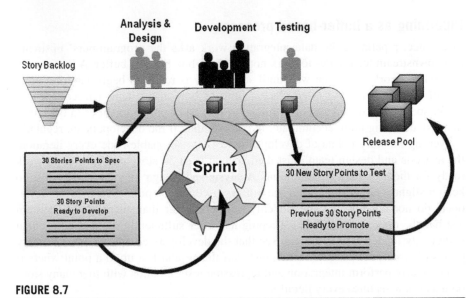

FIGURE 8.7

Using buffers to manage both ends of the pipeline.

next chapter, has the potential to evolve to the point where time boxes and story estimation can be eliminated all roles on the team. This additional streamlining of the development process frees up the time spent on top-of-cycle, noncoding activities, thus allowing even greater team velocity.

Regarding velocity, the pipeline can confuse teams as to where their delivery speed should be measured. Should they track the velocity of the work, leaving coding, or wait until it drops out of the system test into the release pool? In spirit, with keeping their business partners as involved as possible, it works best to measure the velocity by which the programmers demo new features to the product owner at the end of the programming stage. This point is part of the process with the shortest time span between the last discussion of requirements and the first glimpse of the resulting shippable code. By measuring velocity based on what arrives to the small data demos of the programmers rather than to the large data demos of the system test, all teammates will focus upon the development stage of the pipeline and continue viewing it as the heartbeat of the method. This approach also keeps the system test decoupled from coding as much as possible, keeping integration-level validation work easier to visualize and manage separately.

Pipelining is controversial

Pipelining is not universally accepted as a solution to adapting agile for the challenges of data warehousing projects with heavy data integration components. Portions of the agile analytics community believe all the difficulties that make scrum encounters with data integration modules arise from trying to work through "overly fat stories." These practitioners believe teams should ignore developer stories and simply decompose user requests into tasks so simple that the architectural dependencies and intersecting business rules simply disappear.

Some teams make this extreme tasking approach work, but it is natural to ask whether they lose something important through this radical decomposition. The discussion of developer stories in Chapter 6 acknowledged that even stories as "fat" as developer stories were still a challenge for product owners to understand as a unit of business value. Teams have to labor to educate product owner to appreciate developer stories that only bring data to an intermediate layer of the warehouse's macro data architecture, providing nonproduction dashboards on each layer to make these intermediate results seem real. Decompose the work to even smaller units and one must give up entirely on keeping the delivery of each work unit meaningful to the business. Even the perceivable value of an entire iteration may be lost if it does not fulfill a user or developer story. Teams pursuing this strategy will have to take the position of "If the bundle of microstories delivered during one iteration adds up to something that impresses the product owner or his stakeholders, great. If not, perhaps the deliveries of the next iteration will add up to something of value."

The inherent risk of extreme tasking a project's backlog is that the team will no longer be linked hard and fast to delivering tangible value to the product owner with each iteration. This outcome should make many agile practitioners nervous, especially if they are converting from a waterfall method where their business customers had been complaining that the data warehousing department is "too slow and far too expensive." Especially in that situation, building the business' trust in IT through frequent, tangible deliverables is all important.

In contrast to extreme tasking, the pipeline approach described previously works with reasonably small developer stories, and all those developer stories (except those falling within the team's 20% architectural reserve) have been defined in a way that they still represent meaningful progress toward the functional goals set out by the product owner. By emphasizing the "business-valued" component of DILBERT'S test, pipelining teams will allow the product owner to know he is steadily extracting value out of his warehousing team, something he probably does not experience with many other IT projects. Later, when the project portfolio budgets come up for annual review, the business-value oriented agile team may well have a unique advantage that greatly helps their project survive the axe.

Continuous and automated integration testing

In the discussions concerning new team roles, developer data churn, and pipelined delivery patterns, the system tester was the party who should prove that new modules integrate smoothly into a coherent application, that they do not conflict with modules delivered earlier, and that, when viewed as a system, all the modules will be accepted by the operations team for promotion into production. These objectives are crucial for large warehouse projects, especially if they involve the multiple data layers required for significant data integration requirements. They also represent a large amount of work that threatens to exceed the capabilities of one or two testers if they attempt to perform all that work by manual means. Clearly, the generic agile collaboration model could use further modifications to make these quality assurance objectives economically attainable.

Generic agile's quality control revolves around the test-led development technique presented in Chapter 2. For all of its strengths, test-led development emphasizes unit-level quality concerns and therefore cannot guarantee the broader aspects of application quality. As a developer hurries to deliver modules for a given iteration demo, what assurances do his teammates have that those components will operate as expected when combined with the project's other modules? When a developer claims a module is "done," what guarantees that it is truly "done?" Such assurance is the system tester's responsibility. He must validate each iteration's new and modified modules through two styles of validation: (a) *integration testing*, where all the changed components are stitched into a current build and operated in the proper sequence as a logical whole, and (b) *regression testing*, where validation scripts assure that features delivered previously have not been affected adversely.

Integration testing is the process of validating that all the components of an application function together as planned. Whereas developers typically attend to testing the units they build and even the components that two or more units combine into, integration testing on DWBI teams is usually left to a tester because it requires assembling all the components into a build before testing can begin. Regression testing is the process of validating that aspect of a system that worked during a previous build of an application still work, the concern being that coding changes that were intended not to change a particular function did indeed manage to leave it unaffected.

Full integration testing has long been a practice of development teams of all types, but most waterfall-based initiatives undertake integration testing only toward the end of a project, after the bulk of development is complete. Such an arrangement will not work for agile development efforts because the developers commit to delivering "shippable code" with every short sprint and to promoting incremental releases into production every few iterations. Agile teams cannot afford to lose half a week identifying which changes over the last 12 days actually caused three dozen errors to appear. They need to detect coding flaws as soon as they are introduced, when the culprit is still easily identifiable.

For this reason, agile communities urge developers to practice *daily* application assembly and validation. Given that any iteration's user stories may carry programming into unanticipated areas of design, this daily testing will need to span the full application, not just the part the team believed it would touch during the current sprint. However, daily full integration and regression testing increases greatly the total amount of validation effort required far past what a dedicated tester can sustain so that agile teams typically find themselves searching for some form of test automation.

As will be seen in a moment, the layered architecture of most warehouses involves a tremendous amount of "data jockeying" for system testers, making test automation an absolute necessity. Implementing automated and continuous testing requires a nontrivial investment of team resources, yet it rewards that investment by driving the developers to such a high level of quality thinking that all stakeholders can feel confident that their warehouse project is based on "bullet-proof" code, despite the barely controlled chaos sometimes apparent in an agile project room during midsprint.

High quality is a necessity

Data warehousing teams should be aiming for something very close to 100% accuracy. The information their data transforms deliver should be complete and correct, fully enabling the end-user analyses requested. The organization will employ this information to make crucial tactical and strategic choices. If the warehouse is proven wrong even a couple of times, decision makers will find another source that they can trust, and the warehouse will be left without users or sponsors. BI applications in regulated industries face an even higher quality requirement given that errors in their information can risk product recalls, extensive external audits, tort actions, and, in the age of the European Union's BASEL accords and the U.S. SOX act, criminal investigation of company officers. (See [BIS 2012] and [The Economist 2007], respectively.)

For these reasons, a team might first set its quality objectives to the gold standard of data processing: "provably correct," which would require that their validation efforts demonstrate that (a) every feature requested is present in the deliverable and (b) all such features function without error. Demonstrating the latter may well require a cost-prohibitive degree of validation, depending on one's threshold for proof. For example, must a name-cleansing routine be tested with every possible combination of letters up to the full length of the name fields to be considered proven error free? Most warehousing professionals would consider that standard to be overkill.

Realizing that no programming or testing effort can economically prove an application to be absolutely perfect, teams must adjust their goals slightly to "essentially correct and fault tolerant," which asserts that (a) the code is complete with no known bugs *as far as reasonable validation efforts can demonstrate* and (b) when an unanticipated problem does arise, the application follows a planned and constructive response.

In a few situations involving particularly dirty data or deep mysteries at work within complex source systems, the team may negotiate an incremental series of quality goals. Here the objective might be at first to match 90% of a comparison data set, then 95%, and so forth. However, for most BI projects, essentially correct, fault-tolerant code will be the only quality standard that project sponsors and other stakeholders will accept. Indeed, if the BI team were to ask them to accept less, it is doubtful that many warehouse projects would be funded.

However, data integration teams have one large obstacle to surmount before they can deliver upon the high quality standard of *essentially correct*—the complexity of their application.

Agile warehousing testing requirements

Even three decades into the practice of data warehousing, the profession is lamentably weak when it comes to testing our applications. Much of the lapses are due to the fact that traditional methods have left validation to the end of the project, and of course testing gets squeezed down to often only a few days whenever coding takes longer than expected. Because of these time limitations or other scarce resources, most data warehouse teams test their applications with only a couple of data sets. This is woefully inadequate, even for the fairly simple warehouse portrayed in Figure 8.8. Analysis will show that even this basic BI application will need over a dozen test data sets just to span four different types of error scenarios. Let us take a moment to understand why.

In this example, there are only four layers to the data architecture and five major classes of errors to test for. The data layers are the same used in the example of deriving developer stories in an earlier chapter using Figure 6.4. The five classes of data errors in the diagram are as follow:

1. nominal: data that are free of errors and which should load completely and perfectly, also known as "happy path" data
2. incoherent: data including skipped or mis-sequenced extracts
3. missing: data extracts lacking one or more of the values, rows, or tables needed to maintain data integrity relational integrity, for example, orders without a corresponding customer record

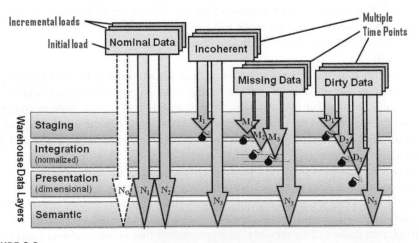

FIGURE 8.8

Testing warehouse applications properly requires many data sets.

4. "dirty data": data with human-visible flaws in the format or content of the values
5. multiple time points: data requiring special processing because it represents either the end or the beginning of an important time period, such as a fiscal year

Table 8.8 lists seven additional classes of errors that data warehousing programs should test for. Even with only the five considerations shown in the figure, it is clear that a testing team cannot get by with just a few data sets, as illustrated in the following discussions of the error classes included in the diagram.

Nominal data testing

With nominal data, data should be perfectly ready for transformation. It should load into every architectural layer without error, and the whole data transform application should execute across its full scope without stopping.

If a team were to test this "happy path" scenario with only one data set, it would necessarily need to be an initial load—data sent to the warehouse when it is first initiated. Initial loads typically involve a large proportion of history records that the organization has been pooling up in some repository. Often these records are found in legacy warehouses and data marts that will be retired once the current project goes live. Data for the second and subsequent loads will be smaller and used to update a previous layer of loaded information incrementally.

So a team cannot fully test the warehouse's happy path logic with just the first nominal data set—N_0 in our diagram—because it represent only the initial load, a process that will run only a few times in the life of the warehouse. The incremental data sets—N_1 and N_2—will be necessary. Why are two incremental loads needed after the initial load? Because initial and incremental data sets come from different combinations of sources, warehouses can suffer one set of errors when developers apply an incremental data set to an initial load and a completely different set of errors when they layer an incremental data set on top of a previous incremental

---

Table 8.8 Important Data-Based Testing Scenarios for Data Integration Projects

- Nominal—"happy path"
- Dirty data—human-visible flaws in formatting or validity
- Corrupted data—machine-detectable, low-level data syntax flaws
- Missing rows/tables—insufficient records for relational integrity, e.g., no customer record or no product file
- Incoherent data—skipped or mis-sequenced files
- Duplicate data—e.g., overlap between extracts
- Time period boundaries—e.g., month, quarter, year
- Archiving—purging of data that are too old to retain
- Catch-up—recover from system outage, usually 3 days per 24 hours of recovery
- Restart—simulate operator's context during abnormal process terminations
- High or full volume—model operational performance and processing of one-in-a-million errors
- Resource outage—e.g., disk fills up or FTP node goes down

load. Many teams have learned the hard way to always test an incremental load against an incremental load before sending their application to production.

Incoherent data

Many data warehouses depend on external feeds of data and must check that these feeds arrive in the proper order. Examples of such feeds would be laboratory reports sent in by participating research facilities for pharmaceutical clinical trials or daily transaction logs from a general ledger system. Any warehouse that maintains a current status for the entities within its domain will need these event records to arrive in the proper order. Many teams program their data transforms to suspend if a metadata value in the extracts indicates a particular feed has been skipped.

In the current example, a special data set is needed for the warehouse to attempt to load after N_2 that contains an invalid sequence number. As shown in the diagram, this data set, I_1, should cause the load to halt during the staging routine. Because warehouse applications must be programmed so that the operations group can work with it following simple instructions, the development teams typically program the data transforms to resume smoothly after the error condition is corrected and to finish loading records without corrupting the information already in the target schema.

To demonstrate such resilience, integration testing will need to load a nominal data set immediately after the application suspends for incomplete data, and which will prove the load routine's ability to restart and eventually generate a usable data set. The diagram assumes that the test suite will attempt to load incomplete data after the nominal test suite completes, thus I_1 is followed with a load of a third nominal data set, labeled N_3, indicating that it is the error-free data set that should logically occur after N_2.

Missing data

When the correct dimension record is unavailable for a given fact event, young data marts will sometimes set the fact table's corresponding foreign key attribute to a special value meaning "missing reference data." Because this is disappointing to users and undermines the credibility of the BI team, warehouses commonly mature to take two other approaches to managing data that are missing information within an extract. Teams operating on a shoestring will often design their loads to just suspend when an extract lacks referential integrity. They will restart the load once missing data are located and placed in staging. Teams with greater budgets often enhance their ETL so that transforms keep running when encountering missing data, placing the unloadable records in "suspense" tables. The unloadable records will be removed from the suspense tables later once data have been repaired on the source systems and the missing information appears in a subsequent extract.

The diagram documents the starter, low-budget case, where the team builds load routines that will stop at any one of several points when they cannot integrate a particular data set. Each stop condition typically has a corresponding piece of restart logic so that the load operators can simply resume the suspended processing step rather than rewinding the entire run back to the staging step. Of course, every restart point implemented in the load application needs to be validated.

To test a restart point, the team will need a data set that has the last extract's referential integrity flaw corrected, only to be replaced by a flaw that triggers the next stop condition.

The sample warehouse of the diagram has three such stop conditions in its integration layer load routine, thus testing for missing data needs three separate data sets, with a further use of the nominal extract N_3 to prove the final restart logic works. One should note that by using N_3 rather than a fourth nominal load, the warehouse has to be reset to the state occurring after the nominal load completed with N_2 before a test case was submitted using a defective data set. This resetting of data to a known state before each special case is tested represents an additional time-consuming task that system testing can eliminate by implementing an automated testing engine.

Dirty data

The final error class in our example involves corrupted or misformatted information, which is frequently called "dirty data." Dirty data occur in several varieties, two of the most important being miskeyed attributes and invalid reference keys. Examples of the former would be letter "ohs" occurring in the place of zeroes in a U.S. postal code or pipes occurring in user comment fields, which can unfortunately mimic the field separators in many source extract files. These flaws can usually be caught all at once, and teams can choose to stop the load while it is at work in either the staging or the integration layer.

The second group of dirty data is invalid references, such as product codes and customer identifiers that have somehow gotten missent so that they point to no record existing in the reference tables that the company maintains. Often these errors cannot be detected until much later in the iteration process or even while dimensionalizing data for the presentation layer or subsetting it out to the departmental data marts.

For example, the load of ERP system data must stop in the integration layer when a vendor cannot be found in the Duns Registry information the company has purchased. Data loading should also halt in the presentation layer when a product cannot be found in the refreshed enterprise product dimension table, perhaps because a standard product code has been retired by finance. Similarly, a portion of the load application should suspend when subsetting warehouse data out to the department if a particular marketing territory cannot be found in the reference tables the departmental staff maintains for their organization.

The diagram shows dirty data conditions halting the loads at each one of these layers using data sets D_1 though D_3, with N_3 again used at the end of the sequence to prove that the final restart point will work.

Multiple time points

As can be counted on the diagram, just 4 out of the 12 error classes listed in Table 8.11 create the need to test a data warehouse load application with more than 10 distinct data sets. This number only grows larger when multiple time points are considered. Data sets for different extract dates are needed because transformation code often employs one set of business rules for data representing a midmonth time point and significantly different business for data corresponding to end-of-month, end-of-quarter, and end-of-year events.

Unfortunately, the team cannot simply pile the records for all these time points into a single extract. At least one version of all the other data sets will be needed for each conceptual time point the team wishes to evaluate for temporal differences in business rules. For example, a sales forecast missing from M_1 might not be important until the last load of a quarter, and sales agent tax ID numbers missing from M_2 may be of little consequence until year end. The integration team may well program the data loads to halt only when these records are crucial for the time period in question.

If the first four error classes raised the number of data sets needed for sufficient warehouse testing to 11, crucial time points may multiply that number by a factor of two or three. Jockeying all those data sets in and out of the integration testing environment will clearly absorb a full system tester or more if this plethora of extracts has to be all staged manually.

The need for automation

All told, if one or two dozen data sets must be employed regularly for a single integration and regression test run for even a simple warehouse application, the team's system tester is going to need some help. True, the tables required for many of the test conditions such as missing data need only a few records each—nothing close to the millions required to do a full volume incremental load test. However, the manual labor burden these data sets place upon a tester is largely unrelated to the number of records they contain. The time needed to tear out one extract, locate, and stage another in its place properly is significant, even if that second data set contains only one record. The frenetic shuffling of records in and out of a staging area also represents a large risk because a tester can easily stage the wrong data and think he has proven something that is actually still left unaddressed.

This data-shuffling burden would be bad enough for a waterfall approaching its next release date, but agile teams have an even greater need to streamline the management of these many data sets. Their programmers are evolving the code rapidly with minimal to-be specifications. They may well instill a defect into the code on any given day. Because an iteration often has developers programming closely interrelated modules in parallel (think of facts and their related dimensions), bugs can compound each other. Interconnected bugs layered upon each other make the individual impact of each defect exponentially harder to assess. In this situation, the coding error causing the first defect is fairly easy to understand and correct, but three errors causing three defects in interdependent code modules will require the team to think through nine possible combinations of cause and effect. It is not uncommon to see teams that have let defects proliferate end up spending over half their time diagnosing, correcting, and/or coding around the errors.

In order to succeed, then, agile teams need to fail fast and fix quickly. When it comes to programming errors, the exponential impact of bugs demands that they catch each defect as soon as it is introduced into the code. Combine this need with the large number of data sets required to prove a load application is essentially correct and the daily testing requirements will grow far beyond what even a half-dozen testers could manage accurately.

Requirements for a warehouse test engine

Many agile warehousing teams decide they need to automate their system validation, both in terms of integration and regression. Although test engines can be elaborate applications in themselves, their basic function is fairly straightforward. Figure 8.9 depicts the primary services agile teams should look for in a testing engine—on the left one can see both the collection of error classes and time points discussed earlier. A list of subject areas has also been added, for agile teams often need to manage and execute tests separately for the different areas of the warehouse so that the scope of their validation work can be focused appropriately when it must fit within a tight time window.

As shown in the diagram, these three components combine into a large cube of test scenarios. There could well be other testing aspects that define the scenarios, such as separate funding programs, individual projects sharing the test server, application release numbers, and even individual developers. The more aspects an engine supports, the finer the subsets of test cases a team can invoke independently. A properly implemented, automatic, and continuous integration testing (ACIT) engine would

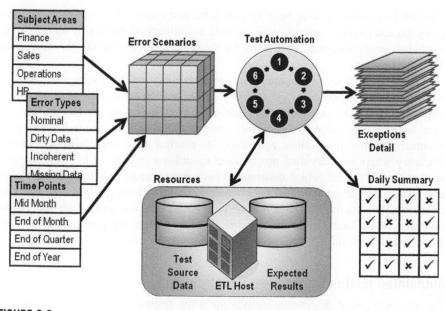

FIGURE 8.9

Warehouse test engines must iterate through numerous scenarios.

then be able to combine all these testing aspects into the "cube" of test scenarios it must iterate through.

For each such a scenario, the team should configure ACIT engine to understand three items:

1. the particular data set required and where each component of it needs to be placed so that the upcoming data transform will find them
2. the ETL module to call and where it will write actual results
3. the resulting values the test team expects to find in those target tables or at least an analytical script to run that will determine properly whether the right results were generated

In practice, the ACIT engine would be invoked regularly by a scheduler such as a Unix's "cron," at which time it would spin through all scenarios in the test case cube. The test engine would then perform six steps:

1. Set data in the staging tables and warehouse target tables to reflect the desired starting conditions
2. Invoke the ETL with the correct parameters for the scenario
3. Fetch the actual results
4. Fetch the expected results
5. Compare actual results against expected or invoke any test-oriented analytical scripts
6. Record any defects to an exception log

After all test scenarios have been executed, the test engine or a reporting tool can query the test engine's repository to compile a summary of defects by subject area, error class, and conceptual time point for the team to review before the next daily stand-up meeting.

Advanced versions of automated test engines adapt to the testing context they run within, intelligently modifying the test scripts, source data, and executables they employ to match the installation they are pointed at, including production, acceptance testing, integration environments—even sandboxes for the individual programmers. Such engines allow agile teams to reach a truly impressive operational efficiency where an individual programmer modifies a module in his sandbox and invokes the test engine, which understands enough to execute only the unit test cases appropriate for that very limited environment. If all unit tests pass, the engine then automatically ports the new code into the build residing in the application integration environment and later invokes the appropriate set of integration test cases against all the ported changes for a day using the data sets needed for integration testing.

Automated testing for front-end applications

The aforementioned discussion focuses upon the testing requirements of a warehouse's back-end processing layer. Because its data are stored in database objects that make it easy to fetch and evaluate, the back end of an application is, in many ways, easier to test than the system's front-end dashboards. Dashboards are graphical applications in which data must be pulled off a screen rather than out of a database, and it has to be acquired from the right area of a screen before it can be validated. A test automation engine would need to know how to find the necessary values by using screen pixels as coordinates, coordinates that change frequently as the programmers fine-tune the dashboard's appearance.

Just arranging for the right display to appear on a dashboard so it can be validated can be a frighteningly difficult process for system testers to consider automating. Causing the desired results to materialize can require clicking on the right menu items, plus filling out the proper values for a query constraint or picking them from a pull-down list of possibilities. The coordinates of all those widgets must be calculated, recorded in the script, and later updated when layouts change. For an agile team adjusting an application to stakeholder requirements as the user stories unfold, script-driven testing will entail far too maintenance to be practical.

On the bright side, the Web applications industry has brought forth many tools for testing graphical user interfaces. The first generation required recording mouse motions and keystrokes so that the resulting scripts were extremely fragile when a developer moved an entry field a few pixels to the left or placed the submit button in another area of the screen. More recent GUI testing tools can read application descriptors, typically exported to XML, and, within limits, adapt their test scripts routines accordingly. Many of these adaptive graphical test tools can be called via the command line, making it possible for the automated testing engine described for the back ends above to simply delegate GUI validation to these partner tools and then record whether the execution of their scripts passed or failed.

Still, involving graphical testing tools to any degree will cause warehouse teams to wrestle with a category of more or less brittle test scripts. Luckily, clever validation planning can extend the reach of the back-end testing tool all the way to the warehouse's semantic layer, obviating the need for most front-end GUI testing. Before considering this technique, one should note that front-end testing actually involves two aspects, with differing benefits for the project sponsors. First, testing should ensure that all the dashboard widgets are in the right place and the GUI menu items are working properly. This functionality is indeed important for user acceptance testing, but those aspects of an application can usually be repaired quickly—sometimes while the user watches—because the GUI controls offered by BI tools have given developers instant command over the visual elements of the display screen.

The portions of a data warehouse that cannot be fixed and demonstrated quickly are the set of business rules that determine the values that the dashboards will have for their front-end displays. These business rules might include flagging a company's top 10 customers or allocating discounts across payments based on the product a customer ordered. Validating these business rules takes a good amount of planning to get right, but then fortunately cannot be broken by something as capricious as moving a widget a few pixels to the right. As shown in Figure 8.10, DWBI applications can implement business rules in many different places within their architecture—some

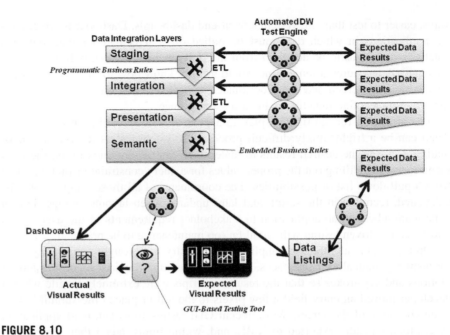

FIGURE 8.10

Extending back-end testing to cover most of a warehouse application.

implemented using a programming language and others embedded within the declarations made within the foundational objects in the semantic layer.

Although it is possible to embed business rules in the code of a GUI application, that architectural decision is counterproductive because testing for these values there is so difficult for the reasons described earlier. High-performance teams restrain themselves from implementing business rules in the graphical layer unless they desperately need a quick fix and then they do so only temporarily. Discipline will lead them to steadily move business rules out of a pixel-based arena toward the back end in order to subject them to the more robust quality assurance process that an automated warehouse testing engine can provide dependably.

As depicted in the diagram, one can employ a data-based testing engine as soon as these business rules migrate just one step back to just the BI tool's semantic layer. In the example, the same semantic layer that powers a BI application's dashboards can be employed to create a data dump via a tabular listing, exporting it to a flat file. For most BI tools, the job that performs this export can be invoked via an operating system command by the same scheduler that calls the ACIT engine.

By regularly calling for a dump from the BI semantic layer, the warehouse test engine can evaluate the business rules embedded in the semantic layer, thus validating the values that are sent to the GUI dashboards. Although this still leaves a small question about whether all the widgets on the front end are working properly, at least this technique covers the tough part—guaranteeing that data flowing through the long processing chain comprising the warehouse have arrived all the way to the BI tool properly transformed.

Evolutionary target schemas—the hard way

The last major adaptation that generic agile methods commonly need to meet the needs of data warehousing is a means of incrementally elaborating the project's physical target data schemas. This need for an evolving target model arises from two sources. First, if the team is going to be responsive to changing requirements, as featured in the agile principles, then occasionally business conditions will demand a few warehouse tables be added, dropped, and/or modified. Second, if the team architect, data architect, and other leaders plan to start module construction with only the most important 80% of an iteration's internals planned thoroughly, they are going to have a few false starts, requiring them to change their minds now and then. The problem with both normalized and dimensional models is that even a small change in target structure's grain or change data capture rules can obviate huge swaths of ETL coding and require many days of emergency programming to fill the holes such changes create.

If agile teams are going to pursue fast starts for their projects, proceed to code with just-in-time requirements, and program with a minimum of to-be specifications, they cannot expect their data architect to provide a definitive target model upon his first pass. Fail fast and fix quickly will require data models to evolve. Accordingly, agile warehousing teams will have to get good at updating their target structures and the ETL that populates them as conditions warrant.

Teams that follow the staffing recommendations listed here will have placed on their teams project architects and data architects who have built several warehouses before. These experienced teammates will be able to greatly anticipate the most common functional changes, allowing the data architect to avoid target models that are brittle and incur devastating levels of rework. Furthermore, giving the project leads Iterations −1 and 0 to prepare for the project will keep big mistakes to a minimum. Slowly changing dimensions provide a good example of such anticipatory data architecting. Every dimension can be structured as a Type 2 dimension whether or not the product owner believes it will need to track history. Reusable modules can be built to populate the row-level meta data columns of a Type 2 dimension, so that when the business suddenly realizes that a current-only qualifier needs to track history, the only coding change needed is call the standardized routine rather than resorting to custom programming.

Nevertheless, there will be occasions where the data model must change, and these could well impact tables that are already in production, loaded with high volumes of data. Having to change production tables is difficult because, in most circumstances, users will not want to lose the span of history already loaded into the warehouse. The team cannot simply throw away existing data when a table structure changes and begin accumulating history from that point onward. Consequently, when tables change, existing data will have to be converted to the new layout and reloaded. Such conversions require a special-purpose program to be written, validated, and executed, with the results carefully reconciled back to the sources. Such work requires a nontrivial amount of time and expense.

Developers on projects based on the new hypernormalized data models mentioned earlier will have tools available that make reengineering loaded tables far easier than teams who have restricted themselves to the traditional Inmon/Kimball data modeling approaches. As discussed in the next volume, hypernormalization techniques convert all links between entities to many-to-many joins and then separate business keys from nonkey attributes, putting their data into separate tables. The tools that teams utilize with the hypernormalized data repositories allow two different styles of reengineering already loaded tables. For those teams who want to maintain some direct involvement with the engineering process, evolving an existing integration layer requires adding only a new table or two and loading them using small, parameter-driven ETL routines. [Linstedt & Graziano 2011] These teams often use a data virtualization product as well so that refreshing the presentation layer requires them to only republish a view rather than building and applying a conversion script to tables full of data. For those teams preferring a more automated approach, evolving both integration and presentation layers consists mostly of updating the business model for the newly required entities, attributes, and relationships and then letting the tools interpret the changes and restructure the existing tables in place. [Kalido 2008]

Teams utilizing traditional Inmon/Kimball designs will have to evolve already loaded tables by hand, which can require considerable effort. In this situation, the DWBI department should invest in learning the skill of "refactoring" databases as a foundation for faster reengineering. Technically, *refactoring* is defined as improving the design of a software component without changing its function. In practice, refactoring blends into reengineering. For example "adding a foreign key" to an existing table can be considered reengineering because it allows data to be queried at a greater level of granularity. It can also be considered refactoring because queries using the previous set of dimensions will implicitly aggregate the retrieved information to the prior level of detail as if nothing had changed.

Perhaps the most important aspect of the entire study of refactoring databases is that there is a cookbook for it. [Ambler & Sandalage 2006] This cookbook contains 68 recipes that span most of the intersections between several data management verbs such as *add*, *drop*, and *merge*, and almost as many major object nouns such as *table*, *column*, and *foreign key*. Table 8.9 lists the nouns and verbs from this collection that pertain most to data warehousing. Table 8.10 provides an example of one of the recipes, listing the recommended steps for *add a foreign key* to link in a table of status codes.

This cookbook in of itself does not make evolving a target data model easier per se. It only codifies the steps one has to take, making it a repeatable process and minimizing the possibility that the team will make a careless mistake. Thus the importance of the cookbook for stakeholders outside the programming staff is reassurance that refactoring actions are well thought out and manageable. The importance of the book within the programming team is to give the developers a starting

Table 8.9 Verbs and Nouns for Refactoring Databases

Major Verbs	Major Nouns
1. Add	1. Table
2. Consolidate	2. Method
3. Drop	3. Column
4. Introduce	4. Default value
5. Merge	5. Foreign key
6. Move	6. View
7. Remove	7. Parameters
8. Rename	
9. Replace	
10. Split	

Table 8.10 Sample database refactoring recipe

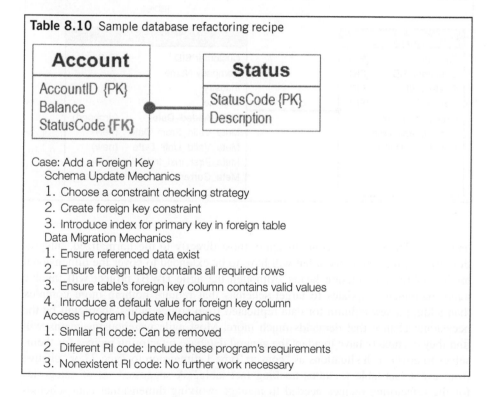

Case: Add a Foreign Key
  Schema Update Mechanics
  1. Choose a constraint checking strategy
  2. Create foreign key constraint
  3. Introduce index for primary key in foreign table
  Data Migration Mechanics
  1. Ensure referenced data exist
  2. Ensure foreign table contains all required rows
  3. Ensure table's foreign key column contains valid values
  4. Introduce a default value for foreign key column
  Access Program Update Mechanics
  1. Similar RI code: Can be removed
  2. Different RI code: Include these program's requirements
  3. Nonexistent RI code: No further work necessary

action list for updating tables and ETL that they can repeatedly refer back to and improve. In fact, each recipe in this book can become the foundation of the "basis of estimate" cards described in Chapter 2, specific to the complex tasks of evolving loaded data tables.

Readers must keep in mind that this cookbook is a guide for refactoring databases in general, and that hence the guidelines for refactoring warehouses are only

Table 8.11 Refactoring Categories for Dimensional Warehouse Schemas

Verbs	Nouns	
	Facts	**Dimensions**
Add/remove	Low impact	High impact upon facts
Split/consolidate	Medium impact + rekeying	High impact upon facts
Increase/reduce table grain	Low impact (equals add fact)	Low impact when supporting new fact tables High impact when dimension-led modification
Alter nature	Switch between: • events • statuses • factless	Switch between Types 1, 2, 3, 4, and 6 Change slow-change trigger columns
Extend	Add drill-across capability	Add snowflake or bridging tables

Sale Event Fact	
Fact SID	{PK}
Customer SID	{FK}
Product SID	{FK}
Date SID	{FK}
Gross Sales Dollar	
Gross Margin Dollar	
Net Margin Dollar	

Customer DIM	
Customer SID	{PK}
Company Name	
Industry	
Channel	
~~Meta_Added_Date~~	(dropped)
Meta_Valid_From_Date	(new)
Meta_Valid_Until_Date	(new)
Meta_First_Inst_Ind	(new)
Meta_Current_Ind	(view only)

half done. The recipes it contains apply most directly to the normalized, integration layer of the warehouses, but will have to be extended to cover the dimensional models of the presentation layers. Although the agile DWBI project will involve many incremental updates to target schemas that require nothing more complex than adding a new column for data replicated from source tables, there will be the occasional change that demands much more. Most agile warehousing teams will find they eventually have to adapt the general database refactoring recipes for themselves to cover such situations as "convert Type 1 dimension to Type 2" or "change from event fact table to status-tracking fact table." A suggested set of categories for the refactoring recipes needed to manage evolving dimensional data schemas is offered in Table 8.11. Data warehousing departments adopting an agile approach will need to begin by elaborating upon the generic database refactoring cookbook to yield dimensional equivalents of its recipes and then accumulate a fuller collection as their programs mature. A sample of what one of those recipes might look like is sketched in Table 8.12.

Table 8.12 Sample Recipe for Converting Type 1 to Type 2 Dimension

Assumptions
1. Persistent staging environment exists
2. Changes made to DEV, validated in SIT environment

Preparation
1. Ensure data for desired date range exist in persistent staging
2. Plan validation
3. Back up existing data objects, ETL, semantic layer, and dashboards
4. Rename existing objects so they can remain online during validation
5. Request temporary storage for transitional objects

Dimension Schema Update Mechanics
1. Alter table—Drop meta_added_date columns
2. Alter table—Add new "meta" columns
3. Add index for meta_valid
4. Alter view—Add derived meta_current_indicator column

Fact Schema Update Mechanics
1. {No changes needed}

Dimension ETL Mechanics
1. Remove find latest record logic
2. Sort customer records by customer and record modification date
3. Alter flow to meta_added_date port to populate meta_valid_from_date instead
4. Add "retire previous record" logic including flow to meta_valid_until_date
5. Add logic for meta_first_instance_indicator column

Fact ETL Mechanics
1. Add criteria to customer dimension lookup to select record valid as of fact event date

ETL Execution Mechanics
1. Clear dimension table
2. Run dimension load
3. Clear fact table
4. Run fact load
5. Validate resulting data, including comparison to previous dimension and fact records

Dashboard Update Mechanics
1. Update SALES EVENT query definition screen(s)—Add "Desired Event Date Range" fields

Wrap-Up
1. Release temporary storage
2. Drop previous version of data objects
3. Plan production and migration for PROD environment
4. Update release install guide
5. Update release operations guide

Summary

When the construction phase of a project begins, agile data warehousing teams will discover that generic Scrum leaves several vital challenges specific to data integration work unaddressed. These challenges include some missing roles, a development period that overly compresses the work of each warehousing specialty, data churn while loading large data sets for each sprint demo, lack of daily integration testing, and already-loaded tables that must occasionally upgrade their form and function. To answer these challenges, Scrum needs to be adapted for data warehousing. It needs four new defined roles who will act as resident resources for the team: project architect, data architect, systems analyst, and system tester. In order to avoid losing days of programming time to data churn, teams will need to create subsets of the company's full volume production data so that it can be loaded quickly for programming and user demos. So that key specialties on the team receive a full iteration to perform their work, the team will need to organize a pipeline of specialties with stations for analysis and design, development, and system testing. Given the complexity of data warehouse macro data architecture and the chance that defects can compound each other's complexity, many agile teams will want to have dozens of test data sets to fully validate their warehouses. With a large number of data sets, automate testing becomes highly beneficial. The test engine will need to be able to manage staging the right data set, execute the right ETL, and evaluate results against the right set of expected values for the large number of permutations created when all the necessary aspects of testing are combined. Finally, agile data warehousing teams working without model-driven design packages or other such DWBI application generators will have to establish repeatable means for updating the structure of already-loaded data tables. A "cookbook" is available for such operations with databases in general. The recipes contained therein are a good start, but will have to be elaborated on for the data warehousing context.

Starting and Scaling Agile Data Warehousing

9

What is the best way to start an agile warehousing team?
How should an organization scale up an agile DWBI program?
What core set of metrics should we use to track an agile warehousing
team's performance?

The preceding chapters provided a deep dive on several practices that agile warehousing teams find essential for business intelligence projects whenever they involve any significant degree of data integration work. Looking back on the depth and breadth of the material covered, the fully adapted agile warehousing method is clearly too much to drop on a new team all at once. The notions of user stories and time-boxed delivery alone may be all the novelty that developers from traditional projects will be able to manage during their first several agile iterations. Because the aspects of iterative and incremental delivery must be introduced over time, data warehousing/business intelligence (DWBI) departments planning to implement agile data warehousing will find it useful to formulate a multipart implementation plan. Many of the components of such a plan can be found in this final chapter.

These components start with a step-by-step path for introducing a new development team to agile data warehousing. It then presents some options for scaling up the method so that several teams can pursue a large endeavor in parallel. Scaling approaches will be followed by techniques that measure and compare the progress of different agile warehousing team so that program managers can coordinate multiple efforts through milestones and even balance work between their iterative teams. Finally, a presentation of a new approach to incremental project management—pull-based work flow systems—will be presented. Many agile practitioners consider pulled-based systems to be the next logical step beyond Scrum, and therefore a likely future for agile data warehousing.

Starting a scrum team

Whereas it would be truly wonderful to simply flip a switch and have all of a department's warehouse project teams suddenly "go agile," the savvy program organizer will

Agile Data Warehousing Project Management.
DOI: http://dx.doi.org/10.1016/B978-0-12-396463-2.00009-0

search instead for a manageable series of transition steps for each group of engineers. He will not want to leave the evolution of each team completely to chance. Although the Scrum approach underlying the agile warehousing method invites teams to innovate the details of their iterative collaboration patterns, new teams often make some big mistakes when first crafting and tuning an iterative approach, especially when deadlines force them to evolve faster than they can experiment and learn. More often than not, they resort to many plan-driven techniques in their search for fast organizing concepts and fundamentally undermine the velocity that an agile approach offers.

Even Scrum's core of self-organized teams and minimal to-be specifications alone can be an uncomfortably big leap for many traditional software engineers. Estimating in story points and switching to test-led development will be overwhelming. An agile program organizer can give his developers an overview of the entire agile data warehousing method so they understand their eventual destination, but then he will have to let them work on just a couple of notions at a time. Once developers get those ideas sorted out, they can then return to the agile data warehousing coach for a few more suggestions on how to streamline their process further. Table 9.1 lists a set of six major stages an agile promoter could use for introducing agile warehousing to a new team. The table also estimates how many sprints the developers will need to work through each stage. It then infers how much the calendar time this introduction process will require based on 2- and 3-week iterations.

With even the first one or two of these suggested steps, teams usually demonstrate noticeably faster delivery speeds than the company experienced with traditional methods. However, as can be seen from the totals at the bottom of Table 9.1, achieving a team's full potential in both velocity and quality will take a good part of a year to complete. Because the full transition requires several steps over many months, agile champions need to plan for regular assessments and increments of coaching to steadily guide their teams through this transition.

Table 9.1 Introducing Agile Data Warehousing to a New Team

Stage	Iterations Required	
	Fast	Slow
1. Generic Scrum: Time box and story points	1	2
2. Pipelined delivery	2	4
3. Delivery stories and current estimates	1	2
4. Managed data and test-driven development	2	4
5. Automated and continuous integration testing	2	4
Total iterations	8	16
Elasped time (2- and 3-week iterations)	16–24 weeks	32–48 weeks
6a: Pull-based workflow control: Add WIP limits	3	6
6b: Pull-based workflow control: Drop iterations	3	6

Automated Testing Shortcut

There is an important point implied by the step-by-step organization of Table 9.1: Because developers need significant time to master each stage, agile data warehousing programs clearly benefit by keeping each team of developers together for the duration of a project, even after their first project comes to an end. By casually disbanding and reformulating teams as if developers are plug-compatible components, a company can require its developers to reestablish the interpersonal arrangement and method customization already perfected in their previous groupings. True, teams need different skills sets as projects change, but with some thought, DWBI management can keep the shuffling of developers to a minimum, thereby letting teams build upon the velocity established on prior projects rather than forcing them to continually starting from scratch.

Stage 1: time box and story points

One of the easiest ways to get a new team of developers started with agile is to simply ask them to see how much shippable code they can demonstrate in 3 weeks. Of course, the agile promoter will have to invest a little up front for this approach to succeed. Working with functional managers so that the team members can focus predominantly on the agile project will do wonders to minimize the velocity lost to multitasking. Arranging for colocation will help tremendously as well. Scheduling a training day to cover the notion of user stories and the phases of Scrum as a suggested collaboration approach will enable the developers to achieve a higher velocity from the start.

In this initial step, the emphasis will be pushing generic user stories through time-boxed iterations with little structure beyond daily stand-ups and an end-of-cycle product demo. The scrum master's primary objective for this stage is to combine the pressure of a short sprint with the convenience of working eye to eye to scrub away the slow work habits that the waterfall's "big design up-front" approach entailed. The key insight one hopes the developers achieve during this stage is that though agile is simple, making it work is hard. Success will depend on their individual desires to deliver business-valued software quickly, plus their ability to work and learn as a team. The fact that programmers can succeed and even perform better with little more than index cards, cork boards, and whiteboards will take them a couple of iterations to accept.

The Scrum/XP community speaks of four generic phases in the development of new teams: forming, storming, norming, and performing. [Tuckman 1965] The first "generic Scrum" step suggested in this table of team maturation steps is the toughest because it involves both *forming* and *storming*. An ordinary team can reasonably require two or three iterations to work through this first increment. For some teams, just getting the daily stand-up meetings to 15 minutes or less will be a major victory. When developers start *norming* their particular work habits, significant leaps in *performing* will result and they will be ready for Stage 2.

Depending on the degree of storming, the scrum coach can introduce additional Scrum elements during this latter portion of this first stage, such as size-based estimation, a task board, burndown charts, a product board, and measures of team velocity. He can touch upon the quality of the estimates, but in this early stage, the objective should be just to quantify the programmers' forecasting accuracy so that it can be improved later. Lofty goals such as 95% forecasting accuracy will have to wait for the introduction of developer stories during a later stage.

Stage 2: pipelined delivery

One purpose of Stage 1 is to let the team experiment with the dysfunctional Waterscrum or Scrummerfall mash-ups, as discussed in the prior chapter. Developers will need a chance to first appreciate how much faster a team can deliver through colocation and generalizing specialists. They will also soon observe first-hand how difficult it is to keep all members of the team productive for the entire sprint if they all try to work their specialty on a module during the same iteration. When the developers in each specialty become clearly vexed with how little time they get in one iteration to complete their work, the scrum master can safely introduce pipelining. Broach it any sooner and the developers may confuse the notion with strict work role assignments and a return to waterfall.

Unfortunately, it will take a couple of iterations just to fill the pipeline. Moving through this step takes longer if the team does not immediately hit upon the best way to define the work stations along the pipeline. One way to know if a team is ready for the next stage is to track the "net promoters' scores," described later, which will measure the quality of hand-offs between the specialties in the pipeline.

Stage 3: developer stories and current estimates

Once a team has their pipeline of generalizing specialists roles worked out, the next discernible impediment upon their velocity will be the stories they are working—the user stories will seem to be "too fat" for quick time-boxed delivery. Furthermore, the sponsors will be by this time undoubtedly demanding to know how long the team thinks the project will take. Both these needs can be addressed at once by transitioning the team from user stories down to the more granular notion of developer stories for their data integration work. As discussed in previous chapters, this transition aligns the work units flowing through the iterations with the natural components dictated by the application's macro data architecture.

The product owner will need to make the mental transition to developer stories as well. So that the transition can be made as soon as the team is ready, scrum masters and project architects can work offline with the product owner, familiarizing him with just the basics of data warehousing ahead of time so that he is ready to work with developer stories when the time for this step comes.

Story points may need to be recalibrated for this next step, as developer stories are smaller and thus the team's velocity measure will be redefined. As a result, this stage can be frustrating for stakeholders because the planning metrics will be in flux for an iteration or two. At the conclusion of this transition, however, the team should feel like their work units are well matched to the tight window formed by the sprint time box and that they have driven out much of the imprecision of their earlier estimates. With such confidence in place, it will be straightforward to take 1 day away from development and produce the team's first current estimate for the benefit of its stakeholder community.

Stage 4: managed development data and test-driven development

Now that work is flowing into the team in bite-sized packets, the developers can turn their attention to perfecting their development process. They may have been following some form of test-driven development up until now, but typically it has been applied inconsistently and shallowly. They may be also losing considerable time to the scourge of *data churn* discussed in the previous chapter.

At this point it makes sense for the teammates to perform a deep think about the awkward volumes of development data they utilize and the limits upon testing it imposes. As discussed in the last chapter, deriving a subset of production data that support quick, representative loads will require analysis. It will also require some scripting to enable the team to occasionally refresh the development records in the test data repository. Such a managed development data set is a natural prerequisite to fast, test-driven development because it will enable the coders to "get intimate" with the native keys and attribute values within their data. Such familiarity allows them to check the output of unit and component tests rapidly by looking for the expected results on the records they have memorized.

Stage 5: automatic and continuous integration testing

The previous chapter recommended that agile warehousing teams subset production data to managed development data sets. With a collection of well-understood and controlled data sets in place, the team can continue driving for rock-solid, quality deliverables by automating the comparisons of actual to expected results. That automation can then be scheduled to run against a nightly build of their application. With automated and nightly integration testing established, the team will have a report each morning indicating whether any modules added during the previous day have failed to integrate properly. It will also be clear where yesterday's changes have caused troubles for untouched modules that were working the day before. Typically this step will require implementing an automated test engine, and sometimes an automated build utility if that feature is not part of the extract, transform, and load (ETL) package the team uses. Given that tool implementation may be involved, project planners may need to anticipate this stage and have an automated testing package waiting for implementation.

For managers of data warehousing programs hoping for a fast conversion to agile, automated and continuous integration (ACIT) testing provides a shortcut across the maturity path outlined earlier. As shown in Table 9.1, the "Automated Testing Shortcut" occurs when the warehousing department implements an automated test engine before an individual agile warehousing team gets underway. This strategy represents test-led development at the whole project level, above the realm of unit and component development.

Of course, at the beginning of the project, the team cannot provide all of the test cases an application will eventually have to pass. But even at that early juncture, the product owner, project architect, data architect, and system analysts should be able to provide dozens of appropriate test cases, such as "targets should reconcile to source tables," "all orders should have one and only one customer," and "all type-two dimensions should have a current record for every natural key."

By putting ACIT in place from the start, the leaders provide for the coders an instant visualization of the whole notion of iterative development. As shown in Figure 9.1, these leaders can set up a few major tests for each topic area of the project and each layer in the data architecture. The quality assurance engine will then run these tests each night, starting from the first day of the project. Getting the team into the mind-set required for fast incremental delivery then becomes as simple as asking the developers "which of these traffic lights on the QA board do you all want to turn green when we run this test suite on the morning of the next demo?"

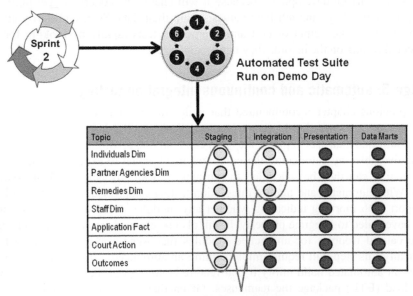

FIGURE 9.1

Automated testing gives team in an incremental point of view.

Such a question makes defining deliverables very tangible and strongly focuses the conversation of the next story conference.

Installing automated testing from the start also puts an instant cap on sloppy coding and careless application design. If a programmer throws a module on the heap that undermines the function of the other modules already in the build, a light that used to turn green suddenly shows red the next morning, making it very easy for the team to figure out which developer probably caused the problem. Automated testing allows the developers to self-police, thus accelerating how quickly a new team will travel down the maturity path laid out earlier.

Stage 6: pull-based collaboration

The final step in maturing an agile warehousing team is to incorporate some or all of the techniques of a newer approach to managing work flow through the project. These techniques are based on "work-in-progress limits" placed on a task board that has been refined for the particular development process a team wants to utilize. With these modifications, work is pulled through the development cycle and time boxes become unnecessary. Because such an approach requires some additional process measurements besides story points and velocity, this discussion will have to wait until later in this chapter after discussing the metrics with which agile teams can quantify and communicate their results.

Scaling agile

Getting one agile team established and performing is only a first milestone for a full iterative warehousing program. More than likely, a company will have this first team try only a modest project, such as a data mart with one or two fact tables. Should this pilot project meet with success, the agile champions in the organization will soon face the challenge of scaling the agile warehousing method to address larger, more complex projects and even multiproject development efforts. To succeed, these planners will need to consider how to coordinate a half-dozen or more agile development teams working through tough requirements and complex corporate situations. Solving these challenges typically requires analyzing what makes growing a program difficult and the best practices for addressing each of those challenges.

Like many engineering disciplines, the software industry has labored for decades to identify *scaling factors* that might reveal how much one should multiply the cost and durations of known projects to create reasonable estimates for a new application that differs along some codified notion of project size. Some algorithmic cost estimation models from the prior century actually quantified these scaling factors into predictive formulas (see, for example, [Barry Boehm et al. 1995]). The agile community has not yet been so bold as to publish such scaling formulas, probably because most agile approaches are closer to adaptive collaboration frameworks

> **Table 9.2** Agile scaling factors
>
> **Application complexity.** More complex and expansive problem domains require more time for exploration and experimentation, including prototyping, modeling, and simulation.
>
> **Geographical distribution.** Effective collaboration becomes more challenging and disconnects are more likely to occur when team members work in different buildings, cities, or countries.
>
> **Team size.** Mainstream agile processes work very well for smaller teams of 10 to 15 people, but paper-based, face-to-face strategies start to fall apart as the team size grows.
>
> **Compliance requirements.** Regulatory issues and international quality standards may impose process standards upon teams that consume velocity and stifle process innovations.
>
> **Information technology governance.** Formal IT process controls can sap a team velocity by imposing ceremonies and audits that run counter to agile notions such as self-organization, fail fast and fix quickly, and 80/20 specifications.
>
> **Organizational culture.** A project team may include members from different divisions or even different companies, thereby increasing the risk to your project greatly.
>
> **Organizational complexity.** An organization's structure and culture may reflect traditional values, increasing the complexity of adopting and scaling modern agile strategies within your organization.
>
> **Organizational distribution.** Teams can lose velocity when they must resolve conflicts between organization units over goals, definitions, access, and funding.
>
> *Adapted from [Ambler 2009].*

than iron-clad methodologies. However, the community has done well at identifying what the most important scaling factors seem to be, as summarized in Table 9.2, which lists a recent IBM summary of agile scaling factors.

Each scaling factor listed in Table 9.2 is a complex topic in of itself. Many may well deserve a book of their own. While there are no silver bullets that solve all of them quickly, a few strategies exist for each that agile project planners can investigate when challenges emerge in that arena as they grow their agile warehousing program.

Application complexity

For all the advances ETL tools have made since the early 2000s, they still leave data warehousing teams with a lot of hard thinking to do when it comes to data architecture and transformation rules for data integration. The primary means for mitigating this complexity was discussed in previous chapters. First, staff the team with project and data architects who spend Iterations −1 and 0 performing business and logical modeling so that they can inform the team where the complexity lies within the scope of the project. Second, staff the team with a systems analyst who can spend Iteration 0 profiling data and identifying the nature of the project's most challenging data transformation requirements. Third, have teams organize these finding using "developer stories," which are each specific to a layer of the warehouse macro data architecture, and thus reasonably sized for iterative development. Fourth, allow the team to conduct a spike (see Chapter 2) to complete some prototyping solutions around any deeply challenging developer stories. Finally, organize the team for a pipelined delivery approach, which will give the leadership subteam time to fill in the remaining gaps concerning data modeling and transformation rules for the developer stories that will be programmed during the next iteration.

Geographical distribution

Agile thrives on close collaboration. Spreading the team across the map requires careful planning and some good remote-presence communication products, as discussed in Chapter 3.

Team size

Because of the time spent planning and estimating during each iteration, generic Scrum teams hit peak effectiveness in the 6 to 10 developer range. Scaling past this point can be addressed by splitting the program into multiple coordinated teams or modifying the collaboration model, both of which are discussed later in this chapter.

Compliance requirements

Many large organizations adopt compliance goals that all information technology (IT) development efforts within the company, including the agile warehousing projects, are expected to uphold. The impetus for adopting these demanding compliance goals may originate with externally imposed regulatory agencies or with voluntary notions to meet international quality standards. The maturity models that companies adopt frequently for their compliance efforts largely predate agile methods. Therefore, many compliance planners have trouble understanding how their models can accommodate iterative development efforts. Such compliance schemes often involve software development process audits, such as those based on SEI's Capabilities Maturity Model (CMM). [SEI 2006] Although large organizations typically interpret these maturity models as if they only supported plan-driven, "command and control" styles of project management, careful reading of their guidance reveals that they have no inherent conflict with iterative methods. [Glazer 2008] Melding the two worlds takes some careful definitional thinking to align the concepts and practices. [See Hughes 2008, Chapter 7] Once management can articulate a combined approach, it then takes a considerable investment to document the new "bilingual" standards to the point where both waterfall and iterative development teams can understand how to work within the process defined. True to the agile manifesto, the iterative teams will want to emphasize whole team solutions over following a formal process. So that they can thrive within an audited environment, it helps for management to emphasize not the audits, but instead the coaching on the adapted method so that the agile teams receive fast and consistent resolutions each time; delivering quickly seems to conflict with the documented process.

Perhaps a more attractive alternative for organizations will be to avoid trying to "agilize" maturity models such as CMM that originated during the waterfall era and employ instead those arising from the agile world itself. These efforts are in their infancy, which is advantageous because young maturity models are less detailed, so they can be read and adapted with relatively little effort. [See, for example, Petit 2006] The disadvantage of new and unelaborated models is that corporate compliance planners who do not trust self-organization to innovate process challenges will view them as incomplete and doubt their potential compared to their waterfall counterparts.

Information technology governance

Information technology governance is a broad set of practices for reliably aligning IT services with the needs of the enterprise. The topics of concern within IT governance can be as broad as the proper definition and approval of projects, as well as their assembly into funded programs and managed portfolios. Governance topics can also be as detailed as the best change control process to follow when stakeholders request new features for an application already under development.

There are several formal definitions of these practices, including the Information Systems Audit and Control Association's COBIT and the United Kingdom's IT Infrastructure Library (ITIL). ITIL's IT Service Management system, for example, focuses upon five service areas that should be placed under governance through definition and periodic assessment: business relationship management, demand management, strategy management, portfolio management, and financial management. ITIL also provides detailed guidance on operational areas such as infrastructure security, application management, and implementation planning. [Cartlidge 2007]

Agile warehousing programs will find IT governance to be a challenging scaling factor when the policy and procedures of IT department preclude many of the shortcuts suggested by agile principles, such as sourcing detailed requirements through eye-to-eye conversations with users and treating source code as a modules working design until it passes validation. Perhaps the fastest approach to resolving such points of conflicts can be found among the agile communities emerging literature on "Lean IT" governance schemes. [Bell 2011] These studies strive to map agile practices arising out of the "lean" family of agile approaches to the general categories of IT governance such as ITIL, including policy and standards, roles and responsibilities, processes, and measures. [Ambler & Kroll 2011]

Organizational culture

Invariably, agile programs encounter a seemingly impenetrable wall composed of the company's beliefs—crystallized in its many policies, templates, and checklists—that allow no room for the innovative philosophies and techniques that agile depends upon. Often, the root causes of these conflicts are summarized by nonagile staff in statements as terse as "iterative methods just won't work in this company." Frustrated by such pronouncements, many agile champions will realize that to succeed, they will have to find a way to change the entire culture of the IT department or the CIO's organization, a daunting proposition at best.

Luckily, the field of *organizational change management* can provide a model for creating opportunities for agile advocates to insert incremental delivery concepts into the corporate culture. Starting in the mid-1990s, the change management industry has been promoting structured approaches to shifting individuals, teams, and organizations from a limited, current state to a desired future orientation with greater potential. These strategies revolve around changing the mind-sets, behaviors, and systems employed by the individuals, teams, and larger groupings that exist within a company. [Anderson 2010]

A fast way for the agile advocate to begin strategizing mechanisms for warming an organization to new ideas such as incremental methods can be found in *Change the Culture, Change the Game.* [Connors 2011] This management consulting book offers aspiring change agents a particularly streamlined approach to planning new experiences for staff and managers that will spark changes in beliefs and practices so that new cultural directions begin to emerge.

Organizational distribution

Because data warehouses are such large, multipurpose applications, often the agile teams building them cannot identify a single product owner who can articulate all the necessary requirements, let alone communicate with all the impacted stakeholders in a large company. Because data ownership is often unclear within large companies, warehouse planners can find it difficult to secure solid definitions of the source and target elements from the many stakeholder groups involved. When the business community gets too large and disjointed, agile teams will need some data-specific groupware tools to secure solid agreements on shared business terms. The next volume of this book set looks at some of those tools and the techniques they make possible in a section that focuses upon requirements management.

Beyond business-term definitions, agile warehouse projects often stumble over organizational politics within a distributed company. Control of legacy BI applications, plus the business rules and staffing that goes with them, can become heavily guarded when new warehousing projects emerge. Although one might cynically look for solutions to this challenge in Machiavelli's *The Prince*, a two-fold contemporary approach will probably lead to more desirable results. First, linking the project to the business's *money-making machine* is always the bedrock of building the political support needed to mitigate an organization obstruction. To this end one can tap into general business management books, such as Charan's *What the CEO Wants You to Know* [Charan 2001], which—title aside—identifies basic business drivers linking the interests of directors, middle managers, and knowledge workers throughout an organization. Second, there are business books specifically about managing tumultuous events, including those that disruptive technologies such as agile frequently set off. *The First 90 Days* provides a quick approach to properly categorizing which of four possible business situations a new project may find itself: start-ups, turnarounds, realignments, or sustained success. This book then provides step-by-step processes for combining elements from the company's structure, systems, strategies, and skills into a 3-month roadmap for success. [Watkins 2003]

Finally, distributed organizations frequently cause tough problems for enterprise data warehousing programs in particular. In many corporate settings, funding for DWBI is allocated through the business departments on a project-by-project basis. This arrangement leaves the enterprise architects without any resources of their own with which they can pursue reusable components to be shared between the departmental projects, inviting a myriad of unmanageable, stovepiped solutions to result. Without shared development, the architects find themselves unable to ensure that an *enterprise* data warehouse will somehow emerge from a long series of many, loosely coupled, agile data mart projects. The enterprise architecture group could have already compiled a comprehensive data architecture for the company and be striving to instill it into departmental projects through mandatory architectural review sessions. However, because enterprise architecture groups rarely have any funding to contribute toward development, the dictates of their review boards are sidestepped easily by the departmental application teams when they do not speak to the immediate objectives of each project.

In practice, enterprise architects facing project-level funding schemes need to offer a set of DWBI services that are so attractive to the departmental development teams that enterprise architecture gets invited to join the agile projects as visiting resources. With a seat at the table, they can begin to steer the individual project designs toward shared enterprise objectives. A recent white paper provides a good list of over 50 such services an enterprise architecture group can offer to departmental development projects. [Hughes 2011] This white paper also provides a balancing framework, reproduced in Figure 9.2, which guides enterprise BI planners in monitoring and optimizing their relationship with each individual project. By managing the balance suggested by this framework properly, the corporate architecture group will find itself providing enough project-level support that it will be able to coax the departmental teams into contributing to enterprise-level warehouse assets. With such participation from the departmental development efforts, an enterprise warehouse *can* emerge from a collection of separately funded agile BI projects.

Coordinating multiple scrum teams

Projects with a long list of stories to deliver within a compressed amount of time will need more developers than a single agile team can support. Project planners naturally need to know the point where simply adding developers to an existing team no longer works and at which point additional teams need to be inaugurated. The answer differs upon the agile method the program has employed. It is easier to discuss Scrum first and then reconsider the answer for pull-based approaches once they have been presented below as an evolution for iterative development schemes.

Roughly, who's working for whom?	Who Owns the Asset that Benefits	
	Departmental Project Team	_Enterprise DWBI_
Who's Doing Design & ETL _Departmental Project Team_	**Quadrant D for D:** You're building something unique to your project...here's some techniques for a good, speedy result.	**Quadrant D for E:** You're building something new that should be reusable...here's some design features we'd like you to build in.
Enterprise DWBI	**Quadrant E for D:** We're building something you could use...please wait for us to complete it.	**Quadrant E for E:** Please use our object, even though it's a lot fancier than what you need, and, oh, you'll have to wait for it, too.

Each quadrant lists a typical request that occurs for its combination of factors.

FIGURE 9.2

Enterprise business intelligence architecture balancing framework.

Using time-boxed Scrum, DWBI departments will need to keep the teams fairly small. Scrum dedicates a full day to the story conference and task planning session. Unfortunately, a team can only decompose a limited number of user stories from product owner concepts to detailed development tasks within a single day. Moreover, Scrum performs its fine-grained developer coordination through the stand-up meetings. Only so many people can check using the three Scrum questions during a short meeting of 15 to 20 minutes.

These factors determine that Scrum teams become ineffective as they approach the 10-member mark. Given that limit, individual teams will have to stay small, forcing program planners to establish many teams for big applications, coordinating between them for the proper sequencing of large deliverables. There are three straightforward means for coordinating a collection of multiple agile teams: "scrum of scrums," milestones marked on time-bracketed backlogs, and the progress visualization made possible by earned-value reporting.

Coordinating through scrum of scrums

The original Scrum book described scrum of scrums as "a daily scrum consisting of one member from each team in a multiteam project." [Schwaber 2004] Perhaps because data integration projects frequently involve _meta data_, which is defined as "data about data," warehousing teams sometimes drop the awkward-sounding "scrums of scrum" and speak instead of _meta scrums_. In the simplest of scaling situations, individual teams will hold their morning stand-ups and then send one member each to program-level scrum of scrums. This meta scrum follows the same format as the project scrums, where each participant quickly covers the three questions:

1. What did your team complete yesterday?
2. What will it complete today?
3. What might be blocking its progress?

Agile coaches make several suggestions to ensure smooth scaling through scrum of scrums:

- Perform sufficient preproject planning to eliminate as many dependencies between the teams as possible by giving them an independent and coherent portion of the program's release backlog.
- Colocate the teams in a single building or small campus so that meta scrums and other incidental communication can occur fluidly.
- Synchronize the teams' iterations if possible so that (a) no team is locked away in a story conference or retrospective when other teams need their input and (b) they can easily include each other's newly produced deliverables in their normal planning phases.

In practice, however, these suggestions do not add up to a robust scaling solution. It is not always possible to assign each team an "orthogonal" portion of a program backlog free of any major dependencies, especially in data warehousing. Far more frequently, these applications serve as key data exchange points for multiple functional groups within the corporation. The clinical trial warehouse shown in Figure 9.3, taken from one of the author's projects in the biomedical industry, is a typical example. As indicated by the differing circles at the end of the lines in this data topology diagram, the warehouse provided a crucial data interchange between multiple lines of business applications, sometimes serving as a consumer of data for information collation purposes and other times serving as a "source of record" once the information has been scrubbed and integrated. Many warehousing thought leaders strongly caution against using data warehouses to feed operational systems, but regardless of guidance, the practice is all too common.

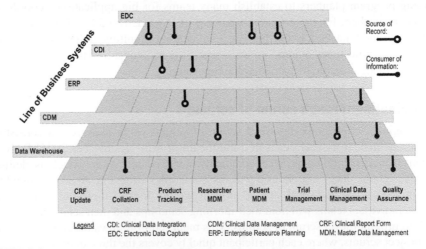

FIGURE 9.3

Data topology diagram for typical warehouse program with extensively interdependent projects.

The program depicted in Figure 9.3 was complicated further by the fact that the warehouse department was organized into several standing teams with widely varying skill inventories and sprint lengths. A single data architecting team owned the company's shared integration layer and followed an 8-week cycle for updating the database, flatly denying the possibility of a shorter time box. Pulling data from the corporate warehouse were several project-based ETL teams that each owned a separate data mart and preferred to work on 4-week cycles. Finally, the multiple BI teams that maintained individual dashboard applications were quite happy delivering on 2-week cycles.

The company truly valued the delivery speed and quality provided by Scrum, but it needed something more robust than simply scrum of scrums to coordinate work across so many teams with such a divergent set of work cadences At first, the program managers tried to synchronize the top of cycles across all three types of teams, but something always occurred with one or another team to knock them off the cadence. Figure 9.4 portrays a far more forgiving arrangement of meta scrums needed to solve this challenge. Although only one instance for each type of team is depicted here, the diagram shows a pipeline with typical stages for analysis and design, coding, and high-volume testing presented in the prior chapter.

Overlaid across the first stage of each pipeline is a meta scrum of project architects, one from each team. Instead of shuttling between short daily scrums at project and program levels, these architects would spend the entire morning with their project teams and then relocate in the afternoon to a project space dedicated for project architects. There they could struggle with and mitigate the interdependencies between their many projects, preparing materials with which to guide their separate project teams on the following morning. In this fashion, development took place at the detailed project level but architecture and design occurred at a comprehensive program level.

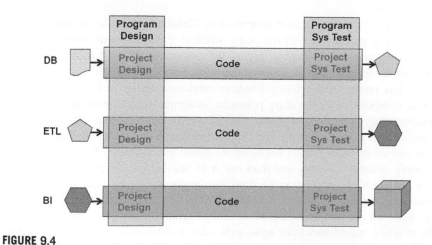

FIGURE 9.4

Specialty-based meta scrums coordinate projects across large programs.

Quality assurance took a similar approach in which the meta scrum for system testers gathered every afternoon in a meeting space the program maintained just for them. Like the architects, these testers spent mornings in the work rooms of their separate project teams, wrestling with the validation issues of their particular development teams. In the afternoon, they met as a cross-project, specialty meta scrum. Together they labored upon a single, all-project build with which they would perform nightly program-level integration testing. As a result, the enterprise data warehouse received unit and component tested at the project level, but integration and regression tested at the program level.

In this manner, an agile data warehousing program can be scaled into the realm of a half-dozen teams or more. The limiting factor is not the number of project teams but the ability of the specialty-driven meta scrums to understand, plan, and disseminate direction back to the individual coding teams. In this variation of scrum of scrums, specialty roles take the place of developers and often have more interdependencies to sift through than coders on a regular development team. Thus, meta scrums can often start to feel too big at even the six to seven member level. With this limit on the scrum of scrum, the ceiling on scaling Scrum to the program level is then in the range of 60 to 70 coders.

Matching milestones

Assuming that they do not share coders or resident scholars, the biggest point of coordination between agile development teams on a program will be the timing of the deliverables that represent the connect points between them. When listed on a project calendar, these major deliverables become project "milestones" that the program managers need the project teams to deliver close to their appointed times, lest other teams fall idle because they have not received the starting components their work requires.

The *current estimate* artifact described in Chapter 7 provides a handy means for identifying milestones and reasoning whether a particular delivery date for a desired component is reasonable. Figure 9.5 depicts the current estimates of two teams and shows a pair of milestones that they have in common. For clarity, this diagram has omitted the velocity brackets employed earlier in Figure 7.5. Those brackets combined with the story points to determine the iteration in which each developer story would most likely be delivered. With current estimates, it is straightforward to determine the iteration during which the producing team will finish the stories its sister project needs for its milestone. One only has to understand the team's delivery velocity and then use it to bracket the developer stories on a team's project backlog. Such projections also make it easy for data architects collaborating in a scrum of scrums to reason about ways to reprioritize their modeling backlogs in the event that a milestone delivery begins to slip in the schedule.

In practice, milestones from agile-style current estimates are far more dependable than waterfall projections for two reasons in particular. First, the story points on the backlogs come from teams that practice their estimating skills every iteration

"Master Data" Team		
User / Dev Story	St Pts	Sprint
Add Master Customer Dimension		
Eastern ERP	13	6
Western ERP	8	7
Add Master Product Dimension		
Eastern ERP	5	7
Western ERP	3	7
♦ Product by Customer Possible -- July		
Add Master Location Dimension		
Eastern ERP	5	8
Western ERP	5	8
Add Master Sales Agent Dimension		
Eastern ERP	3	8
Western ERP	8	9
♦ Agents by Office Possible -- September		

Aligned

Trouble!

"New Metrics" Team		
User / Dev Story	St Pts	Sprint
Integrate Corporate Revenue for External Reporting		
Add Strategic Sales System	8	2
Add Legacy Sales System	3	2
Revenue Smoothing	5	3
G/L Recognition	3	3
♦ Revenue by Customer & Product -- July		
Integrate Corporate Revenue for Internal Management		
Link in Billing Addresses	3	3
Link in Network Addresses	3	4
Link in Strategic Sales Comp Data	5	4
Link in Legacy Sales Comp Data	3	4
♦ Revenue by Agent & Office -- August		

FIGURE 9.5

Using current estimates for milestone planning between agile DWBI projects.

and get regular confirmation of their accuracy. Second, the velocity brackets used to predict the sprint where a particular story will be completed are derived from the actual delivery speeds of the teams doing the work. The milestone predictions are themselves easy to keep up to date. It requires only shuffling items on a simple list of features on a backlog each time priorities change and then rebracketing them whenever a team displays new velocity. This process is far less work than the waterfall equivalent of rebalancing a PERT graph or updating a Gantt chart full of predecessor and successor relationships, which, for large programs, appear more like microcircuitry than project plans. This combined accuracy and ease of update is often the factor that tips the scale in favor of iterative methods for project management offices deciding whether to try an agile approach.

Balancing work between teams with earned-value reporting

Specialty-driven scrum-of-scrums and current-estimate milestones both make coordinating multiple agile warehousing projects possible, but they do not provide a means of tracking how well each team is performing and whether one should consider reallocating work between the teams in order to match their delivery speeds. Naturally, the sooner a program planner can detect a team that is struggling to keep up, the more options he will have for correcting the situation. Traditional project management has many mechanisms for visualizing progress such as Gantt charts, critical paths, and critical chains. All of them require more information than an agile team typically collects. Traditional project management artifacts require managed links between predecessors and successors tasks, plus confidence intervals on the developer's estimates for tasks. In contrast, Agile developers can manage their iterations by revisiting the story point estimated earlier for the project's story cards and then updating each day the remaining labor estimates on a couple of task cards.

Luckily, a technique called *earned-value reporting* can visualize progress and determine slippage given the information the scrum master already gathers from his teammates: value points, story points, and whether stories are accepted or rejected. Earned-value reporting is typically depicted as a set of line graphs as shown in Figure 9.6. To build such a graph for a team, a program planner needs only the following items:

- a project plan that identifies work ahead and when it should be finished (one can use the current estimate described in Chapter 7)
- a valuation of the planned work (one can use the value points the product owner has assigned to the user stories on his project backlog, also described in Chapter 7)
- predefined "earning rules" to quantify the value of the work delivered (a typical schedule of earning ratios as a function of delivery quality is shown in Table 9.3)

Note that the scrum master from each team can provide the first two of these items readily. No additional input is needed from the developers, and thus this reporting device will not interfere with their activities or their velocity.

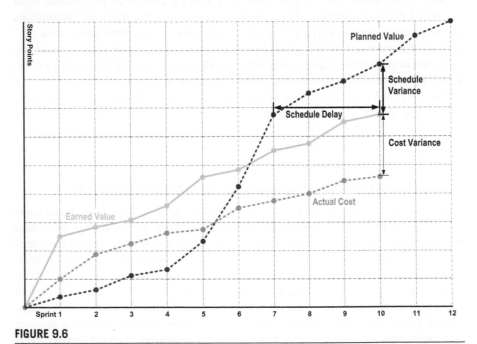

FIGURE 9.6

Typical earned-value reporting graph for a waterfall project.

Table 9.3 Typical Schedule of Earning Rules for Earned-Value Reporting

Quality of Deliverable	Code	Earned
Accepted	ACC	100%
Tech debt	TD	80%
Rejected back to coders	R2C	50%
Rejected to designers	R2D	10%
Rejected to architect	R2A	0%

Lines on the sample earned-value graph mentioned earlier are typical for a waterfall project. The *actual cost* line takes a nonlinear path because all project expenses are being tracked; those costs typically do not accumulate evenly across time. The *planned value* line shows the anticipated cost of deliverables plotted using the dates each item is expected to be complete. The *earned-value* line is the actual cost of deliverables plotted against the date they were actually completed.

The diagram reveals the power of earned-value reporting that makes these graphs so appealing to program manages. Contrasting the earned value against the planned value line for the last time point reveals how far the project is behind in terms of dollars. By examining the time points for the same level of earned versus planned value, one can calculate how far behind the project is running in terms of time. By comparing the earned value to the actual cost line, one can see how much the project is over or below budget. Earned-value graphs are easy to read and quickly answer the crucial questions concerning project spend and performance.

When managing the milestones of an agile data warehouse program, program planners can simplify the earned-value reporting graphs a bit further. For this purpose, one needs graphs for two or more individual teams, as shown in Figure 9.7. The planner will also want to focus upon the performance of the resident team—developers and leadership roles only—leaving participation of visiting resource to be considered later, if there is a problem. By focusing upon just the resident team's expense, the actual cost line becomes very predictable. It is simply the dollar cost of a stable headcount, and therefore linear and uninteresting. Planners tend not to plot the actual cost line when using earned-value reporting to balance work between agile teams.

On graphs for an agile data warehousing project, the planned value line is based on value points awarded to the user stories. To make the earned-value lines more granular and responsive to up-to-the minute events, the planner needs these allocated down to developer stories where data integration work is involved. The scrum master or product owner can make this allocation, usually proportioning the value points to developer stories based on the story points the developers estimated for each. This allocation is illustrated in Table 9.4, which details the earned-value calculation for typical iterative project over three iterations. With this approach, the planned value line is simply the allocated value points that would have been delivered if all the developers' stories were completed in the iterations that the current estimate had scheduled them for.

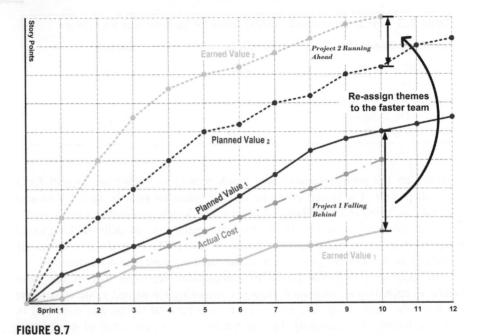

FIGURE 9.7

Balancing work between teams using earned-value analysis.

The earned-value line is even simpler to calculate. It is the allocated value points of the stories delivered, adjusted for the quality of the deliverable. As depicted for this example earlier in Table 9.3, the program planner gives the team 100% credit for stories accepted by the product owner, 80% for modules accepted with tech debt, and only 50% if they are rejected back for more coding. Stories that are rejected for further analysis and design work are credited as being only 10% complete, and if they need architectural work, no credit at all is given.

The graph of a team's earned value versus its planned value is interesting enough, but it becomes truly useful when compared to that of another team, as shown in Figure 9.7. Without earned-value reporting, it is very easy to misjudge the relative situations of the individual agile projects that make up a program. For example, which of the following projects sounds like it is in greater trouble?

- Team 1 has had one story rejected every sprint, and others accepted with tech debt. One of the rejected stories had to go all the way back for rework with the project architect.
- Team 2 has had all its stories accepted, although a couple of them were associated with a bit of tech debt.

Based on these simple descriptions alone, one could reasonably think Team 1 was in worse shape and perhaps some of its work should go to Team 2. However, as a close study of Tables 9.4 and 9.5 will reveal, we must factor in the story points

Table 9.4 Midproject Earned-Value Report for Team 1

Team 1:		Velocity = 16		Planned Value			Deliveries (Earned Value)		
ID	Value Points	Story Point	Allocated Value Pts	1	2	3	1	2	3
US1	**35**	**35.0**							
DS1	8	13.3	13.3	13.3			Acc 13.3	13.3	13.3
DS2	5	8.3	8.3	8.3			Acc 8.3	8.3	8.3
DS3	3	5.0	5.0	5.0			R2C 2.5	Acc 5.0	5.0
DS4	5	8.3	8.3		8.3			Acc 8.3	8.3
US2	**30**	**30.0**							
DS5	5	15.0	15.0		15.0			Acc 15.0	15.0
DS6	3	9.0	9.0		9.0			Acc 9.0	9.0
DS7	2	6.0	6.0		6.0			Acc 6.0	6.0
US3	**25**	**25.0**							
DS8	2	2.8	2.8		2.8			R2D 0.6	Acc 2.8
DS9	8	11.1	11.1			11.1		TD 8.9	Acc 11.1
DS10	3	4.2	4.2			4.2			Acc 4.2
DS11	2	2.8	2.8			2.8			Acc 2.8
DS12	2	2.8	2.8			2.8			Acc 2.8
DS13	1	1.4	1.4			1.4			R2A 0.0
US3	**20**	**20.0**							
DS9	8	10.0							TD 8.0
DS10	3	3.8							
DS11	2	2.5							
DS12	2	2.5							
DS13	1	1.3							
Value/iteration				26.7	41.1	22.2			
Cumulative value				26.7	67.8	90.0	24.2	74.4	96.6
Earned value %							22%	68%	88%
Planned value %				24%	62%	82%	24%	62%	82%
EV/PV %							**91%**	**110%**	**107%**

Table 9.5 Midproject Earned-Value Report for Team 2

Team 2:		Velocity = 16		Planned Value			Deliveries (Earned Value)		
ID	Value Points	Story Point	Allocated Value Pts	1	2	3	1	2	3
US1	**35**		**35.0**						
DS1		3	5.8	5.8			Acc 5.8		5.8
DS2		5	9.7	9.7			TD 7.8	Acc	9.7
DS3		8	15.6	15.6			TD 12.4	Acc 15.6	15.6
DS4		2	3.9		3.9			Acc 3.9	3.9
US2	**30**		**30.0**						
DS5		2	6.0		6.0			Acc 6.0	6.0
DS6		3	9.0		9.0			Acc 9.0	9.0
DS7		5	15.0		15.0			TD 12.0	Acc 15.0
US3	**25**		**25.0**						
DS8		5	6.0		6.0			TD 4.8	Acc 6.0
DS9		1	1.2			1.2			Acc 1.2
DS10		1	1.2			1.2			Acc 1.2
DS11		1	1.2			1.2			Acc 1.2
DS12		5	6.0			6.0			TD 4.8
DS13		8	9.5			9.5			TD 7.6
US3	**20**		**20.0**						
DS9		1	1.3						
DS10		2	2.5						
DS11		2	2.5						
DS12		3	3.8						
DS13		8	10.0						
Value/iteration				31.1	39.8	19.0			
Cumulative value				31.1	71.0	90.0	26.1	66.8	86.9
Earned value %							24%	61%	79%
Planned value %				28%	65%	82%	28%	65%	82%
EV/PV %							**84%**	**94%**	**97%**

and whether stories were delivered before they were expected before drawing this conclusion. Because Team 1's troubles involved only developer stories with very low points, and because its tech debt was incurred on stories that were not expected until the following iteration, they were actually ahead of schedule when calculated using earned-value metrics. Team 2's tech debt centered upon modules with very high story points, bringing their earned-value performance down considerably.

Using earned-value reporting to compare teams can lead to graphs that look very much like the one shown in Figure 9.7. Such graphs provide program planners with the insights they need to rebalance work between teams. In this diagram, Team 1 is clearly ahead of schedule and Team 2 is behind. Especially if the latter team's performance has an important milestone coming due on their project backlog, the program planner would be shrewd to consider Team 2's project backlog in detail and find work he can reassign to Team 1 in order to achieve a more balanced delivery schedule.

In an agile setting, it is important to reallocate work to the teams instead of moving developers between teams. Changing the composition of teams midproject will require the developers to reestablish its internal work patterns and discover its velocity measure from scratch. Although it is better to reassign work to teams, the practice takes a modicum of care. Developer stories are usually difficult to understand and program outside of their context—they make sense only to their parent user story. Furthermore, as discussed in the middle chapters of this book, user stories can also be hard to understand in isolation because they often correspond with an analytical step rather than an obvious business goal, which is more typically linked to their parent theme. It is the themes that represent the "minimally marketable features" of the project, that is, they are the components that make business sense all on their own and thus can be readily designed, programmed, and validated independently. For this reason, when earned-value reporting suggests that work needs to be rebalanced between teams, the scrum of scrums or other program planners should consider reassigning "themes to teams" for their corrective action.

What is agile data warehousing?

So far, this chapter has described how to get agile warehousing teams started and scaled up for multiple projects, plus how to plan and balance multiteam deliveries. As a new agile warehousing program grows, its champions will want to gather some hard statistics to demonstrate that their new approach is working well and has truly benefited the company. Incremental delivery methods do, in fact, provide a large collection of progress metrics, but because tracking each measure requires effort, it is worth identifying a minimalist set if possible. To identify a select few metrics to focus upon, agile programs will need to be clear about what they are trying to demonstrate. They must be clear on what they mean by the terms "agile" and "agile data warehousing."

What is "agile?" The reader will by now understand that agile is such a large change in development practices that it is difficult to provide a definition that is at once concise and comprehensive. Is it iterative? Does it thoroughly involve the customer? How much ceremony must it have? How much ad hoc anarchy will it allow? Even seasoned agile practitioners can debate these points at length. If one considers the dozen different agile approaches—from XP and Scrum, to Kanban and RUP—plus the diverse ways they are implemented across thousands of programs, he will find an argument on both sides of all the fundamental questions such as these. The presentation of agile in this book began with the basic tenets and principles of the agile manifesto and then added suggested patterns for team work to them. That layering indicates that agile is a set of philosophies, principles, behaviors, and techniques for developing software, but we still need to state the end that goes with these means.

Figure 9.8 attempts to present the entirety of the agile approach offered in this book, with the highest objectives depicted on the right and the suggested techniques for achieving them flowing into them from the left. It cannot comply with everyone's definition of agile, but it will make it easy to identify some key metrics for demonstrating to sponsors that the new iterative approach—whether the purist decides to call it agile or not—has made an improvement.

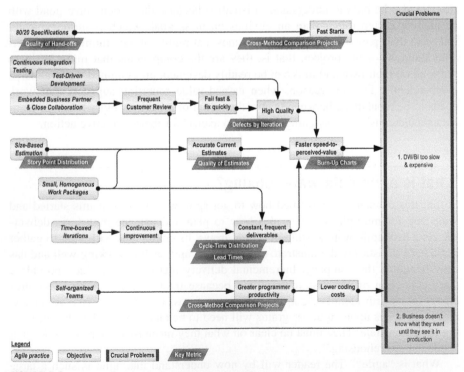

FIGURE 9.8

One answer to "What is agile data warehousing?"

Figure 9.8's definition of agile revolves about solving an urgent existential problem that many DWBI shops face today: their customers think they are too slow to deliver and far too expensive. Added to this challenge is another elemental problem, expressed from the DWBI department's perspective: the business cannot state what it is they want until they first see it on a dashboard. Solving these twin problems calls for a few fundamentally different strategies: faster starts, greater programmer productivity, and—above all else—faster speed to value.

As can be traced to the left side of Figure 9.8, the need for speed requires us to employ many innovative, labor-saving techniques such as self-organized teams, 80/20 specifications, and close collaboration (even colocation, if possible). However, speed to market cannot be a one-time deliverable, so the diagram includes notions such as constant, frequent deliverables and continuous improvement, which suggests an iterative approach, at least at the outset.

As this book further explored techniques for fast delivery, it discussed other priorities of a team's business partners, such as dependable data and clear forecasts for delivery cost and dates. These priorities added the notions of high-quality and current labor estimates to the objectives of agile warehousing as elements of customer satisfaction. The key role of quality also requires several other familiar aspects: test-driven development, frequent customer reviews, and the whole notion of fail fast and fix quickly.

This carefully vetted chain of challenges and solutions, then, results in a single-sentence outline of agile data warehousing that is probably more a good start on a definition than the final formulation:

> *Agile data warehousing is a set of principles, behaviors, and techniques that provides our customers a far shorter time to value for quality business intelligence through fast project starts, high business involvement, frequent increments of value, and regularly updated planning information.*

Any agile warehousing team can test this definition quite easily by compromising on any one aspect. Take a year to start a new project, or 12 months to deliver a first, working product. Alternatively, give the end users less than perfect data or deny them any idea of how much time and money the project will require. Teams that try any one of these compromises will quickly hear the same gripes sprouting among their end users again: DWBI takes too long and far too much money to create anything useful. In the definition given earlier, speed to market is the primary goal. Indeed, we opened this book with one study suggesting that accelerations of two to four times waterfall delivery rates can be achieved based on methods alone. It may be instructive, then, to take a moment and describe where agile gets all its speed. Table 9.6 lists the primary accelerators agile data practitioners emphasize when instructing new teams. Of course, constantly improving, self-organized teams are prominent on the list, as is the deprecation of big, to-be specifications throughout the project. Upon reflection, many of the elements in Table 9.6 provide speed through an indirect mechanism: they help the team avoid big mistakes that would consume inordinate amounts of time. These are noted in Table 9.6 and can be used by agile warehousing champions to counter the notion that fast starts and 80/20 specifications are not disciplined enough to represent a careful approach to building applications.

Table 9.6 Where Agile Gets Its Speed

Aspect	Direct Acceleration	Avoids Time-Consuming Mistakes
Self-organized teams	Y	
80/20 specifications	Y	
Technical leads stay in project room	Y	Y
Customer descopes stories that lose value	Y	Y
More accurate estimation		Y
Test-driven development		Y
Coding starts early→feedback sooner		Y
Business frequently reviews deliverables		Y
Automated testing catches errors		Y
Paying off tech debt early		Y

Communicating success

The quick sketch given of agile data warehousing provides a handy means of identifying a core set of metrics to demonstrate the effectiveness of an iterative DWBI implementation. As indicated by the dark slanted boxes in Figure 9.8, a few key metrics address the value delivered, reveal when teams need coaching, or demonstrate whether a coach's recommendations has helped them improve their agile practices. The descriptions that follow work from the left of Figure 9.8 toward the right. Those metrics to the left are closer to the developers' concerns regarding their collaboration. Those on the right pertain to the higher level issues determining customer satisfaction. As seen from their definitions, all of these metrics besides the cross-method project comparison can be compiled easily by the scrum master and system testers using measures they already have or can acquire quickly during a sprint retrospective. For multiproject environments, these metrics can be displayed on a daily dashboard in order to give both stakeholders and developers the regular feedback needed to monitor performance. Those metrics that change daily will benefit from this regular refresh, of course. Those measures gathered at the end of each iteration may remain static for multiple weeks for a given team. If they are part of larger programs, however, their aggregate value will change more frequently because at least one project will provide an updated input every day or two.

Handoff quality

The development process presented in previous chapters sets up a considerable challenge for the software developers on the team. The process established a pipeline of labor specialties, but still exhorted the members of the team to work quickly, using lightweight specifications that focus upon the most important 80% of the remaining unknowns related to each module. Although such pared-down specs allow us to get a project started after investing only 20% or so of the time waterfall efforts consume, even these minimalist specifications must be of high quality. Despite the fact that the missing details will be supplied via eye-to-eye consultation with the upstream party, if the lightweight sketch prepared ahead of time is grossly incomplete, these discussions will take far too long and project work will grind to a halt.

For this reason, agile warehousing teams need a means for ensuring that these 80/20 artifacts are usable and that the handoffs between teammates are effective. However, in order to measure this effectiveness, scrum coaches do not want to resort to a point-by-point audit of the deliverables exchanged between roles, as is done in many highly elaborate waterfall methods. A better approach is to measure the downstream party's satisfaction with the handoff without trying to define what each handoff must be. Once that satisfaction or lack thereof is measured, the two parties involved in the exchange can work through the details of how to make it better.

Because we want to know whether consumers all along the agile warehousing value chain are happy, why not use the ubiquitous tool that the corporate world uses to measure its customer satisfaction: the net promoter score? For this purpose, the net promoter score can be obtained by asking each "customer" in the value chain a single question: "On a scale of 0 to 10, how likely would you be to recommend your upstream partner to a friend in the company performing the same role as you?" Here "10" is "extremely likely" and "0" is "not at all." Based on their responses, customers are categorized into three groups. Folks responding a 9 to 10 rating are considered "promoters." Customers answering 7 to 8 are "passives," and those replying with anything lower are considered "detractors." The percentage of detractors is then subtracted from the percentage of promoters to obtain a *net promoter score* (NPS). The NPS will range from −100 for those situations where everyone is a detractor to +100 when everyone is a promoter of the teammate in question. In marketing surveys, an NPS score above 0 is considered good, with values of +50 considered excellent.

On an agile team, because the scrum master can collect individual promoter scores quickly during the sprint retrospectives, gathering them will not impact team velocity. He can track them at the developer story level rather than for each task so there will be only a handful of scores to collect for each producer on the team. Even the product owner can be rated by the project architect, which will provide important feedback on this crucial area of business-IT alignment.

For agile warehousing teams, upstream producers in the value chain should be able to do far better than a net promoter score of 50%. The close collaboration and frequent appraisals at the sprint retrospectives should provide the motivation and guidance producers need to please their development partners 90% of the time after a little discussion of each party's expectations. More important than the absolute level, however, is the trend. If the NPS starts low at the beginning of the project, it only points out where work needs to be done. As long as the NPS moves upward quickly and remains high once reaching the 90% level, team leads can be reasonably assured that the developers are communicating well all along the value chain and that the risk of the team making a big mistake in requirements or design has been minimized.

Quality of estimates

On the agile warehousing definition chart shown in Figure 9.8, accurate current estimates build good rapport with business partners by demonstrating a faster speed to value even before the whole project has completed. Scrum coaches need to ensure that the team is honoring these forecasts, so the diagram affixed this objective with a metric called *quality of estimates*. As discussed earlier in Chapter 7, this metric is also pivotal in detecting new troubles within the team's work process. Whereas *time to value* (or, equivalently, *speed to market*) considers "Job Number One" for the developers, the quality of their estimates can only stay high if they are conducting all parts of the method effectively, and therefore this measure serves as their "canary in the coal mine."

To remind the reader, this metric is defined as the number of labor hours originally estimated for tasks on stories accepted at each user demo divided by the estimated hours of all tasks included in the sprint, after subtracting from the numerator the hours estimated for any tech debt carried over into the next sprint. The quality of estimates may start low for new teams but should reach the mid-90 percentage range by the third or fourth iteration. If anything goes wrong with the team's self-organized process, this number will fall, alerting the program that this team in particular could use some coaching.

Defects by iteration

Faster speed to market will not impress a DWBI department's business partner unless its developers are delivering quality data. Without it, they risk losing their product owner's support and their project's funding altogether. True, earned-value reporting does provide some indication of quality by reducing the value credited to the team when stories get pushed back to earlier stages in the pipeline due to defects, but the root cause still remains hidden in the earned-value line.

Figure 9.9 provides a mechanism for making careless coding instantly visible for the team. This *Defects by Iteration* bar chart depicts the number of defects found during integration testing. Defects are categorized by the iteration in which they first appeared, which is important because defects can be fixed only to reappear two or three sprints later if not truly corrected. By measuring quality at the system integration level, this diagram nets out the chaos occurring during unit or component testing, which typically takes place on the developers' workstations.

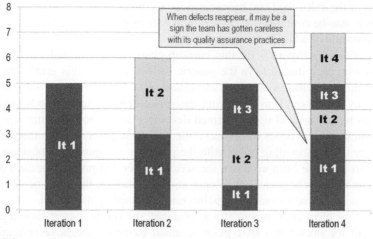

FIGURE 9.9

Tracking defects by iteration.

Instead, Figure 9.9 reveals only the flaws found in modules the developers have sent to integration testing, claiming they were "done" (that is, "error free").

When testing gets particularly busy after the first three or four iterations, the chart in Figure 9.9 can be meaningfully compiled on a daily basis for the team to review before every stand-up meeting. For prior sprints on the diagram, the height of the bars shows the total number of defects open at the end of the iteration. For the sprint in progress, the bar height indicates the number of defects currently open. As defects emerge, the system testers actively identify them in a way that they can be recognized should they reappear after being fixed. Recording the module and error type for each bug is often sufficient.

Ideally, defects appearing in one sprint will be resolved by the time the next sprint concludes, but teams are less than perfect when it comes to resolving coding flaws. Bugs come back "from the dead," as can be seen in the last bar for the current sprint. Teams need some feedback on how they are doing at truly fixing data quality flaws. When supposedly corrected bugs return, it can indicate deep problems with the team's approach to root cause analysis or coordination between the developers. Moreover, as discussed in the last chapter, some defects must go back to analysis and design or even architecture for resolution. By highlighting persistent defects, this diagram can suggest when certain defects may need that extreme level of attention.

Burn-up charts

Because the agile data warehousing definition diagram ties faster speed to market to customer satisfaction, teams must have a measure of their delivery speed to share with their business partners. For this purpose, an agile burn-up chart is a graphical depiction of the value the team has created for the business community to date. This metric, too, can be compiled by the scrum master using data he already tracks with only a minimum of additional effort.

As revealed by Figure 9.10, this burn-up chart reveals the value delivered by the team with each iteration. In the generic agile version of this graph, the scrum master simply adds the value points associated with the user stories that have been accepted by the product owner during the sprint demos. Agile warehousing programs can base it instead upon accepted developer stories to make the graph a bit more granular. The product owner has collected value points for the themes in the backlog by using estimating poker with the project's community of business stakeholders. To build the burn-up chart, the scrum master can proportion each theme's value points to its component developer stories based on the ratio of one story's story points compared to total story points encompassed by the theme.

So that the chart is as meaningful as possible, the scrum master should give his team credit for stories that have been accepted based on the large-volume demo performed by the system tester rather than the programmers' small-volume demo. The former set contains stories that can actually be promoted into user acceptance testing should the product owner call for a new product release, and therefore are the only stories that truly matter to him.

For greater transparency, the sample burn-up diagram uses two overlaid styles of bars. The lower solid bar represents value points associated with themes for which all developer stories have passed system integration testing, the preferred definition of "delivered." The team's developers can use these bars alone to demonstrate to the product owner that they are steadily providing value. They can even remind him which end-user features were delivered in each iteration by reviewing archived versions of the project backlog for those prior sprints. The outlined tip of each bar in Figure 9.10 depicts value points for the additional themes for which developer stories are underway. These "value in progress" bars quantify the additional value that is already in the pipeline for the product owner so that he can gauge the importance of the features coming versus those that have already arrived.

With the burn-up chart in hand, the team can demonstrate to the product owner and his management that the team is delivering upon the business requests that were given to them. For teams that have prioritized their project backlog according to guidelines offered during an earlier chapter with Table 7.4, stories with the greatest value will be located toward the top of the list. With that ordering in effect, the delivered value shown on the burn-up chart should climb steeply during early iterations because the team is delivering the most important features first for the most part. With time, however, the slope of both value delivered and value in progress stacks should soften, making burn-up charts good vehicles for discussing whether coding should continue on a given project. If the business has other warehousing needs waiting, perhaps the organization would be better off at this point filling this team's backlog with stories from those projects, as they will probably result in faster burn-ups bars for the next several iterations.

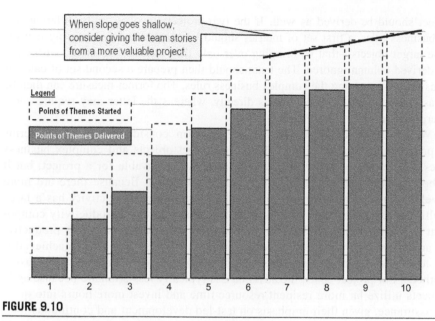

When slope goes shallow, consider giving the team stories from a more valuable project.

Legend

Points of Themes Started

Points of Themes Delivered

1 2 3 4 5 6 7 8 9 10

FIGURE 9.10

Burn-up chart showing value points delivered by sprint.

Cross-method comparison projects

As suggested in the agile data warehousing definition diagram, faster starts and speedier component deliveries are primary objectives of the agile DWBI approach. Yet this notion begs an important question: faster than what? A good answer for a DWBI department would be "faster than the previous method that had frustrated our business partners to the point where we in IT had to start searching for a new method." To prove that "faster" has been achieved, then, the agile team will need a reference point to compare against. Somehow, it must find or derive the delivery speed of a waterfall project that it can use as a reasonable reference.

Especially while IT is still considering whether to switch to agile methods, it may well be possible to identify two warehousing projects of similar scope and source data so that one can be pursued with an agile approach and the other using the department's standard development method. If a pair of comparable project cannot be found in the development queue, then perhaps a single large project can be split into two, with each half pursued by a contrasting method. At worse, a set of baseline statistics can be derived from the records of a previous waterfall project. If at all possible, the two projects should start with definitions provided by the same architect, data architect, and systems analyst so that the only difference is the method, not specification quality.

The easiest and most informative metrics to match between two comparable projects are programmer hours per target data object. Total project costs per target object should be derived as well. If the two projects involve vastly different sets of business rules, a first set of metrics should be calculated for delivering just the base target objects—that is, bringing over only the replicated columns, with work on derived column ignored. The team should then prepare a second set of calculations for programming the complex business rules. The former measure can then be measured between the two projects directly, whereas the latter may require some interpretation.

Well-executed agile projects should perform considerably better in terms of programmer productivity for both base target objects and complex business rules. There may be other productivity metrics conceivable for a project, but it is best to keep the number of metrics to a minimum. Because there are more developers on a team than any other role, programmer productivity has a large multiplier associated with it, making it the most important productivity component of team velocity. Agile practitioners often suggest at least a 40% productivity advantage over waterfall for a first project, although 70% can be achieved if the team's leadership subteam has significant experience with agile warehousing methods. For project costs, the advantage is typically less dramatic because agile projects utilize far more resident resource time and invest more hours into quality assurance, given their emphasis on test-led development and continuous integration testing.

Cycle times and story point distribution

Last but not least are the metrics for lead time and story point distribution metrics. They point the way to the pull-based agile methods such as Scrumban and Kanban that many agile warehousing teams will contemplate after a year or two of iterative delivery practice. *Cycle time* is defined as the number of days that elapse from the moment the team pulls a developer story into the pipeline and the day it passes integration testing after being added to the nightly build. As the team matures, this cycle time should diminish steadily, adjusting for each work package's story points until it reaches a base level that reflects how long it takes a truly high-velocity team to transform a sizable feature request into working software.

The story point distribution chart shows the number of stories in the project backlog for each level of story points estimated. It is an important indicator of how consistently a team is defining its developer stories. By steadily improving the definition of developer stories, the team can narrow greatly the story point range of the items in their project backlog, which will allow them to focus on perfecting their coding habits for a particular size of work units. Backlogs with stories ranging from 2 to 20 points require the team to maintain a wide variety of work patterns, making it hard to know where to optimize. A team performing sprint after sprint on stories mostly in the 3- and 5-point range, however, will be able to finely tune its internal definitions, handoffs, and coding patterns for maximum speed. Figure 9.11 demonstrates a story point distribution chart, and readers will find a cycle time analysis later in Figure 9.14.

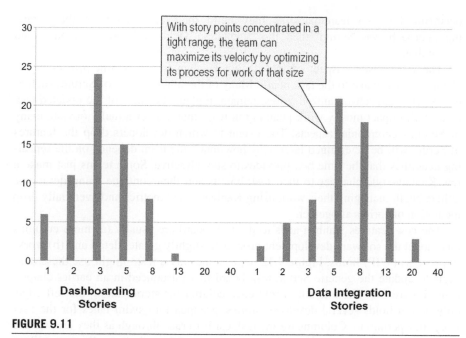

With story points concentrated in a tight range, the team can maximize its veloicty by optimizing its process for work of that size

Dashboarding Stories

Data Integration Stories

FIGURE 9.11

Single team's story point distribution chart by work type.

Moving to pull-driven systems

With cycle times defined, we can now return to the last two steps of the agile warehousing maturity path listed at the bottom of Table 9.1. Recent years have seen a growing consideration of *Kanban* workflow management techniques, which represent another class of agile methods called "pull-based systems." The pull-based approach offers agile data warehousing programs ways to move their teams beyond the need for time-boxed iterations. Without time boxing, teams pursue simply a steady flow of software development, which allows them to continue programming during the 2 days they used to lose to the top-of-cycle stages of Scrum, such as the story conference and sprint retrospective.

Given its potential for greater team productivity, this chapter closes with a glimpse at a pull-based, continuous flow approach and the advantages it might offer. It shows how a pull-based system might be adapted for a DWBI project and then discusses some of the key considerations that will determine if, when, and how far a given agile warehousing program may want to go in that direction.

A glimpse at a pull-based approach

Kanban is a work management approach that emphasizes continuous flow rather than delivery through iterations. Developers that are ready for it can drop it on top of their current process, without needing to alter the pattern of interactions occurring between teammates as they build their application. If their starting approach was Scrum, then this adaptation yields a hybrid method called "Scrumban."

The most visible aspect of introducing Kanban into a Scrum project is the changes it will make to the task board. Many of the other aspects of Scrum, such as user stories and self-organized teams, remain in place. Features of the updated task board will impact mostly work planning in ways that may eventually obviate many of Scrum's ceremonial aspects. The extent to which developers drop the features of Scrum will be determined largely by how much the team depends on the repeating deadlines that the time box provides to stay effective. Some teams just make a few Kanban-style changes to their task boards and then continue using iterations. Others begin managing their work using Kanban's new metrics and eventually drop the notion of sprints altogether.

The new features Kanban adds to the task board are usually (a) more columns that model the software development process in slightly greater detail and (b) work-in-progress (WIP) limits. Figure 9.12 depicts one way a team might use these concepts to update the generic Scrum task board first introduced in an earlier chapter using Figure 3.1. There is still a reference column for stories along the left edge, only now it holds several developer stories, grouped into swim lanes for the user story they pertain to. Columns for the task cards to race through as they are worked have remained the same with *waiting*, *underway*, and *ready for validation* still on the board. For clarity, this diagram has omitted the *test written* column.

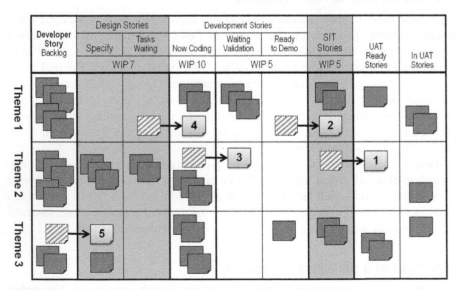

FIGURE 9.12

Scrum data warehousing task board adapted for Kanban concepts.

The task board now has cards for developer stories rather than tasks. The swim lanes have been reset to align with user stories. Moreover, the upstream and downstream work specialties of the pipeline defined in the last chapter now have columns for tracking their work. The new task board has added a set of *design* columns for the data architect and systems analysts to manage on the left and a column dedicated to *system integration testing* on the right. These roles no longer have to manage their own work "off the board," but instead now participate fully with orchestrating the flow of work through the new board. The updated task board also gives the designers ownership of the *tasks waiting* column so that these team leads can use it as their "done" buffer, leaving modules to rest there until coders are ready pull a story into the columns they manage and begin programming it.

As a further change, this updated task board also now contains several *work-in-progress limits*. These WIP limits place a cap upon how many stories each station can have under its management at any one time. The board in Figure 9.12 belongs to a team with five coders, so the WIP limit for their work was set at 10, based on the notion that each developer needs one work unit they can be engaged in actively plus another one on hold due to a dependency. The limit for *waiting validation* was set at one item per developer, thinking that if each developer had a module waiting to be reviewed, programming should stop and the programmers should focus instead on checking each other's work.

The WIP limit for the upstream design work was set at seven thinking that at any one time there should be one item ready to code per programmer plus a couple more in case coding proceeds faster than expected. SIT's limit of five was set based on the system tester's (rather loud) assertion that he wanted to have only one module to discuss with each programmer at any given moment. Tuning a Kanban system for optimal flow is largely a matter of picking the right value for these WIP limits as work cards pile up or become absent in different parts of the task board.

Figure 9.12 also shows how a team would move tasks through this board while honoring the new WIP limits. In the first step, SIT finishes validating a module and moves its task card into *UAT ready*. For the second step, the vacancy just created in his column allows the tester to pull a module from the coders' *ready to demo* column without exceeding his WIP limit. In the third step, the spot just opened by the tester allows coders to advance one of their modules from *now coding* into *waiting validation*. Fourth, the space created by the last action allows one of the programmers to pull a newly designed module from *tasks waiting* into the *now coding* column. Finally, the designers see that their work set has fallen below the WIP limit, so they chose a new story from the backlog and pulled it into their specification activities.

Note that the modules advanced at each step do not have to all lie within the same swim lane, meaning they do not have to all pertain to the same user story. Pull-based systems still rely on self-organized teams. Each time there is an opportunity to pull work forward in the process, the team needs to discuss which module is most important to make new progress upon.

The newly added WIP limits serve as a means of balancing work within the iteration. Without them, all tasks could be started at once, leaving the coders ineffectively multitasking and the tester with too little to do until late in the iteration. By setting some WIP limits, the team forces itself to focus on advancing tasks to the latter columns of the board as soon as possible. Tuning these WIP limits over time ensures that tasks will flow steadily through all stages of the development value chain modeled on the board. When tasks pile up in one column, it indicates a bottleneck. In the short term, the self-organized team can swarm to a particular step in the development process and concentrate their efforts until the log jam has been cleared. Later, during the sprint retrospective, the team can select new values for the WIP limits and even add some new buffer columns in order to avoid such a pile up in the future.

In addition to changing the task board, Kanban principles provide the team with a new artifact for monitoring their development activities—the cumulative flow diagram (CFD). Figure 9.13 provides an example of this diagram and shows some of the performance metrics a team can derive from it. The CFD graphs the cumulative number of stories that have entered each stage across time and, in Scrumban, across all iterations. The units of measure can be number of developer stories or the story points of items added to each work stage.

The vertical height of each band depicts work in progress within that stage at a particular time point. Sudden increases in overall work in progress in any one stage are associated with plateaus along one or more components of the downstream system. These indicate a process bottleneck, such as the ones indicated by asterisks in the diagram. Take the bottleneck farthest to the right, for example. Here the number of modules added to UAT started to lag behind the number of items SIT had

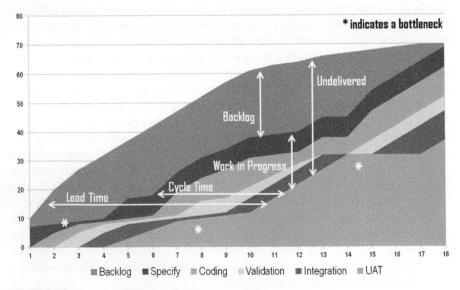

FIGURE 9.13

Cumulative flow diagram and some of the metrics it provides.

finished testing. This plateau alerted the team to the fact that the product owner had gotten distracted by a business emergency back in his department and had to be reminded to continue working the warehouse development project, too.

The horizontal span between units entering *specify* and landing in *UAT ready* is the system's "cycle time." This measure serves as a good indicator for how long the team takes to translate a request into a working module once they start working on it. The other horizontal stretch between *backlog* and *UAT ready* is of great interest to the product owner, for it represents the project's "lead time," that is, the number of days he must wait after giving the project architect a good description of a new feature before he can evaluate the new capabilities in a system test using large-volume data.

Kanban allows one further artifact crucial for considering agile warehousing beyond time boxes—the cycle time distribution analysis, an example of which is shown in Figure 9.14. The middle grid of this analysis shows the lag between *specify* and *UAT ready* for individual work units across the iterations of the project. The "count" column on the right tallies the number of units across all iterations that have taken the given number of days to move through this major portion of the task board. In this example, a good 95% of the work units went from design to UAT in less than the 13 coding days that make up this team's 3-week time box. One can also learn that roughly two-thirds of the time modules are delivered within 8 days or less.

Kanban advocates claim that these cycle time brackets are key to designing truly efficient software development systems. With some thought, a team developer's could base its *service level agreement* (SLA) with customers upon its cycle time distribution plot. An SLA is a promise to a customer to satisfy a request within a certain amount of time. In this case, the team could segment that promise a bit by stating: *From the moment we pull a feature request into our work process, we will deliver it within 8 days 60% of the time and within 13 days 95% of the time.* As will be seen in a moment, that level of insight is key to moving toward agile warehousing without time-boxed iterations.

Days Worked	Number in Tier by Iteration										Count	Tier %	Percentile
	1	2	3	4	5	6	7	8	9	10			
19 +											0	0.0%	100.0%
16 - 18	1										1	1.6%	96.0%
13 - 15		1							1		2	3.2%	95.0%
10 - 12	2			1	2	2	1	2		2	12	19.0%	92.0%
7 - 9					3		1		1		5	7.9%	73.0%
5 - 6		1	2	1				1			5	7.9%	66.0%
3 - 4	1	1	2	3		3	3		1	3	17	27.0%	59.0%
0 - 2	2	4	3	2		2		3	2	3	21	33.3%	33.0%
Totals	6	7	7	7	5	7	5	6	5	8	63		

(Left side vertical label: Iteration Length)

FIGURE 9.14

Cycle time distribution analysis.

Kanban advantages

Kanban offers some very tempting simplifications and expanded capabilities to agile development teams. The value proposition it offers has many layers to it and runs much along the following outline.

1. Building the development process into the task board allows greater visibility as to where work is occurring within the system.
2. WIP limits prevent the team from taking on too much in any one area, thereby leading to higher effectiveness by minimizing multitasking.
3. When work piles up in one process stage, it reveals bottlenecks in the overall development process that can be improved.
4. WIP limits give the team the levers they need to balance their process so that most work units will flow through the system as quickly as possible.
5. With enough data points, the team can identify a service level it can offer dependably to its customer.
6. By switching to a service level agreement with its customers, there is no longer any need for a team to promise delivery of a defined set of features by a certain date—time boxing becomes unnecessary. Iterations can be dropped if the team chooses to do so. In that situation, the team simply pulls work into the development process as needed to keep the leading buffers filled to their WIP limit.
7. Teams that free themselves from formal iterations no longer need to estimate the work to ensure that it will fit into a time box. They only need to define their work consistently and let the SLA reassure the customers that the work will get done expeditiously.
8. Without the need for a time box or estimating, the story conference and task planning become superfluous. Kanban excels when employed upon a backlog of consistently sized work items that all require roughly the same delivery process. The team leadership roles need to focus on providing stories defined so they are congruent with the developers' preferred size and development process. As long as stories entering the development process are congruent with developer expectations for work units, there is no need for the team to halt the production process and discuss a large batch of stories. Stories will be demoed as completed to the product owner.
9. By skipping Scrum's top-of-cycle ceremonies, the team can reclaim 10 to 20% more time for product development.
10. Moreover, now free of these top-of-cycle steps of Scrum, there is no need to keep the team size so small, thus Kanban teams can scale to 50 developers or more.
11. Once free of the iterative structure, there is no longer any need to keep the work definition steps chained to the cadence of delivery steps. Story identification needs to take place whenever coders need more items to program. Deployments can happen whenever it suits the stakeholders to pull finished pieces into production. Retrospectives take place whenever there is an issue serious enough that it merits halting production to discuss or when a certain number of less important issues have been pinned to the team's project board.

There is no reason to throttle one portion of the process to meet the cadence of the other. Groups at both ends of the system can now work at their optimal speed and patterns.

A more cautious view

Waterfall adherents who thought Scrum's iterative development was an outlandish proposition now have a doubly radical proposal to contend with:

> *All a team needs to do to achieve truly remarkable efficiencies is set up the right kind of task board with some work-in-progress limits and track how long it takes a self-organized team to deliver each module of code. No detailed planning or estimating is needed. Eventually, the observed delivery rates will allow program managers to identify the distribution of cycle times, thus enabling them to statistically predict how much projects will cost and how long they will take.*

As attractive as a pull-based approach may be, before a team abandons its familiar iterative method in favor of a completely pull-based system, it should ask a few questions about how well data warehousing projects can meet Kanban's prerequisites.

1 How will a pull-based system respond when stories range too widely in size?

Data warehouses entail multiple categories of work: dashboarding versus data integration, dimensions versus fact tables, replicated columns versus columns derived through complex business rules. These work units can range in story points from 1 to 80. If a team does not estimate work on the front end, what assures us that three 40-point stories do not enter a system designed for 5-point work items, collide in the coding stage, and clog up the entire process?

Because Kanban is only a development-coordination system that drapes over an existing process, it does not preclude us from keeping what works. Teams can still utilize the epic–theme–user/developer story approach developed for Scrum-based warehousing to prevent such blockage from happening. Consequently, the question for the program is something more tractable as "Are my teams' *developer stories* granular and consistent enough to allow a pull-based system to work?" If not, perhaps the team needs to work on its story-definition techniques to make the work units consistently small before moving to a pull-based work management system.

2 Can we really define workable units without keeping our estimating skills sharp?

Doing away with the overhead of estimating sounds appealing, but if a team must keep its story defined so they are small, it will need to maintain its developer's estimating abilities. Without keeping those skills sharp, one or more overly large stories might slip onto the board and jam the process. The best way to stay good at estimating is to practice it regularly. Because iterations regularly require developers to estimate, perhaps teams should continue with the sprints and their story planning component, even if it starts tracking cycle types and using cumulative flow diagrams.

3 Should we categorize our work and adapt the task board in great detail?

Kanban enthusiasts realize that widely varying work units threaten the smooth operations of a pull-based system. They frequently advocate that work that differs in cycle time, skills required, or technology employed be identified with different colored post-its or given their own swim lanes. [Anderson 2010] This segregation will allow WIP limits and service levels to be identified by work type, allowing some process tuning and metric gathering at a medium level of detail. Work types can be depicted on separate cumulative flow diagrams and cycle time distribution plots, allowing the challenges and services levels inherent in each category to be independently understandable. The question then becomes "how many swim lanes will my particular data warehousing program require?" If it runs past five or six, the resulting process may require more tracking effort than it saves on estimating time.

4 Is the underlying process stable enough to have only one optimal set of WIP limits?

Kanban posits that a team needs to set up its task board and then fiddle with the WIP limits until it gets the flow of work just right. That vision presupposes that there is a single stable set of WIP limits (per swim lane) to aim for. Data warehousing projects oscillate between many different kinds of work. A project can start with a large number of easy staging routines and then move into a long spell of very complicated extracts. Data integration modules can be horrendously complex and then give way to a fairly easy ETL transform for star schemas. Program planners should consider whether their teams will have enough time to identify an effective set of WIP limits before the nature of the work changes so much that they will need to start tuning their system all over again.

5 When will we have enough data points to identify a dependable SLA?

The cycle time distribution plot is very handy for identifying actual delivery brackets, assuming one has enough data to reveal the underlying pattern. However, what are those points on the plot? Developer stories? There may not be enough developer stories in a project to provide the high number of data points needed for a good statistical calculation of average cycle times. Especially for teams segmenting the work between several swim lanes, a data mart project may only have a dozen such points to place on each band of the cycle time grid. Can a team truly identify a dependable service level for its customers given this paucity of observations in each category?

6 Aren't there other reasons for having iterations besides estimating?

Moving out of iterations into a pull-based system takes effort and time. If the only objective was to save the time formerly spent on iteration overhead, the proposition might seem compelling. But iterations often fill more purposes than just estimating the next chunk of work. The planning sessions gave the team a moment to think through the upcoming segment of the project from a higher view point, to collectively reintegrate the project in their minds, and to spot some mistaken assumptions. The end-of-cycle demo and retrospective provide a chance to reconnect with the business partner and reflect on the interpersonal dynamics within the team. These needs may not be met easily in an ad hoc fashion or by adjusting a few WIP limits. Perhaps the iterations perform an important social function, one that is necessary for keeping the team interconnected and fully collaborative.

Stages of scrumban

Questions such as those just given reveal that there is still a need for iterative agile methods for many project teams. However, because the WIP limits and cycle time metrics of pull-based systems provide tremendous insight into the dynamics of a project, many agile practitioners now speak in terms of combining Scrum and Kanban into a hybrid approach called "Scrumban." [Ladas 2009]

Scrumban is more an evolutionary process that teams must pursue than a particular method that they can simply switch to. The steps a team would take in this evolution might be as follows.

1. A successful Scum team would update its task board. The developers would add a few columns to reflect their preferred development process and some WIP limits to go with each major work step.
2. Once the team believes it has modeled its work process correctly with the new columns on its task board, it would draft a cumulative flow diagram so that it can visualize and begin discussing issues concerning WIP limits and lead times. WIP limits on the task board can then be tuned to achieve a better overall process using the cumulative flow diagram to monitor whether each change makes the system perform any better.
3. After the lead times stabilize and enough data appear on the cycle time distribution plot to identify a dependable set of service brackets, the team can consider switching to service level agreements rather than time boxes.
4. Should the team prove able to dependably deliver within the time frames promised, they can then consider eliminating the iterations altogether, decoupling planning from delivery.

The Scrumban evolution process will not be quick, and there is no predicting how far along this path the team will go until they decide their method is good enough. Given all the cultural changes discussed throughout this book, it seems that Scrum is a necessary first step to move teams from the deeply wasteful antipatterns of waterfall methods to the high-performance world of close customer collaboration and self-organized teams. At some point though, some very experienced teams working on long-term projects will want to take the next step. At that point, pull-driven systems offer yet another leap in productivity that some agile data warehousing programs will be able to take. It will be exciting to discover just how fast each of these pioneering teams can then go.

Summary

Introducing a new team to agile data warehousing can follow a six-step process. Once one team is performing well, a DWBI department can begin scaling up the practice to a program involving 50 or more developers by instituting a scrum of scrums for the specialty roles at both ends of the development pipeline. Several metrics allow a DWBI department to track how well its agile teams are performing and how much value it is delivering to its business partners. Interproject milestones can be scheduled and monitored by comparing each team's current estimate. When teams start to lag, a modified earned-value reporting graph can reveal which of them can be given additional work in order to let the lagging teams catch up. Cycle time and story point distribution metrics can prepare a team to incorporate some pull-based project management techniques defined by Kanban. These techniques require mostly that the task board be updated with the team's preferred work process and a few work-in-progress limits. These modifications provide greater insights into the work process and keep development work flowing smoothly. Taken a step further, Kanban may allow Scrum DWBI teams to eliminate time-boxed iterations altogether and reinvest the time into generating more value for their customers. However, many data warehousing teams will find their work too erratic in size and temperament to adapt completely to Kanban. They may also want to keep Scrum's iteration structure for important social reasons that contribute as much to team effectiveness as does a well-managed task board.

References

Chapter 1

Ambler, S. (2005), Agile modeling: effective practices for modeling and documentation, <www.agilemodeling.com>.

Ambler, S. (2008, May 7), Has agile peaked? Dr. Dobb's, <http://www.drdobbs.com/architecture-and-design/207600615>.

Ambler, S. (2011). Architecture envisioning: an agile best practice, agile modeling, <http://www.agilemodeling.com/essays/initialArchitectureModeling.htm> Accessed September 2011.

Ambler, S. W., & Lines, M. (2012). *Disciplined agile delivery: a practitioner's guide to agile software delivery in the enterprise*. IBM Press.

Anderson, D.J and Reinertsen, D.G. (2010, April 7). Kanban: successful evolutionary change for your technology business.

Beck, K. and Andres, C. (2004, November 26). Extreme programming explained: embrace change (2nd ed.).

Benefield, G. (2008, January). Rolling out agile in a large enterprise, proceedings of the 41st annual Hawaii International Conference on System Sciences, 1 Location: Waikoloa, HI, 461–46.

Cockburn, A. (2004, October 29). Crystal clear: a human-powered methodology for small teams.

Cohn, M. (2009, November 5). Succeeding with agile: software development using scrum.

Department of Defense, (1985). Military standard: defense system, software development, DOD-STD-2167, Washington, DC, <http://www.everyspec.com> on 2011-09-07T13:00:23 Accessed September 2011.

Ericson, J., (2006, April). A simple plan, information management magazine, <http://www.information-management.com/issues/20060401/1051182-1.html> Accessed September 2011.

Fairbanks, G. H. (2010). *Just enough software architecture: a risk-driven approach*. Marshall & Brainerd.

Highsmith, J.A. (1999, December). Adaptive software development: a collaborative approach to managing complex systems.

Hunt, A., & Thomas, D. (1999, October 30). *The pragmatic programmer: from journeyman to master* (1st ed.). Addison-Wesley Professional. 1999, October 20.

Jacobson, I., Booch, G., and Rumbaugh, J. (1999, February 14). The unified software development process.

Jarzombek, J., (1999). The 5th annual JAWS S3 proceedings; cited in Larman 2004.

Kroll, P., & MacIsaac, B. (2006). *Agility and discipline made easy: practices from openUP and RUP*. Addison-Wesley Professional.

Larman, C. (2004). *Agile and iterative development : a manager's guide*. Upper Saddle River, NJ: Pearson Education.

Maurer, F., & Martel, S. (2002). *On the productivity of agile software practices: an industrial case study*. Alberta, Canada: University of Calgary, Department of Computer Science. T2N 1N4.

Palmer, S.R. and Felsing, J.M. (2002, February 21). A practical guide to feature-driven development.

Poppendieck, M., & Poppendieck, T. (2003). *Lean software development: an agile toolkit.* Addison-Wesley Professional.

Reynolds, C. (2010). *Introduction to business architecture.* Course Technology PTR.

Royce, W. W. (1970, August). *Managing the development of large software systems. Proceedings, IEEE WESCON.* New York: Institute of Electrical and Electronics Engineers.

Schwaber, K. (2004, March 10). Agile project management with scrum (Microsoft professional).

The Standish Group International, 1995. The Chaos Report. <http:// www.standishgroup.com> Accessed February 2007.

DSDM Consortium and J. Stapleton (2003, January 13). DSDM: business focused development, (2nd ed).

The Data Warehousing Institute, 2011. TDWI data modeling: data analysis and design for BI and data warehousing systems (course book), <www.tdwi.org>.

Vingrys, K., 2011m, August 17. Gaining momentum with agile, <www.thoughtworks.com>, <http://www.thoughtworks.com/sites/www.thoughtworks.com/files/files/kristan-vingrys-gaining-momentum-with-agile.pdf> Accessed April 2012.

Chapter 2

Ambler, S. W. (2011). Generalizing specialists: improving your IT career skills. *Agile Modeling* <http://www.agilemodeling.com>.

Advanced Development Methods (ADM) 1995. Controlled chaos: living on the edge. <http:// www.controlchaos.com/download/LivingontheEdge.pdf> Accessed February 2007.

Astels, D. (2003, July 12). *Test-driven development: a practical guide: a practical guide* (1st ed.). Prentice Hall.

Beck, K. (1999). *Extreme programming explained: embrace change.* Addison-Wesley Professional.

Beck, K. (2002, November 18). *Test driven development* (1st ed.). Addison-Wesley Professional.

Behrens, P. (2005). Scrum gathering—enterprise adoption. *Agile Executive Blog* <http:// trailridgeconsulting.com/blog/?m=200511> Accessed February 2007.

Boehm, B. (1988, May). Spiral model of software development and enhancement. Computer; 21, no. 5: 61-72, <http://sunset.usc.edu/csse/TECHRPTS/1988/usccse1988-500/usc-cse1988-500.pdf> Accessed February 2006.

C3 Team, Chrysler goes to extremes. *Distributed Computing* <http://www.xprogramming.com/publications/dc9810cs.pdf> Accessed February 2007.

Control Chaos 2007, Controlled-chaos software development. <http://www.controlchaos.com/download/Controlled-ChaosSoftwareDevelopment.pdf> Accessed February 2007.

Goldratt, E. (1990). *Theory of constraints.* Great Barrington, MA: North River Press.

Péraire, C., Edwards, M., Fernandes, A., Mancin, Enrico, and Carroll, K., (2007, July). The IBM rational unified process for system z, <ibm.com/redbooks>.

Jacobson, I., Booch, G., and Rumbaugh, J. (1999, February 14). The unified software development process.

Lines, M., (2012, April 6). Incremental delivery of consumable solutions requires discipline, disciplined agile delivery, <http://www.disciplinedagiledelivery.com> Accessed May 2012.

McCarthy, J. (2006). *Dynamics of software development*. Redmond, WA: Microsoft Press.

Project Management Institute, *A guide to the project management body of knowledge* (4th ed.). Pmbok Guide.

Royce, W. W. (1970, August). *Managing the development of large software systems. Proceedings, IEEE WESCON*. New York: Institute of Electrical and Electronics Engineers.

Schwaber, K. (2004). *Agile project management with scrum*. Redmond, WA: Microsoft Press.

The Standish Group International 1999, Chaos: a recipe for success. <http://www.standishgroup.com> Accessed April 2006.

Takeuchi, H., & Nonaka, I. (1986). The new new product development game. *Harvard Business Review, Jan.-Feb.*, 137–146.

Chapter 3

Ambler, S. (2008, May 7). Has agile peaked? Dr. Dobb's, <http://www.drdobbs.com/architecture-and-design/207600615>.

Cohen, J. (1988). *Statistical power analysis for the behavioral sciences* (2nd ed.). Routledge Academic.

Collier, K. W. (2011). *Agile analytics: a value-driven approach to business intelligence and data warehousing*. Addison-Wesley Professional.

The Standish Group International. 1999. Chaos: a recipe for success. <http://www.standishgroup.com> Accessed April 2006.

Woodward, E., Surdek, S., & Ganis, M. (2010, July 1). *A practical guide to distributed scrum*. IBM Press.

Chapter 4

Ambler, S. (2003). Introduction to user stories. *Agile Modeling (Web site)* <http://www.agilemodeling.com/artifacts/userStory.htm> Accessed December 2011.

Bower, G. H., Black, J. B., & Turner, T. J. (1979). Scripts in memory for text. *Cognitive Psychology, 11*(2), 177–220.

Bruce, P., & Pederson, S. M. (1982). *The software development project: planning and management*. John Wiley & Sons.

Burton, S. (2011, April 28). *User stories*, <http://blog.chaione.com/better-user-stories>.

Cockburn, A. (2001). *Writing effective use cases*. Addison-Wesley Pearson Education.

Cockburn, A. (2008). A user story is to a use case as a gazelle is to a gazebo (blog), <http://alistair.cockburn.us> Accessed December 2011.

Cohn, M. (2004, March 1). *User stories applied: for agile software development*. Addison-Wesley Professional.

Cohn, M. (2005, September 26). Writing effective user stories for agile requirements, <http://www.mountaingoatsoftware.com/system/presentation/file/64/SDBP2005_EUS.pdf?1267636390>.

Davies, R. (2001). *The power of stories*, white paper presented at XP2001 conference, <http://www.agilexp.com/presentations/PowerOfStories.pdf> Accessed December 2011.

Jeffries, R. (2004, February 4). *Extreme programming adventures in C#*. Microsoft Press.

Leffingwell, D. (2006, April). *Agile Journal* (webzine), "Agile at scale: 7 + 7 practices for enterprise agility, <http://www.agilejournal.com/articles/columns/column-articles/33-agile-at-scale-77-practices-for-enterprise-agility> Accessed December 2011.

Lucas, 2011. <http://www.capitalcamp.org/sites/default/files/slides/Crafting-Great-User-Stories.pdf>.

Haskins, B., Stecklein, J., Brandon, D., Moroney, G., Lovell, R., & Dabney, J. (2004). Error cost escalation through the project life cycle, Proceedings of the INCOSE Symposium. NASA Johnson Space Center. <http://ntrs.nasa.gov/archive/nasa/casi.ntrs.nasa.gov/20100036670_2010039922.pdf> Accessed December 2011.

Pichler, R. ,(2010). Writing good user stories, <http://www.romanpichler.com/presentations/pdfs/WritingGreatUserStories.pdf>.

Pischler, R. (2011, March). *All Things Product Owner* (blog), The product backlog board, <http://www.romanpichler.com/blog/product-backlog/product-backlog-board> Accessed December 2011.

Suzanne and Robertson, J. (1999), Mastering the requirements process.

Rosenberg, D. (1999). *Use case driven object modeling with UML*. Indianapolis: Addison-Wesley.

Wake, B. (2003, August 17). *INVEST in good stories, and SMART tasks*, <http://xp123.com/articles/invest-in-good-stories-and-smart-tasks>.

Chapter 5

Nielsen, (2011). *ConneXions lifestage group distribution*, <www.claritas.com/samples/sitereports/connexions_lg_11.pdf> Accessed January 2012.

Schwaber, K. (2004, March 10). Agile project management with scrum (Microsoft Professional).

Silverston, L. (2001). The data model resource book.

The Data Warehousing Institute 2011, TDWI data modeling: data analysis and design for BI and data warehousing systems (course book), <www.tdwi.org>.

Chapter 6

Spewak, S. H. (1993). *Enterprise architecture planning: developing* (2nd ed.). Wiley.

Kimball Group (2011), *Kimball Forum*, dimensional modeling and data architecture,<http://forum.kimballgroup.com> Accessed February 2012.

Zachman, J. P. (2011). The zachman framework evolution. *Zachman International (Web site)* <http://www.zachman.com/ea-articles-reference/54-the-zachman-framework-evolution>.

Chapter 7

Camerer, C. F., & Johnson, E. J. (1991). The process-performance paradox in expert judgment: how can experts know so much and predict so badly? In K. A. Ericsson & J. Smith (Eds.), *Towards a general theory of expertise: prospects and limits*. New York: Cambridge Press.

Cohn, M. (2005, September 26). Writing effective user stories for agile requirements, <http://www.mountaingoatsoftware.com/system/presentation/file/64/SDBP2005_EUS.pdf?1267636390>.

DeMarco, T. (1986). *Controlling software projects* (1st ed.). Upper Saddle River, NJ: Prentice Hall.

Goode, E. (2000, January 18). *Among the inept, researchers discover, ignorance is bliss.* New York Times. <http://www.nytimes.com/library/national/science/health/011800hth-behavior-incompetents.html> Accessed April 2007.

Jairus, H. and Lum, K.T. (2002). Improving software size estimates by using probabilistic pairwise comparison matrices. <http://trs-new.jpl.nasa.gov/dspace/bitstream/2014/37964/1/04-0903.pdf> Accessed April 2007.

Janis, I. L. (1971). Groupthink. *Psychology Today, 5*(6) 43–46, 74–76.

Jorgenson, M. et al., (2000). Human judgment in effort estimation of software projects, Proceedings of the 22nd international conference on software engineering. <http://www.cs.uvic.ca/icse2000/papers/2_Survey/p12.pdf> Accessed March 2007.

Jorgenson, M., et al. (2004). A review of studies on expert estimation of software development effort. *Document Actions Journal of Systems and Software, 70*(no. 1-2), 37–60. <http://www.simula.no/research/engineering/publications> Accessed March 2007.

Jorgenson, M. and Sjoberg, D. (2006),*Expert estimation of software development work: learning through feedback.* <http://www.simula.no/research/engineering/publications> Accessed March 2007.

Kimball, R. (1997, August). Data warehouse role models. *Data Warehouse Architect* <http://www.kimballgroup.com/html/articles_search/articles1997/9708d05.html> Accessed October 2011.

Kimball, R. (1998, September). *Data warehouse architect,* Help for hierarchies, <http://www.kimballgroup.com/html/articles_search/articles1998/9809d05.html> Accessed October 2011.

Little, T. (2004). *Agility, uncertainty, and software project estimation.* <http://www.agilealliance.org/show/1418> Accessed March 2007.

Miranda, E. (2000). Improving subjective estimations using the paired comparisons method. *International Forum on COCOMO and Software Cost Estimation* <http://sunset.usc.edu/Activities/oct24-27-00/Presentations/Miranda.pdf> Accessed March 2007.

McConnell, S. (2006). *Software estimation: demystifying the black art.* Microsoft Press.

Project Management Institute, (2008), December 31. A guide to the project management body of knowledge (Pmbok Guide,4e).

The Standish Group International. (1999). Chaos: a recipe for success. <http://www.standishgroup.com> Accessed April 2006.

Chapter 8

Bank for International Settlements (2012). About the basel committee, <http://www.bis.org/bcbs/about.htm> Accessed June 2012.

Burns, L. (2011). *Building the agile database: how to build a successful application using agile without sacrificing data management.* Technics publications. LLC.

Date, C. J., Darwen, H., & Lorentzos, N. A. (2003). *Temporal data and the relational model: a detailed investigation into the application of interval and relation theory to the problem of temporal database management.* Oxford: Elsevier Ltd..

Kalido, (2008). *Kalido dynamic information warehouse technical overview*, <www.kalido. com>.

Kent, W. (1983, February). A simple guide to five normal forms in relational database theory. *Communications of the ACM, 26*(2), 120–125. <http://www.bkent.net/Doc/simple5. htm>.

Linstedt, D. and Graziano, K. (2011). Super charge your data warehouse, createspace.

Linstedt, D., Graziano, K. and Hultgren, H. (2009). The new business supermodel. The business of data vault modelling, 2nd ed., <Lulu.com>.

Rönnbäck, L., Regardt, O., Bergholtz, M., Johannesson, P., & Wohed, P. (2010). Anchor modeling—agile information modeling in evolving data environments. *Data & Knowledge Engineering, 69*, 1229–1253.

The Economist,(2007, July 26). Five years of Sarbanes–Oxley.

Zachman, J. A. (1987). A framework for information systems architecture. *IBM Systems Journal, 26*(3), 276–292.

Chapter 9

Ambler, S.W. (2009). *Scaling agile software development: reality over rhetoric*, IBM, <http://aplndc.com/eventSlides/Year2009/2009-03-ScalingAgileSoftwareDevelopment-ScottAmbler-March2009.pdf>.

Ambler, S. and Kroll, P. (2011). *Applying agile and lean principles to the governance of software and systems development* (white paper), IBM, <http://public.dhe.ibm.com/common/ssi/ecm/en/raw14000usen/RAW14000USEN.PDF>.

Anderson, D., & Anderson, L. A. (2010, October). *Beyond change management: how to achieve breakthrough results through conscious change leadership* (2nd ed.). Pfeiffer.

Connors, R., & Smith, T. (2011, January 4). *Change the culture, change the game: the breakthrough strategy for energizing your organization and creating accountability for results*. Portfolio Hardcover.

Charan, R. (2001). *What the CEO wants you to know: how your company really works*. Crown Business.

Bell, S., & Orzen, M. (2010). *Lean IT, enabling and sustaining your lean transformation*. Productivity Press. ISBN 978-1-4398-1757-5. Shingo Prize Research Award 2011.

Clark, B., Horowitz, E., Westland, C., Madachy, R., & Selby, R. (1995). Cost models for future software life cycle processes: COCOMO 2.0. In J. D. Arthur & S. M. Henry (Eds.), *Annals of software engineering special volume on software process and product measurement*. Amsterdam, The Netherlands: J.C. Baltzer AG, Science Publishers.

Cartlidge, A. et al., (2007). An introductory overview of ITIL V3, itSMF Ltd, 2007, itSMF Ltd, <http://www.best-management-practice.com/gempdf/itSMF_An_Introductory_Overview_of_ITIL_V3.pdf>.

Connors, R., & Smith, T. (2011). *Change the culture, change the game: the breakthrough strategy for energizing your organization and creating accountability*. Portfolio Hardcover.

Glazer, H. et al. (2008, November). *CMMI or Agile: why not embrace both!* (CMU/SEI-2008-TN-003), TECHNICAL NOTE, software engineering institute, <http://www.sei. cmu.edu/reports/08tn003.pdf> Accessed March 2012.

Hughes, R. (2008). Agile data warehousing, iUniverse.

Hughes, R. (2011). Enterprise BI architecture groups: the key to effective agile data warehousing programs: *Data Integration, BI & Collaboration.* Arlington, MA: Cutter Consortium. Vol. 11, No. 5.

Ladas, C. (2009). *Scrumban—essays on kanban systems for lean software development.* Modus Cooperandi Press.

Pettit, R. (2006). An 'agile maturity model?'. *Agile Journal* <http://www.agilejournal.com/articles/columns/the-agile-manager/52-an-qagile-maturity-modelq>.

Schwaber, K. (2004, March 10). Agile project management with scrum (Microsoft Professional).

Software Engineering Institute (SEI),(2006). CMMI for Develoment (v1.2). <http://www.sei.cmu.edu/cmmi/models> Accessed August 2007.

Tuckman, B. (1965). Psychological Bulletin. *Developmental sequence in small groups, 63*(6), 384–399.10.1037/h0022100 PMID 14314073.

Watkins, M. (2003, September 18). *The first 90 days: critical success strategies for new leaders at all levels.* Harvard Business Review Press.

Index